COOKSTOWN'S WAR DEAD

1914-1918
1939-1945

Cookstown District Council

Published by Cookstown District Council
Burn Road, Cookstown, Co. Tyrone
BT80 8DT

© Cookstown District Council

October 2007

Compiled and edited by Cookstown District Council
in conjunction with
The Friends of the Somme Mid Ulster Branch

ISBN 978-0-9557462-0-8

Printed by
Coleraine Printing Company
117 Ballycastle Road, Coleraine BT52 2DZ
Telephone: (028) 7035 4873

TO MY COMRADES WHO HAVE SURVIVED 1914-1918

The last goodbyes were whispered and the foe lay straight ahead,
So over the top and the best of luck, or, at worst, a soldier's bed;
A soldier's bed and all that it meant, with a wooden cross above,
A number, a name engraved, and a country's debt and love.
Perhaps the ones who survived it all, and returned to their homes again
Are the ones who long for the battlefield grave, and an end to all their pain.

Have you ever lived alone with the past, and the pals who paid the price
And paused and thought of the comradeship my word but it was nice?
The great hearts of humanity, who laughed at the slush and the mud;
And the shells, and the bullets, and foemen too, and poured out their British blood,
To make the world a heaven where all could live in peace,
And the lamb lie down with the wolf and fellowship never cease.

If you have, you know all about it; if not you have much to learn;
How the times and the people have changed, it makes one's heart to yearn.
For the good old days when pals were pal's, and a man's word was his bond,
And he would stick to his chum to the mouth of the pit and perhaps a bit beyond,
Goodbye, old chap, I am dying, just tell her I loved her so dear;
And you promised you would, if you came through safe, between a smile and a tear.

Life we can smile and face it, and take our medicine still,
But it takes a heap of doing and it makes one use their will,
Yes, the sleepless nights around Ypres and the "Minnies" on the Menin Road,
When we were caught with the rations, and each man had his load
Of food and things that were needed by the boys up in the line;
How we advanced when the straffing ceased, and advanced in double quick time.

The curtain's been down for many years, but we're soldiers all the time,
Though dressed in civilian garb for years and now long past our prime.
The boys of Mons, and Ypres, the Somme and Paschendaele too,
Keep up your hearts, my comrades, 'tis the only thing to do;
We have lived through the noise of battle, we can battle it now on our own,
And await the great Commander's word that will bring his soldiers home.

By William Irvine, Tullyhogue, Cookstown

William Irvine was a veteran of the Great War and served from 1914-1918. His son
William was killed while serving with the R.A.F during World War 2

Postcard photograph courtesy of Tom Jebb

Contents

THE HISTORY OF COOKSTOWN CENOTAPH

The following passage is an extract from the Mid Ulster Mail dated April 1927.

The Cenotaph was unveiled on Easter Monday the 18th April 1927 by Mrs Ricardo, widow of the late General Ricardo C.M.G. who commanded the 36th Ulster Division in the 1914 / 18 Great War in which a great many Cookstown men had served.

When a memorial was originally mooted in 1923, councils were divided as to the best form it should take. After many meetings a proposal was carried to erect an emplematical statue, but the subscription collected were insufficient and it was allowed to be in abeyance; some of the collectors returned their subscriptions and others deposited the amounts in the bank.

In 1926 the matter was revived by the local branch of the Royal British Legion, chiefly on the initiative of the energetic Secretary Mr Rooke and a committee was again formed. In order to avoid a similar hitch it was decided to leave it to the Legion to decide the form of the memorial, as the men who came back should be the best able to judge of what would be appropriate as a memorial to their fallen comrades, and the cenotaph in London recommended itself.

The collection of the subscriptions formerly given or the sums promised was largely in the capable hands of Mr J. D Anderson and it is gratifying to know that in spite of the stringency of money compared with the post war boom the memorial was erected and paid for, and a small remnant of the fund left was given to the local Legion to provide a hut or other meeting place for the ex-servicemen of the town.

The memorial is a replica of the Cenotaph in London, built of silver grey granite from the Moore Quarry, Newry and stands 17 ft high on a granite base 9 ft 9 ins x 7 ft 3 ins which is surrounded by a concrete step 14 ft x 12 ft.

A quote in the Mid-Ulster Mail 27th April 1927 said

"It is situated in the centre of the main street, nearly opposite the Ulster Bank, and with Slieve Gallion mountain in the background it will form not only a permanent memorial but a graceful addition to the street. It is also evident that it will form a new landmark for the town and a centre of interest judging by the number of motorists who stop to admire it".

Panels bearing the names of the fallen in relief, one on the east

and one on the west side are of Castleduff limestone. The tablets are illuminated at night by two flambeaux, electrically lighted and on the narrow sides of the cenotaph are wreaths with the dates inscribed of the commencements and the conclusion of the Great War, with the south side bearing the inscription "OUR GLORIOUS DEAD". On the panels facing east and west is inscribed – "In Grateful memory of the men from Cookstown who in the Great War gave their lives for freedom".
The Memorial was supplied and erected by Purdy and Millard of Belfast.

On the morning of Easter Monday, 18th April 1927, ex-servicemen assembled outside the Post Office in Cookstown, and marched in slow time, headed by Cookstown Pipe Band, led by Pipe-Major McCormack. In the front rank of the procession were Lieutenant Colonel Lewis of Tullylagan, President of the Royal British Legion; Captain J. Leeper, Chairman of the Legion; Captain J.B. Knox, Commander and Lieutenant Hopper. The men marched to the Memorial, where they formed a square, kept by the Royal Ulster Constabulary under the supervision of District-Inspector Hall, M.B.E. On the steps of the memorial stood, a Sergeant, a Corporal, a Lance Corporal and a Fusilier of the Royal Inniskilling Fusiliers acting as escort, one standing at each corner of the Memorial, with two buglers standing at the south side of the Memorial, under the supervision of Major Alexander, D.S.O. Around the square, crowded the relatives and members of the local council. At 11.00am all stood to attention as Mr. Thomas Gibson, Chairman, Urban District Council, gave a short address and paid tribute to those who gave their lives in the war and then introduced Mrs. Ambrose Ricardo, widow of the late Colonel Ambrose Ricardo who commanded the 36th Ulster Division. Mrs. Ricardo thanked the committee and cut the cord unveiling the east and west faces of the Memorial. As the Memorial was unveiled the escort presented arms and the Buglers sounded the "Last Post," followed, after minute's silence, by Reveille. Mr. J.W. Fleming, secretary of the memorial committee read aloud the names

Lieutenant Colonel Gregg D.S.O., Officer Commanding the Depot, The Royal Inniskilling Fusiliers, gave a short address. Mr. J.D. Anderson, on behalf of the War Memorial committee, asked Mr. Thomas Gibson, to accept the monument on behalf of the Cookstown Urban District Council.

The Pipe Band played "The Flowers of the Forest" as relatives of the Fallen placed wreaths on the Cenotaph. The proceedings closed with the playing of the National Anthem.
No special invitations were issued but all ex-servicemen and their friends, and all subscribers were invited to be present on the occasion.

INTRODUCTION

It gives me great pleasure to introduce our District Book of Honour covering the First and Second World War periods.

The Council first considered this project approximately two years ago and with the help of Community Relations funding and support from a local Ad Hoc Committee involving churches and a local interest group the book has gradually taken shape.

My own family have a particular interest in this book as it, among many others, commemorates my Uncle, Able Seaman John McGuckin, Royal Navy, killed during the Battle of the Java Sea during the Second World War.

Cookstown District has become a cosmopolitan, vibrant market town enjoying significant affluence, as part of a peaceful and progressively democratic Europe. It now seems far distant from the dark days of turmoil and conflict that beset Europe twice in the last century. Those periods are now almost beyond living memory.

To a significant extent our comforts and safety today were paid for by the courage and sacrifice of the generations before us who left this island to face those aggressors and foreign foes who threatened our shores. It is to those who did not return that this book is dedicated.

M. J. McGuckin
Clerk/Chief Executive

ACKNOWLEDGEMENTS

The Council wishes to acknowledge the support and assistance of all who contributed to the preparation of this Book of Honour.

The Community Relations section established the Ad Hoc Committee some eighteen months ago and they have contributed significantly to overseeing the project.

Coleraine Printing (the publishers) have been patient and helpful in the many months of compilation of the various drafts. Their associate, Mr Robert Thompson (Great War Research), has worked tirelessly researching and compiling information on casualties from the First World War.

The public and, in particular, family relatives have been helpful in the provision of information, photographs and letters and the like; for this we are indebted.

We would like to acknowledge the help and co-operation of all the clergy throughout the District who have made church records and property readily accessible, particularly to the Friends of the Somme.

Mr Thomas Hutchinson, River Graphics (Cookstown), has provided much help with reprographics.

Thanks also goes to Mrs Mary Mullan, Derrygonigan, Cookstown for her help throughout the project.

The Mid-Ulster Mail Archive, Cookstown has provided much assistance with original photographs and information.

The major thanks must go to the Friends of the Somme, Mid-Ulster Branch without whom this book would not have been possible. The Chairman Mr Wesley Wright, who carried out extensive research before and during the project, his work has been of enormous value. Mr Desmond Gordon (Secretary), Ms Denise Gordon (Administrative Assistant) and Mr Martin Brennan (Vice Chairman) are major contributors.

Mr Brennan has devoted hundreds of hours of his personal time over the past two years in research, both through interviews with families and searching public records. The creation of this book and the detail contained therein is a testament to his commitment to the project.

We have included in the book records of those servicemen and women who died in both World Wars who either were born, lived, worked in, or whose families had a long association with the District Council area. We have also included those whose names appear on the War Memorials situated within the district, some of whom were resident close to the Council boundaries.

The Council has in good faith included information obtained from a variety of sources and has endeavoured to corroborate the accuracy of details using Commonwealth War Grave records, Ministry of Defence information, newspaper archives and family records. In the event of an inaccuracy appearing in the text we take full responsiblity for that and apologise.

Historical Context

This book is about men and women who gave their lives for freedom in World Wars 1 & 2 and who were born or lived in the area of Cookstown District as it is today.

The area now encompassed by Cookstown Council District is very different from the area during World Wars 1 and 2. Then the area would have been covered by Cookstown Urban District Council and Cookstown Rural District Council, and would all have been in County Tyrone and considerably smaller. To-day Cookstown council area stretches into South Derry.

We believe that we have been as accurate as possible but where we found people who were close to and in the vicinity of existing district boundaries then they have been included.

Anyone who served in the various armed services, army, navy, merchant navy and air force is entitled to a commonwealth war grave if they died between 4th August 1914 and 31st August 1921 for World War 1. The World War 2 period extends from 3rd September to 31st December 1947.

There are discrepancies in Merchant Navy procedures. In most cases men who died in the Merchant Navy had to die as the of result of enemy action but this does not always hold true.

Not to be forgotten are civilians who died as the result of enemy action.

World War 1

Most of the men from the area joined the army during World War 1, few were in the Merchant/Royal Navy or in the Royal Flying Corps (became Royal Air Force in 1918)

Men from the area joined mainly Irish Regiments-Royal Inniskilling Fusiliers, Royal Inniskilling Dragoon Guards, Royal Irish Fusiliers, Royal Irish Rifles, Royal Dublin Fusiliers, Leinster Regiment, Connaught Rangers, Royal Munster Fusiliers and Royal Irish Regiment. Reflecting the agrarian nature of the area, men also joined the North Irish Horse and South Irish Horse, yeomanry (Cavalry) regiments. Men from the area also joined Regiments from the mainland, many of them fearing they would miss the action if, as then predicted, the "war would be over by Christmas 1914".

Many also joined the Canadian, Australian, New Zealand and South African armies. Most had emigrated in the late 19th century and some spent leave back in the Cookstown area visiting relatives.

1914

During the summer of 1914 Ireland was very much a troubled state. The Home Rule Act came into force in September 1914 but its implementation was suspended pending the end of the war. Sir Edward Carson representing the Unionists, was bitterly opposed to Home Rule and had formed the Ulster Volunteer Force, 85,000 strong pledging to fight against Home Rule. They were opposed by the Irish Volunteers 180,000 strong determined to ensure that Home Rule would be implemented for the whole of Ireland. They were in the main Nationalists and their leader was John Redmond. The Irish National Voluneers were formed from the majority wing of the Irish Volunteers who split over the issue of supporting the war effort or not. The minority kept the name, Irish Volunteers and eventually rebelled in 1916. Both leaders agreed that Home Rule in the event of war would be delayed for one year or for the duration of the war, whichever was longer. Britain declared war on 4th August 1914 because of Germany's unlawful invasion of Belgium. The Ulster Volunteers and the National Volunteers as they became known would form the backbone of the 36th (Ulster) and the 16th (Irish) Divisions.

Whilst neither the 16th (Irish) Division nor the 36th (Ulster) Division were exclusively Nationalist/Unionist the most diverse division was the 10th Irish Division. The 10th division was the first Irish Division formed and was destined to fight in Gallipoli, Salonkia, Bulgaria and Mesopotamia (Iraq), but they never served in France or Belgium.

Men who died in 1914 from the area were members of regular army regiments or reservists recalled to their regiments and served in the British Expeditionary Force sent to France. Their graves and memorials are widely scattered in France and Belgium indicating the rapid retreat of the Allied forces before the German Army was halted on the River Marne in September.

1915

Men who died in 1915 again were from regular battalions, plus men who joined the 10th Irish Division.

Many men from the area serving in the 10th Irish Division and 1st Royal Inniskilling Fusiliers were to lose their lives in the ill-fated Gallipoli landings. The British Army lost over 21,000 men, the Australians and New Zealanders 11,400 men, and the French over 10,000 men in an ill-fated attempt to knock Turkey out of the war.

The Battles of Loos, Aubers Ridge, and Ypres claimed many local lives as the regular battalions continued to bear the brunt of the casualties.

The 36th (Ulster) and 16th (Irish) divisions completed their training in England and were sent to France in October 1915.

The Germans used poison gas during April in the Ypres Salient for the first time.

Many men who survived the war would return home and suffer horribly from the effects of gas for many years.

1916

This was arguably the most momentous year of the 20th century in the history of Ireland.

The ramifications of the Easter Rebellion and the Battle of the Somme still reverberate throughout both communities to this day.

Almost 2,000 men from the 36th Division and 1200 men from the 16th Irish Divisions died during the Battle of the Somme which began on 1st July and lasted until 18th November. The vast majority of the men who died on the Somme from the 36th (Ulster) Division died on the morning of the 1st July. The 16th (Irish) Division captured the villages of Ginchy and Guillemont between the 3rd and 9th September.

Neither of the two divisions was exclusively Irish in origin, since after the Battle of the Somme, the majority of the replacements came from the British mainland.

When Britain introduced conscription for the first time, this permitted initially all single men to join the armed forces but by 1918 the act covered all males up to the age of 50. Conscription was never made compulsory in Ireland—political pressure from Nationalist politicians ensured it was never introduced in Ireland.

Lord Kitchener, whose photograph looked out of posters urging men to join up, was to lose his life on 5th June due to his ship hitting a mine off the Shetlands. Two men from Cookstown also died in the same incident.

May 21st saw the introduction of *British Summer Time* in the British Isles for the first time.

1917

This year witnessed the first time the 16th (Irish) and the 36th (Ulster) Divisions served adjacent to each other in the Battle of Messines which began on 7th June.

Messines was a well planned action and led to both divisions achieving their initial objectives. However, lack of adequate support and both divisions being kept "in the Line" too long led to many deaths.

Further battles in the Ypres Salient especially the Battle of Paschendale during the summer of 1917 cost many lives. Large parts of Belgium had been flooded deliberately in 1914 to try to prevent the German invasion. This, coupled with a very wet summer, led to men being "swallowed up by the mud".

Both Divisions moved back to France where both took part in Battle of Cambrai from 20th November. This saw the first large scale use of tanks on the battlefield.

The United States of America which had been neutral declared war on Germany on 6th April.

1918

Many of the volunteer battalions in the 16th and 36th Divisions were either amalgamated or disbanded and the men sent to remaining battalions. The regular battalions were brought into the divisions to bring them up to strength.

The Germans launched their last great offensive on 21st March and pushed the allies back over 50 miles inside a few days. Again the 36th and 16th divisions were in the line adjacent to each other. Both suffered heavily during this offensive.

The Allies halted the offensive in late April and whilst the Germans stayed on the offensive until the end of May, they never again made any significant progress.

The Allies (including the Americans who arrived in the spring) went on the offensive at the beginning of August and within 100 days World War 1 was over.

The Germans signed the Armistice at Compiègne on the morning of 11th November. Hostilities ceased on the Western Front at 11am, the Great War as it was known prior to World War 2 was over.

Many historians believe that the harsh economic conditions placed on Germany contributed to the rise of Nazism and led to World War 2.

Women over the age of 30 received the vote in parliamentary elections for the first time. The first woman to be elected was the Countess Markievicz, though born in England she played a significant part in the Easter Rebellion in 1916.

Casualties

Fatal Casualties of Irish Infantry Regiments and numbers of Battalions raised.

N.B.- Second figure indicates the number of battalions who saw active service.

Irish Guards raised 3/2 battalions and 2,191 fatalities

Royal Irish Rifles raised 21/13 battalions and 7,005 fatalities

Royal Inniskilling Fusiliers raised 13/9 battalions and 5,772 fatalities

Royal Dublin Fusiliers raised 11/7 battalions and 4,778 fatalities

Royal Irish Fusiliers raised 14/7 battalions and 3,375 fatalities

Royal Munster Fusiliers raised 10/4 battalions and 2,835 fatalities

Royal Irish Regiment 12/8 battalions and 2,455 fatalities

Leinster Regiment raised 7/4 battalions and 2,067 fatalities

Connaught Rangers raised 6/4 battalions and 1,998 fatalities

The Irish National War Memorial and gardens at Island Bridge commemorate the 49,400 men from Irish Regiments who died in World War 1 and is situated in Dublin near Phoenix Park.

This figure is agreed by most historians of today to be too high. The figure includes all the men in the various Irish regiments plus men who died from Ireland in the various Imperial Forces. Many of the men who joined the various Irish regiments were from the British mainland and the Channel Islands. The figure generally accepted for Irish born fatalities is between 27 and 32 thousand.

Unveiling of Cookstown Cenotaph Easter Monday 18th of April, 1927

Archive photo courtesy of David Lennox

World War One Roll of Honour

11113-Private Richard Cheevers

2nd Battalion Royal Irish Fusiliers
Died of Illness: 20th August 1914
Age: 21
Interred in Quetta Government Cemetery, India 2166
Delhi Memorial, India. Panel 23.

Richard was a son of James and Maggie Cheevers of Waterloo Place, Cookstown. He was a regular soldier and was serving in India at the outbreak of the First World War.

Richard is believed to have died of an illness contracted in India and is interred in Quetta Government Cemetery close to where he was stationed. His Battalion didn't leave India until October 1914.

Richard Cheevers is commemorated on Cookstown Cenotaph and on St. Luran's Church of Ireland Roll of Honour, Derryloran, Cookstown.

10693-Private Patrick Joseph Leo Murphy

2nd Battalion Royal Inniskilling Fusiliers
Died of Wounds: 23rd August 1914
Age: 20
Le Mans West Cemetery, France.   Grave: A-21

Patrick Joseph Leo Murphy was born in Stewartstown and
subsequently moved with his parents to Dublin. He enlisted in
Belfast. Nothing is known of his early life but he was part of the
first draft of men sent to the Western Front on the outbreak of
hostilities in August 1914. Patrick was mortally wounded within
days of arriving in France and was removed to hospital at Le
Mans. In 1914, when St Nazaire and Nantes were British bases,
Le Mans was the advance base and a hospital centre. There were
three Stationary Hospitals situated in Le Mans in September of
1914 and it was to one of these that Patrick was taken. He died
from his wounds there on 23rd August 1914. He is buried in row
A- grave 21 at Le Mans West Cemetery, France,

Le Mans is a large town and the seat of the Prefecture of the
Department of the Sarthe. The Cemetery is in the north-west
suburb of the town, west of the river Sarthe.

Patrick Joseph Leo Murphy is commemorated on Stewartstown
Cenotaph.

7881-Private Robert Falls

2nd Battalion Royal Inniskilling Fusiliers
Killed in Action: 26th August 1914
Age: 29
La Ferte-sous-Jouarre Memorial, France.

Robert Falls was a son of John and Margaret Falls of Blue Doors, Coolkeeghan, Cookstown. Robert enlisted in 1903 and had served for a time in China. He was a life long friend of Private William Nixon. The two friends were almost the same age and lived next door to each other. Tragically they died on the same day.

Robert was well known in Cookstown. He distinguished himself in sporting circles by winning a marathon race in Malta a few years before the war when he defeated several French runners and covered the twenty-six miles in about three hours. His prize was a silver casket priced at the time at £10, which his widowed mother and his brothers at home greatly prized. While serving in China with the British Legation Board, Robert won a medal in a cross-country race promoted by the Army and Navy YMCA, in Peking in 1910. After completing his time of service in the Army, Robert was employed for some time in Scotland. He returned home and found work at the Ulster Dairy School (now Loughry College) where he worked in the farmyard. He was a member of the Church of Ireland and a member of Strifehill L.O.L. At the outbreak of the First World War, Robert joined his old regiment and was posted to the Western Front with the first draft of men.

Robert was killed in action in the battle of Le Cateau on 26th August 1914. His unit was driven back about 200 yards before eventually recovering most of the lost ground. It was during this action that Robert was killed. The Battalion lost thirty-six men on this day. Robert has no known grave and is commemorated on the La Ferte-sous-Jouarre Memorial, France.

He is commemorated on Cookstown Cenotaph and St. Luran's Church of Ireland Roll of Honour, Derryloran Cookstown.

His younger brother, Samuel was killed in action while serving with the Scots Guards on 27th September 1915 at the Battle of Loos.

9413-Private Albert McCluskey
2nd Battalion Manchester Regiment
Died of Wounds: 26th August 1914
Le Cateau Military Cemetery, France. Grave: 4-H-5

Albert McCluskey was born in Stewartstown, County Tyrone. He was living and working in Winsford, Cheshire where he enlisted with the 2nd Battalion Manchester Regiment at Manchester.

On the 17th August 1914 the 1st and 2nd Battalions of the Manchester Regiment landed at Le Harve and almost immediately were engaged in action at the Battle of Mons. The Battle of Mons was the first engagement between the British and German Forces on the Western Front and began on 23rd August 1914. The Battle comprises one of the so-called Battles of the Frontier that took place during August 1914 at Mulhouse, Lorraine, Ardennes, Charleroi and Mons.

Albert McCluskey died of wounds received during the Battle of Mons and is interred in, plot 4, row H, grave 5 at Le Cateau Military Cemetery, France.

Le Cateau is a small town about 27 kilometres east-south-east of Cambrai. The town and the countryside around it were the scene of fierce fighting, fought by British 2nd Army Corps against a greatly superior German force on the 26th August 1914. From that day the town remained in German control until 10th October 1918, when the town was liberated by the 5th Battalion Connaught Rangers.

7871-Private William Nixon

2nd Battalion Royal Inniskilling Fusiliers
Killed in Action: 26th August 1914
Age: 30
Esnes Communal Cemetery, France.

William Nixon was born at Blue Doors, Coolkeeghan, Cookstown, County Tyrone.

William had been on the Reserve Army and prior to the outbreak of the First World War he was employed for nine years in Greenvale Mill (Adair's). He was called up when war was declared and sent to France with the first British Expeditionary Force. On the 26th August 1914, the opening day of Battle of Le Cateau, his Battalion were at first driven back but then recovered most of the lost ground and it was during this recovery that William was killed.

His last letter to his wife was written on the 23rd August and was received by her on the day he was killed. In it he said he had taken God as his guide and if they did not meet on earth his trust was that they would meet in a brighter and better world.

He left a young widow, Emma, (nee Davidson) and two children, William, a boy of four and a half years, and Jean, a girl of three years. Like his good friend, Robert Falls, he was a member of the Church of Ireland and also of the Orange Order.

William Nixon is buried in Esnes Communal Cemetery, France.

He is commemorated on Cookstown Cenotaph and on St. Luran's Church of Ireland Roll of Honour, Derryloran, Cookstown.

Take comfort, Christians, when your friends in Jesus fall asleep
There better being never ends while in dejected weep
Why inconsolable? As those to whom no hope is given
Death is the messenger of peace, and calls the soul to Heaven

Together to thy Father's house, with joyful hearts they go
And dwell for ever with the Lord, beyond the reach of woe
A few short years of evil past we reach the happy shore
Where death divided friends at last, shall meet to part no more.

Obituary inserted by his wife and two children Mid Ulster Mail 1914.

2nd Lieutenant - John Gunning Moore Dunlop

2nd Battalion Royal Dublin Fusiliers
Killed in Action: 27th August 1914
Age: 28
Honnechy British Cemetery, Nord, France. Grave: 2 C 9

John Dunlop was the son of Dr. Archibald Dunlop, St. Helens, Holywood, County Down, and Mrs. Bessie Dunlop (nee Gunning-Moore) formerly of Cookstown, County Tyrone, and nephew of Mr. J.B. Gunning-Moore, Coolnafranky, Cookstown.

John Dunlop was educated at Gonville and Caius College, Cambridge.

In his last will and testament, dated 3rd August 1914 he stated that his executors were to be, "The Masters and Fellows of Gonville & Caius College".

He left his estates and lands in County Tyrone to his brother George Malcolm Dunlop, and to his sister Elizabeth Dorothea he left the contents of his rooms at College.

The rest of his estate was left to the Masters and Fellows of Gonville and Caius College.

He was killed in action on 27th August 1914 and is buried in grave 2 C 9 at Honnechy British Cemetery, Nord, France and is commemorated on Holywood War Memorial, Co. Down.

John's brother, Captain George Malcolm Dunlop was later killed in action at Gallipoli on 25th April 1915.

There is a substantial plaque in memory of the brothers in Holywood Church of Ireland while their mother was given the honour of unveiling the town's main war memorial in 1922.

John Gunning Moore Dunlop was a member of 381 Masonic Lodge, Holywood, Co. Down.

11376- Private Thomas William Steele.

1st Battalion Royal Irish Fusiliers
Killed in Action: 16th September 1914
Age: 20
La Ferte Sous Touarre Memorial, France.

Thomas was born in Cookstown in the summer of 1894. He had just turned twenty when he was killed in action on 16th September 1914 having been in the army for little over a year. When Thomas enlisted he joined the Royal Inniskilling Fusiliers under number 11376 but subsequently transferred to the Royal Irish Fusiliers. Much of his early training took place at Shorncliffe Camp on the south coast of England. Thomas' father had passed away and his mother Catherine had re-married. Her second husband was Robert Martin and they lived at Church Street, Cookstown. Thomas' brother, Robert, also enlisted with the Royal Inniskilling Fusiliers. He survived the war.

The British Army, having forced the Aisne, had seized the high ground to the north and was clinging on to the southern edges of these heights, whilst the French sixth army pivoted on their left. This was the commencement of a prolonged stalemate in trench warfare, for the British found the enemy strongly entrenched. The position held was precarious. Owing to the wide level plain which lay behind the British lines all movement of reinforcement by day was in full view of the enemy. The 1st Battalion Royal Irish Fusiliers, now in support, suffered more from shellfire than troops actually in the line, protected by trenches and natural caves. This action bounded the southern side of Bucy-le-Long, a village which was almost obliterated during the battle. Thomas was the only man to be killed on the 16th September, almost certainly by shellfire, and has no known grave. He is commemorated on La-Ferte-Sous-Jouarre Memorial, France.

Thomas Steele is commemorated on Cookstown Cenotaph and on St. Luran's Church of Ireland Roll of Honour, Derryloran, Cookstown.

9310-A/Corporal Samuel Ballentyne
2nd Battalion Argyll and Sutherland Highlanders
Killed in Action: 21st October 1914
Age: 28
Ploegsteert Memorial, Belgium. Panels: 9 - 10

Samuel was born in1886 and was the son of Thomas J. and Elizabeth Ballentyne.

The family moved to live at 83 Willowfield Street, Belfast. Samuel was working in Scotland before the start of the First World War and enlisted in Stirling.

On the 21st October 1914 the 2nd Battalion were attacked by German troops and were driven back about three hundred yards. They regained their trench after midnight in a courageous counter attack. Men who had been wounded and who could not walk had to be left behind and became German prisoners. Samuel was originally reported missing, later presumed killed in action. He has no known grave and today he is commemorated on panels 9-10 on Ploegsteert Memorial, Belgium.and He is also remembered on the family plot in Cookstown New Cemetery.

His mother passed away on 22nd December 1943 and his father three years later on 17th February 1946.

10097- Private James Sterling Lavery
2nd Battalion Royal Inniskilling Fusiliers
Killed in Action: 21st October 1914
Age: 24
Strand Military Cemetery, Belgium. Grave: 8-O-3

James Sterling Lavery was the son of William James Lavery (Clerk of the Markets, Cookstown) and Ellen Lavery, Cookstown, County Tyrone. He was the husband of Edith Lavery (later Mrs. Wright) of 470 Keppochill Road, Springburn, Glasgow. After leaving school James served his apprenticeship in the offices of Gunning's Factory (Milburn, Cookstown) where the Managing Director, Mr. W. Leper J. P., was a close friend. After serving his time James immigrated to Canada where he remained for two years before returning home. He then joined the army in Cookstown and trained in Omagh.

Soon after the outbreak of hostilities he was sent to Dover, from where he went to France in one of the earliest drafts. His last letter home, written just two days before he was killed, congratulated his brother on gaining his commission in the Royal Garrison Artillery and expressed the hope that they would meet in Germany one day. On the 20th October 1914 the 2nd Battalion Royal Inniskillings were in the front line at Le Gheer, Belgium, and sustained a heavy enemy attack throughout the day. The next day the enemy was strongly re-inforced and attacked again in a dawn mist. With the exception of D company, the Royal Inniskillings were driven back a few hundred yards. They regained their trenches in a counter attack on the afternoon of the 21st October. James Sterling Lavery was killed in action on the 21st October 1914. He is buried in plot 8- row O- grave 3 at Strand Military Cemetery, Belgium. He was survived by his wife Edith and son James Cecil, parents, brothers and sisters. His wife Edith later remarried, as Mrs. Wright, and lived in Glasgow.

He is commemorated on Cookstown Cenotaph and on Second Presbyterian Roll of Honour (Molesworth) Cookstown.

4322-Private David McMenemy

2nd Battalion Royal Inniskilling Fusiliers
Killed in Action: 21st October 1914
Age: 21
Ploegsteert Memorial, Belgium. Panel: 5

David McMenemy was the third son of Samuel and Mrs. M.A. McMenemy of Tullyhogue, Cookstown. He was regarded as a popular young man in the district and a valued member of LOL 111. He was in the Royal Inniskillings Fusiliers Reserves in January 1914 and was called up on the outbreak of hostilities and sent to the Western Front with the first draft. On the 21st October 1914, the 2nd Battalion were involved in a very heavy German attack which drove them back about three hundred yards, in which David was killed. The Battalion held their position from 5.15pm to after midnight when they were able to re-take their former trench. His father, Samuel, had previously spent twenty years serving in the British Army. Private McMenemy's brothers, John, Robert and Samuel also served during the First World War. John had been wounded in action at Gallipoli and again at the Somme. Robert and Samuel had both been gassed but recovered. David McMenemy has no known grave and is commemorated on panel 5 at Ploegsteert Memorial, Belgium. He is also commemorated on Cookstown Cenotaph.

9988-Private Joseph Newell
2nd Battalion Royal Inniskilling Fusiliers
'A' Company
Killed in Action: 21st October 1914
Age: 20
Ploegsteert Memorial, Belgium. Panel: 5

Joseph Newell was a son of Rachel Newell and the late William Newell of North Street, Stewartstown. He joined the army as a boy soldier and for two years prior to the war was an Officers servant. His Master, with whom he was very popular, was medically unfit for active service and it could have been arranged that young Newell could have remained with him at home but Joseph Newell elected to go to the Front. It was a decision that was to cost him his life. When he was killed in action he had three other brothers serving - James in the Army Veterinary Corps, Samuel in India, and John, who was right beside him in the same Company. Sadly, John was to survive his brother by just a little over two weeks. On the 21st October 1914, the Inniskillings came under a ferocious attack and were driven back a few hundred yards. It was during this attack that Joseph lost his life. From about 5.15pm they held the enemy and re-took their former trench after midnight.

On 16th January 1915 the Mid Ulster Mail reported that Mrs Newell had received a letter from the King informing her that he had heard with great interest that she had four sons in the Army and expressing his congratulations and assuring her that His Majesty appreciates the spirit and patriotism which prompted this example in one family of loyalty and devotion to Sovereign and Country. A fifth son had just joined the Army the previous week. In addition to this she also had two brothers and thirteen cousins in the British Army. On New Year's Day she received a small present of rice from children in the United States and a number of cards from comrades of her two fallen sons.

Neither of the boys has a known grave and both are commemorated on panel 5 on the Ploegsteert Memorial, Belgium and on Stewartstown Cenotaph and Donaghendry Church of Ireland Roll of Honour.

8845-Lance Corporal William McCann

2nd Battalion Royal Irish Rifles
Killed in Action: 25th October 1914
Age: 25
Le Touret Memorial, France. Panel: 42-43

William McCann was born in Stewartstown and later lived at 42 Greenville Street, Bloomfield, Belfast. He enlisted in Newry, joining the 2nd Royal Irish Rifles and arrived at Rouen, France on 14th August 1914. He was killed in action on 25th October 1914. William McCann has no known grave and is commemorated on, panels 42-43 at Le Touret Memorial, France.

8215-Rifleman John Crossett

2nd Battalion Royal Irish Rifles
Killed in Action: 27th October 1914
Age: 23
Le Touret Memorial, France. Panel: 42-43

John Crossett was a son of Henry and Mary Ann Crossett of Cookstown.

The family moved to live at 116 Carnan Street, Belfast. John enlisted in Belfast, joining the 2nd Battalion Royal Irish Rifles.

The 1st Battle of Ypres started on 18th October 1914, John Crossett was killed in action on the 27th of October 1914 and has no known grave.

He is commemorated on Le Touret Memorial, panels 42 and 43.

5867-Private Joseph Sloan
2nd Battalion Royal Scots Fusiliers
Died of Wounds: 2nd November 1914
Age: 26
Grangegorman Cemetery, Dublin (Cork Memorials).

Joseph Sloan was a son of George and Elizabeth Sloan of Grange, Cookstown. Shortly after leaving school he went to Scotland in search of work and found employment in Coatbridge. He served in the Royal Scots Fusiliers prior to the war and was called up when war was declared. The regiment embarked for France on 10th September 1914 and he served in the front line almost continuously until he was wounded on 21st October. He arrived at hospital in Cork a week later and died on 2nd November. His sister, Mrs. Cheevers, Cookstown had a number of letters from the Chaplain of the hospital, Reverend J.H. Murphy, telling her of Joseph's condition. He conducted the funeral service on 3rd November 1914 and Joseph Sloan is buried in Cork Military Cemetery. News of his death from wounds was received with shock in Coatbridge where he was fondly remembered. He was an active member of East United Free Church and was well known and held in high esteem in Coatbridge where he was a prominent player with Summerlee Britannia Football Club. Joseph was survived by a brother and two sisters.

The Grangegorman (Cork) Memorial Headstones commemorate the graves of 83 war dead who are buried in Cork Military Cemetery, but whose graves could not be maintained there. The headstones of the 83 War Dead are arranged before the Grangegorman Memorial, which is located in Grangegorman Military Cemetery on Blackhorse Avenue outside the North-East boundary of Phoenix Park.

Joseph Sloan is commemorated on Cookstown Cenotaph and on St. Luran's Church of Ireland Roll of Honour, Derryloran, Cookstown.

Now the labourer's task is o'er
Now the battle day has passed
Now upon the farther shore
Lands the voyager at last
Father, in thy gracious keeping
Leave me now thy servants sleeping.

Obituary inserted by his family Mid Ulster Mail 1914

Captain Hon. Robert Sheffield Stuart (Viscount)
Royal Scots Fusiliers
Killed In Action: 2nd November 1914
Age: 28
Le Touret Memorial, France. Panel 12 - 13

© *Earl Castle Stewart*

He was the second son of Andrew, 6th Earl Castle Stewart and Esme Georgiana, Countess Castle Stewart, Stuart Hall, Stewartstown, County Tyrone, and husband of Nancye Stuart (nee Croker) who was the daughter of Captain Croker, of the Argyll and Sutherland Highlanders. Nancye was a nurse in France during the First World War. Robert and Nancye had no children.

Robert Sheffield Stuart was gazetted to the Royal Scots Fusiliers when he was 20 years old and was well known in Dublin where his regiment was based. Regarded as a splendid horseman, he hunted with the Ward, Meath and Kildare hunts, and played polo, and rode at Fairyhouse and Punchestown. Although at the same time he did not neglect his serious work in which he had passed as a first class interpreter in French and Russian.

His battalion was in South Africa in 1913 and returned to England in March 1914, where it formed part of the first expeditionary force which held back the Germans in their first rush for Paris and the Channel ports. Captain Stuart took part in the retreat from Mons and the Battles of the Marne and the Aisne.

On 2nd November 1914 he led a night attack on an enemy trench at Neuve Chapelle. The party had to retire, but Captain Stuart was not with them. Though hopes were entertained that he might have been captured, as for a long time he had been reported 'Wounded and Missing in Action', it was later accepted that he had been killed. He was 28 years old.

Captain Robert Sheffield Stuart has no known grave and is commemorated on panel 12-13 on Le Touret Memorial, France.

He is also commemorated on Stewartstown Cenotaph and Donaghendry Church of Ireland Roll of Honour.

Captain Stuart's wife Nancye remarried in later years to Mr. Charles Elverson, of Julian Island, British Columbia.

© By kind permission. Earl Castle Stewart, Stuart Hall, Stewartstown, County Tyrone.

3773-Private Abraham Stewart

2nd Battalion Royal Inniskilling Fusiliers
Died of Wounds: 5th November 1914
Wimereux Cemetery, France. Grave: 1-A-112

Abraham was a son of Abraham Stewart of Dunamoney, Magherafelt. He was attached to the Special Reserve which he had joined about 1910. Abraham was called up in June 1914 and sent to Finner Camp for a hurried few weeks of training. He went to the Front with the first draft in October and was mortally wounded and taken to a Casualty Clearing Station where he died a short time later. He is buried in plot 1, row A, grave 112 at Wimereux Cemetery, Boulogne, France. He is commemorated on Cookstown Cenotaph and on St. Luran's Church of Ireland Roll of Honour, Derryloran, Cookstown.

Abraham Stewart had relatives in Dungannon, Cookstown and Magherafelt.

7771-Private Thomas Montgomery

2nd Battalion Royal Inniskilling Fusilers
Killed in Action: 7th November 1914
Age: 30
Ploegsteert Memorial, Belgium. Panel: 5

Thomas Montgomery was a son of Samuel and Nancy Montgomery of Carradarragh, Moneymore, County Londonderry. He had been an Army Reservist and emigrated to Canada a number of years before the start of the First World War. His period of service was due to expire in December but when he saw the mobilisation notices he made arrangements to return home to rejoin his regiment. He enlisted in Cookstown. He arrived in France with the first draft of the British Expeditionary Force, Third Army Corps, 4th Division, 12th. Infantry Brigade. He was killed in action on 7th November 1914. His unit had been sent to recover trenches on the edge of Ploegsteert Wood and two desperate assaults were made. They were eventually driven back with heavy casualties. He has no known grave and today Thomas is commemorated on the Ploegsteert Memorial, panel 5. At the time of his death his brother John was training at Finner Camp, County Donegal. He is commemorated on Moneymore War Memorial (Assembly Rooms) and First Moneymore Presbyterian Roll of Honour.

4069-Private John Newell

2nd Battalion Royal Inniskilling Fusiliers
'A' Company
Killed in Action: 7th November 1914
Age: 18
Ploegsteert Memorial, Belgium. Panel: 5

John Newell was a son of Rachel Newell of North Street, Stewartstown, and the late William Newell. John was born in Stewartstown and educated in the local school. He enlisted in Cookstown but probably had some initial experience of army life. John had served along with his elder brother, Joseph; when Joseph was killed in action just over two weeks earlier and had to cope alone with the knowledge that his brother was dead. John was killed in action on 7th November 1914 when his unit was sent out to recover trenches on the edge of Ploegsteert Wood. Two desperate assaults were made during which John was killed. There is no known grave and John is commemorated along with his brother on the Ploegsteert Memorial, Panel 5. Both brothers are commemorated on Stewartstown Cenotaph, and on Donaghendry Church of Ireland Roll of Honour.

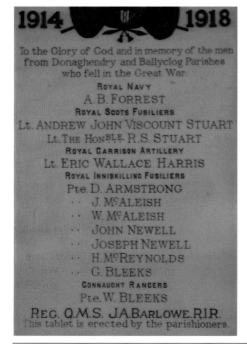

Donaghendry Church of Ireland
WW1 Roll of Honour

6792-Private James Herbert Clarke

2nd Battalion Royal Inniskilling Fusiliers
Died of Wounds: 8th November 1914
Age: 32
Bailleul Communal Cemetery, Nord, France. Grave: B 23

James Herbert Clarke was the husband of Elizabeth (Lilly) Helen Clarke (nee Steenson) of Milburn Street, Cookstown and later of 24005, St. Dominique, Montreal, Canada., and the son of Henry and Mary Clarke, Coleraine, County Londonderry., and brother of Jack Clarke who worked for the 'Ulster Gazette' in Armagh.

James Herbert Clarke was born and educated in Coleraine. He worked as a telegraphist in Coleraine before joining the army in 1899. He served throughout the Boer War in South Africa and went from there to Cairo, Egypt in 1905, where he served as a training instructor at a regimental school. He left Egypt in 1908 and returned to Cookstown where he married Lilly, who was the daughter of Mr James Steenson, Milburn Street.

James and Lilly left Cookstown and settled in Scotland where they lived at 2 Springbank Road, Paisley. He worked as a Red-leader in the shipyard there for the Fullerton Company.

At the outbreak of World War 1 he was called to Cowshot, Hampshire to rejoin the army. He and his family returned to Cookstown from where he went to Omagh and joined up with his old regiment.

The 2nd Battalion Royal Inniskilling Fusiliers were part of the 4th Division sent to the Western Front on 22nd August 1914 as part of the British Expeditionary Force and they took part in the action at the Battle of Messines between 10th October and 2nd November 1914.

James Clarke was severely wounded at St. Marguritte on 7th November 1914 and was taken to Number 10 Field Ambulance Hospital where he died from his wounds the next day.

He was 32 years old and left a widow and four children.

James Herbert Clarke is buried in grave B 23 at Bailleul Communal Cemetery, Nord, France. He is commemorated on Coleraine Memorial, Coleraine Congregational Church and at The Irish Society School where he was educated.

Weep not, mourn not,
For our Hero hath gone,
To reap in heaven,
His true reward.

Inserted for publication in Mid Ulster Mail by Mrs Lilly Clarke and children, 1916

8608-Guardsman Charles Montgomery

1st Battalion Scots Guards
Killed in Action: 11th November 1914
Menin Gate, Ypres (Ieper), Belgium.

Charles Montgomery was a son of Robert J. and Agnes
Montgomery of 10 Killymoon Street, Cookstown. He was born in
Ballymena and lived in Cookstown. He enlisted with the Scots
Guards in Glasgow, Scotland, and arrived in France in August
1914 with the British Expeditionary Force as part of First Army
Corps, 1st Division, First Guards Brigade. Charles Montgomery
was killed in action on 11th November 1914. He has no known
grave and is commemorated on panel 11 on the Menin Gate,
Ypres, Belgium. He is also commemorated on Cookstown
Cenotaph and Molesworth Presbyterian Roll of Honour. Charles
Montgomery was survived by his parents and his brothers,
William and John.

4065-Private John Joseph McCaffrey

2nd Battalion Royal Irish Fusiliers
Died of Wounds: 16th November 1914
Age: 19
Cite Bonjean Military Cemetery, Armentieres, France. Grave: 9-
B-72

John McCaffrey was born in Moyglass, County Fermanagh. He
was the son of John and Anne McCaffrey of 26 Blackhill,
Cookstown.

John worked at Adair's Mill at Greenvale, Cookstown, and his
father was a gardener on the Adair Estate. Two brothers of his
Grandmother fell in action while storming the heights of Alma
during the Crimean War (1854) and another grand-uncle on his
father's side was a veteran of the Indian Mutiny (1857-58).

John was a section leader with Cookstown Corps of Irish
Volunteers and regularly played football with the local Greenvale
Swifts Football Club, which included many of the workers from
the mill. Many of these lads eventually joined the Royal
Inniskillings. Lads such as Paddy Corey, Michael Lawn, James
King and Jacob Wilkinson (John McCaffrey's friend), all lost
their lives in the First World War. John enlisted in Cookstown
with the Inniskilling Fusiliers. He trained at Finner Camp and
was posted to Malin Head and Magilligan. On 18th September
1914 he was transferred to the 2nd Battalion Royal Inniskilling

Fusiliers and went to France. Many of the letters written to his father still exist to this day. In these letters he would refer to his friends back home and those with whom he joined the army, but had been sent elsewhere. While on service John received the following letter from his father:

Dear John, Just a few lines to let you know we received your kind and welcome letter this morning and glad to see by it that you are well as we are all well ourselves. Thank God. We are sending you some garters and we hope you get the medals and things we sent you, we sent cups and all in one box. Owen O'Lone was asking for you, the Blackhill team is starting up again and James Hamill says you will be back in time to play for them. Paddy Corey is at home yet and so is Johnnie Hampsey. We had a letter from the Maguires and Paddy is a prisoner of war in Germany. Francis Mullan was asking for you. Tell Robert Lawless we were asking for him and we were glad to hear he was well. Felix and Pat were asking for you and I heard that Jimmy McCaffrey and Pat were passed for the Police, so I think this is all at present. Goodbye from your loving father.

John McCaffrey. God Bless you, Write soon.

The above letter refers to names such as Paddy Corey, later killed at Bethune, Johnnie Hampsey who was wounded at Mons, and Robert Lawless, later killed in action at Festubert. John McCaffrey died of wounds on 16th November 1914. He is interred plot 9- row B- grave 72 at Cite Bonjean Military Cemetery, Armentieres, France.

John McCaffrey is commemorated on Cookstown Cenotaph.

90597 – Gunner Archibald Cooke
51st Battery Royal Field Artillery
Killed in Action: 18th November 1914
Menin Gate, Ypres Belgium. Panel 5 - 9

Archibald Cooke was born in Coagh and lived near Springhill, Moneymore before he enlisted with the Royal Field Artillery at Stockton-on-Tees.

He was killed in action on 18th November 1914 and is commemorated on Panel 5 – 9 on the Menin Gate Memorial, Ypres, Belgium.

Sergeant William Taylor
Royal Inniskiling Fusiliers Depot
Died of Illness: 20th January 1915
Cookstown New Cemetery, Cemetery Road, Cookstown.

William Taylor was one of 3 brothers who served in the army during the Boer War in South Africa. After his term of service had expired he returned to Cookstown to work.

He was married with 7 children and was a regular attendant at St Lurans's Church of Ireland, Church Street, Cookstown. His services were called upon in 1912 on the formation of the Ulster Volunteers where he acted as an instructor with the Cookstown company. At the outbreak of the First World War he joined his old regiment as a recruiting officer. During this time he contracted pneumonia and died on 20th January 1915. He received a full regimental funeral, with the service overseen by Reverend F.M. Moeran A.M. and Reverend J. Bloomer A.B. Funeral arrangements were carried out by Mr. Robert Steenson. William Taylor is buried in Cookstown New Cemetery. He does not have a commonwealth war grave.

Sergeant William Taylor was a brother of Private Joseph Taylor (2nd Royal Inniskilling Fusiliers) who was later killed in action on 5th May 1915.

3802 - Private James McGurk
1st Battalion Royal Scots
Died Of Wounds: 25th February 1915
Dickebusch New Military Cemetery, Belgium. Grave: A-5

James McGurk was born in Cookstown. The family appears to have moved to live in Glasgow. James enlisted at Weymouth in Dorset, joining the 1st Battalion Royal Scots. He died of wounds on 25th February 1915 and is interred in row A, grave 5 at Dickebusch New Military Cemetery, Belgium.

7867-Private Henry Campbell

2nd Battalion Royal Inniskilling Fusiliers
Died of Wounds: 7th March 1915
St. Sever Cemetery. France. Grave: A-5-7

Henry Campbell was the eldest son of William Campbell of Desertcreat, Tullyhogue, Cookstown, County Tyrone. He enlisted in Cookstown just after the outbreak of war. The Battalion arrived in France on 22nd August 1914 and William joined them later after his initial training had taken place. He died from wounds at Rouen on 7th March 1915 and is interred in plot A-row 5- grave 7 at St. Sever Cemetery, France.

He is commemorated on Cookstown Cenotaph.

On the anniversary of his death the family put the following verse in the Mid Ulster Mail, in his memory.

The Lord took him to himself
He knew his time had come
And we mourn the loss of one so dear
Our own beloved son

Henry Campbell is commemorated on Desertcreat Parish Church Roll of Honour.

19978-Private William Stewart

9th Battalion Royal Inniskilling Fusiliers
Died of Illness: 9th March 1915
Lissan Church of Ireland Graveyard. 407 A

William was born at Rossmore near Lissan, Cookstown. He enlisted in Cookstown, joining the 9th Battalion Royal Inniskilling Fusiliers. William's health began to deteriorate in January of 1915 while training with the Inniskillings at Randalstown, and he died on the 9th March 1915. He is interred in Lissan Church of Ireland graveyard, 407a.

8954-Rifleman Michael Curtiss

1st Battalion Royal Irish Rifles
Killed in Action: 10th March 1915
Le Touret Memorial, France. Panel: 42-43

Michael Curtiss was born in the Shankill, Belfast, but some time later his family moved to live at Churchtown, Cookstown. He went back to Belfast to enlist in the 1st Battalion of the Royal Irish Rifles. He was killed in action in the Battle of Neuve Chappelle on 10th March 1915. There is no known grave and Michael is commemorated on Le Touret Memorial, panels 42 and 43.

Neuve Chappelle was a battle designed to distract the Germans on the Western Front as much as possible. It was also the first planned battle on the Western Front with an initial bombardment of the enemy lines, which began at a quarter past seven on Wednesday 10th March. By 7.30am a heavier more concentrated bombardment became more intense and by 11.00am Neuve Chappelle was in British hands. It was during this early morning fighting that Michael was killed in action.

9323-Lance Corporal Robert Ross

1st Battalion Royal Irish Rifles
Killed in Action: 11th March 1915
Le Touret Memorial, France.   Panel: 42 - 43

Robert Ross was the son of Robert and Julia Ross, of 20 Linview Street, Grosvenor Road, Belfast. He worked at Gunning's Factory at Milburn in Cookstown.

He enlisted with the 1st Battalion Royal Irish Rifles and was posted to France. He was killed in action at the Battle of Neuve-Chapelle on 11th March 1915 and has no known grave. He is commemorated on panel 42-43 at Le Touret Memorial, France.

He is also commemorated on Gunning's Factory War Memorial (Royal British Legion, Cookstown).

18089-Private James Nelson
9th Battalion Royal Inniskilling Fusiliers
Died of Illness: 24th March 1915
Ballygoney Presbyterian Churchyard, Coagh

James Nelson was born at Lismoney, Cookstown, County Tyrone.

He was a member of Tamlaghtmore Flute Band and a member of Lissan Company of Ulster Volunteers. He enlisted in Cookstown, joining the 9th Battalion Royal Inniskilling Fusiliers. James Nelson was at Randalstown with his brothers, Thomas and William, training with their battalion when he fell ill with a severe throat infection.

He died from sceptic poisoning on 24th March 1915. His remains were brought back to Cookstown and met by members of the local Ulster Volunteers who escorted the remains from Cookstown train station at 7.45pm on Thursday 25th March to his home at Lismoney. James was buried the next day and his funeral was escorted by a party of local Volunteers along with his brothers Thomas and William. Privates Alexander McLernon and William Riddle both received special permission to leave the Randalstown Camp to escort their friend's remains to his last resting place.The service was taken by the Reverend John Entrican B.A. and funeral arrangements were undertaken by Mr. Robert Steenson. James Nelson was interred in Ballygoney Presbyterian Church Graveyard.

He is commemorated on the Roll of Honour in Molesworth, Presbyterian Church, Cookstown and Cookstown Cenotaph.

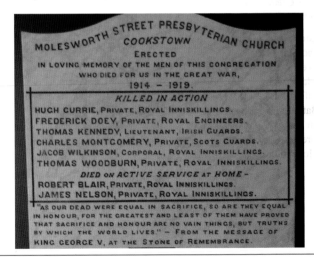

3035-Private Francis O'Neill

2nd Battalion Royal Inniskilling Fusiliers
Killed in Action: 29th March 1915
Age: 31
Browns Road Cemetery, Grave: 2-E-6

Francis O'Neill was a son of Joseph O'Neill of Ruskey, Coagh, County Tyrone. He and his wife, Annie, lived at Ballygruby, Moneymore. He was a brother of Margaret O'Neill of Rousky, Ballygruby. On the 29th March 1915 the 2nd Inniskillings were in trenches at Festubert. Six men were wounded and one was killed, Francis O'Neill. He is buried in plot 2- row E- grave 6 at Browns Road Cemetery, France. He is commemorated on Coagh War Memorial (Royal British Legion, Cookstown) and Moneymore War Memorial (Assembly Rooms).

Sleep! Soldier! Sleep! Thy warfare o'er
Not thine own bugles loudest strain
Shall ever break thy slumbers more
With summons of the battle plain
A trumpet-note more loud and deep
Must rouse thee from that leaden sleep!

Verse appeared with Obituary in Mid Ulster Mail in April 1915.

7678-Private James Devlin

2nd Battalion Cameronians (Scottish Rifles)
Killed in Action: 30th March 1915
Age: 18
Bois Grenier Communal Cemetery, France.
Grave: I - 2

James Devlin was born in Moneymore, and was the son of Henry and Mary Devlin. The family moved to work in Scotland and lived at 15 Union Place, Anderston, Glasgow. James enlisted in Glasgow, joining the 2nd Battalion Cameronians (Scottish Rifles). He was killed in action on 30th March 1915. The Battalion were just to the south of Armentieres, and lost six men on this day. James was interred, in row I- grave 2 at Bois Grenier Communal Cemetery, France. He is commemorated on Moneymore War Memorial (Assembly Rooms).

Staff Surgeon-Thomas Dickson Liddle
Royal Navy
H.M.S. Thames
MB
Died: 2nd April 1915
Age: 35

Sheerness, (Isle of Sheppey) Cemetery, Kent. Grave: C-C- 49.

Thomas Dixon Liddle was born on 23rd January 1879 and was the son of Edward and Eliza Liddle of Cookstown. Thomas's father was also a doctor who later moved to Hungerford Road, Crewe. His brother was a doctor and practised at Market Street, in Portadown.

Thomas passed his surgical exams, graduating from Queen's University Belfast on 23rd November 1903 and immediately joined the Admiralty. Eight years later, on 23rd November 1911, he became a Staff Surgeon. Over the years he worked on many different ships and had at least two spells in Haslar Hospital. His last ship was H.M.S. Thames which he joined on 7th January 1913. When he died on 2nd April 1915 there were extenuating circumstances which called for a post mortem to be held. The results of the post mortem were read by Staff Surgeon Hughes. The cause of death was given as morphia poisoning, self administered, but whether by intent or misadventure, there was insufficient evidence to prove. Thomas was interred in Sheerness (Isle of Sheppey) Cemetery, C-C-49. Kent, England and is commemorated on Queen's University Belfast War Memorial.

8092 - Private Robert Blair
Royal Inniskilling Fusiliers (Omagh Depot)
Died of Illness: 8th April 1915
Cookstown New Cemetery: J 1491

Although Robert Blair died at home, he was still an army
reservist with the Royal Inniskilling Fusiliers. Originally a native
of Castlecaulfield he had served many years overseas in Egypt.
He had been employed in Orritor quarry where he lost an eye in
an accident with a traction engine. At the beginning of the war
he was called up but owing to the defect in his sight he was not
sent to the Western Front but was employed as a cook in the
depot in Omagh. Whilst at home for Easter holidays, 1915 where
his wife resided at Toberlane, he became ill suffering from a
severe cold. Later influenza developed and cardiac trouble. He
was described as a quiet inoffensive man and respected by all
who knew him. He had been married about a year to Miss Sarah
Jane Kempton. Robert was a valued member of R.B.P. 598
Montober. He passed away on the 8th April 1915 and is interred
in Cookstown New Cemetery.

In later years Robert's wife would often say that she was married,
widowed, and became a mother, all in the one year. Robert Blair
is commemorated on Cookstown Cenotaph, St. Luran's Church
of Ireland Roll of Honour, Derryloran, Cookstown and
Molesworth Presbyterian Roll of Honour.

Captain George Malcolm Dunlop

1st Battalion Royal Dublin Fusiliers
Killed in Action: 25th April 1915
Age: 26
'V' Beach Cemetery, Turkey. Special Memorial: A 46

George Malcolm Dunlop was the son of Dr. Archibald Dunlop of "St Helen's" Holywood, County Down, and Mrs. Bessie Dunlop (nee Gunning-Moore) formerly of Cookstown, and nephew of Mr. J.B. Gunning-Moore, Coolnafranky, Cookstown.

George was educated at Cheltenham and joined the Royal Dublin Fusiliers in 1906.

He was promoted to Captain in December 1914.

He was killed in action on 25th April 1915 and is commemorated on special memorial A 46 at 'V' Beach Cemetery, Turkey. He is also commemorated on Holywood War Memorial.

Captain George Malcolm Dunlop was the brother of 2nd Lieutenant John Gunning Moore Dunlop who was killed in action on 27th August 1914.

Both brothers are commemorated on the Roll of Honour at Holywood Church of Ireland.

10838: Regimental Sergeant Major James Weir

1st Battalion Kings Own Scottish Borderers
Killed in Action: 26th April 1915
Tilloy British Cemetery, France. Grave: 6-B-22

James Weir was born in Moneymore but had been living in
Glasgow. He enlisted in Glasgow joining the 1st Battalion
King's Own Scottish Borderers. He was killed in action on 26th
April 1915 in fierce fighting around the Southern edge of the city
of Arras, France. His body was recovered and he is interred Plot
6, Row B, Grave 22 at Tilloy British Cemetery, France.

13206-Private Edward McGeown

1st Battalion Royal Inniskilling Fusiliers
Killed in Action: 28th April 1915
Age: 20
Helles Memorial, Turkey.   *Panel: 97-101*

Edward McGeown was born in Cookstown and was the son of
James and Mary Jane McGeown of Killymoon Street,
Cookstown. The family later moved to live at 27 Milfort Avenue,
Dunmurry.

In 1913 Edward joined the 4th Hussars. After one year of service
he underwent surgery for appendicitis. He was subsequently
considered unfit for cavalry work and, refusing to transfer to a
foot regiment, he was discharged. He re-enlisted with the
Inniskillings in Cookstown at the outbreak of war and was sent to
the Gallipoli Peninsula. Edward was killed in action during the
first Battle of Krithia on 28th April 1915. This was just a few
days after landing on the Peninsula. He has no known grave and
is commemorated on panels 97-101 on the Helles Memorial,
Turkey. Private McGeown had an older brother who had served
in a Derbyshire Regiment and had gone through the Boer War
without a scratch, and who was to die later in Singapore as a
result of sunstroke. Just before Edward was killed, his parents
received a letter from him in which he said:

*"We have not done any fighting yet, but by all appearances it
won't be very long now. We are all ready to face the music and
the men are all in the best of health."*

Edward McGeown is commemorated on Cookstown Cenotaph
and St. Luran's Church of Ireland Roll of Honour, Derryloran,
Cookstown.

2445- Private Joseph Taylor
2nd Battalion Royal Inniskilling Fusiliers ('C' Company)
Killed In Action: 5th May 1915
Age: 48
Cuinchy Communal Cemetery, France. Grave 2-C-6

Joseph Taylor was born in Dungannon and was the husband of
Mary Taylor, and father of Jane Taylor, Coolreaghs, Cookstown.
He was a brother to Sergeant William Taylor who died of illness
while on home service on 20th January 1915.

Joseph and William had both served with the Inniskilling
Fusiliers during the Boer War in South Africa and both men
retired from the army to work in Cookstown. Joseph was called
back to his old regiment at the outbreak of the First World War.

On 25th January 1915 the 2nd Inniskillings were posted to 5th
Infantry Brigade, 2nd Division, but came into no serious action
for some time. At the opening of the Battle of Festubert the
Battalion was called upon to show their mettle in attack. Up until
15th May 1915 they had encountered little resistance and it was
reported that there had been 6 men killed and 40 wounded.
Joseph Taylor was reported as killed in action at around 6 a.m. on
the morning, 5th May 1915 and was buried at 4 p.m. later that
day in Plot 2, Row C, Grave 6 at Cuinchy Communal Cemetery,
France.

His wife Mary and daughter Jane received a letter of condolence
from Quarter-Master Sergeant M. Mehaffey.

Joseph Taylor is commemorated on Cookstown Cenotaph and St.
Luran's Church of Ireland Roll of Honour, Derryloran,
Cookstown.

My darling sleeps, but not forever,
There will be a glorious dawn,
Where we meet to part, no, never,
On the resurrection morn.
It's hard to part with one so dear,
And say, 'Thy Will Be Done'.
But he who chose him for his own,
Will keep him 'til we come.

Submitted by his wife Mary and daughter Jane Taylor, Mid Ulster Mail 1915.

9419-Rifleman Patrick Sweeney

1st Battalion Royal Irish Rifles
Killed in Action: 9th May 1915
Age: 23
Ploegsteert Memorial, Belgium. Panel: 9

Patrick Sweeney was born at Ballygillan, near Ballinderry
Bridge, County Londonderry. Although living at Ballynure, near
Ballyclare, he enlisted in Belfast into the 1st Battalion Royal Irish
Rifles. The Battalion had been in billets at Bac St. Maur since the
5th May 1915 and left at 11.00pm on the 8th to march to the
assembly trenches at La Cordonnerie Farm. The operation was
part of an attempt to take Aubers Ridge co-ordinated with the
French attack at Souchez. Patrick was killed in action on 9th
May during the Battle of Aubers Ridge close to Festubert. There
is no known grave and Patrick is commemorated on panel 9 at
Ploegsteert Memorial, Belgium.

6915-Private Peter Tohill

(Served as Private Patrick O'Neill)
1st Battalion Royal Irish Rifles
Killed in Action: 9th May 1915
Age: 30
Ploegsteert Memorial, Belgium.   Panel: 9

Peter Tohill was the son of Hugh and Elizabeth Tohill of
Stewartstown, County Tyrone. There is some dispute as to
whether Peter was born in Belfast or Londonderry. When he
enlisted in Banbridge he did so under a false name. He used the
name of Patrick O'Neill on his enlistment and it is stated that
Patrick O'Neill was born in Belfast, but according to
Commonwealth War Graves details, he was born in Londonderry.
Either way, at the time he enlisted in Banbridge, he gave his
address as Stewartstown, County Tyrone.

He joined the 1st Battalion Royal Irish Rifles and served with
them in most of the early fighting of the First World War. Peter
was killed in action on Sunday 9th May 1915 during the Battle of
Aubers Ridge. This was an attack that resulted in heavy losses
and the 1st Battalion lost one hundred and seventy-nine men on
that one day. As was to be expected with such heavy losses and
with the front line moving backwards and forwards as the battle
swayed one way then the other, there is no known grave. Peter is
commemorated on panel 9 on Ploegsteert Memorial, Belgium.

217-Private Hugh Robinson

2nd Battalion Australian Infantry, Australian Imperial Forces.
Killed in Action: 10th May 1915
Age: 26
Lone Pine Cemetery, Anzac, Turkey. Grave: 2-C-11

Hugh Robinson was born in Stewartstown and was the son of William Stewart Robinson and Mary Jane Robinson, Stewartstown County Tyrone, and later of, Fort William, Ontario, Canada.

Hugh was living in Radwick, New South Wales, Australia, where he worked as an iron monger. His brother Benjamin was living and working in Ballarat, Victoria, Australia. Hugh enlisted with the 2nd Battalion Australian Imperial Force on 28th August 1914.

He left Sydney, Australia on 18th October 1914 and arrived at Alexandria, Egypt on 18th December 1914. He was part of the ANZAC forces (Australia/New Zealand Corps) which landed on the Gallipoli peninsula in April 1915 at Gaba Tepe, an area known as Anzac Cove. The force made little headway in the intense heat and with the Turkish forces holding the high ground, casualties were very high.

Hugh Robinson was killed in action on 10th May 1915 and was originally interred in Brown Dip North Cemetery, 500 yards behind the lines. He was later reburied in plot 2, row C, grave 11 at Lone Pine Cemetery, Turkey, about 18 miles from Anzac Cove.

3525-Private John Jordan
2nd Battalion Royal Inniskilling Fusiliers
Killed in Action: 14th May 1915
Age: 22
Rue-de-Berceaux Cemetery, France. Grave: 2-D-34

John Jordan was a son of Mrs. M.A. McAtee of Hammond Street, Moneymore. She had re-married after the death of her first husband. John had been a Reservist and was called up on mobilisation and left for France on 22nd August 1914. He had been through several actions including the Battle of Mons. Another brother was serving in the same Battalion and they had left for France at the same time. On the 12th May 1915 the 2nd Battalion marched through Richebourg to take the line in preparation for the Battle of Festubert. It wasn't so much trenches that they were holding as a series of frontline breastworks which had been erected and was the only possible means of shelter in the water logged country. These give little or no protection from enemy artillery fire and up until 15th May there had been 6 men from the Battalion killed and 40 wounded. John Jordan was killed by enemy shell fire on 14th May 1915 and is interred in plot 2- row D- grave 34 at Rue-de-Berceaux Cemetery close to Richebourg. Of the three men killed with him or who subsequently died from wounds, two lie in Rue-de-Berceaux and are: E. Manning buried in plot 2- row D- grave 21 and P. McGuigan buried in plot 2- row D- grave 32.

The other man, Sergeant Francis McGartland, was seriously wounded and taken to Boulogne and died there of his wounds. He lies in Boulogne Eastern Cemetery, plot 8- row C- grave 42.

At the time of John Jordan's death he had two other brothers training at Shane's Park Camp at Randalstown with the 36th Ulster Division.

John Jordan is commemorated on Moneymore War Memorial (Assembly Rooms).

8172-Private John Arbuthnot

2nd Battalion Royal Inniskilling Fusiliers
Killed In Action: 16th May 1915
Age: 27
Le Touret Memorial, France. Panel 16-17

John Arbuthnot was born in Stewartstown, County Tyrone and enlisted in Dungannon, and lived at Rathnew.

On 15th May 1915, on the eve of the Battle of Festubert, the 2nd Battalion Inniskillings were preparing for an attack at night as recent daylight attacks had failed to gain any ground.

In the aftermath of this action the Battalion casualties were high. 240 were men killed, including local men, John Arbuthnot, James Hamilton, Edward Lavery, Robert Lawless, James Lawlor, Patrick Taylor, James Owens, Alex McIlree and Michael Lawn who died of his wounds on 17th May 1915. John Arbuthnot has no known grave and is commemorated on Panel 16 -17 on Le Touret Memorial, France.

3699 - Private James Hamilton

2nd Battalion Royal Inniskilling Fusiliers
Killed in Action: 16th May 1915
Le Touret Memorial, France. Panel: 16 - 17

James Hamilton was the brother of Mrs. Cassie Hampsey, of Irish Street, Dungannon and Miss Kate Hamilton, of Church Street, Cookstown.

James had three brothers serving in the Army, Charles and Edward were in France and John was stationed in England.

James was killed in action on the 16th May 1915 during the Battle of Festubert.

10739-Private Edward Lavery

2nd Battalion Royal Inniskilling Fusiliers
Killed in Action: 16th May 1915
Age: 18
Le Touret Memorial, France. Panel: 16-17

Edward Lavery was the son of Mr. J Lavery of 10 Old
Hillsborough Road, Lisburn. He was living in Cookstown at the
beginning of the First World War but returned to Lisburn to
enlist. He was killed in action on 16th May 1915, during the
Battle of Festubert. There is no known grave and Edward is
commemorated on the Le Touret Memorial, panels 16 and 17.
At 9.00pm on the 16th May 1915 the 2nd Inniskillings formed up
in breastworks for an attack, A and D Companies were in the
front line with B and C in support. It was a costly attack which
claimed the lives of two hundred and forty men, 9 of them from
Cookstown district.

8016-Lance Corporal Robert Lawless

2nd Battalion Royal Inniskilling Fusiliers
Killed in Action: 16th May 1915
Age: 30
Le Touret Memorial, France. Panel 16 - 17

Robert Lawless was born in Cookstown. He was the son of John
Lawless, Church Street, Cookstown.

He worked and lived in Belfast and enlisted in Cookstown at the
outbreak of war. He was a close friend of John McCaffrey's and
was often referred to in Private McCaffrey's letters.

Robert Lawless was killed in action on 16th May 1915 in the
same attack on the first night of the Battle of Festubert where 8
other Cookstown men also died.

Private Shields who took part in the attack was home on leave
soon after and told Robert's family that he'd seen him fall in
action but had not seen or heard from him since.

Robert has no known grave and is commemorated on Le Touret
Memorial, France, Panel 16 - 17, and on Cookstown Cenotaph.

10479 - Private James Dominic Lawlor

2nd Battalion Royal Inniskilling Fusiliers
Killed In Action: 16th May 1915
Le Touret Memorial, France.   Panel 16 - 17

James Lawlor was born at Ballymacarrett, County Down. He lived and worked in Cookstown. He went back home to enlist at Ballymacarrett. He was killed in action on the eve of the Battle of Festubert.

He has no known grave and is commemorated on panel 16-17 on Le Touret Memorial, France.

The Inniskillings marching in Cookstown

Photo courtesy of David Lennox

4304-Private Alexander McIlree

2nd Battalion Royal Inniskilling Fusiliers
Killed in Action: 16th May 1915
Le Touret Memorial, France. Panel 16 - 17

Alexander McIlree was born at Annahavil near Cookstown and
worked for Alexander Barclay at Drapersfield before joining the
Inniskillings in November 1913. He was one of eight boys from
the same family to join up for service during the First World War.

He was a member of Knockinroe LOL. 194.

Early in 1915 his mother received a letter from Buckingham
Palace after the Rector of Ardtrea, the Reverend W.E.R. Scott,
wrote and told the King about Mrs. McIlree having 8 sons
serving in the army.

Madam, I have the honour to inform you that The King has heard
with much interest that you have at present eight sons in the
army. I am commanded to express to you The King's
congratulations and to assure you that His Majesty much
appreciates the spirit of patriotism which prompted this example,
in one family, of loyalty to their Sovereign and the Empire. I have
the honour to be, Madam, your obedient servant.

F. Ponsonby.
Keeper of the Privy Purse, 1st February 1915.

Alex McIlree was killed in action during a night attack on enemy
positions on the eve of the Battle of Festubert. A report in the
Mid Ulster Mail, Cookstown the following month stated:

"Alexander McIlree's body was discovered on the battlefield by
two soldiers from the 1st Manchester Regiment. In forwarding
home his personal belongings they sent a letter saying that he
had fallen in action near them, being struck by shell shrapnel and
had died a soldiers death, fighting for King and Country."

Alexander McIlree has no known grave and is commemorated on
panel 16-17 on Le Touret Memorial, France. He is also
commemorated on Cookstown Cenotaph and St. Andrew's,
Ardtrea Church of Ireland, Roll of Honour.

3620-Private James Owens
2nd Battalion Royal Inniskiling Fusiliers
Killed in Action: 16th May 1915
Age: 24
Le Touret Memorial, France. Panel 16 - 17

James Owens was born at Lissan, Cookstown. He lived and worked in Cookstown prior to enlisting in the army with the 2nd Battalion Royal Inniskillings. James Owens was later killed on the eve of the Battle of Festubert.

On the 12th May 1915 the 2nd Battalion marched through Richebourg to take their positions in waterlogged breastworks (makeshift trenches) near the front line getting ready for an attack on the strongly held German lines as repeated attacks had been made by other regiments since the 9th May without success.

All attacks during daylight had failed. On the night of May 15th 1915 a night attack was attempted. On the 2nd Division front, two brigades were entrusted with the task, 6th Brigade on the right of attack and 5th Brigade on the left which included 2nd Inniskillings along with the Worcestershire Regiment which would lead the attack. Their objective was to seize and consolidate the first and second lines of Germans trenches. "D" Company of the 2nd Inniskillings were successful with "C" company in their support. Unfortunately as the attack progressed, "A" company on the left of the attack suffered very heavy casualties, the Worcestershire Regiment failed to consolidate their efforts and "B" company in support also suffered quite badly. A and B companies were obliged to fall back to their own lines. C and D companies were ordered to fall back to the first German line and consolidate there, which they held until they were relieved the next evening. The 2nd Inniskillings lost 240 men in the attack including Private James Owens.

The 2nd Worcestershire's lost 64 men including Sergeant James Toole from Bray, County Wicklow, and Private Henry Nash from Limerick.

Private James Owens has no known grave and is commemorated on panel 16-17 on the Le Touret Memorial, France. He is also commemorated on Cookstown Cenotaph and Moneymore War Memorial (Assembly Rooms).

3543-Private Patrick Taylor
2nd Battalion Royal Inniskilling Fusiliers
Killed in Action: 16th May 1915
Age: 27
Le Touret Memorial, France. Panel: 16-17

Patrick Taylor was a son of Mrs. Sarah Taylor of Moneymore, County Londonderry. His father had died before the outbreak of the First World War. Patrick enlisted in Cookstown at the same time as James Owens and both men joined the 2nd Battalion Royal Inniskilling Fusiliers. They went out to France together in the same draft. Patrick was killed in action at the Battle of Festubert on Sunday 16th May 1915. He has no known grave and is commemorated on panels 16-17 on Le Touret Memorial, France. Patrick Taylor is also commemorated on Moneymore War Memorial (Assembly Rooms).

Second Lieutenant Robert James Noel Stuart
3rd Battalion Royal Scots Fusiliers
(attached to 2nd Battalion)
Killed in Action: 16th May 1915
Age: 29
Guards Cemetery, Windy Corner, Cuinchy, France. Grave - 5 L 3

Robert James Noel Stuart was born on 23rd October 1886, the only child of Horace Noel Stuart and Madeleine Frances Stuart (nee Hemming) of 'Wilminster', Richmond Road, Staines, Middlesex. He was a great grandson of Robert, 2nd Earl Castle Stewart. Robert's father Horace was half-brother to Andrew 6th Earl Castle Stewart, Stuart Hall, Stewartstown, County Tyrone.

Robert James Noel Stuart received his commission in 1914 and was killed in action at about 08.00 hours on the morning of 16th May 1915. His commanding officer later wrote:

"He was a very good reliable Officer and a very good fellow, we are all much grieved at his death, he was a thorough soldier."

Robert James Noel Stuart was a cousin of Robert Sheffield Stuart who was killed in action on 2nd November 1914, and Andrew John Stuart killed in action on 25th September 1915.

Lieutenant Stuart is buried in plot 5, row L, grave 3 at Guards Cemetery, Windy Corner, Cuinchy, France.

© By kind permission 8th Earl Castle Stewart

4064-Private Michael Lawn
2nd Battalion Royal Inniskilling Fusiliers
Died of Wounds: 17th May 1915
Lillers Communal Cemetery, France. Grave: 3-A-44

Michael Lawn was born at Urney, County Tyrone, and lived at Blackhill, Cookstown.

He worked in Adair's Mill at Greenvale, Cookstown and was well known in the area as a football player. He had played with some of the local clubs including Greenvale Swifts where quite a few of his colleagues were reserve soldiers, including, John McCaffrey, James King and Paddy Corey. He was 19 years old when he was called up at the outbreak of the First World War. He had spent almost eight months at the Front and was involved in several engagements with the enemy, before he was severely wounded in fierce fighting on the 16th May 1915 during the opening of the Battle of Festubert. He was taken to a Casualty Clearing Station, situated close to Lillers, a town to the west of Bethune. Casualty Clearing Stations were situated here for most of 1915 and 1916 and again during the German Spring Offensive of 1918. On the day on which he was wounded, 240 men of the 2nd Inniskillings were killed. Michael Lawn died of his wounds on the 17th May 1915 and is interred in plot 3- row A- grave 44 at Lillers Communal Cemetery, France. He is also commemorated on Cookstown Cenotaph.

At a meeting of Greenvale Swifts Football Club which was held on Wednesday 9th June 1915, the following resolution was passed.

That we, the members of Greenvale Swifts Football Club, express our deepest sympathy with the relatives of Private Michael Lawn, Blackhill, Cookstown, who was severely wounded on 16th May and died the following day.

Michael Lawn was a worthy member of the above club. His position in the club was left back and he was a great sportsman and took a real interest in the game. He joined the Royal Inniskillings at an early age and we are all much grieved at his death. He was a thorough soldier.

Signed by, James Field (Captain of the club) and John Cooney (Hon Sec).

We mourn the loss of one so dear
So good, so kind, so brave,
Who died on the battlefields of France,
And lies in a hero's grave,
He'll never see another fight,
His earthly conflicts past,
For folded in his Saviour's arms
He's safe, safe home at last.

The above verse appeared in the Mid Ulster Mail on 12th June 1915, deeply regretted by his stepfather, mother, brothers and sisters.

9584-Private William George Little
1st Battalion Royal Inniskilling Fusiliers
Died of Wounds: 17th May 1915
Twelve Tree Copse Cemtery, Turkey. Special Memorial C-188

William George Little was born in Moneymore and lived at
Coolkeeghan, Blue Doors, in Cookstown. He enlisted at Finner
Camp, Ballyshannon, County Donegal, when he was 16 and
served with the 1st Battalion Royal Inniskilling Fusiliers for 8
years in China and Trimulgherry, India, where he served with
Robert Falls and William Nixon, two of his childhood friends.

In early December 1914 the Battalion returned to England,
arriving at Avonmouth on 10th January 1915. They were based at
Rugby with the 87th Brigade of the 29th Division until they
sailed for the Mediterranean in March 1915 arriving at Mudros
on the island of Limnos in the Aegean Sea in April. They landed
at 'X' beach just inside the Gulf of Saros on the Gallipoli
peninsula on 25th April 1915, where they suffered very heavy
casualties. The open terrain often left the men exposed to enemy
fire. On 13th May 1915 the 1st Battalion Royal Inniskilling
Fusiliers were attached to the Indian Brigade, which also
included the 1st Battalion Lancashire Fusiliers and battalions of
the Ghurkas and Sikhs. Their objective was to hold the line
between Ghurka Bluff and Big Nullah on the Gallipoli
Penninsula, Turkey. During this action on 17th May, William
George Little was wounded and died from his wounds a few
hours later.

Between April 1915 and January 1916 the battalion lost 436 men
in this campaign.

In a letter to William's mother, the Reverend O. Creighton,
Church of England Chaplain with Mediterranean Forces at
Gallipoli (89th Field Ambulance, M.E.F. May 18th 1915) stated:

*"I buried Private William Little, No.9584, Inniskilling Fusiliers
who died of wounds yesterday on a hill just above 'Y' beach, next
to one or two of his comrades, at about 8.30pm last night and
concealed his grave. He lies among the hills over looking the sea.
Everything had been done that was possible for him by the
R.A.M.C., but his wound was fatal."*

William's mother received a letter from his friend, Private Espie
who told her that he and William were treated at the same
hospital and he had only lived for 6 hours after being wounded.
Subsequently the whereabouts of the marked grave was lost and

William is commemorated on Special Memorial, C-188 at Twelve Tree Copse Cemetery, Turkey. At the time of William's death his brother, Robert, was serving with the 36th Ulster Division.

William Little is commemorated on Cookstown Cenotaph and St. Luran's Church of Ireland Roll of Honour, Derryloran, Cookstown (as William Lyttle).

He sleeps upon a foreign shore,
But when his mortal life is o'er
May we reunite in Heaven
Clasp him again the one we love
Rest evermore in Heaven above.

Verse chosen by his mother, appeared in Mid Ulster Mail 1915

Twelve Tree Copse Cemetery Special Memorial commemmorates 10 men from the Cookstown District.

Recruiting advertisement in the Mid Ulster Mail, circa 1915

4686 - Private Oliver Bates
1st Battalion Irish Guards
Killed in Action: 18th May 1915
Le Touret Memorial, France. Panel: 4

Oliver Bates was born in Willenhall, Warwick, and was residing in Cookstown, County Tyrone when he enlisted. He served with 1st Battalion Irish Guards, 4th Guards Brigade, which made up part of the 2nd Division on the Western Front. They took part in the Battle of Festubert which began on the eve of 15th May 1915. On the morning of the 18th of May, the day dawned with driving rain and mist, so the attack was postponed until 4.30pm in the late afternoon because of the poor conditions. By the following morning the 1st Battalion Irish Guards had lost 22 men killed in action, 284 wounded and 86 missing. Oliver Bates was one of those killed in action. He has no known grave and is commemorated on panel 4 at Le Touret Memorial in France.

Le Touret Memorial commemorates those men from the United Kingdom who have no known grave and who fell in the Battles of La Bassee, Neuve-Chapelle, Aubers Ridge and Festubert up until 25th September 1915, (the eve of the Battle of Loos).

In all there are, 13,377 men (including 14 from Cookstown) remembered on the memorial which is located near Bethune in France.

9634-Lance Corporal Alexander Freeburn
1st Battalion Royal Inniskilling Fusiliers
Killed in Action: 18th May 1915
Twelve Tree Copse Cemetery, Turkey. Special Memorial: C-119

Alexander Freeburn was born in Killymoon Street, Cookstown, and was a son of David Freeburn who worked at Greenvale Mill (Adair's) and brother of Thomas John Freeburn who served with the Royal Garrison Artillery during the First World War. Prior to enlisting, Alexander, worked as a solicitor's clerk in Omagh. He joined the Army in Cookstown in 1910 and was drafted into the 1st Battalion Royal Inniskilling Fusiliers. He went with them to China and later was stationed in Secunderabad in India, and later at the Gallipoli Peninsula, Dardenelles in April 1915. He was killed in action on the 18th May 1915 while the 1st Inniskillings were holding the line between Ghurka Bluff and Big Nullah on the Gallipoli Peninsula. He is commemorated on Special Memorial C 119 in Twelve Tree Copse Cemetery, Turkey. He is also commemorated on Cookstown Cenotaph and on Second Presbyterian Cookstown, Roll of Honour (at Molesworth).

21318-Private Daniel Charles

10th Battalion Canadian Infantry (Alberta Regiment)
Died: 22nd May 1915
Age: 25
Vimy Memorial, France.

Daniel Charles was born in April 1890 at Low Cross, Tullyhogue, Cookstown. He was the son of Henry Richard Charles, Low Cross, and later of 52 Palestine Street, Belfast and later of 35 Burmah Street, Belfast.

Daniel emigrated to Canada and enlisted in the Canadian Infantry on 24th September 1914 at Valcartier which was a large training camp near Quebec city.

His enlistment papers show that he was 5'7" and worked as a clerk before enlisting.

The Commonwealth War Graves Commission lists Daniel as having served with the 10th Battalion, but per list of Officers and men serving with the First Canadian Contingent of the Expeditionary Force 1914, he was in the 4th Infantry Brigade, 'B' company, 11th Battalion.

Daniel sailed with the battalion from England in early October 1914 and would have seen action in the Battle of Ypres which was fought between 22nd April and 25th May 1915. This officially named Battle consisted of a number of individual battles and Daniel Charles would have been involved in the gas attack on the Canadian lines during the Battle of Gravenstafel. He would have seen action at the Battle of St. Julian where he was most likely wounded and died sometime later.

He died 22nd May 1915 and has no known grave. He is commemorated on Vimy Memorial, France.

The memorial commemorates 11,170 Canadian Servicemen who died in World War1.

9270-Private John McBride

1st Battalion Royal Inniskilling Fusiliers
Killed in Action: 22nd May 1915
Twelve Tree Copse Cemetery, Turkey.
Special Memorial C-184.

John was the youngest son of Hugh McBride of William Street, Cookstown.

By October of 1914, John McBride had served seven years in the Army and the last four years had been in India. He arrived back in England in January 1915 and got four days leave to Cookstown. John was sent to the Dardanelles and survived several actions. He wrote his last letter home just three days before he was killed:

"Just a few lines to let you know, I am getting along fine at present. I am up in the trenches now for the second time. We were fifteen days in them the first time. The weather is fine out here with a very strong sun during the day. The enemy never trouble us during the day except for a few snipers. But night is the time we want to watch them. I am writing this in my dugout and they are still sniping away over my head. They start shelling about five o'clock every day. Cigarettes and notepaper are very short here, so do not forget to send me some. Remember me to all my old friends. All the Cookstown boys are still kicking. If the war lasts very much longer there will be no turkeys for Christmas. We are now back in our little houses and this leaves me well."

John was killed in action three days later at Gurkha Bluff during very heavy and intense fighting among rocky terrain. Trenches could not be dug to sufficient depth in the stony ground and the men had to build up the front of the trench with stones to provide cover. Forty-nine men from his unit were killed on the 22nd May 1915.

John McBride was buried close to where he fell. When the war was over and the Commonwealth War Graves Commission tried to discover the location of graves, John's could not be found. Today he is commemorated on Special Memorial C 184 in Twelve Tree Copse Cemetery, Turkey. He is also commemorated on Cookstown Cenotaph.

409A-Private Martin McFlynn

Australian Army Service Corps (1st Company, Division Train)
Died of Wounds: 23rd May 1915
Age: 23
Beach Cemetery, Anzac, Turkey. Grave: 1 E 12

Martin Mc Flynn was born and raised in Sydney, Australia, the son of Michael McFlynn, Keenaghan, Cookstown, and Mrs. Ellen McFlynn of 58 Annadale Street, Annadale, Sydney, New South Wales, Australia.

Michael McFlynn served his apprenticeship as a joiner with Mr. John Kane, Gortalowry, Cookstown before emigrating with his family to Australia where he married and started a career as a building contractor. His son Martin served with the Australian Expeditionary Force attached to the Army Medical Corps at Gallipoli.

The eight month campaign in Gallipoli was fought by Commonwealth and French forces in an attempt to force Turkey out of the war, to relieve the deadlock of the Western Front in France and Belgium, and to open a supply route to Russia through the Dardanelles and the Black Sea. The Allies landed on the Gallipoli peninsula on 25th - 26th April 1915. The 29th Division landed at Cape Helles in the south and the Australian and New Zealand Corps landed north of Gaba Tepe on the west coast, an area that became known as Anzac Cove.

The following letter by Martin's Commanding Officer was sent to Michael McFlynn in Sydney, following the death of his son.

"I feel it is my duty to write and explain the circumstances under which your son met his death, as I am his commanding officer. He was working with me in a very exposed position, subject to shrapnel and rifle fire, and was carrying on his work in a most able manner, so much so that I had occasion to compliment him very highly.

He not only attended to many wounded with absolute coolness, receiving many suffering, but saved a man's life earlier in the day by holding his finger over the man's bleeding artery for over half an hour, under very heavy shell fire, until help came. A most excellent piece of work."

Later that evening when the shelling had stopped, Martin McFlynn was struck in the head by a bullet and died a few hours later from the wound. He was buried at Hillside cemetery close to Anzac Cove and the Military service was conducted by Reverend J. Green C.F. Martin McFlynn's remains were re-interred in grave 1 E 12 at Beach Cemetery, Anzac, Turkey. Beach Cemetery was used almost from the moment of the first landings, until evacuation 8 months later. There are a total of 391 commonwealth servicemen buried or commemorated at the cemetery, 369 can be identified.

16868-Corporal Robert Forde
9th Battalion Royal Inniskilling Fusiliers
Died of Illness: 27th May 1915
Age: 23
Antrim New Cemetery, County Antrim, Northern Ireland.
Grave: K-1-3

Robert was a son of Robert Forde of Bardahessiagh, Pomeroy.

Before enlisting in the Army, Robert Forde was a section leader with Pomeroy Company of Ulster Volunteers.

He joined the 9th Battalion of the Royal Inniskilling Fusiliers at Finner Camp, Ballyshannon, County Donegal. Robert had attained the rank of Corporal and while the Battalion was training at Randalstown, County Antrim, he contracted Scarlet fever and was taken to hospital in Antrim where he died of his illness on 27th May 1915. He is interred in Antrim Cemetery, County Antrim in grave K-1-3.

Major Hugh Quinn
15th Battalion Australian Infantry, A.I.F.
Killed in Action: 29th May 1915
Age: 27
Shrapnel Valley Cemetery, Turkey. Grave: 3 C 21

Major Hugh Quinn was the son of John Quinn, formerly of Pomeroy, County Tyrone, and son of Mary J. Quinn (nee Irwin), of 14 Robert Street, Springhill, Brisbane, Australia, and nephew of Mrs. Flanagan, Church Street, Cookstown, and Mrs. Lavin, Ann Street, Dungannon. The family were well known in Pomeroy where John's father, Mr. Hugh Quinn was a merchant in the village and John's brother Francis was a local Publican. John Quinn emigrated to Australia in 1881and was married with 2 sons.

His son Hugh was born on 6th May 1888 at Rutherford Street, Charter Towers, Queensland, Australia, and educated at Millchester State School, Charter Towers, and The Southport Church of England Grammar School for Boys (Dixon's), Queensland.

From an early age he showed great skills as an athlete and all-round sportsman. He received many plaudits for his boxing skills and was well known in the sport throughout the country, becoming Northern Queensland Light Heavyweight Boxing Champion.

Hugh worked as a Public Accountant, Local Authorities Auditor, Stockbroker and Auctioneer before joining the Commonwealth Defence Force (Kennedy Regiment) as a private. He rose through the ranks to acting Quartermaster Sergeant and was commissioned as Second Lieutenant on 6th April 1908 and subsequently to Lieutenant on 25th September 1911. Hugh's father, John died 3rd May 1912.

Hugh Quinn served with the 2nd Infantry Naval and Military Expedition in the Pacific Ocean for a number of years before the outbreak of World War 1, when he volunteered for overseas service on 16th August 1914 and was appointed Captain on 16th December 1914 and attached to15th Battalion Australian Infantry Force. He was 'Mentioned in Dispatches' because of his gallant action when leading his men on 26th April 1915, on the first day of the landings at Anzac Beach. The objective was to capture an area known as Baby 700. It was to become one of the most advanced and dangerous of the Anzac posts, the site of incessant fighting between the Anzacs and the Turks at Gallipoli. At some points the front lines were only 15 metres apart. The area would become synonymous with Hugh Quinn's name and was subsequently known as, "Quinn's Post." He was promoted to the rank of Major on 1st May 1915 and by all reports he was regarded highly by all those who served with him. The welfare and comfort of his men were always his first priority.

The following letter was written by Sergeant McKay 15th Battalion A.I.F. and sent to Major Richardson, of Omagh, County Tyrone.

"I knew the late gallant Major Hugh Quinn well, both in private and military life. I had the honour of serving under him with the military from New Guinea to the Dardenelles. You know the sport he was in civil life, so you can understand how we appreciated the different tournaments he used to get up to on board ship and during our severe training in Egypt. We left Helliopolis on April 10th 1915, for Linnes and stayed there for a few days before going to the now historic landing at Gaba-Tepe.

The Major (then Captain) took his company of men to what is now known as 'Quinn's Post' (named after him). It was one of the hottest of hot spots. The first week was one continual fight, night and day, and our battalion suffered heavily. The work done by the Major was really great, ably seconded by Captain Corier (later wounded) and Lieutenant Armstrong (later killed).

On 29th May 1915, at about 8am, the Turks made a desperate attack on our positions, and a few of them penetrated into a section of our trenches. They did not remain there long, as the boys of the 13th and 15th Battalions got to work with the bayonet. Major Quinn lost his life as the Turks retired back to their own trenches. He stood on top of a parapet and fired at them with his revolver. It was there that he was shot through the heart, to the great sorrow of the Brigade and especially the boys of his own company."

A party of Turks had broken into no:3 section of 'Quinn's Post' on 29th May 1915, after having fired a large mine which killed most of the Australians there at 3.20am. From this section they began to penetrate through the post, but were pushed back and confined. Cut off from retreat or reinforcement, their surrender was only a matter of time, but Major Hugh Quinn was ordered to attack over an exposed crest and retake the trenches 'at all costs'.

Quinn twice placed his whistle between his teeth to give the signal for attack, but removed it again, deciding to move up the front line to reconnoitre the scene for himself before he ordered his men to charge. Colonel Chauvel had arrived on the scene during the fighting and gave the order for Major Quinn to take the charge, but Quinn was reported to be argumentative and refused to give the order. Finally Captain McSharry and Major Quinn moved up the line where they took their positions. Hugh Quinn is reported to have stood on a parapet with his revolver when he was struck by an enemy bullet and fell back into the arms of his comrade, Captain McSharry.

Hugh Quinn was buried at New Monash Cemetery with the Military Service conducted by Reverend J. Green. His remains were later re-interred to grave 3 C 21 at Shrapnel Valley Cemetery, Turkey. The cemetery is situated 400 yards south-east of Anzac Cove and got its name because of the heavy shelling it was given by the Turks on the 26th April 1915.

After his death, Hugh's mother, Mary Quinn was awarded a pension of £52 per year, this increased to £104 and finally to £255

On 21st September 1915, in Charter Towers, Queensland, in the town hall, at the request of the Mayor, Councillors J. Millican and Mr. Pritchard performed a ceremony, unveiling the pictures of Captain S.W. Harry and Major Hugh Quinn. The Mayor spoke highly of the qualities of both officers who were natives of the town.

Major Quinn, Captain Walsh and Captain Harry, all killed in action at Gallipoli, were boyhood friends in Charter Towers, Queensland.

12124- Private Peter O'Neill
1st Battalion Royal Inniskilling Fusiliers
Killed in Action: 30th May 1915
Twelve Tree Copse Cemetery, Turkey. Memorial C 157

Peter O'Neill was born at Loup, County Londonderry. He lived with his wife, Esther, at Ballygillen, Ballinderry Bridge, Coagh.

He enlisted in Cookstown with 1st Battalion Royal Inniskilling Fusiliers and was posted to Gallipoli. He was killed in action, on 30th May 1915, while his battalion was in Brigade reserve at White House, Gallipoli. He has no known grave and is commemorated on Memorial C-157 at Twelve Tree Copse Cemetery, Turkey.

Queen of the Most Holy Rosary pray for him.
Departed, yes, but not forever,
We shall meet him by and by,
Where no partings e'er shall sever,
Where no tear shall dim the eye.
His pain is past, his joys are full,
His heart can ask no more,
Save the dear ones he left at home,
May meet him on that shore

Submitted by Mrs. Esther O'Neill to the Mid Ulster Mail, 1915

6686 Private John Harvey

1st Battalion Royal Inniskilling Fusiliers
Killed In Action: 5th June 1915
Twelve Tree Copse Cemetery, Special Memorial C 333. Turkey

John Harvey lived in Union Street, Cookstown, with his wife and 5 children.

He was born at Tullygare in the parish of Derryloran and was raised as a child by Mr. John Shaw, one of whose daughters John Harvey would later marry.

John Harvey originally enlisted in the Inniskiling Fusiliers at the age of 18, during the Boer War, and went to South Africa in December 1900. He served under Colonel Allenbury, first in the Cape Colony, then tracked up country to the Kronstat-Lindley blockhouse, and assisted in keeping the lines until peace was declared in 1902.

He transferred to the 2nd Battalion Inniskilling Fusiliers in which he remained in South Africa until the end of 1903 when they went to Egypt. He was in Cairo until the troubles in Crete broke out in 1906, when along with 375 men they were relieved by an English regiment. He went back to Cairo when it was thought there may be trouble with Turkey. The battalion eventually left Alexandria in 1908.

He left the army and got married in Belfast to the daughter of John Shaw. He was employed in Belfast, where he worked in the jack shop for the Great Northern Railway Company. After 18 months in Belfast, a vacancy became available in Cookstown and he returned home and worked as an examiner with the railways.

He still kept connections to his old regiment though, firstly serving with the 'B' reserves for 4 years and then the 'D' reserves for a while. At the outbreak of the First World War, he rejoined his old regiment along with 4 other soldiers, Nixon, Speers, Falls and Taylor. They were escorted to the train depot in Cookstown by a section of Ulster Volunteers of which they were all members. John Harvey was the section leader of No.1 Section, 'A' company of the 5th Tyrone Regiment. They left Southampton to go to the Western Front on 23rd August 1914. It was while serving at the front that John Harvey received a shot to one of his legs during the retreat from Mons and returned home to recover in September 1914. While at home recuperating he supported General Sir William Adair's call for recruits, declaring:

"I hope to be back in the fighting line within a month, myself."

He was back at the front even before his wound had healed properly, but was invalided home again with severe frost bite. While back at home he was confined to Depot Duties.

He was later shipped out to Gallipoli with the Inniskillings and had written a letter home in early June 1915 enquiring about the Army in France and stating that he was well.

On 4th June 1915 the 1st Battalion Royal Inniskillings were to participate in a break out against the Turks, but this didn't occur, even though the planned attack was supported by a Naval bombardment from the sea. Heavy and concentrated machine gun fire from the Turks repelled any notion of attack and the Battalion was not called upon to leave their trenches. John Harvey was killed in action on the 5th June 1915, he has no known grave and in commemorated on Special Memorial C 333 at Twelve Tree Copse Cemetery in Turkey. He is also commemorated on Cookstown Cenotaph.

12095 - Private William Mills

2nd Battalion Royal Irish Fusiliers (Princess Victoria's)
Killed in Action: 15th June 1915
Houplines Communal Cemetery Extension, France. Grave: 2-C-18

William Mills was born in Carrickmore, County Tyrone, and lived in Pomeroy.

He was living and working in Scotland, at the outbreak of the First World War. William Mills enlisted in Ayr, Scotland, with the Royal Irish Fusiliers. He was killed in action on 15th June 1915 and is buried in plot 2, row C, grave 18 at Houplines Communal Cemetery Extension, France.

11113-Private James Espey

1st Battalion Royal Inniskilling Fusiliers
Killed in Action: 28th June 1915
Twelve Tree Copse Cemetery, Turkey. Special Memorial: C-244

James Espey was born in the parish of Derryloran, Cookstown. He and his wife, Mary, lived in Chapel Street, Cookstown.

Soon after the outbreak of the First World War, James enlisted in Cookstown with the 1st Battalion Royal Inniskilling Fusiliers. They were posted to Gallipoli, a strange and hostile environment for men unaccustomed to the hot climate. Clean drinking water was constantly in short supply and men fought to secure a tenuous foothold.

The 1st Battalion lost 10 men on the 28th June 1915, among them, James Espey and James McGhee, from Cookstown. Both were killed in action in the assault on the Turkish trench J11 during the Battle of Gully Ravine. James' body was recovered and buried at the time, but when the Commonwealth War Graves Commission came to build the cemeteries his grave could not be found. He is commemorated at Special Memorial C. 244 at Twelve Tree Copse Cemetery, Turkey.

He is also commemorated on Cookstown Cenotaph and at St. Luran's Church of Ireland Roll of Honour, Derryloran, Cookstown.

4428-Private James McGhee
1st Battalion Royal Inniskilling Fusiliers
Killed in Action: 28th June 1915
Age: 19
Twelve Tree Copse Cemetery, Turkey

James McGhee was born in Desertmartin, County Londonderry, the son of John McGhee. The family later moved to live in Magherafelt. James enlisted in Cookstown, with the Royal Inniskilling Fusiliers, and was killed in action in Gallipoli, during the Battle of Gully Ravine on 28th June 1915. He has no known grave and is commemorated on Special Memorial C. 295 in Twelve Tree Copse Cemetery, Turkey.

Private William Oliver Hardy
14th Battalion Royal Irish Rifles (Young Citizen Volunteers)
Died of Illness: 13th July 1915

William Oliver Hardy was the son of Mr. Joseph Hardy, Stranmillis Road, Belfast, and formerly of Lissan House, Cookstown.

William Hardy lived and worked in Cookstown for the Great Northern Railway as a ticket clerk. He eventually found work with the railways at Annaghmore and in Dromore, County Down, before settling in Belfast where he enlisted with the 14th Royal Irish Rifles, Young Citizen Volunteers. He took ill and was hospitalised while he was training with his battalion and died soon after.

He was buried with full military honours at Stewartstown Churchyard, Belfast.

77056-Private Robert Henry Norris
7th Battalion Canadian Infantry (British Columbia Regiment)
Killed in Action: 21st July 1915
Berks Cemetery Extension, Belgium.   Grave: 3-B-1

Robert Henry Norris was born 23rd March 1882 and was the son
of Mr and Mrs G.S. Norris, Tamlaghtmore, Stewartstown,
County Tyrone. He was a member of Tamlaghtmore LOL 198
and RBP 518. He emigrated to Canada in 1906 and prior to
active service he worked as a stoker before enlisting in the 7th
Canadian Infantry on 7th November 1914 at Victoria, British
Columbia.

He was killed in action when he was struck in the neck by a
bullet while returning to his Battalion trench on 21st July 1915
and was buried with full military honours in plot 3, row B, grave
1 at Berks Cemetery Extension in Belgium. He is
commemorated on Stewartstown Cenotaph.

Derryloran Football Club 1910-11
Harry Tohill (7th from left back row), Thomas Darragh (9th from left middle row)
and Paddy Corey (far right middle row) all killed in action during the
First World War.

8022-Private Patrick Corey

2nd Battalion Royal Inniskilling Fusiliers
Killed in Action: 22nd July 1915
Age: 29
Bethune Town Cemtery, Pas de Calais, France.   Grave: 4-D-22

Patrick Corey was the husband of Mary Corey of Blackhill, Cookstown. Prior to the war he was well known and very popular in Cookstown, being a footballer of considerable ability, playing both Association and Gaelic games. He was a member of Derryloran Football Club 1910-1911, Cookstown Whites Football Club 1909-1910 and played Gaelic football with Cookstown Brian Og in 1909. Patrick was also selected to play for Tyrone in 1909 and played in the Ulster Senior Gaelic Football final at Clones when Tyrone lost 1 - 6 to 2 - 4 to Fermanagh on 22nd August 1909.

He was an army reservist and had gone out with the British Expeditionary Force at the outbreak of war and was present at the Battle of Mons. He had been seriously wounded in October 1914 and after a long term in hospital was allowed home on leave in January 1915. On returning to the Colours he was stationed in Londonderry and went out with a draft of Inniskillings in May 1915. It is thought that he was killed by shellfire while billeted in the town of Bethune.

Sergeant McAtackney, who was a friend of Paddy Corey said in later years, that while they were billeted in Bethune, the town came under a bombardment from the Germans. It was while the men were at rest and McAtackney was helping an illiterate soldier compose a letter home, that a shell hit the building. Sgt. McAtackney was immediately thrown into a water trough where he was sitting, and when he regained his composure he went to the building to find Paddy and others had been killed by the blast. Altogether fifteen men were killed in the explosion.

Paddy is buried in plot 4- row D- grave 22 at Bethune Town Cemetery, France. He is commemorated on Cookstown Cenotaph.

5185- Private Henry (Harry) Tohill
(Formerly-16922 Royal Inniskilling Fusiliers)
6th Battalion Royal Munster Fusiliers
Killed in Action: 7th August 1915
Helles Memorial, Turkey. Panel 185 – 190

Private Harry Tohill was born and lived at Rainey Street
Magherafelt, County Londonderry. He was the son of Henry and
Margaret Tohill (nee Lavelle). Henry Tohill was a butcher by
trade and a close friend of Mr. Bobby Allen, Cookstown.

Harry was the eldest of 5 boys who served in the army during the
First World War. His bother James was wounded in Egypt where
it was discovered that he was actually under age and was
promptly sent back home to recuperate, but rejoined the army
later on. Harry's other brothers, John and Francis, survived the
war.

Although a resident of Magherafelt, Harry Tohill was well known
in the Mid Ulster area as a footballer and keen sportsman, and
was friends with Cookstown soccer players, Thomas Darragh and
Paddy Corey. During the soccer season, Harry was brought to
Cookstown every Friday evening to stay overnight by Mr. Bobby
Allen, a butcher by trade, so Harry could qualify as a resident,
making him eligible to play for popular local team, Derryloran
Football Club.

At the outbreak of war, Harry along with his team mates, Thomas
Darragh and Paddy Corey joined the ranks of the Inniskilling
Fusiliers. Harry later transferred to the Royal Munster Fusiliers
and was killed in action at Gallipoli on 7th August 1915. He has
no known grave and is commemorated on panels 185-190 on
Helles Memorial, Turkey.

Harry Tohill's team mates, Thomas Darragh and Paddy Corey,
were also killed in action during the First World War.

10653-Rifleman Francis Carron

6th Battalion Royal Irish Rifles
Killed in Action: 8th August 1915
Age: 27
Helles Memorial, Turkey. Panel 177 - 178

Francis was the son of Daniel and Mary Carron, Stewartstown, County Tyrone.

He enlisted in Lisburn, County Antrim. His brother John Carron served with the 8th Battalion Royal Inniskilling Fusiliers throughout World War 1.

Francis Carron was killed in action in Gallipoli on the 8th August 1915. He has no known grave and is commemorated on Helles Memorial, Turkey, on panel 177 - 178, and also on Stewartstown Cenotaph.

18065-Private Joseph Morgan

1st Battalion Royal Dublin Fusiliers
Killed in Action: 8th August 1915
Pink Farm , Helles, Turkey. Grave: 3-A-2

Joseph Morgan was born in Cookstown. He enlisted in Dublin with the 1st Battalion Royal Dublin Fusiliers. The Battalion was sent to Gallipoli early in 1915. Joseph was killed in action at the Southern Barricade near Gully Ravine on 8th August 1915. The Battalion lost ten men on that day. Joseph Morgan was buried in plot 3, row A, grave 2 at Pink Farm Cemetery at Helles, Turkey.

11099-Sergeant John McGarvey

6th Battalion Royal Irish Rifles
Killed in Action: 11th August 1915
Age: 38
Helles Memorial, Turkey. Panel: 177-178

John McGarvey was a son of Thomas McGarvey of Cookstown, County Tyrone, and by 1914 the family had moved to Belfast.

John McGarvey enlisted with the 6th Battalion Royal Irish Rifles in Dundalk, County Louth, and before he arrived in Gallipoli he was promoted to the rank of Sergeant. He was killed in action near The Farm, Anzac, on 11th August 1915. The battalion suffered very heavy losses on this day of intense fighting and fifty men were killed. There is no known grave and John McGarvey is commemorated on panel 177-178 on Helles Memorial, Turkey.

1234 - Rifleman Charles Symington

6th Battalion Royal Irish Rifles
Killed in Action: 11th August 1915
Age: 30
Helles Memorial, Turkey. Panel 177 - 178

Charles Symington was born in Cookstown and enlisted in Belfast where he was living.

His sister Margaret Hughes of 55 Rockville Street, Belfast was listed as his next of kin.

He was killed in action in Gallipoli on 11th August 1915 and has no known grave. He is commemorated on panel 177-178 on Helles Memorial, Turkey.

Albert Turkington

Cattleman / Mercantile Marine
S.S. "Jacona" (Dundee)
Died: 12th August 1915
Age: 22
Tower Hill Memorial, London

Albert Turkington was born in Cookstown, County Tyrone.

He worked as a cattleman on board S.S. "Jacona" (Dundee), a 2,969 tons Merchant Vessel which was part of the Cairn Line of Steamships built in 1889. Official records state that SS Jacona was sunk on 12th August 1915 when it struck a mine and sank 25 miles North/North West of Troup Head near Fraserburgh, Bannfshire, with a loss of 29 crew, including Albert Turkington. He has no known grave and is commemorated on Tower Hill Memorial, London

Horseman J. McLaughlin (age 45) from Kilwinning, Scotland was also lost.

Albert Turkington's colleague, Cecil Hetherington (apprentice) on board S.S. Jacona survived the sinking and struggled to a drifting life boat and after reaching it, returned to rescue the other 9 survivors, including the Captain. He was awarded The Board Of Trade Sea Gallantry Medal for his action on 12th August 1915. He was later presented the Stanhope Medal for Bravery. The Stanhope is a very prestigious award as only one medal is struck each year. Cecil's brother Archie was killed in an accident in June 1915 while training with 19th Northumberland Fusiliers and is buried at Masham, Yorkshire.

Both boys were the sons of Peter Hetherington, a cabinet maker and painter, and Mrs. Jane Hetherington of Cross Keys House, Allendale, Northumberland.

4444 - Private James King

1st Battalion Royal Inniskilling Fusiliers
Died of Wounds: 14th August 1915
Age: 23
Helles Memorial, Turkey. Panel 97 - 101

James King was the son of John and Mary King, of Blackhill, Cookstown.

James worked at Adair's Mill, Greenvale, Cookstown, and played regularly for the local Greenvale Swifts Football Club, alongside his team mates, Michael Lawn and John McCaffrey who were both killed in action. James enlisted with the Inniskillings at Omagh and was posted to the 1st Battalion, and subsequently to Gallipoli. The 1st Battalion Inniskillings were in the Helles sector at Gallipoli and were soon to leave for the Suvla Bay area, but on the night of August 14th 1915 the Turks exploded a mine that had been tunnelled towards the Inniskilling trench lines. This precipitated wave after wave of Turkish attacks, which were beaten back from the Inniskilling lines. Captain O'Sullivan and Sergeant Somers beat back the advancing Turks with bomb after bomb and held their line, an action that would warrant both men the Victoria Cross. James King was seriously wounded in the attack and died a short time later. He has no known grave and is commemorated on panel 97-101 at Helles Memorial, Turkey. He is also commemorated on Cookstown Cenotaph.

Greenvale Swifts FC 1913-14
Front row: J. Lawn, T. Kelly, J. McCaffrey, J. Corey, J. Fields
Middle row: F. Mullan, M. Lawn, F. McCaffrey, J. King, J. McCaffrey,
J. Somerville
Back row: W. Moore, J. Hamill, P. McKeown, W. Lawn, F Harris

12084-Private James Gormley
1st Battalion Royal Inniskilling Fusiliers
Killed in Action: 15th August 1915
Helles Memorial, Turkey. Panel: 97-101

James Gormley was born in Shettleston, Lanarkshire, and was the son of William and Annabella Gormley (nee Breslin) from Dunamanagh, Cloughcorr, County Tyrone. In the early 1900's the family settled in Cookstown. James had three brothers William, John and Edward, and four sisters, Bella, Margaret, Kate and Brigid.

James Gormley was working in Cookstown prior to enlisting with the 1st Battalion Royal Inniskilling Fusiliers. The Battalion was sent to Gallipoli as part of 29th Division in April 1915. James was reported killed in action during the assault on Kidney Hill at Suvla, on 15th August 1915. One of James comrades returned from Gallipoli and told his family that James had volunteered to bring back some fresh water from a well, where it is thought he was killed by a Turkish sniper. He has no known grave and is commemorated on panel 97-101 on the Helles Memorial, Turkey. His nephews and nieces still live in the Cookstown area.

James Gormley is commemorated on Cookstown Cenotaph.

Second Lieutenant Donald James Grubb
5th Battalion Royal Inniskilling Fusiliers
Killed in Action: 15th August 1915
Age: 20
Helles Memorial, Turkey. Panel: 97 -101

Donald James Grubb was the only son of the Reverend James Grubb and Mrs. Jessie Grubb of 24 Stranmillis Road, Belfast, and nephew of Captain J.J. Grubb, Royal West Surrey Regiment. He was educated at Wesley College, Dublin, and was a member of the Officers' Training Corps at Queens University, Belfast.

He spent some time in Cookstown before he enlisted with the 5th Battalion Royal Inniskilling Fusiliers, 31st Brigade of the 10th Irish Division and served in Gallipoli.

On the 15th August 1915 the 5th Inniskillings were appointed the task to take Kidney Ridge, and shortly after noon that day, they advanced and made moderate progress until they reached the plain at the foot of the hill. The advance then stopped due to very heavy artillery and enemy machine gun fire. More advances were made, but all were in vain. By 8pm that evening orders were sent from Brigade Headquarters to withdraw back to the position they held at noon that day. An order was sent out by Captain Adams to go out and collect the wounded, and by midnight the Captain had retrieved over 100 wounded men. The task was completed by 4am the next morning.

The casualty count was high, 6 Officers had been killed and 14 wounded, with 28 other ranks killed and 230 wounded. 78 men were posted as missing. Almost half the Battalion strength had gone since landing at Suvla Bay in early August.

Donald James Grubb was one of those killed in action on 15th August 1915. He has no known grave and is commemorated on panel 97-101 on the Helles Memorial, Turkey. His obituary appeared in the London Illustrated News on September 18th 1915,

Donald Grubb is commemorated on Gunning's Factory Memorial at the Royal British Legion, Cookstown and is commemorated at Seymour Street Methodist Church, Lisburn, Lisburn War Memorial and also commemorated on the war memorials of Donegall Square Methodist Church (now closed), Queen's University Belfast and Wesley College, Dublin.

1845- Private Samuel James MacFarlane
13th Battalion Australian Infantry
Died of Wounds: 20th August 1915
Age: 21
Lone Pine Cemetery, Lone Pine Memorial-38, Turkey

Private Samuel James MacFarlane was born at Doons, Orritor, Cookstown on 17th March 1894. He was the youngest son of James MacFarlane, who owned the Skerry Bhan Hotel in Portrush.

He received his education at the Royal Academical Institution, Belfast and Coleraine Academy. On leaving school he served his apprenticeship as a mid-shipman with the Henderson Line of Steamers, trading between Glasgow and Rangoon. He was a life long abstainer and an ardent unionist, and on a visit home in 1913 he assisted in the training of the Signalling Corps of the Ulster Volunteers at Portrush. He later went to work in the Coast Trade in Australia. On his arrival in Sydney he found that war had broken out in Europe and immediately volunteered his services in the Naval and Military Expedition. He took part in the New Guinea Campaign and on his return to Sydney he was offered a commission if he would return for a further three months to assist in training other volunteers. He preferred, however to volunteer for active service in Europe and was at first posted to Cairo and then Gallipoli. He was fatally wounded at Gallipoli on 20th August 1915 and died a short time later on an Australian Hospital Ship, having been recommended for a medal. His grave was subsequently lost and he is commemorated on Lone Pine Memorial- 38 at Lone Pine Cemetery, Turkey. He is also commemorated on Portrush War Memorial.

4442-Private Thomas Devlin

1st Battalion Royal Inniskilling Fusiliers
Killed in Action: 21st August 1915
Age: 17
Helles Memorial, Turkey. Panel 97 - 101

Private Thomas Devlin was born near the village of Coagh, Cookstown, County Tyrone and was the son of Joseph and Catherine Devlin, Coagh, Cookstown, later of 40 Mill Street, Whiteabbey; Belfast. Thomas lived and worked in Cookstown and at the outbreak of the First World War. He enlisted in the army at Omagh and was posted to the 1st Battalion Royal Inniskilling Fusiliers in Gallipoli.

The 21st August 1915 was a day in hell for the 1st Battalion Inniskillings. The objective that day was regarded by Sir Frank Fox (The Royal Inniskillings in the Great War) as 'The final effort at Suvla Bay.'

The 1st Battalion had to cross 400 yards of ground. Their objective was Scimitar Hill. The initial attack was left until mid afternoon as it was thought that the declining sun in the sky would obscure the enemy's vision, but the weather turned dull and misty, coupled with the dense smoke of burning scrub. It didn't deter the enemy though as they had trained their sights on the Inniskilling positions. At 15.00 hours the allied artillery bombardment began. The enemy responded at once but caused little damage. At 15.30 hours the Inniskillings advanced and by that time the dry scrub and foliage on the ground had begun to burn as a result of the shellfire. The advance continued up the hill to the first line enemy position but was beaten back by constant shell and machine gun fire, Officers and men were cut down. Every effort to move forward to the second line trench was beaten back and the order was given to fall back 400 yards or so to a small gulley to regroup for another attack. Captain Pike, commanding the battalion in reserve couldn't endure the agony of remaining behind in support so he moved to the front and called for a charge, and every man who could follow him charged over the crest of the hill. No man returned. Then Captain O'Sullivan V.C., an Officer who had proven his mettle many times at Gallipoli, appealed to the few men who were left. "One more charge for the honour of the Old Regiment", he was heard to call out. Any man that could move responded. A small band of about 50 men rushed forward to the crest of the hill. Only one man, a wounded Sergeant returned.

126 men of the 1st Battalion Inniskillings were killed in action and 6 others died of their wounds the following day.

Thomas Devlin, aged 17 was killed in action in the assault at Scimitar Hill. He has no known grave and is commemorated on panels 97-101 on Helles Memorial in Turkey.

Thomas Devlin is also commemorated on Coagh War Memorial (Royal British Legion Cookstown).

3768-Private William George Graham

"A" Company-1st Battalion Royal Inniskiling Fusiliers
Killed in Action: 21st August 1915
Age: 24
Helles Memorial, Turkey. Panel 97 - 101

William Graham was born in the parish of Derryloran, Cookstown, County Tyrone, the son of Mary J. Graham, of Milfort Avenue, Dunmurry, County Antrim and the late William Graham of Cookstown. He enlisted in the army at Cookstown and was posted to 1st Battalion Royal Inniskilling Fusiliers.

He was killed in action along with Thomas Devlin and John Rafferty during the assault on Scimitar Hill, Gallipoli, on August 21st 1915. He has no known grave and is commemorated on panel 97-101 on Helles Memorial, Turkey.

4608-Private Patrick Murphy

1st Battalion Royal Inniskilling Fusiliers
Killed In Action: 21st August 1915
Age: 18
Helles Memorial Turkey. Panel 97-101

Patrick Murphy was a son of Patrick and Mary Murphy. His father had married Mary O'Reilly, of Chapel Street, Cookstown and they went to live at 105 Stockwell Road, Glasgow. Patrick (junior) was born in Whiteinch, Lanarkshire, on 7th February 1897. His father had served with the Royal Inniskilling Fusiliers and had been through the Boer War. The family returned to Belturbet, County Cavan, where Patrick (senior) originally came from. He eventually brought his family to Cookstown to work for Thomas Adair & Sons.

After leaving school young Patrick also found work with Thomas Adair & Sons. He was known to have a kindly and obliging disposition, and was popular with all who knew him. He possessed considerable ability as a humorous vocalist and was ever ready to assist in the programmes of public entertainment. His father rejoined the army in 1914 serving throughout the war in Londonderry.

Patrick (junior) enlisted in Cookstown with the 1st Battalion Royal Inniskilling Fusiliers and went to Gallipoli as part of the 29th Division in April 1915. The heat during the day was almost unbearable and fresh water was virtually impossible to find. Fighting in this environment with steep rocky hillsides and very shallow trenches was difficult and losses were heavy. Patrick was killed in action on 21st August 1915 close to Scimitar Hill. Dense scrub covered this part of the countryside and it burnt with a thick acrid smoke. This scrub had been set alight by the constant shelling and the British were forced to fight among the many fires here and this hampered their movements. Patrick Murphy has no known grave and is commemorated on panels 97-101 on Helles Memorial, Turkey. He is also commemorated on Cookstown Cenotaph.

19245-Private John Rafferty
1st Battalion Royal Inniskilling Fusiliers
Killed in Action: 21st August 1915
Age: 43
Helles Memorial, Turkey. Panel: 97-101

John Rafferty was born in Cookstown but enlisted in Newcastle-upon-Tyne while he was living and working there. He was serving in the 1st Battalion Royal Inniskilling Fusiliers at Gallipoli when he was killed in action along with Thomas Devlin and William Graham at Scimitar Hill on 21st August 1915. He has no known grave and is commemorated on panels 97-101 on Helles Memorial, Turkey.

Irish Recruiting Poster from the First World War

Major Algernon Hubert Cuthell

9th Battalion West Yorkshire Regiment (Prince of Wales's Own)
Killed in Action: 22nd August 1915
Age: 36
Helles Memorial, Turkey. Panel: 47 - 51

Algernon Cuthell was the husband of Mrs. Rhona K. Cuthell (nee Adair), Cookstown, County Tyrone, and the son of Lieutenant Colonel T.G. Cuthell (late of 13th Hussars and 38th South Staffordshire Regiment) and Mrs. Edith E. Cuthell, of Sloane Gate Mansions, London. He was brother-in-law to Louis and John Adair, Greenvale and Glenavon, Cookstown.

Major Cuthell had served 16 years in the Army, receiving his first commission on 11th February 1899 when he was posted to South Africa. During the Boer War he took part in the relief of Ladysmith and other actions at Colenso, Spion Kop, Vaal Kranz, on the Tugela Heights and at Pieter's Hill. He was awarded the Queen's Medal with three clasps and King's Medal with two clasps. He served later with the West Yorkshire Regiment when they were stationed in Belfast where he was a prominent member of the North of Ireland Cricket Club, and was regarded as a keen sportsman with a genial temperament. It was while based in Ulster that Major Cuthell married Miss Rhona Adair, youngest daughter of Mr. Hugh Adair J.P., Glenavon, Cookstown.

Rhona held the Ladies Golf Championship in 1900 and 1903. They had two children, and Rhona's father Hugh Adair, passed away at his home in Glenavon, Cookstown, in March 1916, aged 68.

At the out break of World War 1, Major Cuthell was in charge of the Regimental Depot in York when his regiment returned from Malta where they had been based. He helped assist in the training of the 'new' volunteer army before leaving with the 9th Battalion West Yorkshire Regiment when they where posted to Gallipoli.

Major Algernon Hubert Cuthell was killed in action at Gallipoli on 22nd August 1915.

He has no known grave and is commemorated on panels 47 - 51 at Helles Memorial, Turkey.

Major Cuthell was also Mentioned in Dispatches.

17804- Private James McClean
9th and 12th Battalion Royal Inniskilling Fuiliers
Died of Illness: 6th September 1915
Belfast City Cemetery, Belfast, Northern Ireland. Screen Wall
Memorial H.533

James McClean was the son of James McClean, Builder and Contactor, Belturbet, County Cavan.

James served his apprenticeship in the Drapery business with Mr. A.W. Richardson in Cookstown, where he came to live with his family after his father and mother had died in 1903 and 1908 respectively.

James had two brothers and one sister, and all three boys joined the army.

He joined the local section of the Ulster Volunteers shortly after its formation, and despite his youth and poor eyesight he proved to be very capable and greatly admired by both the Officers and men for his pluck and adaptability.

Shortly after the outbreak of war in Europe he volunteered for the army, but was rejected on account of his defective eyesight. He persisted however with every visit to recruiting stations until recruiting Sergeants and examining Doctors finally accepted him as fit for service and he was posted to the 9th Inniskilling Fusiliers in October 1914. He was stationed at Finner Camp, County Donegal and Shane's Park Camp at Randalstown, County Antrim, where he contracted Scarlet Fever in the spring of 1915. He made a good recovery and upon his discharge from Antrim Hospital he returned to Cookstown and spent a few days with his old employer Mr. Richardson, who thought highly of the young boy.

Shortly after returning to Randalstown Camp he took ill again, and from June 1915 until he passed away he was under constant care and treatment at the Military Hospital, Donegal Road, Belfast and later at Purdysburn Hospital.

He had two brothers already serving in the Army. One was a prisoner of war in Germany.

James' cousin was Sergeant James Somers who received a Victoria Cross at Gallipoli in August 1915.

James McClean died on the 6th September 1915. His funeral took place on Wednesday 8th September with full military honours and an escort of Royal Inniskilling Fusiliers, accompanied by a band.

The service was conducted by the Rev. M. Archdale, Chaplain to the Forces. A firing party fired 3 volleys and a bugler sounded the 'Last Post'.

James McClean's grave is now sadly lost and he is commemorated on Screen Wall H.533 at Belfast City Cemetery, Belfast, Northern Ireland.

S/2753-Private John McNeill
1st Battalion Gordon Highlanders
Killed in Action: 25th September 1915
Age: 36
Menin Gate Memorial, Ypres, Belgium.

John McNeill was born in Cookstown, County Tyrone, and was living and working in Cambuslang, Glasgow, Scotland, when he enlisted with the Gordon Highlanders. He was killed in action on 25th September 1915. He has no known grave and is commemorated on the Menin Gate Memorial, Ypres, Belgium.

S/3848- Company Sergeant Major William Murdock.

9th Battalion Black Watch
Killed in Action: 25th September 1915
Age: 43
Loos Memorial, France. Panel 78 - 83

William Murdock was the eldest son of Richard Murdock of Unagh, Lissan, Cookstown. At the outbreak of the First World War William had already served twenty-one years in the British Army. He first saw action in South Africa at the time of the Jameson raid. He later went to India and was stationed there until the Boer War started. He was then sent back to South Africa and took part in a number of engagements without injury. He served six more years in India and the last two years of his service were spent in Perth. In July 1914 he retired on a pension and went to live in Edinburgh. When war was declared he was called up and was engaged for several months training troops in England. He was sent to France with his Regiment during the summer of 1915. By September 1915 plans were in place for what became the Battle of Loos and it was during the first morning of the offensive that William was killed in action. The attack began at 6.30am and by about 7.20am the 9th Battalion had taken the second German line and were fighting their way through the village of Loos when William was killed. There is no known grave and William is commemorated on the Loos Memorial, panels 78 to 83. At the time of his death he left a widow and 5 children.

William Murdock is commemorated on Cookstown Cenotaph, and First Presbyterian Roll of Honour, Cookstown.

Lieutenant Andrew John, Viscount Stuart

6th Battalion Royal Scots Fusiliers
Killed In Action: 25th September 1915
Age: 34
Loos Memorial, France. Panel 46 - 49

Lieutenant Andrew John, Viscount Stuart, 6th Royal Scots Fusiliers was killed in action in France on 25th September 1915. He was thirty-four years of age and unmarried. He was the eldest son of the 6th Earl Castle Stewart (late of Madras Civil Service) who succeeded to the title in 1914 and Emma Georgiana, Countess Castle Stewart, the youngest daughter of General Arthur Stevens, an Indian mutiny veteran. Viscount Stuart was educated at Shrewsbury and Corpus Christi College, Oxford, with intentions of entering the Indian Civil Service. On failing to pass the necessary exams, he turned to Literary and Scholastic work, interesting himself in the questions of the day, notably education and agriculture. His chief pastime was rowing, for which he was awarded prizes at school and he rowed in the College boat at Oxford. He combined a taste for literature and fine arts with a love for the open air life and did everything he could to encourage games, both at home and when at the Front. He also travelled a great deal on the continent, in Egypt and the Holy Land.

© *Earl Castle Stewart*

He was private secretary to Mr Turner, of Stoke, Rockford, when war broke out. He volunteered for active service and obtained a commission with the Royal Scots in May 1915. He took part in the great advance at the Battle of Loos which commenced on 25th September and he died defending captured ground. His Colonel supplied the following particulars of his last action.

"Lord Stuart was holding a very advanced trench near Haisnes (Hohenzollern Redoubt) when he was shot through the heart, so death was instantaneous. The trench had to be evacuated so his body could not be recovered. The Officer who informed me of this was himself killed soon afterwards. Lord Stuart was a favourite with all ranks and was ever thoughtful for the comfort of his men, who, consequently, would follow him anywhere. In short, he was a very gallant gentleman."

Lieutenant Stuart's Sergeant went on to say:

"As you might have expected he died a very gallant death, like the brave Officer he was. Having led his men in attacking the enemy, we were in turn counter attacked and the Viscount was shot through the lungs. He did not speak beyond saying "Oh Sergeant",

and died by my side. May I respectfully offer my deepest sympathy on your sad loss, a loss that is shared by every man in the regiment."

Andrew has no known grave and is commemorated on panel 46-49 on the Loos Memprial, France.

He is also commemorated on Stewartstown Cenotaph and Donaghendry Church of Ireland Roll of Honour.

At the time of Viscount Stuart's death the search was still going on for his brother, Robert, who had been reported wounded and missing since November 1914.

Sailor, what of the debt we owe you.

Sailor, what of the debt we owe you?
Day or night is the peril more?
Why so dull that he fails to know you
Sleepless guard of our island shore?

Safe the corn to the farmyard taken
Grain ships safe upon all the seas
Homes in peace and faith unshaken
Sailor, what do we owe for these?

Safe the clerk at his desk; the trader
Counts unruined his honest gain
Safe, though yonder the curs't invader
Pours red death over hill and plain

Sailor, what of the debt we owe you?
Now is the hour at last to pay
Now is the stricken field to show you
What is the spirit you guard today?

This poem was written by Andrew John Viscount Stuart and was published in the "Times" on September 16th 1914. In commenting upon them a writer in the "Spectator" remarked upon the fine spirit expressed in them, and that fine spirit expressed in the verses found full expression in the author's life.

© By kind permission 8th Earl Castle Stewart, Stuart Hall, Stewartstown

A/7697 Private John Coyle
1st Battalion Cameronians (Scottish Rifles)
Killed in Action: 27th September 1915
Loos Memorial, France.   Panel 57 - 59

John Coyle was born in Castelderg, County Tyrone, and lived and worked in Cookstown.

He was in Glasgow, Scotland, before he enlisted in the Cameronians.

He was killed in action during the Battle of Loos. He has no known grave and is commemorated on the Loos Memorial France, panel 57 -59

The Battle of Loos formed a part of the wider Artois-Loos Offensive conducted by the French and British in the autumn of 1915, and is sometimes referred to as the second Battle of Artois. The Loos Offensive began on 25th September 1915, following a four day bombardment in which 250,000 shells were fired, and was called off in failure on the 28th September. The Offensive had been presided over by Douglas Haig who committed six Divisions to the attack, despite serious misgivings. He was concerned at both the marked shortage in available shells (sparking the shell shortage scandal in Britain in 1915), and at the fatigued state of his troops; he was further concerned at the nature of the difficult terrain that would need to be crossed. All considered he favoured a delay in the attack. Set against these concerns however was the reality that the British out-numbered their German opposition, almost 7 to 1 in some places along this front line. After the first day's attack, supply problems and a serious need for reserves brought the attack to a halt. Haig asked the Commander-in-Chief, Sir John French, to make available 9 Corps as a potential reserve to use on the same day as the first attack, but French argued that these troops would not be needed until the next day. These troops, including two new army Divisions at the time, 21st and 24th Divisions arrived late that night. Along the line, little progress was made, however 7th and 9th Divisions managed to establish a foothold at the Hohenzollern Reboubt. The delay in making available these reserves was however crucial to the success of the attack. On the second day the Germans brought in reserves to defend the lines at Hulluch and Hill 60 and were stronger than they were at the start of the attack.

By now the British no longer had the benefit of a preliminary bombardment. As British Troops advanced toward the German lines that afternoon without the artillery cover fire, they were decimated by repeated machine gun fire, the Germans were astonished that the second attack had been launched without adequate cover. After a few days of sporadic fighting, the British were forced to withdraw. The Loos attack was renewed on the 13th October 1915, when further heavy losses combined with the poor weather conditions caused the Offensive to be called off. During the Battle of Loos, the British suffered 50,000 casualties. German casualties were estimated to be approximately half of that. The British failure at Loos contributed to Sir John French being replaced as Commander-in-Chief by Douglas Haig at the close of 1915.

11097-Private Samuel Falls
1st Battalion Scots Guards
Killed in Action: 27th September 1915
Age: 26
Loos Memorial, France. Panel 8 - 9

Samuel Joseph Falls was born in Tempo, County Fermanagh, he was the son of John and Margaret Falls, of Blue Doors, Killymoon, Cookstown, and brother of Robert Falls (killed in action on 26th August 1914).

He was working in Glasgow when he enlisted in the Scots Guards. His father had passed away by this time. Samuel Falls was killed in Action on the 27th September 1915 during the Battle of Loos. He has no known grave and is commemorated on Panel 8-9 on Loos Memorial, France.

He is also commemorated on Cookstown Cenotaph and St. Luran's Church of Ireland Roll of Honour, Derryloran, Cookstown.

Inscription on Loos Memorial

11030 - Private William John Whann
1st Battalion Scots Guards
Killed in Action: 27th September 1915
Age:22
Loos Memorial, France. Panel 8 - 9

William John Whann was born in Cookstown, he was the son of Robert Whann, later of Straits, Lurgan Road, Banbridge, County Down and the grandson of William Whann of Cookstown, County Tyrone. William enlisted in the Scots Guards in Glasgow, while he was living and working there. He was originally reported as missing in action and has no known grave and is commemorated on panels 8-9 on Loos Memorial, France.

William Whann is commemorated on Cookstown Cenotaph and First Presbyterian Cookstown Roll of Honour.

6770 - Lance Corporal Bryce M. Gilmour
2nd Battalion Irish Guards
Killed in Action: 30th September 1915
Loos Memorial, Dud Corner Cemetery, France. Panels: 9 - 10

Bryce Gilmour was born in Roscommon and lived in Ballymoney. He was the third son of Bryce Gilmour, senior. He served as a police constable with the Royal Irish Constabulary in Cookstown until February 1915, before enlisting with the Irish Guards in Dublin and trained at the old Warley Barracks. They did their first route march on the 6th August. He left with his battalion from Brentwood Station for France on 16th August 1915.

On the 26th September, the 2nd Battalion was instructed to advance to and take possession of a captured German trench at La Rutoire, Loos. Later that day their objective was to take Chalk Pit Wood in the same sector of the front, but a heavy bombardment over the following hours and days made the task almost impossible. The battalion had been under considerable strain. It was reported that Bryce Gilmour died as a result of a bayonet wound while attacking the enemy positions at Loos, on 30th September 1915.

He has no known grave and is commemorated on panels 9 - 10 at Loos Memorial, Dud Corner Cemetery, France, and on Cookstown Cenotaph and on Second Cookstown Presbyterian Roll of Honour (at Molesworth)

On Sunday 24th October 1915, at 2nd Presbyterian Church, Cookstown, Reverend D. Maybin, B.A. spoke highly of Bryce Gilmour who was an esteemed member of the congregation.

3022 - Private Joseph Bayne
1st Battalion Royal Inniskilling Fusiliers
Died of Wounds: 1st October 1915
Age: 30
Derryloran (St Luran's) Roman Catholic Churchyard, Chapel Hill, Cookstown

Joseph Bayne resided in Orritor Street, Cookstown with his wife Catherine (nee Rooney) prior to active service with the Royal Inniskilling Fusiliers. He had previously been employed at Gunning's factory. He went with his Battalion to Gallipoli where he was seriously wounded and was sent back to England for hospital treatment. His condition gradually deteriorated and he died from his wounds on Friday 1st October 1915. The military authorities asked if the family wanted his remains returned to Cookstown. This was the family's wish and on Tuesday 5th October his remains were met at Cookstown by a large crowd. Much sympathy was felt for his young wife and her only child, a little boy who had been born after his father had left for active service. His aged mother wept over the coffin of her son.

Joseph Bayne was a member of the William Orr Branch, Irish National Forresters, Cookstown, and the members showed their respect for their late brother by assembling and marching in processional order in front of the funeral cortege, headed by Messrs Lewis Devlin (Chief Ranger), John Hagan (S.C.R.), Dr Gillespie (Branch surgeon), and Patrick McClarnon (Sec). His remains were taken to Holy Trinity Church, Cookstown where the Rev. Father McLaughlin, CC, officiated at Requiem Mass. Funeral arrangements were conducted by John Mulgrew and Son, Cookstown. Joseph is interred in St. Luran's, Old Roman Catholic Churchyard, Chapel Hill, Cookstown

He is commemorated on Cookstown Cenotaph and Gunning's Factory Memorial (Royal British Legion, Cookstown).

6453 - Lance Sergeant William Boyd
2nd Battalion Irish Guards
Died of Wounds: 6th October 1915
Age: 28
Janval Cemetery, Dieppe, France. 1 - A - 6

William Boyd was the son of Eliza Boyd, of Mabouy, Pomeroy, County Tyrone, and the late John David Boyd. William Boyd served as a police constable with the Royal Irish Constabulary and was based at Craven Street Barracks, Belfast, before enlisting with the Irish Guards.

The following is his last known letter to a police colleague:

"Just a line in haste to say I am well and have stuck some very stiff marches in order to get here. We are getting nearer the danger zone every minute, in fact we are right up to it now, and shall have the honor of taking part in one of the greatest battles in history. I must face it bravely and do my part well, as the fate of the Empire and future generations depend on what is about to be done and how we do it. If you do not get a personal correspondence from me in a few days you may guess what has happened; but death's sting will lose its sharpness if I am spared long enough to see Old England's troops carrying the positions and proving victorious once more."

William Boyd was severely wounded by shell fire in the attack that followed during the Battle of Loos, he was taken to hospital in Dieppe, and died of his wounds there. He is buried in grave 1-A-6 at Janval Cemetery, Dieppe, France.

The Mid=Ulster Mail
SOUTH DERRY EDITION
VOL. XIV No. 1??? COOKSTOWN, SATURDAY, NOVEMBER 6, 1915. PRICE ONE PENNY

Irishmen!
YOU cannot permit your Regiments to be kept up to strength by other than Ireland's sons! It would be a deep disgrace to Ireland, if all her regiments were not Irish, to a man
A Call to 50,000 Irishmen
TO JOIN THEIR BRAVE COMRADES IN IRISH REGIMENTS

27927 - Private John McKenna
2nd Battalion Royal Inniskilling Fusiliers
Killed in Action: 23rd November 1915
Thiepval Memorial, France.   Panel 4D-5B

John McKenna was born in Kildress, Cookstown, County Tyrone.

He was working in Govan, Scotland when he enlisted in the army at the outbreak of war.

On 16th November 1915 the 2nd Battalion Royal Inniskilings were posted to 14th Infantry Brigade, 5th Division, and held the position at Suzanne, on the Somme. John McKenna was killed in action here on 23rd November 1915. He has no known grave and is commemorated on panel 4D-5B on Thiepval Memorial, France.

5240-Private Robert Montgomery
1st / 5th Battalion Welsh Regiment
Killed in Action: 1st December 1915
Age: 30
Helles Memorial, Turkey.   Panel: 140-144

Robert Montgomery was the son of Alexander and Margaret Jane Montgomery, Wellbrook, Cookstown, and husband of Alicia Montgomery, Drum Manor, Cookstown

Robert had worked as a Butler in County Cork and later in Merthyr, Glamorgan, Wales, where he lived with his wife and 3 children before enlisting in the army at Pontypridd, in July 1915. He was killed in action on 1st December 1915 while serving with the 1st/5th Welsh Regiment, Mediterranean Expeditionary Force. He has no known grave and is commemorated on panel 140-144 on Helles Memorial, Turkey. He is also commemorated on Cookstown Cenotaph and Orritor Presbyterian Roll of Honour.

9357-Corporal Joseph O'Neill
5th Battalion Connaught Rangers
Killed in Action: 6th December 1915
Dioran Memorial, Greece.

Corporal Joseph O'Neill was born in Magherafelt and was the son of Joseph and Lizzie O'Neill, Rouskey, Coagh. He was living and working in Glasgow at the outbreak of war when he enlisted with the Connaught Rangers. He was killed in action in Salonika on 6th December 1915. He has no known grave and is commemorated on Dioran Memorial, Greece. He is also commemorated on Coagh War Memorial (Royal British Legion Cookstown).

21979-Private Patrick Carson

6th Battalion Royal Dublin Fusiliers
Killed in Action: 9th December 1915
Age: 18
Dioran Memorial. Greece

Patrick was the son of Robert and Lizzie Carson of Church Street, Cookstown. He was however born in Belfast and the family appears to have moved to Cookstown at a later date. He enlisted in Omagh into the Royal Dublin Fusiliers and the Army Service Corps as a baker. He was reported killed in action on 9th December 1915 during a major offensive in the Balkans which cost the Battalion twenty one men. Patrick has no known grave and is commemorated on the Dioran Memorial, Greece, and on Cookstown Cenotaph.

57550-Company Sergeant Major Francis McMath

Royal Engineers, 122 Field Company
Killed in Action: 11th December 1915
Age: 40
Louvencourt Military Cemetery, France. Grave: 1-C-20

Francis McMath was the son of James and Margaret McMath of Drumfad, Donaghadee, County Down. He worked and lived in Cookstown while he was an instructor with the Ulster Volunteer Force in County Tyrone. He was regarded as a man of great energy and enthusiasm, carrying out his duties in a most efficient manner. He was well known in all parts County Tyrone and his battalion colleagues placed great trust and confidence in his work as Company Sgt. Major. He was killed in action on 11th December 1915 aged forty and is interred in plot 1, row C, grave 20 at Louvencourt Military Cemetery, France.

3/8605-Sergeant William R. Bridgett
6th Battalion Yorkshire Regiment
Killed in Action: 12th December1915
Age: 37
Hill 10 Cemetery, Turkey. Grave: 2-I-8

Sergeant William R. Bridgett was the second son of James and Matilda Bridgett, Tamlaght, Coagh, later of Coagh Street, Cookstown, and husband of Esther Bridgett, 41 Victoria Road, Darlington, County Durham. William Bridgett had previously served with the Inniskilling Fusiliers during the Boer War in South Africa and his brother Alfred was killed at Middleburg, Transvaal in 1901. William joined the Yorkshire Regiment, enlisting in Middlesbrough at the out break of the First World War, and married his wife, Esther, in May 1915. William was killed in action in Gallipoli on 12th December 1915 and is buried in plot 2- row I- grave 8 at Hill 10 Cemetery, Turkey.

William R. Bridgett is commemorated on Cookstown Cenotaph and on First Presbyterian Roll of Honour, Cookstown.

At the time of William's death, his brother Samuel James Bridgett was also serving in the army. At the weekly meeting of Cookstown YMCA on Tuesday 11th January 1916, Mr. John Glasgow presiding, on the motion of Mr. George Ramsey, seconded by Mr. William Warnock, a resolution of sympathy was passed to William Bridgett's brother, John, who was a member.

One Sunday 16th January 1916, at First Presbyterian Cookstown, the Reverend R. Hyndman, B.A. said:

"We are all deeply grieved to hear of the death of Sergeant-Major William R. Bridgett."

95897-Gunner John Devlin
Royal Field Artillery -'C' Battery, 53rd Brigade
Killed in Action: 19th December 1915
Ypres Reservoir Cemetery, Ypres, Belgium. Grave: 1-B-55

Gunner John Devlin was born in Ballinderry, County Londonderry.

Prior to the outbreak of war he was working in Stockton-on-Tees, England.

At the age of 19 he volunteered and went to the Western Front in May 1915 where he took part in many fierce engagements, including the Battle of Loos. He had written a letter home prior to Christmas 1915 saying that he hoped to get leave for a week in the New Year of 1916, but his family received no more news until the report of his death was sent to his uncle, James Devlin, Churchill, Ballinderry Bridge. John Devlin is buried in plot 1- row B- grave 55 at Ypres Reservoir Cemetery, Belgium. He is commemorated on Coagh War Memorial (Royal British Legion Cookstown).

Mentioned in Dispatches

Lieutenant Colonel-William John Law

7th (Territorial) Battalion Lancashire Fusiliers
Killed in Action: 19th December 1915
Age: 38
Twelve Tree Copse Cemetery Memorial C.305. Turkey

William John Law was born in Cookstown. He was the only son of ex-Sergeant Law, assistant Petty Sessions clerk of Portadown, and formerly of Cookstown.

William was educated at Derryloran School, Cookstown and then in Dundalk. He was a graduate of the Royal University of Ireland and had also studied at Trinity College, Dublin. He played Rugby for three clubs: Portadown, Lansdowne and Dublin University.

He subsequently received a Home Office appointment as inspector of factories in the Manchester district. In 1906 he joined the 7th (Salford) Battalion Lancashire Fusiliers (Territorial) and at the out break of World War 1. He was promoted to the rank of Major and accompanied his battalion to Egypt and subsequently to Gallipoli where he took part in some severe engagements. He was 'Mentioned in Dispatches' by Sir Ian Hamilton in September 1915 and soon after took over temporary command of his battalion with the rank of Lieutenant Colonel.

He was killed in action on 19th December 1915 during the Gallipoli campaign and has no known grave. He is commemorated on Twelve Tree Copse Memorial, Turkey. C.305

Many letters of condolence and respect were sent after the death of William John Law.

A letter from, Major-General Sir William Douglas described Lieutenant Colonel Law's Gallant Actions and his keenness and energy which deserved all praise.

Lieutenant-Colonel A.F. McClure wrote:

In front of our firing lines was a large crater (formed by a mine explosion) and which practically joined the firing lines. On the 19th December 1915 we exploded a further mine and increased the size of the crater and blew in a portion of a Turkish trench which formed a loop almost directly in front. After the explosion we scaled with ladders the near lip of the crater, sending bombers into each of the enemy's trenches right and left, and by this means driving them back. Our men, however, were driven out of the crater for a few minutes, but later regained it.

General Davies telegraphed the Battalion:

"My congratulations on your success, with many regrets for the death of your gallant C.O., Major Law, a great loss to the corps."

He is commemoriated on the war memorials of the Landsdowne Club and in the Hall of Honour at Trinity College, Dublin.

M 16047–Carpenter's crew Thomas McKeown

Royal Navy
H.M.S "Natal"
Died: 30th December 1915
Age: 25
Chatham Naval Memorial: 12

Thomas was the youngest son of Samuel McKeown of Burn Road, Cookstown, a building contractor. Thomas joined the Royal Navy and was serving on H.M.S. Natal as part of the carpenter's crew. Natal was a heavy cruiser of the Warrior class and got her name because the funds required to build her came from Natal Province. The ship was completed in 1905 and had a displacement of 13,550 tons. She was re-commissioned at Sheerness on 17th September 1912. Natal was at anchor in Cromarty Firth when she exploded on the afternoon of 30th December 1915. 388 members of the crew lost their lives in the explosion including Thomas McKeown, who has no known grave, though many of those who were killed are buried in the Churchyard at Cromarty. Deterioration of explosives was blamed for the disaster at the time, which happened in the after magazine. Thomas McKeown is commemorated on panel 12 on Chatham Naval Memorial, Kent.

He is commemorated on Cookstown Cenotaph and, First Presbyterian Cookstown Roll of Honour.

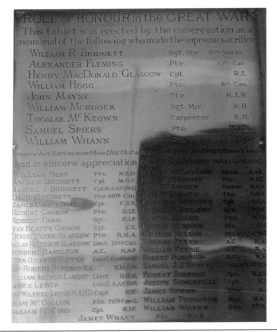

First Cookstown Presbyterian Roll of Honour.

Photo courtesy of Rev. Dr. Isaac Thompson

Helles Memorial, Turkey

The Helles memorial stands on the tip of the Gallipoli peninsula. It takes the form of an obelisk over 30 metres in height that can be seen by ships passing through the Dardanelles

The Memorial serves the dual function of Commonwealth battle memorial for the whole Gallipoli campaign and place of commemoration for many commonwealth servicemen who died there and have no known grave. The United Kingdom and Indian Forces named on the memorial died in operations throughout the peninsula, the Australians at Helles. There are also panels on the memorial for those who died and were buried at sea in Gallipoli waters.

The Helles Memorial bears the names of 21,000 service personnel who have no known grave including 13 men from Cookstown District..

There are four other memorials to the Missing at Gallipoli.

The Lone Pine Memorial (4,933 names), Hill 60 Memorial (183 names), Chunuk Bair Memorial (850 names) commemorate the Australian and New Zealanders at Anzac. The Twelve Tree Copse Memorial (179 names) commemorates the New Zealanders at Helles.

M1/08974- Private John Patrick Tohill
Royal Army Service Corps
(Royal Engineers, attached to 179 Tunnelling Company)
Killed in Action 26th January 1916
Age: 40
Albert Communal Cemetery Extension, France.   Grave 1 B 9

Private John Patrick Tohill was born in Belfast. He was the eldest son of Mr. George Tohill and the family moved to Cookstown where John grew up. John went to live and work in Dublin where he was in business partnership with Mr. Lewis McNally in the Motor and Cycle trade. He married Henrietta McNally, the daughter of Mr. John McNally J.P. and lived at 67 Hollybank Road, Drumcondra, Dublin. John Tohill was a keen sportsman, a skilled motorist and motorcycle rider. At the outbreak of war he offered his services as a dispatch rider but wasn't accepted. John's brother had been invalided in action in early 1915.

In November 1915 John Tohill volunteered for motor transport work with the Royal Army Service Corps. Almost immediately he was in the thick of things in the British front lines, supplying all the Camps in the Loos sector of the Western Front. He was subsequently offered a commission for his work in that sector but turned it down to stay with transport duties. He was then attached to the Royal Engineers for transport work and was at home in Dublin shortly after Christmas 1915 until the New Year 1916.

While back at the front and involved in transport duties again, he was killed by shell fire on 26th January 1916. He is buried in Plot 1, Row B, Grave 9 at Albert Communal Cemetery Extension, France.

John Tohill left a widow and 2 children, a boy aged 9 and a girl aged 12.

7980 - Private Thomas Woodburn
2nd Battalion Royal Inniskilling Fusiliers
Killed in Action: 12th February 1916
Age: 31
Authuille Military Cemetery. France. grave A 33

Thomas was the son of Samuel and Elizabeth Woodburn, and brother of Miss M. Woodburn, Tyressan, Cookstown, County Tyrone.

Captain and Adjutant C.A.M. Alexander reported that Private Woodburn was killed while doing his duty in the trenches on the 12th February 1916. Sergeant J. Preston who was in Private Woodburn's company indicated that Thomas Woodburn was killed instantly when he was struck down by shell fire. At the time of his death, Thomas had over 12 year's military service. His brother William was serving with the 36th Ulster Division in France at the same time.

Thomas Woodburn is buried in Row A, Grave 33 at Authuille Military Cemetery, France. He is commemorated on Cookstown Cenotaph and on Molesworth Presbyterian Roll of Honour.

Authuille Military Cemetery. France.

24273-Private Henderson Moore

10th Battalion Royal Inniskilling Fusiliers
Killed in Action: 10th March 1916
Age: 19
Authuille Military Cemetery, France. Grave C 42

Henderson Moore was the son of William Moore, Ballymacombs, Bellaghy, County Londonderry. He lived and worked in Moneymore for Mr. W. Hunter at Turnaface for about 5 years and was member of Moneymore Company of Ulster Volunteers before enlisting with the 10th Battalion Royal Inniskilling Fusilers in Moneymore, in June 1915.

On the cold Friday morning of March 10th 1916, the 10th Inniskillings were posted at Thiepval Wood. Some of the men were posted to 'saps' which were small dugouts, well camouflaged just beyond their front line trench. The enemy had spotted movement early that day and had trained their mortars and artillery on the Inniskilling positions.

In the afternoon the 10th Battalion was strafed with shells and again later in the day.

The enemy bombardment lifted at 1.30 am the next morning. 7 men of the 10th Inniskillings were killed in action or died of wounds as a result of this attack, including Henderson Moore who was struck by shell shrapnel. He was buried on Saturday morning 11th March in Authuille Military Cemetery, France, in grave C 42. He is commemorated on Moneymore War Memorial (Assembly Rooms).

Soon after Henderson Moore's death, the Reverend J. Jackson Wright, B.A. Chaplain to the 36th Ulster Division wrote a letter to the Reverend T. McCrea of Bellaghy, explaining the circumstances of Private Moore's death and extended sympathy to his family.

23188-Private Hamilton Patterson McReynolds
9th Battalion Royal Inniskilling Fusiliers
Died of Wounds: 12th March 1916
Age: 19
Doullens Communal Cemetery Extension No: 1, Somme, France.
Grave: 2-E-9

Hamilton McReynolds was the second and youngest son of Hugh and Jean McReynolds of Killymoon Street, Cookstown. He was born at Donaghey, Sherrygroom. Hamilton was a popular member of Sherrygroom section of the Ulster Volunteers and was a valued member of L.O.L. 126. Prior to enlistment he was employed by Mr. Glendinning, Sessiagh, Stewartstown. He enlisted with the 12th Battalion Inniskillings on 15th May 1915 and later transferred to the 9th Battalion when they were posted to France with the Ulster Division.

He was severely wounded by shrapnel from enemy shell fire on the 9th March 1916 and taken to Number 19 Casualty Clearing station where he died of wounds on 12th March 1916.

In a letter to his mother Jean, the Reverend J.H. Kidd, Chaplain of Forces said:

"Your son died at no: 19 Casualty Clearing Station on 12th March and was buried on the 14th in a single grave with full Military Honours. Thirty men attended the funeral and a party of six carried the coffin from gate to the grave. The Church of England service was used, and the Last Post was sounded by three buglers and a cross has been erected over the grave and a box edging, and some flowers will be planted as soon as possible."

Hamilton McReynolds is buried in plot 2- row E- grave 9 at Doullens Communal Cemetery Extension No: 1, Somme, France. He is also commemorated on Stewartstown Cenotaph and Donaghendry Church of Ireland Roll of Honour, Stewartstown.

3190 – Private Robert King Holmes Burgess
East African Pioneers
Died of Wounds: 17th March 1916
Age: 36
Taveta Military Cemetery, Kenya. Grave: 7-B-10

Robert King Holmes Burgess was the eldest son of Dr. Robert
Burgess, JP. Coagh. He was educated at the Academical
Institution in Derry and Royal School, Dungannon. He served his
apprenticeship in Messrs Coombe, Barbour & Coombe
Engineering Works in Belfast. At the outbreak of the Boer War he
volunteered for the Imperial Yeomanry and was sent to Rhodesia,
seeing action at Mafeking. At the end of the Boer war he received
the Queen's Medal with four clasps which was presented by King
Edward VII. He also received the City of Derry's gold medal,
presented by the Mayor and Corporation to old boys who had
volunteered from the City. At the conclusion of the war in South
Africa he returned to Rhodesia and worked for a mining company.
At the outbreak of the First World War he again volunteered,
joining the East Africa Pioneer Company, and served with General
Smuts in the East African Campaign. He was wounded in action
on 11th March 1916 when the Imperial Forces routed the Germans
at Taveta. He later succumbed to his wounds and is buried in plot
7- row B- grave 10 at Taveta Military Cemetery in Kenya.

He is commemorated on Coagh War Memorial (Royal British
Legion, Cookstown)

23668-Private Peter Little
7thBattalion Royal Inniskilling Fusiliers
Killed In Action: 2nd April 1916
Age: 21
Philosophe British Military Cemetery, Mazingarbe, France. Grave 1-B-13

Peter Little was the son of Joseph and Maggie Little, Coagh, County Tyrone.

He was educated at Tamlaght National School, Coagh and enlisted with the Inniskillings in Omagh, in June 1915. He was posted to the 7th Battalion for training at Randalstown, County Antrim and Finner Camp, Ballyshannon, County Donegal. The 7th Battalion Royal Inniskilling Fusiliers were part of 49 Brigade, 16th Irish Division and went to the Western Front in February 1916. The Division was split up for training in battle practice with other experienced units which were familiar with the Front and, by St. Patrick's Day 1917, all Inniskilling Battalions had settled back into the line. The 7th Battalion took to their positions again at Philosophe East in the Hulluch sector, close to where many men of the Battalion are buried in the cemetery nearby. Peter Little was killed in action on 2nd April 1916 along with his comrades, John Burns from Belfast, Alex Thompson and Denis Gallagher from Donegal and John Richard Poller from Birmingham.

The following letter was sent to Mrs. Maggie Little in Coagh, from Sergeant A. Hester:

Dear Madam, I write to let you know that it is impossible to convey to you and all relatives of our late comrade, our sincere regret at your great loss. He was a nice, quiet, unassuming lad, attentive to duty, and also his religious duties, and he died a happy death, and suffered no pain. I have handed his belongings into headquarters, and also a letter and parcel which came for him the day he was hit. It was on Sunday 2nd April, about 8 am, the Germans sent over four shells. A piece of shrapnel penetrated his helmet and rendered him unconscious. He never regained consciousness, and died about an hour after. I am certain it was a happy day, as he was well prepared. I shall conclude, hoping that God will comfort you all in your great sorrow. Your heartfelt, friend Sergeant A. Hester.

Private Peter Little is buried in plot 1- row B- grave 13 at Philosophe British Military Cemetery, Mazingarbe, France. He is commemorated on Coagh War Memorial (Royal Britsh Legion, Cookstown).

Second-Lieutenant Newton Henry Collins
7thBattalion Royal Inniskilling Fusilers
Killed in Action: 27th April 1916
Philosophe British Military Cemetery, Mazingarbe, France.
Grave: 1-C-9

Newton Henry Collins was born in 1889, the son of Dr. James and
Mrs. Harriet Collins of Laghey, County Donegal.

He was educated at Mountjoy School in Dublin and subsequently
taught in Cookstown, County Tyrone, as an assistant at Cookstown
Academy where he was described as extremely popular with the
teachers and pupils. He was a well known member of two Dublin
Cricket Clubs, Leinster CC and Civil Service CC. He joined the
Irish Guards and later received his commission with the
Inniskilling Fusiliers in March 1915 and was for a time stationed
in Londonderry before being posted as recruiting officer with the
5th Inniskillings at Magherafelt.

He was killed in action on the morning of 27th April 1916 during
the Battle of Hulluch, which also claimed the lives of Privates
John O'Neill and William Wilson.

Newton Henry Collins is buried in grave 1-C-9 at Philosophe
British Military Cemetry, Mazingarbe, France.

The cemetery was started in August 1915. In 1916 it was taken
over by the 16th (Irish) Division, who held the Loos Salient at the
time, and many of their dead are buried here.

After the Armistice, many isolated graves from the Battle of Loos
were brought here including 41 men of the 9th Black Watch. There
are a total of 1,996 Commonwealth burials here, 277 of these can
not be identified.

He is commemorated on the War Memorial of Mountjoy School,
Dublin.

20502-Private John O'Neill
7th Battalion Royal Inniskilling Fusiliers
Killed in Action: 27th April 1916
Age: 19
Philosophe British Military Cemetery, Mazingarbe, France.
Grave: 1-D-18

John O'Neill was born on 17th February 1897, at Aughacolumb, Ardboe, Cookstown, the second son of John (Jack) O'Neill and Mrs. Rose O'Neill (nee Campbell, of Motherwell, Scotland). John and Rose had 14 children.

Prior to enlisting in the army John O'Neill worked as a farm labourer for Mr. Robert Orr, Ballysudden, Cookstown.

John's sister, Mrs. Rose Carty, Lissan Cookstown, recounted in later years about her brother, John's disappearance one weekend early in 1915:

"John left Robert Orr's farm one Saturday evening on his bicycle, as he did every Saturday night to cycle home to Ardboe to stay for the weekend, but one weekend he didn't show up and this caused a bit of concern. My mother asked my father to go to Robert Orr's to find out if John was okay, but my father said he'd leave it until Monday. On Monday my father spoke to Robert Orr who told him that John had left on Saturday as usual and was expecting him to return to work on Monday, as he normally would. The two men made enquiries in Cookstown and later found out that some boys had gone off with the army who were recruiting in Cookstown that weekend. When my mother found out she was beside herself with grief. He was tracked down in Randalstown and my Mother made enquiries if he could come home explaining that he was just a boy and needed at home. John was adamant that he wanted to stay with his friends and was enjoying the army life and told his superiors that he wasn't needed at home as his father, older brother and younger sister were both in employment. My mother still wasn't happy about all this. John even pawned his good bicycle and brand new suit. We never did find out where he pawned them."

John O'Neill stayed in the army and finished his training at Randalstown, County Antrim and later at Finner Camp, Ballyshannon, County Donegal.

He had enlisted with the 7th Royal Inniskilling Fusiliers.

Mrs. Rose Carty recounted:

John came home on leave a couple of times when he was still in training, I used to polish the buttons of his tunic and polished his boots, he used to laugh that they weren't done right, but he was just joking with me. His last time home on leave before he went to France really upset my mother because he was going away, but he assured her he would be back before long. On the journey from our house in Aughacolumb to Stewartstown train station he told my brother Pat and my sister Kathleen that he had a feeling he would never see Stroud's Corner again. Stroud's Corner was, where he hung out with his friends at the weekends, and he never did see it again, it wasn't long after that we got the word that he had been killed.'

7th Inniskillings formed part of 49 Brigade of the 16th Irish Division and on December 2nd 1915 the Division was inspected by Her Majesty Queen Mary.

In February 1916, 49 Brigade which included the 7th and 8th Inniskillings was the last Brigade of the division to arrive in France. Their first posting was to the Loos Salient sector of the Western Front.

On the 26th April 1916 the 7th Inniskillings were holding the line near Hulluch when word was given of a possible gas attack by the Germans. According to reports a German deserter had come across to the British lines and informed them. Everything was done to strengthen the lines of defence, dugouts were provided with blanket curtains as protection against the gas. In the early hours of the morning of the 27th April 1916 enemy action began with bursts of rifle and machine gun fire, followed by a heavy artillery bombardment, and about 04.45 hours gas was released, the wind carrying it in the direction of the Inniskilling front lines. The Germans left their trenches, suffering some casualties as they crossed the open ground but succeeded in penetrating the trench lines of B and C companies. Hand to hand fighting ensued, with the Germans retreating with a few prisoners. At 08.00 hours the Germans released more gas and advanced again, but their attack broke down under very heavy fire when Lieutenant HBO Mitchell with his Lewis-gun team stopped their advance. By 11.00 hours the crisis had passed and the Inniskilling set about re-building their defences and counting their casualties.

Of the 24 Officers and 603 other ranks that came into the line, 10 officers and 253 others ranks were listed as casualties. 8 men were missing, 52 wounded, 137 gassed and 66 dead including Private John O'Neill. Private William Wilson from Cookstown died of his wounds on the 28th April. Subsequent actions over the next few days brought the total to 71 dead of the 7th Inniskillings and 57 dead of the 8th Inniskillings.

John O'Neill is buried in plot 1- row D- grave 18 at Philosophe British Military Cemetery, Mazingarbe, France.

John O'Neill is commemorated on Stewartstown Cenotaph.

27041-Private William Wilson

7th Battalion Royal Inniskilling Fusiliers
Died of Wounds: 28th April1916
Age: 31
Philosophe British Military Cemetery, Mazingarbe, France.
Grave 1-D-11

Private William Wilson was born in Ballyronan, County Londonderry and was the son of Mr. and Mrs. Samuel Wilson. Church Street, Cookstown

At the outbreak of war, William had been working and living in Scotland, with his sister Mrs. McGlade, 94 Aitchison Street, Airdrie, and William enlisted in the ranks of the Inniskilling Regiment there. The 7th Inniskillings were trained at Randalstown, County Antrim and Finner Camp, Ballyshannon, County Donegal. They were posted to France in February 1916, with the battalion losing many of its ranks in early engagements with the enemy soon after at the Battle of Hulluch. In the early hours of the morning of the 27th April 1916, the 7th Inniskillings were subject to ferocious machine gun and rifle fire, followed by an artillery bombardment and the release of gas.

Private William Wilson died of wounds as a result of the gas attack and is buried in plot 1- row D- rave 11 at Philosophe British Military Cemetery, Mazingarbe, France

William Wilson is commemorated on Cookstown Cenotaph and St. Luran's Church of Ireland Roll of Honour, Derryloran, Cookstown.

At a special meeting of Tullyhogue L.O.L. 111 on Monday 22nd May 1916, Bro. Robert Mullan (Chair) assisted by Bro. Henry Steenson (vice chair) instructed Bro. James Davidson (secretary) to forward the following:

"We, the members of the Lodge, wish to express our deepest sympathy with you in the loss which you have sustained by the death of your dear son, and we pray that the Great Comforter may strengthen you in your time of trial."

William's brothers, Thomas, John and Adam also served during the First World War, and his father, Samuel died as a result of an accident in Glasgow, on 8th March 1919, age 63.

For many years our family chain
Was closely linked together,
But, oh! That chain is broken now
One link has gone forever.
But the hardest part is yet to come,
When heroes do return;
When I miss among the cheering crowd
My, dear beloved son

Submitted to the Mid Ulster Mail, by Samuel Wilson, May 1916

13935-Private Robert J. Little

9th Battalion Royal Inniskilling Fusilers
Died of Wounds: 8th May 1916
Age: 22
Forceville Cemetery, France. Grave: 1-C-2.

Robert Little was the son of William and Eliza Jane Little of Killymoon, Blue Doors, Coolkeeghan, Cookstown, and brother of William J. Little 1st Battalion Royal Inniskilling Fusiliers who was killed in action on 18th May 1915.

Robert was born at Ballyeglish, Moneymore, and lived with his parents in Cookstown. He was a member of Strifehill LOL 628 and a member of Cookstown Company of Ulster Volunteers. He enlisted in the 9th Battalion Inniskillings at Finner Camp, Ballyshannon, County Donegal.

Mrs. Eliza Jane Little received the following letter from Lieutenant-Colonel Ambrose Ricardo:

"The battalion made a successful raid on the enemy's trenches on Sunday 8th May, and inflicted serious loss. We were subjected to a heavy bombardment for over 2 and a half hours, and had considerable casualties, which included Private Little, who was fatally wounded in the attack, and died a short time later."

Captain Cruickshank wrote:

We have lost a fine Soldier and true comrade.

In a letter dated 10th May 1916, the Church of Ireland Chaplain wrote:

I conducted the funeral service of Private Little who was taken from 108th Field Ambulance. I hope that the present sorrow is overshadowed by the love of God, and that this life is but the beginning.

Robert Little died from wounds soon after the attack on the night of the 8th May 1916.

He is buried in plot 1- row C- grave 2 at Forceville Communal Cemetery, France.

He is also commemorated on Cookstown Cenotaph, St. Luran's Church of Ireland Roll of Honour, Derryloran, Cookstown and Moneymore War Memorial (as Robert Lyttle).

17808-Private John McMullan

9th Battalion Royal Inniskilling Fusiliers
Killed in Action: 8th May 1916
Age: 25
Authuille Military Cemetery, France. Special Memorial: A-2

John McMullan was the son of Mr. and Mrs. James McMullan, of Ruskey, Coagh.

John was educated at Tamlaght National School, Coagh and was a member of Carryhill L.O.L. 188 and R.B.P. 243.

In a letter dated 22nd March 1916, Private Edward McGuckin from Coagh wrote home to say:

"All the Coagh boys at the front are doing well and in good fighting form, although they have been constantly in the trenches for the past eight weeks. They are well accustomed to Jack Johnstons, whizz-bangs, trench mortars and other such scrap as the Germans treat them to. John McMullan is going strong, so strong in fact that he has now been nick-named 'whizz-bang'. We have nicknamed the other Coagh lads as well, 'rifle-grenade' Sands, 'trench-mortar' Currie, and 'barbed-wire' Hudson. Sands and Hudson are a bit sore at the some recent marriages in Coagh and are afraid that there won't be any Coagh girls when they return victoriously home."

John McMullan and Robert Sands were killed in a heavy bombardment by the Germans after the Inniskillings had carried out a successful night raid on the German lines on 7th/8th May 1916. Both men are buried in Authuille Military Cemetery, France. They are also commemorated on Coagh War Memorial (Royal British Legion, Cookstown).

When the Commonwealth War Graves Commission came to make the cemeteries which we visit today they discovered that a mistake had been made in the case of John McMullan. They knew that he had been interred in Authuille Cemetery, but could not determine where. The resulting row of headstones at the side of the cemetery is testimony to this. John McMullan is commemorated at Special Memorial A. 2.

At a special meeting of Carryhill LOL 188 on Tuesday 23rd May 1916 the secretary reported the deaths of John McMullan and Robert Sands. On a motion of Bro. Thomas J. McKeown, W.M., seconded by Bro. S. McComb, D.M., the secretary was instructed to forward a letter of sympathy to the relatives of the deceased.

We mourn the loss of one so dear
So good, so kind, so brave
He died on the battle field of France
And lies in a soldier's grave

Obituary inserted by John McMullan's family Mid Ulster Mail 1916.

13890Private Robert Sands

9th Battalion Royal Innskilling Fusiliers ("C" company)
Killed In Action: 8th May 1916
Age: 23
Authuille Military Cemetery, France. Grave D 45

Robert Sands was the son of William and Ellen Sands, Urbal, Coagh, Cookstown.

Before joining the army, Robert was a member of Coagh Company of Ulster Volunteers, and was a member of Drumconvis LOL 794 and acted as Chaplain there. He had one other brother on active service with the army.

Robert was killed in action on the night of 7th/8th May 1916, soon after a successful trench raid against the enemy. The 9th Battalion Inniskillings came under a heavy bombardment in retaliation. 19 other men lost their lives that night, including John McMullan from Coagh and Robert Little from Cookstown. Two other men died of their wounds the next day. Robert Sands is buried in row D, grave 45 at Authuille Military Cemetery, France.

Corporal Mitchell from Coagh, sent a letter of sympathy to Robert's sister soon after his death, saying:

"I'm very sorry to inform you of the death of your brother Robert, who lost his life on the night of 7th May 1916. It was during a heavy bombardment of our lines and his death was instantaneous, so he suffered no pain. He was the favourite of the platoon whose members all join me in offering our heartfelt sympathy in your sad bereavement."

In a letter to Robert's father, his Commanding Officer, Lieutenant-Colonel Ambrose Ricardo, said:

"I wish to convey to you the sympathy of all the ranks of the Battalion in the sorrow that has come to you on the death of your son. The battalion carried out a successful raid on the enemy trenches last Sunday night, inflicting severe loss on them. We were subjected to a very heavy bombardment for over 3 hours, and we had considerable casualties. Your son was a gallant soldier and a good comrade, and we mourn his loss."

His Warfare is over, his battle fought,
His Victory won, though dearly bought;
His fresh young life could not be saved;
He slumbers now in a soldier's grave.
We Loved him in life, he is dear to us still,
In grief we must bend to God's Holy will;
The trial was great, the loss heavy to bare,
The Angels, dear Robert, will tend to your care.

Submitted for publication in Mid Ulster Mail by Robert's parents, June 1916

A Call From The Trenches

By Robert Sands

"Fall in! Fall in! We're out to win!" the country calls today
The raging hun, his worst has done, and soon he'll have to pay.
We dozed a bit, before we hit, but now we'll face about,
With open eyes and brave allies, to knock the beggars out.

Then bustle along with a cheery song, as long as there's work to do
For Kitchener's lot are on the spot, with plenty of work for you.
We're on the scene 'til France is clean and brave little Belgium free,
We've started the job in earnest and we'll finish it on the 'spree'.

We are not great at Hymns of fate, but this we are gained to swear-
We'll make them howl, for fighting foul, and beat them by fighting fair;
To keep our word may seem absurd but that's what Briton's do,
And they may bet our teeth are set, to see the business through.

So pull up your boot and learn to shoot, and march with the army swing,
Get thoroughly fit to do your bit along with our Gracious King.
We've got it in hand to sweep the land as Jellicoe swept the sea,
We're starting the job in earnest and we'll finish it o the 'spree'.

Then off we'll go to face the foe, who laughs at old John Bull?
But some must stay to work and play, and keep the convoy full.
They serve King George in mine and forge, although they can't be here,
So while we spend the shells they send, we'll give them all a cheer.

Then Stand to the front and bare the brunt, for ours is the team to stay
And now that we're in, we mean to win, whatever the croakers say.
We carry a pill for Kaiser Bill, for all the Allies agree
They'll stick to the job in earnest, 'til they finish it on the 'spree'.

3579-Private Alexander Steenson

6th Battalion Connaught Rangers
Killed in Action: 30th May 1916
Age: 48
Loos Memorial, France. Panel 124

Alexander Steenson was born in Stewartstown, County Tyrone, the son of Alexander and Mary Steenson, Cookstown. He had gone to live and work in Belfast where he married his wife Jane and lived at 59 Campore Street, Belfast.

He has no known grave and is commemorated on panel 124 on Loos Memorial, France.

27475 - Private Francis McManus

(Formerly 21324 - Royal Dublin Fusiliers)
7th Battalion Royal Inniskilling Fusiliers
Died of Wounds: 31st May 1916
Age: 25
Philosophe British Military Cemetery, Mazingarbe, France.
Grave 1 D 27

Francis McManus was born Pomeroy and lived in the parish of Kildress, County Tyrone.

He enlisted in the army in Cookstown with the Royal Dublin Fusiliers (21324). He subsequently transferred back to the 7th Royal Inniskilling Fusiliers, as he had previously been with the Inniskilling Reserve since December 15th 1913, when he enlisted with them in Dungannon.

It is not recorded how Francis McManus received his wounds. The 7th Inniskillings lost 13 other men throughout the month of May 1916. 7 men were listed as killed in action and 6 men listed as died of wounds, 4 of those men were formerly of other regiments. After the enemy attack of 27th April 1916, the 7th Battalion Royal Inniskilling Fusiliers was almost at half its normal strength.

Frank McManus is buried in plot 1, row D, grave 27 at Philosophe British Military Cemetery, Mazingarbe, France.

Lieutenant Robert Cecil Wallace
10th Regiment South African Infantry
Killed in Action: 31st May 1916
Age: 33
Dar es Salaam War Cemetery, Tanzania, Africa. Grave: 5-L-3

Robert Cecil Wallace was born on 20th March 1883. He was the eldest son of the Reverend Robert Wallace of Ballygoney, Coagh, and later of Omagh, County Tyrone, grandson of the Reverend John Knox Leslie of Cookstown, and a nephew of Dr. Richard Whytock Leslie of Cookstown who was the first Doctor of Campbell College, Belfast and a respected physician at the Ulster Hospital for Women and Children.

Robert Cecil Wallace was a pupil at Campbell College, Belfast between February 1898 and July 1901, and was regarded as one of the most promising Rugby footballers of his time. He played for the Old Mount Club and Knock, and was living with his widowed mother at 26 Cromwell Road, Belfast before emigrating to South Africa where he was employed at the Standard Bank in Johannesburg. He joined the Imperial Light Horse of the South African Field Force as a Trooper and subsequently received a commission. At the outbreak of the First World War, Tanzania was the core of German East Africa, with Dar es Salaam as its capital. From the invasion of April 1915, Commonwealth Forces fought a difficult and protracted campaign against a relatively small but highly skilled German Force under the command of General von Lettow-Vorbeck. By 1916 the Commonwealth Forces came under the command of General Jan Smuts.

Trooper Jack Burrowes from Dungannon served with the South African Horse during the campaign and described the country as, *"a 'natural zoo' and news often reaches us from the outside world rather slowly and fever is very prevalent among the men."*

By 9th March 1916, British and Colonial Forces had taken and occupied Taveta and by 29th May 1916 the War Office announced a new invasion of German East Africa.

On 31st May, the Germans retreated from Mombo on the Tanga railway towards Hendeni.

Dar es Salaam surrendered to British Forces on 3rd September 1916, but the war in this part of Africa continued until the Germans finally surrendered on 23rd November 1918, twelve days after the European Armistice. By this stage their numbers being reduced to 155 European and 1,168 African troops. General Paul

Emil von Lettow-Vorbeck returned to Germany a national hero but in later years he became destitute, and on hearing of his former opponent's plight, General Jan Smuts arranged (along with some former British and South African officers) a small pension to be paid to him until his death on 9th March 1964 at the age of 94.

Lieutenant Robert Wallace was killed in action on 31st May 1916, during the campaign in German East Africa and is buried in Plot 5, Row L, Grave; 3 at Dar es Salaam War Cemetery, Tanzania, Africa. Robert Wallace's cousin, 2nd Lieutenant James Lytton Millar, age 18 (whose mother came from Cookstown), was killed in action on 28th July 1916. He was the youngest former pupil of Campbell College to die in the First World War, and he is buried at Vermelles British Cemetery, France.

2612-Lance Corporal Charles George Lord
7th Battalion Leinster Regiment
Killed in Action: 2nd June 1916
Age: 32
Philosophe British Military, Cemetery. Mazingarbhe, France.
Grave: 1 – D - 5

Charles George Lord was a son of Thomas and Mary E. Lord of Loy Street, Cookstown. Although he lived in Cookstown, he enlisted while he was in Dublin. The 7th Leinsters were formed at Fermoy in October 1914, went to Blackdown in September of 1915 and landed at Le Havre on 18th December 1915. By the early summer of 1916 the battalion were near Mazingarbhe and it was here that Charles was killed. He was the only casualty in his Battalion on that day and is buried in Philosophe British Military, Cemetery. Mazingarbhe, France.

Charles George Lord is commemorated on Cookstown Cenotaph.

602253-Private Robert Howe
13th Battalion Canadian Infantry
Died of Wounds: 3rd June 1916
Age: 27
Lijssenthoek Cemetery, Belgium Grave: 7-B-3a

Robert Howe was born on 29th November 1889 and was the son of William and Mary Howe of Coagh and later of 22 St. Ives Gardens, Stranmillis, Belfast.

He was educated at Tamlaght National School, Coagh.

Before emigrating to Canada he served his time in the drapery business with Mr. Joseph Geddes, Cookstown and spent six years in the Royal Irish Constabulary being stationed in Queens County and Lurgan, and also at Cullingtree Road Barracks, Belfast. While living in Belfast he was attached to Abercorn Memorial Masonic Lodge No 347. He volunteered on 11 January 1915 at Guelph, Ontario, naming his mother as next of kin, and joining the 13th Battalion Canadian Infantry. Much of his training took place at Shorncliffe and Bramshott Camps. In May 1916 he was seriously wounded, and died in hospital on 3rd June 1916. Robert is buried at Lijssenthoek Military Cemetery, Belgium in plot 7, row B, grave 3a, and commemorated on Coagh War Memorial (R.B.L. Cookstown).

Mrs. Howe received the following letter from the Rev. A.D. Brooke, Chaplain to the Forces.

"I am very sorry indeed to tell you that your son, Sergeant Robert Howe, died in hospital on 3rd June. He was admitted just a few hours before with serious wounds in the abdomen and thigh and was conscious only a short time, during which I was with him and prayed with him and did all I could to help to comfort him. I told him I would write to you and he sent you his dearest love. That was his only message. He soon became unconscious and later, in spite of all the doctor's efforts, he passed quietly away without feeling any pain. He was buried with Church services in the Military Cemetery on the Poperinghe-Baeschepe Road. His grave will be marked with a cross bearing his name. Please accept my deepest sympathy and I hope you will feel he was not alone but with friends who did their very best for him. His personal effects will all be sent to you later by the authorities."

At the time of Robert Howe's death his brother Charles was attached to the Royal Irish Rifles as a drill instructor in Celley Park, Reading. He was a former member of the RIC.

He was one of many, who with patriotic pride
Unto their country's clarion call courageously replied
To duty stern he did respond, his youthful life he gave
He died a fearless death and fills an honoured grave
Though the years have passed away, we still miss him day by day
His battles fought, his trials o'er, and he has gained the brighter shore.

Submitted by his mother, brothers and sisters to Mid Ulster Mail 1916.

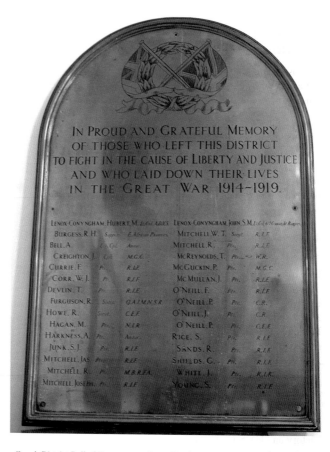

Coagh District Roll of Honour now situated in the Royal British Legion, Cookstown

5057/S - James Devlin (Stoker)
Royal Naval Reserve
HMS "Hampshire"
Died: 5th June 1916
Age: 40
Chatham Naval Memorial, Kent, England (19)

James Devlin was the son of John and Hannah Devlin, and brother of Michael John Devlin, Killeenan, Cookstown.

Before joining the Royal Naval Reserve, James was employed in Iron Works at Port Clarence-on-Tees, where he had lived and worked for over 20 years

He was serving as a stoker on board HMS Hampshire and was lost at sea when the ship struck a mine off the Orkney Isles on 5th June 1916.

HMS Hampshire was a first class armored cruiser of the Devonshire class, with a weight of 10,850 tons and a length of 473ft 6 inches, with a beam of 68ft 6ins and a draught of 24 feet. It was powered by a two shaft, four cylinder engine, six boilers aft and 17 Yarrow water tube boilers distributed between the three forward boiler rooms. The ship could carry up to 1,950 tons of coal and had a maximum speed of 22 knots. To crew the ship it needed a full complement of 655 men. It was built at Chatham dockyard in Kent, between 1902 and 1904 with a cost of £900,000. The ship was commissioned in 1905.

In its time the Hampshire had an eventful 11 years at sea, traveling to the Mediterranean and the Far East. The ship was involved in the hunt for the SMS Embden which was attacking Allied shipping at the start of World War 1 and took part in the Battle of Jutland. Hampshire was heavily armor plated and well equipped with 4x7.5in Guns, 6x6in Guns, 18-three pounders and 2x18in torpedo tubes.

At 4.40pm on Monday 5th June 1916, HMS Hampshire left Scapa Flow and took the route through Hoxa Sound to the south and then turned westwards into stormy weather just off south-west Hoy where it rendezvoused with the escort destroyers, HMS Victory and HMS Unity, the two destroyers then following behind the Hampshire. After failing to keep up to speed with the Hampshire over the next 2 hours both destroyers were signalled and asked to return to base.

At 7.40 pm, the Hampshire was struggling through a force 9 gale with an approximate speed of 13.5 knots between Marwick Head and the Brough of Bisray when the ship took an explosion after striking a mine which shook the whole vessel. The explosion ripped through the port side just forward of the bridge, with the helm jammed and the power cut the ship could not make radio contact with the authorities on shore to ask for assistance.

A telegraph message was sent from Bisray Post Office to Kirkwall and Stromness which read: "Battle cruiser seems in distress between Marwick Head and Brough of Bisray."

By 7.50pm within minutes of striking the mine, HMS Hampshire began to sink. She went down, bows first and leaning to the starboard side.

643 sailors lost their lives with the sinking of the Hampshire. Lord Kitchener, John Forrest and James Devlin were amongst the dead.

James Devlin is commemorated on Chatham Naval Memorial, Kent, England.

K/27693 Stoker 1st Class - John Forrest
Royal Navy - H.M.S. "Hampshire"
Died: 5th June 1916
Age: 24
Portsmouth Naval Memorial, England.

John Forrest was the son of John and Rachel Forrest, High Cross, Tullyhogue, Cookstown. John had gone to work in the United States of America for a few years before returning to Britain in January 1915 when he was employed in the production of torpedoes in Scotland. He was highly regarded by all who knew him and by all reports he had a kind good-natured disposition. He joined the Royal Navy in August 1915 and received his training in Portsmouth. He later qualified as a 1st Class Stoker and was posted to H.M.S Victory and later joined H.M.S Hampshire in early 1916. H.M.S Hampshire struck a mine off the Orkney Isles and was sunk on 5th June 1916, taking the lives of 643 sailors including John Forrest and James Devlin (stoker) from Killeenan, Kildress, Cookstown, and Earl Lord Kitchener who was travelling to Russia on Diplomatic Duties. John Forrest is commemorated on Portsmouth Naval Memorial, England. He is also commemorated on Stewartstown Cenotaph and Donaghendry Church of Ireland Roll of Honour, Stewartstown.

In July 1916 John Forrest's Lodge published the following notice in the Mid Ulster Mail.

Magill Orange Standard LOL 158.

"The officers and members of the above lodge deeply regret the death of Bro. John Forrest, junior, Highcross, who was such a loyal and well beloved member of same.

Shortly after the outbreak of war he volunteered and joined the Navy to help defend the Empire, and after a term of service lost his life on HMS Hampshire of the Orkney Islands along with others. Bro. Forrest was always ready to help with both money and deed, and gained for himself the esteem and good wish of all. Great sympathy is felt for his parents and the rest of the family on their sad bereavement."

Perhaps one of the most familiar names relating to the First World War is that of Earl Lord Herbert Kitchener, who was born at Ballylongford in County Kerry in 1850.

He had served with great distinction in the Middle East, Egypt and the Boer War. He became the Secretary of State for War at the out break of World War 1 and was the distinctive face of recruitment posters and advertising campaigns the length and breadth of Britain and Ireland.

He was lost at sea while on a diplomatic mission to Russia, when HMS Hampshire was sunk. In subsequent years many conspiracy theories have risen surrounding his death and the sinking of the Hampshire.

22853-Private Peter Biggar
13th Battalion Royal Scots
Killed in Action: 12th June 1916
Age: 19
Vermelles Communal, Cemetery. Pas De Calais, France.
Grave: 3-D-3

Peter Biggar was born in Addiewell, Midlothian, Scotland. He was the son of Patrick and Elizabeth Biggar, and lived in Stewartstown, County Tyrone. Peter moved back to Scotland and was living in Edinburgh when he enlisted in with the Royal Scots.

It was reported that he died as a result of an accident, though he is listed as killed in action. Three men from the 13th Battalion Royal Scots were listed as killed in action on 12th June 1916 Peter Biggar, Matthew Laurence and Ernest Corbett.

Peter Biggar is buried in plot 3- row D- grave 3 at Vermelles Communal Cemtery, France.

23667-Private George Shields

7th Battalion Royal Inniskilling Fusilers
Died of Wounds: 15th June 1916
Age: 18
Philosophe British Military Cemetery, Mazingarbe, France.
Grave: 1-F-30

George was a son of Hugh and Alice Shields of Urbal, Coagh, and later lived at Ballybeg, Coalisland, County Tyrone. He joined the army on 1st June 1915 and was sent to the front on 1st February 1916 as a despatch rider. He died of wounds on 15th June 1916 and is interred in Philosophe British Military Cemetery Mazingarbe, France in plot 1- row F- grave 30. He was eighteen years of age. Only one other man was killed in the battalion on that day, James Barrett. He lies close to George in grave 27. James came from Londonderry and was the husband of Mary Barrett of Abbey Street.

George Shields is commemorated on Coagh War Memorial (Royal British Legion, Cookstown).

1st July 1916
The Somme Offensive

The Somme Offensive was a joint, French and British operation which had originally been planned for late 1915, but owing to the German onslaught of January 1916 at Verdun, where the German Army Chief of Staff, von Falkenhayn promised to 'Bleed France White', resulting in the diversion of virtually all French manpower to Verdun.

The German Offensive at Verdun had transformed the intent of the proposed Somme Offensive, and to relieve the pressure of Verdun, the French demanded that the planned date of 1st August 1916 be brought forward by one month.

On the 1st July 1916, the attack was launched along a 25,000 yard (nearly 14 miles) front, from north of the Somme River between the towns of Maricourt in the south, northwards to Serre, with a diversionary attack at Gommecourt, two miles further north. 27 Divisions comprising of 750,000 men, 80% of which were comprised from the British Expeditionary Force, opposed to 16 Divisions of the German Second Army.

The attack was preceded by an eight day artillery bombardment of the German lines which began on 24th June 1916. The expectation was that the bombardment would destroy all forward German defences, therefore enabling the attacking British troops to practically walk across "No Man's Land" and take possession of the German front lines. 1,537 British Guns, together with a similar number of French Artillery were used in the bombardment. It was the heaviest concentration of guns gathered for an offensive in the war so far.

The bombardment was followed by the detonation of a series of 17 mines along the German front lines which began at 07:30 am and was followed by the advance of troops into "No Man's Land", but the artillery had failed to destroy much of the German defences, including the barbed wire, as many of the allied munitions had failed to detonate.

The Infantry Troops emerged from their trenches carrying up to 60 pounds of equipment on their backs and advanced in extended lines at a slow steady pace across the grassy expanse of "No Man's Land". There they met a hail of rifle and machine gun fire from the surviving German defenders. Accurate German artillery barrage immediately added to the chaos, as shells engulfed the attackers and wrecked the crowded British assembly trenches. The advancing infantry and those in support waiting to advance suffered tremendous losses.

Many of the Cookstown men who were lost or wounded that day, served with one of the three Irish Regiments in the 36th Ulster Division.

The Ulster Division was one of those selected to make the initial assault at The Battle of Albert (first phase of The Battle of the Somme). Their objective on 1st July 1916 was to capture the strongly held and fortified German position at Schwaben Redoubt. The Germans had prepared their defences meticulously on the Somme front. Three principle lines of trench systems existed, several hundred yards deep and reinforced by natural and man made strong points. Elaborate subterranean barracks, installed with electric lighting, were dug out of the chalky earth. The Germans were exceptionally well positioned here.

The 36th Ulster Division (almost exclusively Ulster-raised volunteer Battalions) was flanked on either side by 32nd Division on its right, facing the high ground toward Thiepval village, and on its left by 29th Division, facing Beaumont-Hamel on the Ancre River. The 29th Division included two Irish regiments, 1st Battalion Royal Innsikilling Fusiliers (87th Brigade) and 1st Battalion Royal Dublin Fusiliers (86th Brigade). 32nd Division included the 2nd Battalion Royal Inniskilling Fusiliers (96th Brigade)

The opening day of the Battle of the Somme, 1st July 1916 has the onerous distinction of being the worst day in the history of the British Army.

It is often forgotten though, that three Divisions captured their objectives, and that several others while not doing so did perform exceptional feats. The 36th Ulster Division was one of them. It captured and held the Schwaben Redoubt, and held it for a considerable time for part of the day, despite little or no progress being made by any of the Divisions on its flanks. It was forced to withdraw through lack of support, and German reinforcements being brought in.

By the end of the day, the British Army had inccurred more than 58,000 casualties. Over one third of them had been killed including over 2,000 (killed) and 3,000 (wounded and missing) men of the Ulster Division.

The Somme Offensive continued until the 18th November 1916.

16273 Corporal Isaac Black
9th Battalion Royal Inniskilling Fusiliers
Killed in Action: 1st July 1916
Mill Road, Cemetery. Thiepval, France Grave: 1-B-34

Isaac Black was born at Sandholes, Cookstown. He was the son of William Black and Elizabeth Black (nee Vance). The family farmed and also owned the grocer shop in Sandholes village. He had four brothers and four sisters, Robert, Ezekiel, James, George, Jane, Elizabeth, Mina and Georgina.

Before enlisting in the army, Isaac worked on the family farm and was an active member of the local Tullylagan Company of Ulster Volunteers, where part of his duties was as a semaphore signaller with his good friend Alexander (Sandy) Little.

Isaac Black's sister, the late Mrs Jane Swaile, related a story of how as a young girl she watched Isaac and Sandy carry out their duties, signalling to one another from their respective homes up at Killyneedan, Sandholes, a distance of approximately 1000 yards. When members of the Ulster Volunteers joined the colours in 1914, Isaac enlisted at Finner Camp, Ballyshannon, County Donegal, and trained at Shane's Park Camp at Randalstown, County Antrim. He was promoted to Corporal during his early training and early in September 1915 the 9th Inniskillings went to Bordon Camp in England and from there to France in October.

Corporal Isaac Black was killed in action on 1st July 1916, as he encouraged his men to cross 'No Man's Land'. He was buried in Mill Road Cemetery close to where he fell. He is buried in plot 1- row B- grave 34. His family worshipped in Sandholes Presbyterian Church and following Isaac's death the Minister spoke in the most glowing terms of Isaac's life and worth.

Isaac Black is commemorated on Cookstown Cenotaph and on Sandholes Presbyterian Church, Roll of Honour.

16290-Lance Corporal William John Campbell
9th Battalion Royal Irish Rifles
Killed In Action: 1st July 1916
Thiepval Memorial, France. Panel: 15A - 15B

William John Campbell was born in Cookstown, County Tyrone, and enlisted with the Royal Irish Rifles in Belfast. He was killed in action on the 1st July 1916 and has no known grave and is commemorated on panels 15A - 15B on Thiepval Memorial, France.

21869-Private Robert Cander
1st Battalion Royal Dublin Fusiliers
Killed in Action: 1st July 1916
Age: 42
Auchonvillers Military Cemetery, France. Grave: 2-A-4

Robert Cander was born at Clare, Kildress, Cookstown, and was the son of Joseph and Ellen Cander, 47 Stewart Street, Mossend, Lanarkshire, and husband of Catherine McGrath Cander. He enlisted in Hamilton in Scotland. He was killed in action on 1st July 1916 and is buried in grave plot 2- row A- grave 4 at Auchonvillers Military Cemetery, France.

14065-Lance Corporal George Chambers
9th Battalion Royal Irish Fusiliers
Killed in Action: 1st July 1916
Age: 19
Ancre Valley Cemetery, France. Grave: 8-A-37

George Chambers was born at Sherrygroom, Newmills, County Tyrone about 1897. The family moved to live at Milford, Co Armagh. George enlisted in Armagh with the 9th Battalion, Royal Irish Fusiliers. This Battalion was raised from the Armagh, Monaghan and Cavan Volunteers and after training at Seaford arrived at Boulogne in October 1915. George was killed by machine gun fire as he attempted to cross 'No Man's Land' on the 1st July 1916, the first day of the Somme Offensive. He is buried in plot 8- row A- grave 37 at Ancre Valley Cemetery, Somme, France.

17434-Rifleman Francis Cheevers

13th Battalion Royal Irish Rifles
Killed in Action: 1st July 1916
Age: 21
Thiepval Memorial, France   Panel: 15A-15B

Francis Cheevers was a son of John and Sarah Cheevers of Cookstown. The family lived for a time in Killyleagh, County Down, and Francis enlisted in Downpatrick, joining the 13th Battalion Royal Irish Rifles. The 13th Battalion was raised from the ranks of the County Down Volunteers in September 1914, and after training at Clandeboye and Seaford, landed at Boulogne in October 1915. Preparations were under way for the Somme Offensive. He was killed as he attempted to cross 'No Man's Land' on the morning of 1st July 1916, he has no known grave and is commemorated on panel 15A-15B on the Thiepval Memorial, France He is also commemorated on Cookstown Cenotaph and St.Luran's Church of Ireland, Roll of Honour, Derryloran, Cookstown.

Inscription on Thiepval Memorial

24764-Private Francis Donaghy

1st Battalion Royal Inniskilling Fusiliers
Killed in Action: 1st July 1916
Thiepval Memorial, France. Panel: 4D-5B

Francis Donaghy lived at Coagh Street, Cookstown, and for a number of years before the outbreak of the First World War had worked as a barman in the Railway Bar in Cookstown. He enlisted in Cookstown on 15th July 1915 and was killed in action near Thiepval on the first day of the Somme Offensive. He was listed as missing and has no known grave. He is commemorated on panel 4D-5B on Thiepval Memorial to the Missing of the Somme, France. He is also commemorated on Cookstown Cenotaph.

14512 Private Frederick Donnelly
10th Battalion Royal Irish Rifles
Killed in Action: 1st July 1916
Thiepval Memorial, France.   Panel: 15A-15B

Frederick Donnelly was born in Stewartstown, County Tyrone and
enlisted with the Royal Irish Rifles while he was living and
working in Belfast.

He was killed in action on the first day of the Somme Offensive.
He has no known grave and is commemorated on panel 15A-15B
on Thiepval Memorial, France.

27220-Private Samuel Donnelly
15th Battalion Royal Scots
Killed in Action: 1st July 1916
Age: 26
Thiepval Memorial, France. Panel: 6D-7D

Samuel was a son of Mr. and Mrs. Joseph Donnelly of Linneyglass, Stewartstown. After Samuel was killed in action at the Somme his close friend, Private Donald Garden, wrote to Samuel's parents at Stewartstown from his hospital bed in Aberdeen. The letter is as follows:

"I was a chum of Samuel's in the Royal Scots and I feel I should write you a few lines. We went into action on Saturday, 1st July. I am sorry to say Sam was struck with a bullet just before the German lines and he died immediately. It may be some consolation for you to know that he suffered no pain. I was with him at the time and he never spoke. He was a great friend of mine and well-liked in the Company, and I greatly feel the loss of such a friend. I offer my deepest sympathy. I was wounded the same day. We were in a big open bit of country between Albert and La Boisselle, and the Germans were firing very heavily. I was along with Sam all the way across and our men were falling around us. I spoke to him and the Sergeant also, but he was dead, we had no doubt about it. The Sergeant was also badly wounded and so was I soon afterwards so we had no opportunity of seeing him again. I had a number of shrapnel wounds, but am about alright again now. I am sorry I cannot tell you where he is buried."

In a letter to Stewartstown Shooting Club, Sergeant Urquhart of the Royal Scots writes to Mr. Thomas Ferguson (Secretary) and says:

"If your club had many more members of his stamp it would indeed be a fine one. As a quiet unassuming worker he was of great service to his Platoon. I regret his loss very much."

Samuel Donnelly has no known grave and is commemorated on panels 6D-7D on Thiepval Memorial, France. He is also commemorated on Stewartstown Cenotaph.

Second Lieutenant-Leslie Montrose Ekin M.C. (age 22)
Second Lieutentant-James Ekin (age19)

8th Battalion York and Lancaster Regt
Killed in Action: 1st July 1916
Blighty Valley Cemetery, France. Grave: 5-C-13
Lonsdale Cemetery, France. Grave: 6-O-1

Leslie Montrose Ekin and James Ekin were the sons of Mr. James
Ekin and Mrs. Josephine Alice Ekin of De Walden Court,
Eastbourne London. They were the nephews of Messrs. W. and J.
Ekin of Ballymoyle, Coagh, and Mrs. Sanford, Moneymore, and
were cousins of Mr. Hugh Thompson, a Cookstown councillor.

Their father, James had worked for many years in the Belfast
Bank in Cookstown and Dungannon.

Leslie was educated at Sydney Grammar School and had returned
to England with his parents, selecting law as his profession. He
was a member of the Middle Temple and was intending to go to
Oxford University when war broke out. He joined the Inns of
Court O.T.C. and received his commission in December 1914. He
was attached as a machine gun officer to the York and Lancaster
Regiment. On 1st July 1916 as the two brothers led their men
across 'No Man's Land' and, though seriously wounded, Leslie
managed to hold his line of advance with his machine gun team,
then taking control of the gun himself before he was cut down.
For his bravery he was awarded the Military Cross. His younger
brother James had been reported missing on 1st July 1916 and his
body was found later.

In writing to their father, their Commanding Officer said:

Your two sons led their men across No Mans Land with the utmost
gallantry, and with the rest of the Battalion, earned undying fame.

Today the two boys lie less than a mile apart in France.

Leslie Montrose Ekin is buried at Blighty Valley Cemetery in plot
5 - row C - grave 13.

James Ekin is buried at Lonsdale Cemetery in plot 6 - row O -
grave 1.

Leslie was twenty-two years of age, his brother James, nineteen.

The following Citation in reference to Leslie Ekin's Military Cross was published in the London Gazette on 22nd September 1916.

For conspicuous gallantry as Officer in command of a Lewis gun team. He led his men across the open under heavy machine gun and shell fire, in which they all became casualties and he himself wounded. Not withstanding, he took the gun forward alone, and continued to serve it until it was knocked out of action and he was seriously wounded again.

15511-Lance Corporal Charles Eyre

10th Battalion Royal Inniskilling Fusiliers
Killed In Action: 1st July 1916
Thiepval Memorial, France. Panel: 4D - 5B

Charles Eyre was born in Sligo, County Sligo. He was for many years employed in Cookstown as an undertaker's assistant with Mr. John Mayne and was an active member of Cookstown Boy's Brigade. He enlisted in Coleraine, County Londonderry, while he was working there. On the 1st July 1916, 109 Brigade which included the 10th Inniskillings, was given one of the most heavily defended positions on the German front line. At 7.30 am the bombardment of trench mortars launched at the German lines stopped, the bugle called and the 10th Inniskillings made their advance. Things were going well for the 9th and 10th Battalions until German machine gunners placed at Thiepval village trained their guns on the advancing men. They suffered terrible casualties and most were left where they fell as their comrades advanced.

Lance Corporal Charles Eyre was killed in the advance. He has no known grave and is commemorated on panel 4D - 5B on the Thiepval Memorial, France. He is also commemorated on Cookstown Cenotaph, and on Coleraine War Memorial

6329-Rifleman John Faulkner

14th Battalion Royal Irish Rifles (YCV)
Killed in Action: 1st July 1916
Age: 19
Thiepval Memorial, France. Panel: 15A-15B

John Faulkner was the son of William and Sarah Jane Faulkner (nee Speer) of Coolkeeghan, Cookstown. At the outbreak of the First World War he enlisted at Randalstown, County Antrim, and was trained at Finner Camp, Ballyshannon, County Donegal. The 14th Battalion Royal Irish Rifles went to France in October 1915 as part of the 36th Ulster Division. John was killed in action in his first major engagement, the Somme Offensive. He has no known grave and he is commemorated on panel 15A-15B on the Thiepval Memorial, France.

He is also commemorated on Cookstown Cenotaph and on Second Presbyterian Church Roll of Honour (at Molesworth).

14603-Corporal John Henry Fitzsimons

14th Battalion Royal Irish Rifles (Young Citizen Volunteers)
Killed in Action: 1st July 1916
Connaught Cemetery, Thiepval, France. Grave: 1-A-8

John Henry Fitzsimons was born in Coagh, County Tyrone. He enlisted in Belfast, joining the 14th Battalion Royal Irish Rifles. This Battalion had been raised in Belfast from the Belfast Volunteers in September 1914 and were trained at Randalstown and Ballyshannon. During training at Seaford John was promoted to Corporal. They landed at Boulogne, France in October 1915. He was killed in action in his first engagement when he went over the top on the first of July 1916. His body was recovered and today he is buried in plot 1, row A, grave 8 at Connaught Cemetery near the Ulster Tower at Thiepval in France.

6362-Lance Corporal William Furgrove

12th Battalion Royal Irish Rifles
Killed in Action: 1st July 1916
Ancre Valley Cemetery, France. Grave: 2-E-19

William was born at Moneymore but moved to live at
Cullybackey. When war broke out he went to Ballymena to enlist
into the 12th Battalion Royal Irish Rifles. They did much of their
training at Clandeboye and Seaford, and were sent to France in
October 1915, landing at Boulogne. Their first major engagement
with the enemy was to be the Somme Offensive. Wet weather had
delayed the attack until the 1st July 1916. Some of the trenches
close to the River Ancre were flooded and men were moved to the
front of Thiepval Wood to drier ground. This meant that machine-
guns at St Pierre Divion would not be attacked and silenced.
These same guns were then able to fire across the river into the
side of the attacking 12th Battalion, causing heavy casualties. It
was during this attack that William was killed in action. The 12th
Battalion had attacked across the Ancre valley close to where
William Furgrove is buried in plot 2- row E-grave 19 at Ancre
Valley Cemetery, France.

1290-Corporal David Glendinning

11th Battalion Royal Irish Rifles
Killed in Action: 1st July 1916
Age: 22
Thiepval Memorial, France. Panel: 15A-15B

David Glendinning was the son of David and Mary Glendinning
of Randalstown. He lived with his wife, Ellen, in The Cottage,
Ballyronan, Magherafelt. David enlisted with the 11th Battalion,
Royal Irish Rifles at Lisburn. He was killed in action at the Battle
of the Somme on 1st July 1916. There is no known grave and is
commemorated on panel 15A-15B on Thiepval Memorial, France.
He is also commemorated on Woods Church Roll of Honour,
Ballyronan, Magherafelt.

Inscription on Thiepval Memorial

3645-Rifleman William James Greer
10th Battalion Royal Irish Rifles
Killed in Action: 1st July 1916
Thiepval Memorial, France. Panel: 15A-15B

William James Greer was born at Mawillian, Cookstown. He enlisted in Belfast, with the 10th Battalion Royal Irish Rifles. This Battalion was raised in Belfast from the Belfast Volunteers and did much of their training at Newcastle, Ballykinlar and Seaford. They landed at Boulogne in October 1915. Their training continued until just prior to the start of the Somme offensive. William James was killed on the first day of the battle as he tried to cross 'No Mans Land'. There is no known grave and William James is commemorated on panel 15A-15B on the Thiepval Memorial, France. He is also commemorated on Coagh Presbyterian Roll of Honour.

19308-Private George Hamilton
9th Battalion Royal Inniskilling Fusiliers
Killed In Action: 1st July 1916

Private George Hamilton was born at Lissan, County Tyrone and enlisted in the Inniskilling Regiment at Finner Camp, Ballyshannon / Bundoran, County Donegal.

He served with the 9th Royal Inniskilling Fusiliers and is thought to have been killed on the morning of 1st July 1916 when the battalion attacked the Schwaben Redoubt near Thiepval. Little is known of George Hamilton's background. He has no known grave and does not appear to be commemorated with the Commonwealth War Graves Commission. He is however commemorated in, "Soldiers, Died in the Great War" published by the Naval and Military Press, Sussex, England. He is also commemorated in, "Ireland's Memorial Record", soldiers who died, 1914-1918, and listed among the Inniskilling Roll of Honour in "The Royal Inniskillings in the Great War" by Sir Frank Fox.

George Hamilton was reported missing presumed killed in action 1st July 1916.

19977-Private William John Hamilton

9th Battalion Royal Inniskilling Fusiliers
Killed in Action: 1st July 1916
Age: 23
Thiepval Memorial, France. Panel: 4D-5B

William John Hamilton was the husband of Isabella Hamilton of Hillhead, Stewartstown, and was born at Lissan, Cookstown. He enlisted in Cookstown with the 9th Battalion Royal Inniskilling Fusiliers. They were raised at Omagh in September 1914 and were sent to France in October 1915. Their training continued up until the start of the Somme offensive. It was during the first day of the battle that William John lost his life as he tried to cross "No Man's Land". His body was never recovered and he is commemorated on panel 4D-5B on the Thiepval Memorial, France. He is also commemorated on Cookstown Cenotaph and is remembered at Church of Ireland, Lissan, on Remembrance Sunday.

13411-Private John Lavery

15th Battalion Durham Light Infantry
Killed in Action: 1st July 1916
Thiepval Memorial, France. Panel: 14A-15C

John Lavery was born in Pomeroy, County Tyrone. At the outbreak of the First World War he was living in Blaydon-on-Tyne and enlisted in Newcastle-on-Tyne with the 15th Battalion Durham Light Infantry. The Battalion was formed in Newcastle in September 1914 and trained at Halton Park and Witley. They landed at Boulogne on 11th September 1915. As a volunteer battalion, they were posted to further training with other experienced units on the Western Front, before their first action, during the Somme Offensive. John Lavery was killed in action on 1st July 1916. He has no known grave and is commemorated on panel 14A-15C on Thiepval Memorial, France.

16285-Private Sandy Little
9th Battalion Royal Inniskilling Fusiliers
Killed in Action: 1st July 1916
Age: 20
Connaught Cemetery, Thiepval. France 5. D.10

Sandy Little was born at Killyneedan, Sandholes, the son of Alexander and Clara Little. Before the war he worked as a farmer and was an active member of the Tullylagan Company of Ulster Volunteers with his close friend Isaac Black, where they practiced semaphore signalling. He travelled to Finner Camp to enlist with the 9th Battalion Royal Inniskilling Fusiliers ('C' company) and was sent to France in October of 1915.

He was killed in action on 1st July 1916 as he tried to cross 'No Mans Land' close to where the Ulster Tower now stands at Thiepval. At first a slight rise in the ground covered movement but as soon as the Battalion crested this rise they became a target for machine-gunners in the German front line. Most were simply cut down and only a few reached the Schwaben Redoubt, which they captured and held all day. It was a magnificent achievement by the Inniskilling Fusiliers and only shortage of ammunition forced their withdrawal. Sandy Little is buried close to where he fell near Thiepval Wood in row 5D- grave 10 at Connaught Cemetery, Thiepval, France. He is commemorated on Cookstown Cenotaph (as Alexander Lyttle) and on Sandholes Presbyterian Roll of Honour (as Alexander Little).

21164-Private Edward Mallon
1st Battalion Royal Inniskilling Fusiliers
Killed in Action: 1st July 1916
Age: 19
Thiepval Memorial, France. Panel: 4D-5B

Edward Mallon was the son of Mrs. Mary Ann Donnelly of Aughacolumb, Ardboe, Stewartstown. His father seems to have died as a young man and Mary Ann had married, Mr. Mick Donnelly. Edward enlisted in Londonderry with the 1st Battalion Royal Inniskilling Fusiliers. He was nineteen years of age when he was killed at the Somme and it is unlikely that he had served with the Battalion in Gallipoli. Edward Mallon has no known grave and is commemorated on panel 4D-5B on the Thiepval Memorial, France and on Stewartstown War Memorial.

19123-Rifleman John Mayne

13th Battalion Royal Irish Rifles
Killed in Action: 1st July 1916
Mill Road Cemetery, Thiepval, France. Grave: 12-A-2

John and his wife lived at Union Street, Cookstown. His mother, sisters and brothers were living in Church Street. John had a sister employed as a forewoman in Hopper Brothers dressmaking department in Cookstown. John Mayne served his time to the linen trade with Adairs Mills, Greenvale, Cookstown, after which he spent fourteen years at Stevensons of Moygashel, Dungannon. For several years prior to joining the army he was foreman finisher with Martin's in Rostrevor and from there he enlisted into the Royal Irish Rifles. He was home on leave in February of 1916.

The following piece was published in the Newry Telegraph and Mid-Ulster Mail when he returned:

Rostrevor people gave a most cordial welcome to Private John Mayne on his recent visit direct from the front trenches in France. He is a married man with wife and several children, and was happily and comfortably at the out break of war. He was not a reservist, but he heard the call and decided on doing his bit for the protection of the country, his wife and children, and at once joined the 13th Royal Irish Rifles, Ulster Division. Private Mayne is a splendid fellow and suggests the fellowship that exists among men at the front, who are determined to fight for their country, their women and children, and incidentally for the young slackers at home. A married man with a wife and seven children doing his duty! What about single young men? What is keeping you back from joining the army? Married folks say you are afraid – are you?

About this time John's wife and family returned to Cookstown from Rostrevor and his eldest daughter found work in Mr. Hugh McAdoo's drapery department.

John Mayne was killed in action on the first day of the Battle of the Somme and is buried in plot 12- row A- grave 2 at Mill Road Cemetery, Thiepval, France.

He is commemorated on Cookstown Cenotaph and First Presbyterian Roll of Honour, Cookstown.

6794-Lance Corporal James McAleece
11th Battalion Royal Irish Riles
Killed in Action: 1st July 1916
Thiepval Memorial, France. Panel: 15A-15B

James McAleece was born in Stewartstown, County Tyrone, and at the start of the War he was living at Ballyveney, Stewartstown. He enlisted at Clandeboye with the 11th Battalion Royal Irish Rifles. The Battalion was raised in County Antrim from the Antrim Volunteers and trained at Clandeboye and Seaford. They arrived at Boulogne in October 1915 and the Battalion underwent further training, being posted to other more experienced units on the Western Front. On the 1st July 1916 they were in the front line in readiness for the Somme Offensive.

By the end of that day, 133 men of the 11th Royal Irish Rifles had been killed in action, including Lance Corporal McAleece. He has no known grave and is commemorated on panel 15A-15B on the Thiepval Memorial, France.

James McAleece is commemorated on Stewartstown Cenotaph and on Donaghendry Church of Ireland Roll of Honour (as James McAleish), Stewartstown.

20773-Private Wilson McConnell
9th Battalion Royal Inniskilling Fusiliers
Killed in Action: 1st July 1916
Thiepval Memorial, France. Panel: 4D-5B

Wilson McConnell was a son of John and Elizabeth McConnell of Ballinamallard, County Fermanagh. He had lived for a time in Moneymore. Wilson and his wife, Sarah Loughlin McConnell, were living at Brown's Land, Gartgosh, Glasgow, when war broke out. He enlisted at Coatbridge with the 9th Battalion Royal Inniskilling Fusiliers, 36th Ulster Division, and arrived in France in October 1915. They were encamped at the small French villages of Mesnil and Martinsart, and much of the following months was spent training with more experienced units on the Western front. On the morning of the 1st July 1916, Wilson McConnell was killed in action as the troops set out to cross 'No Mans Land'. He was listed as missing and has no known grave. He is commemorated on panel 4D-5B on the Thiepval Memorial, France.

24271-Private Joseph McGall
10th Battalion Royal Inniskilling Fusiliers
Killed in Action: 1st July 1916
Age: 19
Thiepval Memorial, France. Panels: 4D – 5B

Joseph McGall was a son of Ignatius and Margaret McGall, of Ballydonnell, Ballinderry Bridge. He enlisted at Randalstown, and was serving in "C" Coy of the 10th Battalion Royal Inniskilling Fusiliers. He was killed in action as his battalion made their advance into No Man's Land on the morning of the 1st July 1916. The 10th Battalion attacked close to where the Ulster Tower now stands, and at first were shielded from the worst of the machine-gun fire by a rise in the ground, but as soon as they crested this rise they were subjected to heavy and accurate machine-gun fire. Joseph has no known grave. He is commemorated on panels 4D-5B on the Thiepval Memorial, France. He was a member of Salterstown L.O.L. 482 and is also commemorated on Ballinderry Church of Ireland Roll of Honour.

17806-Private William McGookin
9th Battalion Royal Inniskilling Fusiliers
Killed in Action: 1st July 1916
Aged: 19
Thiepval Memorial, France, panel 4D – 5B

William McGookin was the second son of William and Rachel McGookin and the brother of John and Margretta of Donaghrisk, Tullyhogue, Cookstown, and later of Blackhill, Cookstown.

William was a member of Tullyhogue Company of Ulster Volunteers and a member of Derryraghan L.O.L. 131. He was posted as Missing in Action on the 1st July, 1916. Two members of his Company wrote to his home to say that they had seen William being hit by a bullet and he had died instantly. He seemed to suffer no pain and according to them he was a gallant soldier and a good comrade. The last words they heard him say as he went over the parapet were, *"Come on lads don't be afraid, if God is on our side, who can be against us?"*

William has no known grave and is commemorated on panel 4D-5B on Thiepval Memorial to the Missing on the Somme, France. He is also commemorated on Cookstown Cenotaph.

19304-Private Alexander McLernon
9th Battalion Royal Inniskilling Fusiliers
Killed in Action: 1st July 1916
Thiepval Memorial, France. Panel: 4D-5B

Alexander McLernon was born in the parish of Derryloran, Cookstown, the husband of Sarah Jane McLernon (nee Nelson).

He was employed at Gunning's Factory, Milburn, Cookstown, before he enlisted with the 9th Battalion Royal Inniskilling Fusiliers. He was training at Shane's Park camp Randalstown, when his brother in law and close friend Private James Nelson took ill and died some time later from septic poisoning. Alexander received permission to leave the camp to act as pall bearer at Private Nelson's funeral on Friday 26th March 1915 at Ballygoney Presbyterian Church, Coagh.

On 1st July 1916, when the 9th Inniskillings made their advance toward the Schwaben Redoubt, Alexander McLernon was seen to have been severely wounded. This was reported later in a letter by Private Thomas Taylor of Waterloo Terrace, Cookstown. At the end of July, Mrs. Sarah Jane McLernon received a letter from Colonel Ambrose Ricardo, stating that all efforts to find her husband had failed and he hoped that he may still be alive and a prisoner of war.

Alexander McLernon has no known grave and is commemorated on panel 4D-5B on the Thiepval Memorial to the Missing on the Somme. He is also commemorated on Cookstown Cenotaph, Gunning's Factory Memorial (Royal British Legion Cookstown) and on St. Luran's Church of Ireland, Roll of Honour Derryloran, Cookstown.

13322- Lance Sergeant Robert J. Millar

9th Battalion Royal Inniskilling Fusiliers
Killed in Action: 1st July 16
Age: 35
Thiepval Memorial. France.   Panel: 4D-5B

Robert Millar was a son of Joseph and Mary Millar of Millburn Street, Cookstown. He was married to Elizabeth Jane Millar of Eagerlougher, Loughgall, County Armagh. He enlisted at Kingstown with the 9th Battalion Royal Inniskilling Fusiliers and was sent to France in October of 1915 in time for the build up to the Somme Offensive.   He was killed in action on the 1st July 1916 in 'No Mans Land'. He has no known grave. Robert is commemorated on panel 4D-5B on Thiepval Memorial, France.

He is commemorated on Cookstown Cenotaph and St. Luran's Church of Ireland Roll of Honour, Derryloran, Cookstown and the war list of Cookstown Masonic Lodge 396.

11676-Corporal John Ramsay
1st Royal Inniskilling Fusiliers
Killed in Action: 1st July 1916
Age: 23
Thiepval Memorial, France. Panel: 4D - 5B

John Ramsay was son of John and Annie Ramsay, of 22 Wilmont Terrace, Lisburn Road Belfast, and the nephew of Mr. George Ramsay (National School Teacher), Mountain View, Cookstown, County Tyrone. George Ramsay was at this time the President of the National School Teachers' Association.

John Ramsay was born at Shankhill, Belfast and enlisted in the army there in August 1914. After their return from service in India the 1st Battalion Royal Inniskilling Fusiliers were attached to 87th Brigade, 29th Division, and landed at Gallipoli in April 1915, where John Ramsay was wounded in action. After Gallipoli, the 29th Division was moved to France. As part of 87th Brigade, 29th Division, the 1st Battalion Royal Inniskillings were given the task of capturing German-held positions between the village of Beaumont Hamel and the Ancre River as part of the 'Big Push' on July 1st 1916. The frontage of the advance was 2,000 yards on the morning of July 1st and 10 minutes before the advance, a mine containing 40,000 pounds of Ammonal was exploded at Hawthorn Redoubt, in front of the enemy positions. It was hoped that the brigades in advance in this sector would consolidate at the crater, but the Germans took advantage of the 10 minute delay between the explosion and the infantry advance, and the oncoming troops were cut down by rifle and machine gun fire. At roll call, the casualties of the 1st Battalion were high, 4 officers killed (including Lieutenant Colonel Robert Campbell Pierce). Total casualties amounted to 549, over half the strength of the battalion. The published figure in the aftermath of the war is 228 other ranks of 1st Battalion Inniskillings killed on 1st July 1916.

John Ramsay was reported missing on 1st July 1916, later listed as killed in action. He has no known grave and is commemorated on panels 4D - 5B on the Thiepval Memorial, France.

16318-Private James Smyth
9th Battalion Royal Inniskilling Fusiliers
Killed in Action: 1st July 1916

James Smyth was born in the parish of Derryloran, Cookstown, He was working at Clydebank, Scotland, at the out break of war but returned home to enlist at Finner Camp, Ballyshannon, County Donegal, joining the 9th Battalion Royal Inniskilling Fusiliers.

On the morning of 1st July 1916, the 9th Inniskillings attacked close to where the Ulster Tower now stands and were successful in capturing the Schwaben Redoubt, and holding it until being forced to withdraw through lack of ammunition and support on there left and right flanks. In a letter by Private Thomas Taylor of Waterloo Terrace, Cookstown, he reported that James Smyth was listed as missing after 1st July and no confirmation had been received at that time as to his whereabouts.

James was listed as killed in action on 1st July. He has no known grave and does not appear to be commemorated with the Commonwealth War Graves Commission.

His is commemorated on Cookstown Cenotaph and on St. Luran's Church of Ireland Roll of Honour, Derryloran, Cookstown.

St. Luran's, Derryloran Church of Ireland Roll of Honour

27688-Private Hugh Taylor
9th Battalion Royal Inniskilling Fusiliers
Killed in Action: 1st July 1916
Mill Road Cemetery, Thiepval, France.   Grave: 1-C-20

Hugh Taylor was born in Cookstown. He was the son of James
and Elizabeth Taylor, and brother of Hetty, Emma, Mabel,
Margaret, Thomas, Samuel, Oliver and William. Hugh Taylor
worked at Gunning's Factory, Milburn before enlisting with the
9th Battalion Royal Inniskilling Fusiliers in Cooktown.

Miss Annie Taylor, Milburn Street, Cookstown, received the
following letter from Major Peacock of the 9th Inniskillings:

*"I regret to inform you that your brother, Private Hugh Taylor, of
my Battalion is missing since the 1st July. He took part in the
gallant attack made by the Ulster Division on that date. Every
enquiry has been made regarding his fate, but without result. I
cannot ask you to entertain any forlorn hopes of his turning up
alive as I am afraid he fell on that occasion. He was a good
soldier and a loyal comrade. Please accept my sincere sympathy
from all the ranks in the Battalion in your great loss."*

Hugh Taylor was killed in action on Saturday 1st July 1916, and
is one of the few Cookstown men killed on that day to have a
known grave. He is buried in plot 1, row C, grave 20 at Mill
Road Cemetery, Thiepval, France.

He is commemorated on Cookstown Cenotaph, Gunning's Factory
Memorial (Royal British Legion Cookstown) and St. Luran's
Church of Ireland Roll of Honour, Derryloran, Cookstown.

16320-Corporal William Nathaniel Thom
9th Battalion Royal Inniskilling Fuiliers
Killed in Action: 1st July 1916
Age: 27
Thiepval Memorial, France. Panel: 4D-5B

William Nathaniel Thom was the youngest son of William and Margaret Thom, of The Poplars, Cookstown. He was known among his friends as "Nat Thom". William had been a National School Teacher in Cookstown before serving his time to the linen trade at Gunning's Factory, Milburn. Shortly after being promoted as under-manager, the war broke out and he promptly responded to the call of King and Country, joining the Royal Inniskilling Fusiliers. He soon gained the rank of Lance Corporal, and preferring to remain among his pals, he declined a commission in another regiment.

On the 1st July 1916, the 9th Battalion attacked up a slight rise which at first shielded them from the worst of the machine-gun fire but as they crested that rise they became a target for heavy German machine-gun fire which decimated their numbers, causing a huge loss of life. Private Thomas Taylor from Waterloo Terrace, Cookstown, wrote home to say that he was with 'Nat' Thom as they approached the enemy lines, and that Corporal Thom was struck in the head by a bullet.

William Nathanial Thom has no known grave and is commemorated on panel 4D-5B on Thiepval Memorial to the Missing of the Somme. He is also commemorated on Cookstown Cenotaph, Gunning's (Milburn) Factory Memorial (Royal British Legion Cookstown) and St. Luran's Church of Ireland Roll of Honour, Derryloran, Cookstown and is commemorated on the war list of Cookstown Masonic Lodge 396.

After his death his mother received letters of sympathy from Lieutenant E.W. Crawford, 9th Royal Inniskilling Fusiliers and from Mr. W Leeper, JP, on behalf of Gunning's Factory.

13585 Corporal Jacob Wilkinson
9th Battalion Royal Inniskilling Fusiliers
Killed in Action: 1st July 1916
Age: 31
Thiepval Memorial, France.   Panel 4D - 5B

Jacob Wilkinson was born on 25th May 1885, and was the eighth child of Henry and Isabella Wilkinson (nee Black), 1 Blackhill, Cookstown. The family had moved from Killycurragh, to the Blackhill, where Jacob worked at Adair's Mill, Greenvale, Cookstown with his father. Jacob was a close friend to John McCaffrey (killed in action on 16th November 1914) who he lived next door to, and played football for the local Greenvale Swifts and often referred to John in his correspondence.

Jacob's older brother, King William Wilkinson had served overseas in India and China, in 1904-1906. Jacob enlisted with the 9th Royal Inniskilling Fusiliers at Finner Camp, Ballyshannon, County Donegal, and trained at Randalstown before moving out with the 36th (Ulster) Division to Seaford, England and then to France. He was promoted to the rank of Corporal shortly before the Somme Offensive.

Henry Wilkinson received a postcard from Jacob on 16th July 1916, stating that he was quite well. It appears that the postcard was not sent on until after that fateful morning, 1st July 1916 when Jacob was killed in action on the first day of the Somme offensive, he has no known grave and is commemorated on panels 4D-5B on Thiepval Memorial, France. He is also commemorated on Cookstown Cenotaph and Molesworth Presbyterian Roll of Honour.

Greenvale Mill (Adairs) Cookstown, where Jacob Wilkinson, Michael Lawn, James
King and John McCaffrey worked before the outbreak of war.

Photo by kind permission of David Lennox

4679-Rifleman Robert James Wright

14th Battalion Royal Irish Rifles
Died of Wounds: 1st July 1916
Aged: 20
Thiepval Memorial, France. Panel: 15A – 15B

Robert James was a son of Thomas and Sarah Wright of
Ballylifford, Moneymore, County Londonderry. He joined the
14th Battalion Royal Irish Rifles, (Y.C.V.) Young Citizen
Volunteers. It is recorded that Robert died of wounds received on
1st July 1916. He has no known grave and is commemorated on
panel 15A-15B on the Thiepval Memorial, France and at
Ballinderry Church of Ireland Roll of Honour. He was also a
member of Salterstown L.O.L. 482

23/548-Private Andrew Wylie

23rd Battalion Northumberland Fusiliers (Tyneside Scottish)
Killed in Action: 1st July 1916
Aged: 40
Thiepval Memorial. Panel: 10b-11b-12b. France

Andrew was a son of George and Margaret Wylie of Mobuy,
Lissan, Cookstown. Andrew was born at Ryton, Northumberland
and enlisted at Newcastle-on-Tyne. He was killed in action on 1st
July 1916 and has no known grave. He is commemorated on
panels: 10B-11B-12B on the Thiepval Memorial, France. His wife
later remarried as, Mrs. Eliza Jane Thompson and lived at 2 Store
Street, Lemington-on-Tyne.

1157-Rifleman Robert Fulton

16th Battalion Royal Irish Rifles
(Formerly of 9th Battalion Royal Inniskilling Fusiliers)
Killed in Action: 2nd July 1916
Age: 21
Thiepval Memorial, France. Panel: 15A-15B

Robert Fulton was born in Newmills. He was the eldest son of
Robert and Mary A. Fulton of Tullaghmore, Sherrygroom,
Cookstown. He was a member of Newmills Company, Ulster
Volunteers, before he enlisted with the Royal Inniskilling
Fusiliers in Dungannon at the outbreak of the First World War
and subsequently transferred to the 16th Battalion Royal Irish
Rifles. Robert survived the first day on the Somme but was killed
in action on 2nd July 1916. He has no known grave and is
commemorated on panels, 15A-15B on the Thiepval Memorial.
He is also commemorated in Newmills Presbyterian Church and
Dungannon War Memorial. On Sunday 16th July 1916 at a
special service at Newmills Presbyterian, Reverend Dr. Logan
spoke of Private Robert Fulton and paid tribute to him. A vote of
sympathy was passed by Mr. Elliot and Mr. McCrum (Robert's
Sunday School Teacher) to his family.

17774-Private Robert Thompson

108th Company Machine Gun Corps
Died of Wounds: 2nd July 1916
Age: 21
Warloy Baillon Communal Cemetery Extension, France.
Grave: 1, A, 2,

Robert Thompson was born in Cookstown, County Tyrone and
was the son of Thomas and Matilda Thompson of Dundonald,
Belfast. He enlisted with the Machine Gun Corps in
Downpatrick.

He was seriously wounded on the first day of the Somme
offensive and was taken to a field ambulance at Warloy Baillon.
His injuries were critical and he died the following day. Robert
was interred in Plot 1, Row A, Grave 2 at Warloy Baillon
Communal Cemetery Extension, France.

10534-Private William McAleece
2nd Battalion Royal Inniskilling Fusiliers
Killed in Action: 10th July 1916
Thiepval Memorial, France. Panel: 4D-5B

William McAleece was born at Ballyclog and was the eldest son of Mrs. McAleece of Ballynuey, Stewartstown, County Tyrone. He enlisted in the army in Cookstown.

On 22nd August 1914 the 2nd Battalion Inniskillings landed at Le Havre and went on to take part in engagements at Le Cateau, The Marne, The Aisne, Meteren, Armentieres, Douve Farm and Ploegsteert Wood in 1914. In January 1915 the Battalion was posted to the 5th Infantry Brigade, 2nd Division was saw action at Festubert and Richebourg. By December 1915 the Battalion was posted to the 96th Brigade, 32nd Division and took part in the Somme offensive in July 1916. At 9pm on 9th July 1916 the Battalion moved out into the shell torn No Man's Land north-west of Ovillers with the objective to take a series of enemy trenches. These were quickly captured overnight and the enemy launched a counter attack which was beaten back by the Lewis-gunners. Early on 10th July 1916 the Battalion spent their time strengthening their captured position and that night were ordered to exploit their gains by pushing forward to take a further German position. Before they could achieve this they were engaged in some heavy hand to hand fighting with the enemy in which William McAleece was killed.

He has no known grave and is commemorated on panels 4D-5B on the Thiepval Memorial, France.

William McAleece is commemorated on Stewartstown Cenotaph and on Donaghendry Church of Ireland Roll of Honour (as William McAleish), Stewartstown.

24085-Private Andrew McCord

2nd Battalion Royal Inniskilling Fusiliers
Killed in Action: 10th July 1916
Thiepval Memorial, France.   Panel: 4D-5B

Andrew was born at Ballynulty, County Tyrone, and enlisted in Cookstown.

He was killed in action in the same engagement as William McAleece. Andrew McCord has no known grave and is commemorated on panel 4D-5B on the Thiepval Memorial, France. He is also commemorated on Cookstown Cenotaph.

22764-Private John Timoney

2nd Battalion Royal Inniskilling Fusiliers
Killed in Action: 11th July 1916
Thiepval Memorial, France. Panel: 4D-5B

John Timoney was a son of Edward and Brigid Timoney of Loy Street, Cookstown.

He enlisted with the Royal Inniskilling Fusiliers in Londonderry.

On the 9th July 1916, the 2nd Battalion Inniskillings were temporarily attached to the 14th Infantry Brigade and marched to Ovillers-la-Boiselle. Their objective was to take a series of enemy trenches nearby, which they captured. The Inniskillings spent the next day strengthening their positions. On the night of the 10th July they were ordered to further exploit these positions by pushing the Germans out of a forward trench. Hand to hand fighting ensued, with many casualties before accomplishing this task. Over the next two days, the 2nd Inniskilling had captured and consolidated their objective, but with the loss of 55 other ranks dying of wounds or killed in action between 9th and 15th July. John Timoney was killed in action on 11th July 1916 and has no known grave. He is commemorated on panels 4D-5B on Thiepval Memorial to the Missing of the Somme, France.

Edward Joseph Timoney was another son of Edward and Brigid Timoney of Loy Street, Cookstown and a brother of John. Edward was married and lived with his wife, Catherine, at 45 Churchtown Cottages, Dundrum, County Dublin. After serving throughout the First World War, Edward returned to India with the 36th Division Signals Company and died on 17th September 1920. Edward is commemorated on Face: 1 of the Delhi Memorial in India.

11380-Private Edward McNamee

9th Battalion Cameronians (Scottish Rifles)
Killed in Action: 18th July 1916
Thiepval Memorial, France.   Panel: 4D

Edward McNamee was born in Cookstown. He was living and working in Scotland when he enlisted with the 9th Battalion Cameronians in Hamilton. They were formed at Hamilton in August 1914 and landed at Boulogne, France on 12th May 1915.

On 18th July 1916, the 9th Battalion Cameronians lost eighteen men, including Edward McNamee, during the fighting for High Wood on the Somme. Edward has no known grave and is commemorated on the Thiepval Memorial, 4D.

7692-Lance Corporal James McGuckin

1st Battalion Cameronians (Scottish Rifles)
Killed in Action: 20th July 1916
Caterpillar Valley Cemetery, France. Grave: 7-D-37

James McGuckin was born in Stewartstown, County Tyrone. At the outbreak of the First World War was living in Glasgow. He enlisted in Hamilton with the Cameronians. They were formed at Hamilton and landed at Le Havre on 15th August 1914. James had gained promotion to Lance Corporal and it is thought he joined the 1st Battalion early in 1916. By the 20th July the Cameronians were engaged in very heavy fighting in a desperate attempt to take High Wood and Delville Wood. 107 men of the Battalion were killed, including James McGuckin.

He is buried in plot 7, row D, grave 37 at Caterpillar Valley Cemetery, France.

S/13837-Private Archibald McAllister
1st Battalion Gordon Highlanders
Died of Wounds: 21st July 16
Age: 25
St. Sever Cemetery, France. Grave: A-15-53

Archie McAllister was the eldest son of John McAllister of
Killymoon Street, Cookstown. He was member of Cookstown
True Blues L.O.L.

Prior to enlisting in the army he had been working in Noble's
Explosive Works in Stevenston in Ayrshire. He came home at
the end of 1915 and enlisted in Cookstown with the 1st
Battalion Gordon Highlanders. He was seriously wounded
during the Somme offensive and he endured a difficult journey
to hospital in Rouen. By the time he reached hospital in the
early hours of the morning, he was unconscious and the doctors
could not save him. He had suffered serious gunshot wounds to
the head. The Reverend Dr. Richards, a Chaplain at the
hospital was called and remained with him until his death, he
did not regain consciousness. Dr. Richards wrote a letter of
sympathy to the family at Cookstown.

Archie McAllister is interred in grave A-15-53 at St. Sever
Cemetery at Rouen, France. He is commemorated on
Cookstown Cenotaph and St. Luran's Church of Ireland Roll of
Honour, Derryloran, Cookstown.

*Cookstown Orange Hall, used extensively for recruiting
during the First World War.*

Photo courtesy of Tom Jebb

S/13144-Private Silas Lennox
2nd Battalion Black Watch (Royal Highlanders)
Died of Illness: 22nd July 1916
Age: 21
Basra War Cemetery, Iraq. Grave: 6 – E - 7

Silas Lennox was a son of Eccles and Martha Lennox, of Coagh Street, Cookstown, and later of 61 Cowlairs Road, Springburn, Glasgow. He was born at Bellaghy but lived with his parents in Cookstown, where he worked for awhile as a messenger boy with a relative, Mr. A. Lennox who owned the "The Arcade".

When he moved to Glasgow he was employed in one of the shops of the Maypole Dairy Company, where he received promotion and his job seemed secure before he enlisted with the Argyll and Sutherland Highlanders and later transferred to the Black Watch (Royal Highlanders)

While on active service in Mesopotamia, Silas Lennox contracted a fever and died a few days later, on 22nd July 1916. He is interred in plot 6, row E, grave 7 at Basra War Cemetery, Iraq.

At the time of his death, Silas had two brothers on active service in the army.

Hugh Lennox was serving with Argyll and Sutherland Highlanders and died of wounds on 9th October 1916.

Now the earthly fight is over,
And in perfect peace he sleeps,
Till he meets again with his loved ones
Angels, carefully him keeps.
Short was your life, my darling son,
But peaceful is your rest
Your mother misses you most of all,
't was she who loved you best.
The news was sad, the blow was hard,
God's will is shall be done!
With a manly heart, he did his part
My dear beloved son

The above piece submitted to Mid Ulster Mail by Mrs. Martha Lennox in 1916.

12396 - Private James P. Cassidy
1st Battalion Royal Inniskiling Fusiliers
Died : 23rd July 1916
Engelbelmer Communal Cemetery Extension, Somme, France.
Grave D5

James Cassidy was the husband of Annie Cassidy, Coagh Street, Cookstown. He was an army veteran, having had 12 years experience, originally joining the army as a drummer boy and went on to see action during the Boer War.

After leaving the army he lived and worked in Cookstown as surface man on the roads between Orritor and Cookstown. At the outbreak of the First World War, he volunteered and was called to the front, being posted to Gallipoli. He was wounded twice in action, in June and again in August 1915, when he was returned to Redlands War Hospital, Reading, Berkshire, with a severe wound to his left arm that almost invalided him out of the war. He was later posted back to his battalion in France. He died on 23rd July 1916. At the time of his death, his mother was employed at the Police Barracks in Toome, County Antrim where the family originally came from.

James is buried at Engelbelmer Communal Cemetery Extension, Somme France., in grave D5. The cemetery was used extensively during this period to bury those from Field Ambulance Hospitals.

His wife Annie received the following letter (undated, but postmarked "Field Post Office – 26th July 1916") from the Reverend Francis Charles Devas, S.J. Chaplain of Forces:-

Dear Mrs Cassidy, You will by this time have heard from the War Office of the death of your husband. I can say nothing to console you except that he died a most holy death. He received the last sacraments and the last blessing. He was quite resigned to God's Holy will and I feel sure that his purgatory must have been a short one and that he is now in heaven. He asked me to send you his prayer book and Rosary beads, which I have done. Your registered letter arrived shortly before he died and he asked me to write you and his mother. God Bless and strengthen you in your sorrow. In these sad days if we do not put our trust in God there is no happiness for us anywhere.

Ever Yours,

Sincerely, F.C. Devas, S.J. CF

Father Francis Charles Devas was born in 1877 and educated at Beaumont College, Old Windsor. He entered the Society of Jesus in 1895 and taught in the Jesuit Colleges of Beaumont, Wimbledon and Stamford Hill. He received his commission to the Army on 14th November 1914 and was chaplain attached to 1st Royal Inniskilling Fusiliers throughout the Gallipoli Campaign, and again on the Western Front in France and Flanders. He received an OBE in 1916 and a DSO in 1917.

2503-Private Hubert David William Thompson

8th Battalion Australian Infantry, A.I.F
Killed in Action: 25th July 1916
Age: 26
Gordon Dump Cemetery, Ovillers La Boiselle, France.   Grave 1
B 42

Private Hubert Thompson was the second son of Joseph Thompson and Mrs. Sarah Thompson of Hazelmount, Krowera, Victoria, Australia, and formerly of Windmill Farm, Coagh, County Tyrone. He was a nephew of Dr. George Thompson and cousin to the Duff family in Coagh.

Hubert was one of three brothers who served during the Gallipoli Campaign with the Australian Imperial Forces, where he contracted dysentry and was hospitalised.

He arrived in Marseilles, France from Alexandria, Egypt with the A.I.F. on 26th March 1916. The 8th Battalion Australian Infantry took part in the action during the Somme Offensive. Hubert was a stretcher bearer serving with the 8th Australian Battalion when he was killed in action on 25th July 1916. He is buried in Plot 1, Row B, Grave 42 at Gordon Dump Cemetery, Ovillers La Boiselle, France.

23851-Private Charles Mulholland

5th Battalion Oxfordshire and Buckinghamshire Light Infantry
Died of Illness: 28th July 1916
Kildress Old Church of Ireland Churchyard, Cookstown

Private Charles Mulholland of the Oxford and Buckinghamshire Light Infantry was the fifth son of Robert Mulholland of Mackney, Cookstown. He had served his time in the grocery and provisions business with Mr. Joseph Stewart in Cookstown. When his apprenticeship was almost complete he decided to enlist in the Army, joining the Royal Irish Fusiliers. After a spell on home service, he went out to India with his Battalion. When war was declared in 1914 he was sent to France arriving in December. He was attached to the Cyclist Corps for a considerable time. He appeared in good health until the 1st July 1916 when he contracted pericarditis. He was promptly sent to England where he was carefully nursed and it was hoped his life would be prolonged. While in hospital in Manchester his brothers went over to see him twice, and on the last occasion he told them he expected to be home in a couple of weeks. His condition worsened on 28th July and he died at the 2nd Western General Hospital, Manchester. His remains were returned home to the family burying ground at Kildress on Wednesday 2nd August 1916. The chief mourners at his funeral were his father, Robert, his brothers Richard, Albert, Thomas and George. In addition to these brothers at home his brother William James lived in South Africa, his brothers Robert and John in Canada and Joseph and Samuel in the United States. Much sympathy was felt in the surrounding area and a wreath was placed on his grave from the Officers and members of Orritor L.O.L. 686.

Kildress Church of Ireland Old Churchyard is about one and a half kilometres east of the present church. It contains the ruins of the former church burnt in 1641, restored in 1698 and used until 1818.

Charles Mulholland is commemorated on Cookstown Cenotaph.

Second-Lieutenant Albert Victor Morrison
2nd Battalion Royal Scots Fusiliers
Killed in Action: 30th July 1916
Age: 21
Thiepval Memorial, France Panel: 3-C

Albert Victor Morrison was the eldest son of Alexander and Margaret Elizabeth Morrison of Innisfallen, Cookstown and later of 38 Hopefield Avenue, Antrim Road, Belfast. Before the war Victor was a medical student at Queen's University and a member of the University O.T.C., and was a prominent football player.

He volunteered for service with the Royal Scots Fusiliers, passed his exams and became a Second Lieutenant.

He was wounded in the arm on 11th June 1916 but recovered and was sent back to his unit at the front. He was reported missing on 1st August 1916 along with his fellow officer, Lieutenant Small from Markethill, County Armagh, who was the nephew of the Reverend J. Entrican, B.A., Cookstown.

Lieutenant Morrison's parents received the following telegram in Cookstown:

Lieutenant-Colonel Walsh to Alexander Morrison at Innisfallen, Cookstown, on 13th August 1916

"I very much regret that I am unable to give you any definite news regarding your son, Lieut. A. Victor Morrison. The fighting that day was such that the very greatest uncertainty is bound to exist concerning many. Both Officers and men, who either fell or became detached from their comrades. I have made enquiries, but am unable to discover any trace of what befell your son that day. Nothing to amplify, in any way my original report. That I made on 31st July as to his being "Missing". There is, of course, the chance that he is in German hands, either as a wounded or unwounded prisoner, and I sincerely trust that such may be the case"

Victor's body was never found and today he is commemorated on the Thiepval Memorial, France on panel 3-C. He is also commemorated on Cookstown Cenotaph, on St. Luran's Church of Ireland Roll of Honour, Derryloran, Cookstown and on Queen's University Belfast War Memorial.

24762-Private James McCaughey

8th Battalion Royal Inniskiling Fusiliers
Killed in action: 2nd August 1916
Bois-Carre Military Cemetery, Haisnes, France.   Special
Memorial: 27

James McCaughey was born in Clogher, County Tyrone, but lived and worked with his brother in Cookstown. He enlisted in the army on 12th July 1915 and was posted to the 8th Battalion Royal Inniskilling Fusiliers.

He was killed in action on 2nd August 1916 and news of his death was reported to the family in a letter by a fellow soldier who was serving with James, before official confirmation. He is commemorated on Special Memorial 27 at Bois-Carre Military Cemetery, Haisnes in France. His name does not appear on Cookstown Cenotaph. The name J. McGahey appears on the Cenotaph and this is possibly who the inscription refers to.

4795-Private Frederick William Ekin

Royal Fusiliers (Old Public Schools Battalion)
Died of Wounds: 18th August 1916
Age: 23
Belfast City Cemetery, Belfast, Northern Ireland   L.1-548.

Frederick William Ekin was the eldest son of Mr. John Ekin of Ashley Park, Belfast and the Grandson of Mr. William Ekin of Ballynuey, Coagh.

Prior to active service he worked with his father at Messrs. Ekin & Prenten of Waring Street, Belfast. On enlistment he served with the Royal Fusiliers (Old Public Schools Battalion) and was seriously wounded, having received a gunshot to his arm at the Battle of the Somme on 20th July 1916, which was his 23rd birthday.

He was brought back to Edinburgh War Hospital, Bangor, Scotland where he died as a result of septicaemia on 18th August 1916. His remains were brought back to Belfast on Tuesday 22nd August 1916, where he was buried with full military honours at Belfast City Cemetery. L.1-548.

Lieutenant James Greer McKay

Australian Machine Gun Corps
Killed in Action: 19th August 1916
Serre Road Cemetery No: 2, France. Grave: 20-B-16

James Greer McKay was the fourth born son of Mr and Mrs. W.C. McKay of Consort Terrace, Leeds and later of 8 St. John's Terrace, Belle-vue Road, Leeds. His Uncle was Mr. Foster McKay, Petty Sessions Clerk, Aughnacloy.

James Greer McKay was born in Cookstown, County Tyrone and his father and grandfather, Mr Samuel Smart, were in business in the town for many years. The family were prominently connected with First Presbyterian Church, Cookstown. The family left Cookstown for Leeds, where James was educated at Belle-vue Road School, and Leeds Central High school. He was also actively associated with Cavendish Road Presbyterian Church, and was a member of the choir. He served with the territorial regiment, Yorkshire Hussars before he emigrated to Australia in 1909. At the outbreak of the First World War he enlisted at Broadmeadows as a private on 27th August 1914. His attestation papers show that he was 6 feet tall. He left Australia on HMAT Wiltshire (A.18) on 19th October 1914 and landed at Gallipoli where he received his Commission for services in the field. After leaving Gallipoli he was sent to France, where he was attached to the 1st Battalion Australian Machine Gun Corps. He was promoted to Lieutenant on 2nd July 1916 and was killed in action on 19th August close to Mouquet Farm, know as 'Mucky Farm' to allied troops. The gun crew under Lieutenant J.G. McKay were about to move off when they were all killed or wounded. He is buried in plot 20, row B, grave 16 at Serre Road Cemetery No: 2, France. It is one of the largest cemeteries on the Somme.

3731-Private Thomas Darragh
6th Battalion Connaught Rangers
Killed in Action: 3rd September 1916
Thiepval Memorial, France.   *Panel: 15A*

Thomas was the husband of Sarah Jane Darragh of Chapel Street, Cookstown. Prior to joining the army he worked in Cookstown as a builder's labourer and was well known in local football circles having played for both Cookstown and Derryloran Football Clubs. He joined the army soon after the outbreak of hostilities and had been in action for many months and was wounded in May 1916. The 6th Battalion Connaught Rangers was formed in County Cork in September 1914 and included a company of men from West Belfast Nationalist Volunteers and were attached to 47th Brigade (Redmonds Volunteers) of the 16th Irish Division. The 6th Battalion made their advance on the village of Guillemont on 3rd September 1916, and suffered heavily, losing fifty-one men, including Private Thomas Darragh and Lieutenant Colonel J.S.M. Lenox-Conyngham. Later that day the village fell to the British after repeated attempts over the previous two months. During one week's fighting the Battalion would lose 23 officers and 407 other ranks. Thomas Darragh has no known grave and is commemorated on panel 15A on Thiepval Memorial to the Missing of the Somme. He is also commemorated on Cookstown Cenotaph.

The following piece appeared in the Mid Ulster Mail, following new of his death.

Farewell dear wife, I now must go
And leave you in this world of woe
Weep not for me or sorrow take
But love my children for my sake

He sleeps far away in a foreign land
In a hollow grave unknown
But his name is written in letters of gold
On the hearts he left at home

May the Heavenly wind blow softly
O'er that sweet and hallowed spot
Though the sea divides his grave from me
He will never be forgot.

May the Lord have mercy on his soul,
Sadly missed by his sorrowing wife and three little sons.

Thomas Darragh's son William was killed during World War 2, while serving on board HMS Grenville on 19th January 1940.

Lieutenant Colonel-
John Staples Molesworth Lenox-Conyngham
6th Battalion Connaught Rangers
Killed in Action: 3rd September 1916
Age: 54
Carnoy Cemetery, France.Grave: R-33

John Staples Molesworth Lenox-Conyngham was the third son of Sir William F. Lenox-Conyngham K.C.B. of Springhill House, Moneymore. John S.M. Lenox-Conyngham joined the army in January 1881 and got his promotion soon after. He served with the 1st and 2nd Battalions of the Connaught Rangers, and was promoted again to the rank of Captain in 1889. He was married to Miss Violet Donaldson, second daughter of Henry Beveridge Donaldson of Melbourne, in 1891. He attained a field rank in July 1900, and was appointed second in command of the 2nd Battalion Connaught Rangers in February 1906. He retired from the Army on half pay in January 1912. At the out break of the First World War he promptly returned to his old regiment and was immediately gazetted as Commanding Officer of the 6th Battalion Connaught Rangers, a new volunteer Battalion, which was formed at Kilworth, County Cork in September 1914, and assigned to 47th Brigade, 16th Irish Division. On two occasions while the Battalion were in training at Fermoy, County Cork and again at Blackdown, Hampshire, he personally received Mr. Joseph Devlin, M.P. At the outbreak of the First World War, Joe Devlin had actively supported and encouraged men of the National Volunteers to enlist for service. Many of these men were working class Nationalists from West Belfast who went on to join the 6th Connaught Rangers. The Battalion was posted to France in December 1915. He was killed in action on 3rd September 1916 as he led his men in North Street, Guillemont, during the Battle of Guillemont. He was seen carrying his walking stick in one hand and his revolver in the other. He is buried in row R- grave 33 at Carnoy Military Cemetery, France. The temporary wooden cross erected over his grave by men of the 6th Connaught Rangers was later brought home and erected as a memorial to him in Armagh Church of Ireland Cathedral. The cross has recently been restored and is in temporary possession of the Royal Irish Fusiliers Museum, Armagh. Lieutenant Colonel Lenox-Conyngham is commemorated on Coagh War Memorial (RBL Cookstown), Moneymore War Memorial (Assembly Rooms) and St. Mary's Church of Ireland Memorial Cross, Anglesea Road, Dublin

He was remembered as a deeply caring Officer, the welfare of his men being of great concern to him. Fellow officers remembered him dispersing them all to the cook house to ensure the men were served first. His death cut across the political divide in Ireland. Stephen Gwynne, a Captain in the 6th Connaughts, and a Nationalist M.P. at the time stated:

No Commanding Officer was more beloved by those he commanded and I have known no better Irishman than this son of an Ulster House, whose kindred was deep in the Ulster Covenant.

In just over one week's fighting on the Somme, the 6th Connaught Rangers had lost 23 Officers and 407 other ranks. The battalion would go on to fight throughout the rest of the war, and was almost annihilated during the German breakthrough at St. Emilie, in March 1918.

His brother Lieutenant Colonel W.A. Lenox-Conyngham (a veteran of the Boer War) served throughout the First World War with the Worcestershire Regiment and the Carnarvon and Anglesey Territorial Battalion of Welsh Fusiliers. Another brother, Colonel G.P. Lenox-Conyngham served throughout the war with the Royal Engineers.

His brother Lieutenant Colonel Herbert Lenox-Conyngham served with the Army Veterinary Corps. His nephew, Lieutenant Commander J. Lenox-Conyngham Clark served with the Royal Navy and received a D.S.O. in recognition for his services with a destroyer flotilla in operations at the Dardenelles, during the Gallipoli Campaign.

21646-Private Samuel Moore (aka: Samuel Moore Freeman)

7th Battalion Royal Irish Fusiliers
Killed in Action: 5th September 1916
Age: 28
Combles Cemetery, France Grave: 6-D-4

Samuel Moore (Freeman) was a son of Samuel Freeman and Mary Freeman of Donnybraggy, Muff, Cookstown. He enlisted in Randalstown, County Antrim, using his mother's maiden name. The reason for this is unknown. He joined the 7th Battalion Royal Irish Fusiliers. After considerable training they were taken to France and by September 1916 were close to Combles. On the 5th September they were to attack and take a trench which ran from Leuze Wood to Combles. At 4.00pm 'B' Company advanced in two lines followed by 'C' company in similar formation. They advanced about 800 yards and met comparatively little opposition until they found themselves held up by very thick and uncut barbed wire. As they attempted to break through this they were met by a withering fire from enemy machine-guns. They then attempted to dig in where they were. 'A' and 'D' companies were moved up but despite repeated gallant attempts they were unable to break through the wire. During this attack the battalion lost forty two men. For considerable time Samuel Moore was officially reported as missing after this attack. His father Samuel Freeman had made numerous enquiries to the 'War Office' and for a long time little was known. It was later accepted that Samuel Moore was killed in action. He is buried in plot 6- row D- grave 4 at Combles Cemetery, France.

Samuel Moore is commemorated on Moneymore War Memorial (Assembly Rooms). On the memorial he is listed as S.M. Freeman.

17355-Private Joseph Boyle
8th Battalion Royal Inniskilling Fusiliers
Killed in Action: 6th September 1916
Peronne Road Cemetery, Maricourt, Somme, France.   2 - E - 1

Joseph Boyle was born at Derryarden and enlisted in Cookstown.

By September 1916, the 8th Inniskillings were posted to the Somme. On September 6th the Inniskillings came under intensive shellfire with one of the major casualties of the 7th Battalion being Lieutenant Colonel H.N. Young who was wounded by an enemy sniper. That night the enemy made a determined attack on Leuze Wood, preceding it with an intensive bombardment, which was beaten off by the Inniskillings. The action concluded with 14 men of 8th Battalion, killed in action including Joseph Boyle and Corporal Joe Quinn from Drumglass, Dungannon.

Private Joseph Boyle is buried in plot 2- row E- grave 1 at Peronne Road, Cemetery, Maricourt, Somme, France. He is commemorated on Cookstown Cenotaph.

17494-Private Hugh Currie
9th Battalion Royal Inniskilling Fusiliers
Killed in Action 8th September 1916
Age: 20
Pond Farm Cemetery, Belgium. Grave: A-18.

Hugh was the youngest son of Mrs Jane Currie of Drapersfield, Cookstown. He was described as a quiet, good natured lad and before joining the army he was a member of the local Ulster Volunteers and a member of Knockinroe L.O.L. 194. He enlisted in Cookstown on 5th September 1914, and trained at Finner Camp, Ballyshannon, County Donegal and Shane's Park Camp, Randalstown, County Antrim.

He was wounded in action on the 1st July 1916, and was posted back to his Battalion after he recovered.

In a letter to Mrs. Jane Currie, from Private Joseph Crooks, he expresses his deepest sympathy, stating that he and Hugh Currie were chums and that he had been beside him when he was struck by shrapnel and removed to the Dressing Station. Hugh had been on sentry duty in the trenches on 8th September 1916 when the enemy started shelling their front line. He had been struck by shrapnel from a shell which exploded nearby. On hearing of Hugh's death, his cousin Private Joseph Currie wrote to Mrs. Jane Currie from the Front saying,

"When I heard of Hugh's death I got leave and went to see if it were true. I trust that God may comfort you."

Hugh is interred in Pond Farm Cemetery, row A, grave 18. He was twenty years of age and was the only man from the 9th Battalion to die on that day. The Dressing Station was close to where Pond Farm Cemetery now stands

Hugh Currie is commemorated on Cookstown Cenotaph and Molesworth Presbyterian Roll of Honour.

27973-Private Hugh McIvor

10th Battalion Royal Inniskilling Fusiliers
Killed in Action: 8th September 1916
Age: 31
Pond Farm Cemetery, Belgium. Grave: B-19

Hugh McIver was born in Moneymore. He was a son of Francis and Nancy McIvor of Moneymore and husband of Maud McIvor of Queen Street, Magherafelt.

He enlisted with the 10th Battalion Royal Inniskilling Fusiliers in Newtownards. In February 1916 the Battalion arrived in France. It is believed that Hugh was killed by a sniper. He was the only man from the Battalion to be killed on that day. He was buried in Row B, Grave 19 in Pond Farm Cemetery, Belgium. After the war when these Cemeteries were being built his wife had the following inscription engraved on the headstone, *"Thy will be done, In Loving Memory of my dear Husband"*, *Maud McIvor.*

Lieutenant Thomas James Kennedy
8th Battalion Royal Inniskilling Fusiliers
Killed in Action: 9th September 1916
Thiepval Memorial, France. Panel: 4D-5B

Thomas James Kennedy was the eldest son of Samuel and Mary Kennedy of Tyresson, Cookstown. Before the war he had served his apprenticeship in the offices of the Mid Ulster Mail as a reporter, and was well known in journalistic circles in Dungannon, Londonderry, Dublin and Dundalk. He was, for a while, the editor of the "Northern Standard" in Monaghan. He had been in service with the South Irish Horse and a prominent Officer in Monaghan Ulster Volunteer Battalion. He volunteered on the outbreak of war and was given a Commission in the 36th Ulster Division, but was later transferred to the 16th Irish Division. During the Dublin rebellion in April 1916 he was recommended for promotion for services in the field.

While attached to the 12th Inniskillings he was deployed to the Pro-Cathedral in Dublin, where he signalled to have the iron gates and doors open, and arranged to have his men cross under heavy fire without loss. It was through his courtesy afterwards that arrangements were made for a fifteen minute ceasefire so as to enable the Rev. Richard Bowden, Administrator and Parish Priest at the Pro-Cathedral to procure provisions for a large number of refugees who were compelled to take refuge with the men in the building. Lieutenant Kennedy was widely praised by Catholic clergy and by Nationalist newspapers afterwards and it was seen as significant that such a prominent former UVF officer, had behaved with such courtesy.

Lieutenant Kennedy was attached to the 8th Inniskillings at the Somme where he was killed in action on 9th September 1916.

In a letter to his father Major A.J. Walkey of the 8th Inniskillings wrote:

I regret to inform you that your son was killed while leading his men during an attack on the 9th September. I have gathered that he was going down a trench with his bombers, when they met a party of Germans, who put up a fight, one of them throwing a bomb which killed your son. I am glad to say that afterwards some of his men got him away and buried him in decency.

In a letter to his father, the Reverend P.D. McCaul of St Eunan's College, Letterkenny, wrote:

During the week of the Dublin rebellion I met with Lieutenant Kennedy a good deal, and I must say that he was a general favourite with all the people staying in the Hamman Hotel. He was more than kind to myself, personally. He was affable, gentlemanly, fearless, and good humoured. I am deeply touched by his death. The loss of such a noble son is a crushing blow. His parents and other members of the family have my deepest sympathy. May God comfort you in your sorrow is the earnest prayer of one who greatly admired your darling son.

Thomas J. Kennedy was buried at the time of his death but his grave could not be found later by the Commonwealth War Graves Commission. He is therefore commemorated on the Thiepval Memorial to the Missing of the Somme, France. He is also commemorated on Cookstown Cenotaph and Molesworth Presbyterian Roll of Honour, Cookstown. He was a member of Masonic Lodge 55 in Monaghan and a fine memorial portrait of Lieutenant Kennedy was unveiled in the hall there in 1917.

23065-Private Michael McWilliams
7th Battalion Royal Inniskilling Fusiliers
Killed in Action: 9th September 1916
Thiepval Memorial, France.   Panel: 4D-5B

Michael McWilliams was born in Cookstown, and enlisted with the 7th Battalion Royal Inniskilling Fusiliers there.

The 7th Inniskillings formed part of 49 Brigade of the 16th (Irish) Division and were moved to the Somme in August 1916. On the 8th September 1916 the 7th Inniskillings spent the night at Carnoy and then moved to Guillemont for the attack on Ginchy the following day. During the attack on the 9th September, the 7th Inniskillings moved across the open ground, encountering an intense enemy barrage of machine gun fire and shrapnel in which 3 Officers and 43 other ranks of the Battalion were killed, including Michael McWilliams. He has no known grave and is commemorated on the panel 4D-5B on Thiepval Memorial, France.

Inscription on the base of 16th Irish Division Memorial Cross at Ginchy, France

11084-Sergeant William T. Mitchell
9th Battalion Royal Inniskilling Fusiliers
Killed in Action: 9th September 1916
Age: 22
Pond Farm Cemetery, Belgium Grave: A-20

William Mitchell was a son of Thomas and Hannah Mitchell of Coagh, and was educated at Tamlaght National School. Prior to military service William was an active member of Coagh Company of Ulster Volunteers and a valued member of Drumconvis L.O.L. 794. He joined the army, volunteering in August 1914 and while training at Randalstown Camp he was promoted to the rank of Corporal, finally becoming a Sergeant in June 1916. While serving in the trenches on 9th September 1916, he was shot by a German sniper. He is buried in row A, grave 20 at Pond Farm Cemetery, Belgium.

Lieutenant J.B. Anderson ('C' company), wrote a letter to William's father:-

He was a gallant soldier and a good comrade, one of the best of my Sergeants. His death is a great loss to my company, and I will never get another man who will carry out his duties more cheerfully or promptly. He was always very bright, and set such a fine example to his men, often under the most trying circumstances. He is mourned alike by all the Officers and men of his company.

The Battalion lost three men on the 9th September - William Mitchell, John Parke, who died of wounds at Bailleul and William James Elliot.

After the war the family had the following inscription engraved on his headstone, "Thy will be done". William Mitchell is commemorated on Coagh War Memorial (Royal British Legion, Cookstown).

No mother or father saw him die
No brother or sister to say goodbye
No friends or relations to clasp his hand
But they hope to meet in a better land

His warfare is o'er, his battle fought
His victory won, but dearly bought
His fresh young life could not be saved
He slumbers now in a soldier's grave

In a foreign distant land
There our darling Willie sleeps
Nothing now can hurt or harm
Jesus safe his spirit keeps

Mid Ulster Mail in September 1916, by his family in Coagh.

17665-Private John Parke
9th Battalion Royal Inniskilling Fusiliers
Died of Wounds: 9th September 1916
Bailleul Cemetery, France. Grave: 2-F-210

John Parke was the third son of James Wilson Parke and Mrs. Jane Parke of Craigs, Orritor, Cookstown. Before the war John was employed by the Midland Railway Company in Moneymore as a clerk. He enlisted in Cookstown, joining the 9th Battalion Royal Inniskilling Fusiliers. He fought at the Battle of the Somme and was then moved to Belgium. On 9th September 1916 he suffered severe shrapnel wounds to his back and abdomen and was hurriedly removed to No2 Casualty Clearing Station at Bailleul. A number of Casualty Clearing Stations were situated here during the war and the resulting Cemetery is a large one. John's wounds were serious and he died later that day. Doctors and nurses in these stations were overwhelmed with work. Wounded soldiers were brought in constantly and most were forced to lie on their stretchers in the open awaiting the attention of overworked medical staff. John is buried in plot 2-row F- grave 210 at Bailleul Cemetery, France

In a letter to John's parents, Reverend James T. Hall, Presbyterian Chaplain at the Casualty Clearing Station said:

Your sons grave has been marked by a cross on which will be inscribed his name, number, regiment, rank, and date and cause of death. Our Soldiers graves are most carefully protected and preserved and the Cemetery, in which your boy's body lies, is very beautiful, as it has been nicely laid out with flowers and grass borders. The Cemetery faces the rising sun, and I like to think of this God's acre as I frequently see it with the sunshine of God's peace and benediction falling across it. He has given his life for others, following the example of him who died for us. May God comfort and sustain you and yours in this time of loss and trial.

John Parke is commemorated on Cookstown Cenotaph and on Orritor Presbyterian Roll of Honour.

11417- Private John James Beach

5th Battalion Royal Inniskilling Fusiliers
Killed in Action: 10th September 1916
Aged: 30
Struma Military Cemetery, Greece. Grave: 5–A-1

John James Beach was born at Annagh, Belturbet, County Cavan. His parents, James and Annie Beach, moved to 9 Stream Street, Newry and John came to Cookstown to work at Orritor quarry. John had a great deal of experience on active service having served throughout the Boer war. At the outbreak of the First World War he rejoined the army and spent a long time in service before his death. He was killed in action during the Salonika Campaign on 10th September 1916. At the time of his death his wife and son were living at Church Street, Cookstown. John was killed during very heavy fighting close to the Struma River and is buried in Plot 5, Row A; Grave 1 at Struma Military Cemetery, Greece

John James Beach is commemorated on Cookstown Cenotaph

Far and oft my thoughts do wander to the grave in foreign lands
When they laid my darling husband, placed by strange but tender hands
Yet some day I hope to meet him when my days in life are fled
Then in Heaven I hope to greet him, where no farewell tears are shed.

May the Lord have mercy on his Soul

Submitted to Mid Ulster Mail by his wife and baby son. Church St, Cookstown.

Five men of the 5th Inniskillings were killed on the 10th September and all are interred in Struma Cemetery. William Ferguson from County Leitrim, William McConkey, from Belfast, George McCutcheon from Edenderry, and Joseph McGowan of Glasgow

477620-Private Harrison Moore Murphy
Royal Canadian Regiment
Killed in Action: 16th September 1916
Age: 30
Vimy Memorial, France

Private Harrison Moore Murphy was the only son of Captain Moore Murphy and Mrs. Elizabeth Murphy of Gortreagh, Cookstown. Harrison was born in Kent, England. He graduated with a BA, from Queens University, Belfast, before going to live and work in Toronto, Canada. At the out break of war he volunteered and joined the Royal Canadians, and spent some time in England training with his regiment in February 1916, when he visited his parents in Cookstown for a few days leave.

Harrison's father Captain Moore Murphy was an invalid and had spent most of his life in Military service, being 15 years in India and was posted to South Africa where he commanded a company of South Wales Borders, he had many active service and campaign medals before retiring due to illness. Harrison's parents received a letter from him, dated 15th September 1916 which was full of hope and cheerfulness. Harrison was killed in action the following day.

He has no known grave and is commemorated on Vimy (Canadian) Memorial, France.

Captain Moore Murphy sold his home at Gortreagh soon after and returned to England to live with his daughter. He died in December 1916.

144825-Private Louis Boyle
24th Battalion Canadian Infantry
Killed in Action: 17th September 1916
Age: 24
Vimy Memorial. France.

Louis Boyle was born on 27th September 1891 and was the son of Joseph Boyle of Cookstown, County Tyrone. As a young man Louis emigrated to Canada where he worked as a painter and decorator. He was unmarried and enlisted in the Canadian Infantry at Ottawa on 18th August 1915. His enlistment papers state that he was five feet four and a half inches tall with grey eyes, light brown hair and a fair complexion, and that his religion was Roman Catholic.

His battalion arrived in the United Kingdom and trained close to the South coast of England. He was later killed in action in France on 17th September 1916. There is no known grave and Louis is commemorated on the Vimy Memorial. He was ten days short of his twenty-fifth birthday.

Louis Boyle is commemorated on Cookstown Cenotaph.

Leeds Training College also known as Second General Hospital, Leeds, where Private Frederick Currie was treated for his wounds.

Photo by kind permission of Eleanor Seffen.

19319-Private Frederick Currie

9th Battalion Royal Inniskilling Fusiliers
Died of wounds: 22nd September 1916
Aged: 20
Leeds (Harehills Cemetery) Screen wall G 26. Yorkshire, England

Frederick Currie was the youngest son of Thomas and Margaret Currie of Tamlaght, Coagh. He was born on 8th August 1896 and baptised at Tamlaght Church on 26th October 1896 by Reverend A.S.Irwin. He was educated at Tamlaght National School.

Prior to enlisting, Frederick was a member of Carryhill LOL 188, Coagh and a member of Coagh Company, Ulster Volunteers. He enlisted in the 9th Battalion Royal Inniskilling Fusiliers on 29th December 1914 and after training was sent to France with the battalion where he experienced a few engagements with the enemy. He was seriously wounded at the Somme on the 1st July 1916 and lay on the open battlefield for four days with nine shrapnel wounds in one leg and a wound to the groin, before being discovered and brought back to England for treatment at Second General Hospital Leeds.

The following letter was received by the family from the Reverend J. Jackson Wright, dated 5th July, 1916:

Your boy was wounded on Saturday owing to a German artillery attack and unable to return to his battalion. He was found early on Tuesday morning, and I am glad to say, the wound and exposure have not done him as much harm as expected. He came here for medical treatment and rest, and was sent to a base hospital. I saw him while here and he was quite cheery and wonderfully strong. His platoon did splendid in the attack and I hope he will soon recover.

In August around the time of his twentieth birthday he had a visit from his mother at the hospital in Leeds and was expected to recover. His mother Margaret received a letter at home in Coagh on the 19th September stating that her son's recovery was in doubt. In spite of all that could be done for him at Second General Hospital, Leeds, he died of his wounds there on 22nd September 1916. He was buried with full Military Honours in Leeds (Harehills) Cemetery and is commemorated there on Screen wall G26. Frederick Currie is commemorated on Coagh Presbyterian Church Roll of Honour and on Coagh War Memorial (Royal British Legion Cookstown).

He died for his country, what more could he do?
No more he'll answer the roll call, or rush to the bugle sound
But Lord, when the roll is called in Heaven
May his name in Thy Book be found.

Submitted to the Mid Ulster Mail by his parents, September 1916

2nd Lieutenant Charles Richard Cooney
7th Battalion Royal Dublin Fusiliers
Killed in Action: 9th October 1916
Thiepval Memorial. France. Panel: 16 C

Charles Richard Cooney was born on 13th March 1894 and was the only son of James L. Cooney of 3 High Street, Moneymore.

He was a nephew of the Reverend E. Stewart Cooney, MA, LL B, St John's Church, Belfast, and the Rev Charles R. Cooney BA, Fairview, Dublin. He received his primary education in the National School in Moneymore and in October 1904 went to Cookstown Academy. He continued at the Academy until the summer of 1911 having passed with Honours. In August 1911 he entered Connell's Civil Service Institute, Belfast, to prepare for the C.S. Intermediate Examination and on the advice of his teacher, for the experience, he competed in the second division C.S. examination and passed practically without preparation. He began duty in March 1913 in the local Government Board Office, Dublin and was subsequently transferred to the Finance Department of Dublin Metropolitan Police at Dublin Castle. He was regarded as having a warm and quiet disposition.

He received a commission in 1915 to the 7th Battalion Royal Dublin Fusiliers and was sent to Ipswich for a preliminary course on 1st November 1915. He was then attached to the 5th Battalion Royal Dublin Fusiliers for training at Curragh Camp and Moore Park, near Fermoy, and subsequently to the 10th Royal Irish Rifles.

He arrived in France on 20th July 1916 and was attached to the 2nd Royal Irish Rifles and appears to have taken his turn in the trenches from the day of his arrival. While serving with them in France he was killed by shellfire on 9th October 1916.

A Memorial Service was held in St John's Church, Moneymore, on Sunday 15th October, in his memory. The hymns that were selected were "Christ will gather his own" and "Peace, perfect peace". At the conclusion of the service the "Death march in Saul" was played by Mrs Byrne the organist with the congregation standing with bowed heads.

Charles Richard Cooney has no known grave and is commemorated on panel 16-C on the Thiepval Memorial, France. He is also commemorated on Moneymore War Memorial (Assembly Rooms).

602 - Lance Corporal Hugh Lennox

1st Battalion Argyll and Sutherland Highlanders (Princess Louise's)
Died Of Wounds: 9th October 1916
Age: 22

Lance Corporal Hugh Lennox was the son of Eccles and Martha Lennox, Coagh Street, Cookstown and a brother to Silas who died of illness on 22nd July 1916.

He had been a pupil at Oldtown National School, Cookstown and was employed in Milburn Factory in the town.

Hugh was well known as a football player at the time and by all reports was a clean living straight forward lad.

He enlisted in the army in Glasgow where he was working. He joined the Argyll and Sutherland Highlanders. His other brother Eccles, had been discharged early in the war after he'd been gassed.

While on active service, Hugh Lennox was wounded in action in Salonica on 30th September 1916.

In a letter to his mother, while he was in hospital he said:-

Dear Mother,

I got a little bit of a shot on 30th September so I must stay in hospital. Of course, my right hand and arm is a bit sore. The doctors and nurses say I am very good at healing. I expect to be home soon to look after the old dear.

Your Loving Son, Hugh

Hugh Lennox died from his wounds a few days later.

In another letter dated 9th October 1916, the Rev. S.J.M. Campton, Presbyterian Chaplain to the Forces writes:-

Dear Mrs Lennox

I regret very much I have to write you concerning the passing of your son on active service. He was wounded on the chest when his regiment was advancing against the enemy on 30th September and was sent down here from the front. While in hospital here his condition was regarded as dangerous for a time, but we had hopes that he would recover and be restored to health. God willed otherwise, and your son is now numbered among those, 'Who fought the good fight and finished their course.' I was with him when he passed away at 7 o'clock on Monday evening, October 9th . He just slipped away without any pain and in peace. This thought of his end, I am sure, will comfort you, and you can be easy in your mind about the care and attention which he received since he came to the hospital, shortly after his wounding. He had the best surgical treatment and his nurses were very kind to him. They thought him patient and without any trouble.

At the time of his death Hugh Lennox had 3 brothers-in-law on active service, one was a prisoner of war in Germany.

25665-Private Patrick H.J. Monaghan
8th Battalion Royal Dublin Fusiliers
Died of Wounds: 9th October 1916
Age: 24
Bailleul Cemetery, France. Grave: 2-F-249

Patrick Monaghan was a son of Charles and Rose Monaghan of Loup, County Londonderry. He enlisted with the Royal Dublin Fusiliers in Castlerea, Co Londonderry. In early October 1916 Patrick was seriously wounded and taken to one of the Casualty Clearing Stations situated at Bailleul. His condition gradually deteriorated and he died of his wounds on the 9th October 1916.

9956-Sergeant Frederick Wilson
1st Battalion Kings Liverpool Regiment
Died of Wounds: 14th October 1916
Fort Pitt Military Cemetery, Kent. Grave:1415

Frederick Wilson was born in Warrington but eventually came to live in Cookstown. He enlisted in London into the 1st Battalion King's Liverpool Regiment. He had attained the rank of Sergeant by the time of his death. He died of wounds in hospital in England on 14th October 1916 and is buried in Fort Pitt Military Cemetery in Kent. This Cemetery has burials from both wars.

22086-Private Patrick Owens
1st Battalion Royal Dublin Fusiliers
Died of Wounds: 23rd October 1916
Age: 30
Longueval Road Cemetery, France. Grave: F-17

Patrick Owens was a son of Mrs. Margaret Owens of Mount Royal, Tullagh, Cookstown. He was born at Lisbellaw, County Fermanagh, but later moved with his family to Cookstown. He enlisted at Enniskillen with the Connaught Rangers but later transferred to the 1st Battalion Royal Dublin Fusiliers. Patrick Owens died of wounds and is buried in row F- grave 17 at Longueval Road Cemetery, France.

27880-Private William Norman Davidson
15th Battalion, 48th Canadian Highlanders
Killed in Action: 4th November 1916
Zouave Valley Cemtery, Souchez, France.   Grave: 2-H-7

Norman Davidson was born in Moneymore on 2nd June 1894. He was the son of Harper C. and Mrs. M.E. Davidson. They moved to live at 5 Golf Terrace, Portrush, County Antrim. Norman emigrated to Canada to join his older brothers Harry and Jack. Norman enlisted in the army on 22nd September 1914 at Valcartier.

Valcartier was a large training camp a few miles north-west of Quebec. It was hastily set up to take the large numbers of men who were joining up at that time in Canada. An estimated 32, 665 volunteers were brought in by over 100 trains from all over Canada, between August and September 1914. William Norman Davidson was part of 'G' Company of 15th Battalion and sailed for England on 3rd October 1914. In January 1915, he was taken to hospital, where he spent the next two months, with an unknown illness. He rejoined his Battalion on 16th May 1915 and formed part of 1st Canadian Division. The Division fought later at the Battle of the Somme. In October 1916 Norman attended 'Bombing' school and shortly after returning to his regiment he was killed in action, on 4th November 1916. He is buried in plot 2, row H, grave 7 at Zouave Valley Cemtery, Souchez, France. He is commemorated on Portrush War Memorial and Portrush Prebyterian Roll of Honour.

17827-Private Samuel Spiers

9th Battalion Royal Inniskilling Fusiliers
Killed in Action: 7th November 1916
Age: 33
Pond Farm Cemetery, Belgium. Grave: E-14

Samuel Speirs was a son of Robert and Ellen Spiers of Gortalowry, Cookstown. Prior to the war he lived in Church Street and was employed in Greenvale Mill (Adair's). He was a member of Tullyhogue L.O.L. He married circa 1912.

The 9th Battalion were in the front line trenches having arrived there on the 5th November and were not due to be relieved again until the 11th. Samuel Spiers was killed action on 7th November 1916 by a trench mortar and was the only fatal casualty. Two others were wounded in the same incident.

His wife at this time was residing with relatives at Ardtrea where she received the following letter from Reverend J.G.Paton of Terrace Row Presbyterian Church who was at that time a Chaplain to the Forces.

"Dear Mrs Spiers,

I'm sorry to have to tell you that your husband, 17827 Pte Samuel Spiers was killed yesterday by a rifle grenade. He lived for a few minutes afterwards but so far as I know was unconscious, and so did not suffer. I conducted the funeral service today in a little cemetery which is very carefully kept, just behind the lines. Your husband was a good soldier and did his duty like a man, and died like a hero, so you may well be proud of him. The Officers and men send you their warmest sympathy in your sad loss. Rev. R. Hyndman of Cookstown is nearby at present. I will ask him to visit the grave so that he can tell you about it when he returns. I pray that Almighty God will comfort and sustain you and yours with the thought of meeting again where there will be no sorrow."
Yours, with sincere sympathy.

Samuel Spiers was buried in row E, grave 14 at Pond Farm Cemetery, Belgium.

He is commemorated on Cookstown Cenotaph and First Presbyterian Roll of Honour Cookstown.

Clyde Z / 3809-Able Seaman Malachy Hannon

Royal Naval Volunteer Reserve
Hawk Battalion (Royal Naval Division)
Killed in Action: 13th November 1916
Age: 23
Thiepval Memorial, France. Panel (MR 21)

Malachy was born on 14th June 1893. He was the son of James Hannon, Railway Cottage, Stewartstown, County Tyrone and later of, 7 Grove Street - New City Road, Glasgow, Scotland. He worked as a labourer in Glasgow and enlisted with the Royal Naval Volunteer Reserve on 12th April 1915. He was drafted to the Mediterranean Expeditionary Force on the 9th September that year. He served with the Hawk Battalion (Royal Naval Division) from the 21st September to 18th November 1915 when he was posted to Gallipoli, where he received shrapnel wounds to the right side of his face and shoulder and was subsequently hospitalised in Malta. He rejoined Hawk Battalion at Mudros on the island of Limnos, in the Aegean Sea on the 9th February 1916.

The Royal Naval Division was unique in its formation. It consisted mostly of sailors with naval ranks, yet almost none of them served at sea. The Battalions carried the names of distinguished sailors rather than numbers as in the army; Hood, Nelson, Howe, Drake, Hawk, etc. Initially the Division consisted of men from the Royal Naval Volunteer Reserve and the Royal Marines. Subsequently due to a shortage of sailors, a third brigade was formed of soldiers from various regiments. After early action in the defence of Antwerp, the division was posted to Gallipoli, where Malachy Hannon joined it.

The Division saw its posting through to the end of the Gallipoli campaign and in April 1916 it was taken over from the Admiralty by the War Office and was posted to France and the Western Front the following month. In July 1916 in was given the number 63rd Division and remained on the Western Front for the rest of the war. The Division was formed around cadres of Officers and NCO's from Royal Navy and Royal Marines and supported by a sprinkling of retired Officers of high quality, mostly from the Brigade of Guards. A very large proportion of reservists were miners and labourers from the North of England, Scotland and Ulster and this trend continued through to the war's end.

Malachy Hannon was listed as missing, killed in action on 13th November 1916.

He has no known grave and is commemorated on Thiepval Memorial MR 21, and on Stewartstown Cenotaph.

9237-Private George Brown M.M.

1st Battalion Royal Inniskilling Fusiliers
Died of Wounds: 21st November 1916
Thiepval Memorial. France. Panel: 4D-5B

George was born in the parish of Derryloran, Cookstown. He was the only son of James and Jane Brown of Crossnarea, Moneymore. George was awarded the Military Medal. As there is no citation for a military medal we may assume it was for gallantry. He is recorded as having died of wounds on 21st November 1916 and has no known grave. He is commemorated on panels 4D-5B on Thiepval Memorial, France.

After he died his mother and sister inserted the following verse in the local Mid Ulster Mail newspaper:

"It is hard to part with those we love
Though parting days will come
Yet let us hope we meet above
For this is not our home.

George Brown M.M. is commemorated on Moneymore War Memorial, (Assembly Rooms, Moneymore)

Moneymore War Memorial (Assembly Rooms) which commemorates the names of 26 men.

Photo courtesy of Tom Jebb

24193-Private Samuel J. Curran

87th Company Machine Gun Corps
Killed in Action: 21st November 1916
Thiepval Memorial, France. Panel: 5C-12C

Samuel J. Curran was a brother of Miss Lizzie Curran, Oldtown Street, Cookstown. Samuel was an enthusiastic member of Cookstown company of Ulster Volunteers, and was described as having a cheerful, happy disposition and popular with all, who knew him. He had been employed by, Adair & Company, Greenvale Mill, Cookstown.

He enlisted in Cookstown with the Royal Innskilling Fusiliers, army number: 4421. He later transferred to the Machine Gun Corps, where he was attached to the 87th Company. He was killed in action on 21st November 1916 along with Peter Begley of Antrim. Peter, like Samuel had enlisted into the Royal Inniskillings and later transferred to the Machine Gun Corps. Neither of them has a known grave and both are commemorated on panel 5C-12C on Thiepval Memorial, France.

Samuel Curran is also commemorated on Cookstown Cenotaph and St. Luran's Church of Ireland, Roll of Honour, Derryloran, Cookstown.

The following is a letter written by 2nd Lieutenant Leonard K. Norris and addressed to Miss Lizzie Curran:

Dear Madam, It is my painful duty to inform you of the death of your brother, Pte S.J.Curran. He was killed instantly by a bomb and I'm glad to say he didn't suffer any pain. He was buried in the evening and a cross marks the spot where he lies. I may say that your brother will be greatly missed in our section as he was always a bright and cheerful lad and an excellent soldier in all respects, and it will be some consolation for you to know that he died as a good and brave man.

3853-Private John Donaldson

2nd Battalion Royal Inniskilling Fusiliers
Killed in Action: 23rd November 1916
Age: 20
Thiepval Memorial, France. Panel: 4D-5B

John Donaldson was a son of John and Mary Donaldson of Drumglass, Dungannon. John lived with his wife Mary in North Street, Stewartstown.

He was killed in action on 23rd November 1916, when his unit had been ordered to attack Munich trench and succeeded in entering it but were unable to reach their second objective. Four men were killed in this attack with forty-two wounded and nineteen missing. John Donaldson was listed as missing. He is commemorated on panels 4D-5B on Thiepval Memorial to the Missing of the Somme.

Inscription on Thiepval Memorial

25242 - Private Andrew Thomas Booth

11th Battalion Royal Inniskilling Fusiliers
Killed in Action: 24th November 1916
Aged: 20
Pond Farm, Cemetery. Belgium Grave: F-11

Andrew T. Booth was the eldest son of Mr. Thomas Booth of Ballyriff, Loup, Moneymore. He was a member of Ballyronan Company, Ulster Volunteers and was an active member of Woods Church, Magherafelt. He joined the Royal Inniskilling Fusiliers on 2nd August 1915 and was killed in action on 24th November 1916. He is buried in row F- grave 11 at Pond Farm Cemetery, Belgium He is also commemorated at Woods Church, Ballyronan and Moneymore War Memorial (Assembly Rooms)

While serving at the front he was trained as a Lewis gunner. Lieutenant H. P. Fitzgerald Uniacke wrote home to Private Booth's father expressing his sympathy and said:

Pte Booth was one of the best Lewis gunners and a man on whom I could always rely. His place will be extremely difficult to fill.

Rev Alexander Spence C.F. said:

On Friday night the 24th November 1916, the front line was heavily bombarded by the Germans. Pte Booth was asleep at the time in the dugout attached to his Lewis Gun post. The first or second shell landed right on top of the shelter and all the men in the dugout were killed instantaneously. He suffered no pain but passed into the presence of his master in a moment of time. When the debris was cleared away the five men were found killed just as they lay. Your son was a first class soldier, ready for anything and as brave as a lion. I knew him well and he always attended my services. I am sure he was well prepared to die.

The bombardment was in the Spanbroek sector and started at 10.00pm. It lasted for an hour. Altogether that day the battalion lost nine men and a further twelve were wounded. The five men killed in the dugout were those listed below. They are all buried together in plot F at Pond Farm Cemetery, Belgium.

- 16833   J. Bowes, of Enniskillen.- grave 9
- 15256   W. Nixon, of Enniskillen. – grave 10
- 25242   A.T. Booth, of Moneymore.- grave 11
- 27137   J. McGuckin of Desertmartin.- grave 12
- 18633   J. Averill of Co; Durham.- grave 13

For ever with the Lord
Amen so let it be
Life from the dead is in that word
Tis immortality

Obituary inserted in the Mid Ulster Mail 1916 by his Family

Second Lieutenant James McNeill McKinstry

2nd Battalion Royal Inniskilling Fusiliers
Died of Wounds: 2nd December 1916
Age: 21
Warloy Baillon Communal Cemetery Extension, France. Grave: 8-C-16

James McNeill McKinstry was born in Cookstown. He was the son of Dr. Robert and Mrs. A.R. McKinstry, 61 Rugby Road, Belfast.

He was originally commissioned into the 12th Inniskilling Fusiliers having joined the QUB Officers Training Corps after the war began. His father was a Doctor in Bessbrook, Co. Armagh before moving to Belfast. No specific details are available about which action Lieutenant McKinstry was wounded in. In November 1916 the 2nd Inniskillings attacked a series of German held trenches near the Munich line on the Somme and though they reached their objective, many men were lost and wounded. It is recorded that one officer was killed and three severely wounded, but they are not named. James McNeill McKinstry was wounded at this time and taken to hospital. He died of his wounds on 2nd December 1916. He is buried in plot 8- row C- grave 16 at Warloy-Baillon Communal Cemetery Extension, France and commemorated on Bessbrook War Memorial.

17517-Private Robert Hogshaw
9th Battalion Royal Inniskilling Fusiliers
Killed in Action: 6th December 1916
Aged: 21
Pond Farm Cemetery, Belgium. Grave: F-5

Robert Hogshaw was the youngest son of James and Martha Hogshaw of Crossglebe, Sandholes, Cookstown. He was an active member of Sandholes Presbyterian Church and Sandholes LOL, and was a member of Dungannon Company of the Ulster Volunteers.

After his death the Minister of Sandholes Presbyterian Church spoke very highly of the work done by Robert Hogshaw. When the Ulster Division was formed he volunteered for service though only seventeen years of age. He was trained at Finner Camp and Randalstown and went out with the first draft of the Ulster Division. Robert survived the first day of the Battle of the Somme where he was wounded and spent some time in base hospital before rejoining his unit in Belgium.

A letter by Rev J.G.Paton of Coleraine, who was a Presbyterian Chaplain at the Front, said that:

Robert Hogshaw was killed by a trench mortar. He was just
leaving to go to a new line when the incident took place and he
died without pain.

Two other men were killed along with Robert in the same incident. They were W. Ferguson, and R.Gallery, from Castlecaulfield

Mrs. Jane Swail (Isaac Black's sister) remembered "wee Bob", as she knew Robert Hogshaw, and said that Robert was working at the Manse in Sandholes when he signed up for active service. At the time Rev. Dr. Logan occupied the Manse.

Robert Hogshaw is buried in row F- grave 5 at Pond Farm Cemetery, Belgium along with a number of Cookstown men.

He is commemorated at Sandholes Presbyterian Church Roll of Honour and on Cookstown Cenotaph.

28910-Private James Joseph McGhie

11th Battalion Royal Inniskilling Fusiliers
Killed in Action: 7th December 1916
Age: 27
Hyde Park Corner (Royal Berks) Cemetery, Belgium.
Grave: A-16.

James Joseph McGhie was born is Stewartstown and was the son of Henry McGhie of Gortgonis, Coalisland. He enlisted in Motherwell, Scotland, where he had been working and joined the 11th Battalion Royal Inniskilling Fusiliers.

On the 4th December 1916 the 11th Battalion left Wakefield Huts, Dranoutre, at 2.15pm and marched via Neuve Eglise to Bulford Camp, Kortepyp, remaining there for the night. Next day they left Bulford Camp at 10.00am and marched via Red Lodge to relieve the 8th South Lancashire Regiment in the trenches, taking over the Douve sector in the Bois de Ploegsteert. Relief was completed by 12.00 noon. The next day, the 6th, was quiet. On the 7th December James was killed by rifle fire, the only man in the battalion to die that day

James is buried in row A, grave 16 at Hyde Park Corner (Royal Berks) Cemetery at Ploegsteert, Belgium.

20760-Private William Clark

6th/7th Battalion Royal Scots Fusiliers
Killed in Action: 27th December 1916
Thiepval Memorial, France.   Panel 3C

William Clark was born in Cookstown, County Tyrone but lived in Scotland. He enlisted with the Royal Scots Fusiliers in Irvine, Ayrshire. He was killed in action on 27th December 1916 and has no known grave. He is commemorated on panel 3 C on Thiepval Memorial, France.

Thiepval Memorial

Thiepval Memorial was opened in 1932 by the then Prince of Wales.

It records the names of 73,357 missing on the Somme between the time of arrival of British troops in 1915 and the withdrawal of German troops in 1917. It does not record all of the missing on the Somme, as Australians, Canadians, Newfoundlanders, New Zealanders and Indians are commemorated on other Memorials

Most of the recorded names are from British Army Units except for 858 South Africans and one man from the West Indian Regiment.

There are 7 Victoria Cross recipients named on the Memorial, 4 of them Irishmen.

The regiment with the highest recorded missing casualties is the London Regiment (Territorials), with 4,348.

The Commonwealth War Graves Commission makes no distinction of how men died and it also records the names of 3 men who faced Military Courts Martial and were shot at dawn.

The Memorial includes the names of former East Tyrone M.P. Tom Kettle and 43 men from Cookstown District Council area.

A cemetery in the grounds around the Memorial was added later and includes the graves of 300 British and French soldiers, only one of these men can actually be identified as having been killed on 1st July 1916, James Ritchie, 14th Royal Irish Rifles (YCV).

Part of the ground around the Memorial belongs to a pre- war Chateau. The Memorial stands at 45 metres in height and dominates the sky-line for many miles. In the 1970's it had fallen into disrepair, but more recently due to a resurgence of interest it has been restored to it's former glory.

A Visitors Centre and car & coach park has recently been opened in September 2004 to help facilitate the growing numbers of pilgrims who visit there annually.

The finances for the new centre were by public subscription and Cookstown based Mid-Ulster Branch, "Friends of the Somme" contributed £1000 to the cost.

Lieutenant Cecil William Glenn
Army Service Corps
(Attached) 1st Battalion Royal Inniskilling Fusiliers
Killed in Action: 28th January 1917
Thiepval Memorial, France. Panel: 4C-5C

Cecil William Glenn came from Cookstown graduated from Trinity College Dublin in 1915 with a BA and an LLB. He was commissioned into the ASC from the Trinity OTC in January 1915. After gaining promotion he was attached to 1st Battalion Royal Inniskilling Fusiliers. He was killed in action on the night of 27th/28th January 1917, during an attack in which the 1st Inniskillings and 1st Border Regiment attacked strong German held positions south of Le Transloy. The 1st Inniskillings lost eighteen men, but the two battalions managed to capture 394 prisoners. Both battalions were highly commended by Sir Douglas Haig and Sir Henry Rawlinson, Commander of the 4th Army. Sergeant Edward Mott of the 1st Borders received a Victoria Cross for gallantry during the attack. Cecil William Glenn has no known grave and is commemorated on panel 4C-5C on Thiepval Memorial, France.

28205-Private Hugh McKeown
1st Battalion Royal Inniskilling Fusiliers
Killed In Action: 28th January 1917
Thiepval Memorial, France. Panel: 4D-5B

Hugh McKeown was born in Cookstown and enlisted with the Royal Inniskilling Fusiliers there.

Hugh was killed in action as part of a night patrol led by Lieutenant Cecil W. Glenn when the 1st Battalion attacked enemy positions on 28th January 1917, south Le Transloy. Even though the mission was a success, the battalion lost eighteen men. Hugh has no known grave and is commemorated on panel 4D-5B on the Thiepval Memorial, France.

268272-Private Joseph Wilson (age 21)
268276-Private Thomas Wilson (age 24)
1st/6th Battalion Black Watch (Royal Highlanders)
Killed in Action: 1st April 1917
Mareouil Cemetery, France.   Graves: 4-B-9 and 4-B-10

Joseph and Thomas Wilson were sons of William and Jane Wilson of Shivey, Sandholes, Cookstown. The family later moved to Scotland and settled at 74 Grey Street, Shettleston, Glasgow. The two boys enlisted together being numbered only four digits apart and were both in the 1st/6th Battalion Black Watch. On the night of 31st March 1917, a raid on the enemy lines was carried out and it was discovered that the 2nd Bavarian Reserve Infantry Regiment, considered to be one of the bravest and most stubborn in the German Army, was holding the line opposite. The plan was that on the following day, 1st April, they would attack and drive the Germans out of the salient into which they had advanced as a result of fighting on the Somme between the Ancre and the Scarpe. The task given to the 51st Highland Division (in conjunction with the Canadians on the left and the 34th Division on the right), was to capture the southern shoulder of Vimy Ridge. It was during a German bombardment on the morning of the 1st April 1917 that the two brothers were killed in action together as a result of shellfire. They are also buried side by side in Mareouil Cemetery. Thomas is buried in plot 4- row B- grave 9 and Joseph is buried in plot 4- row B- grave 10. Joseph Wilson is commemorated on Cookstown Cenotaph. It is not known why Thomas's name is not commemorated. On the first anniversary of their death their devoted parents, brothers and sisters put the following verse in the Mid Ulster Mail:

"Sleep our dear sons in a foreign grave
Your lives for your country you nobly gave
No friends stood near you to say goodbye
But safe in God's keeping now you lie

Though one year has passed and gone
Since that great sorrow fell
Yet in our hearts we mourn the loss
Of those we loved so well

You have left behind some aching hearts
That loved you very dear
Hearts that never can forget
For still your memory's written here."

552736-Private Samuel Alexander Fleming
10th Battalion Canadian Infantry
Killed in Action: 9th April 1917
Vimy Memorial, France.

Samuel Alexander Fleming was born on 20th November 1893. He was the son of John Wilson Fleming and Annie Fleming of James Street, Cookstown.

John Wilson Fleming was Clerk of Petty Sessions, secretary of the Gas & Light Company, and the Lime Company in Cookstown.

Samuel Alexander Fleming was educated at Campbell College, Belfast, between September 1909 and December 1910.

As a young man he emigrated to Canada, where he settled close to Calgary and worked at the Canadian Bank of Commerce. He enlisted at Calgary on 26th August 1915 and was sent with the draft to England for training. He was six feet two inches tall (above average for an Infantry soldier). He is described on his attestation papers as having, blue eyes, brown hair and a fair complexion. On the opening day of the Battle of Arras, 9th April 1917, the four Divisions of Canadian Corps, fighting side by side for the first time, scored a huge tactical victory in the capture of the 60 metre high Vimy Ridge. Samuel Alexander Fleming was killed in action at the Battle of Arras on Vimy Ridge on 9th April 1917. He has no known grave and is commemorated on the Vimy Memorial, France.

After the war the ridge was chosen as the site to commemorate those Canadians who served and died in France. The Memorial bears the names of 60,000 men who died on the Western Front and 11,000 who perished in the taking of Vimy Ridge. The Impressive Vimy Memorial overlooks the Douai Plain from the highest point of Vimy Ridge, about 5 miles north-east of Arras.

Samuel Alexander Fleming is commemorated on Cookstown Cenotaph, First Presbyterian Roll of Honour, Cookstown and Campbell College War Memorial.

25208-Private Patrick Johnston

1st Battalion Royal Irish Fusiliers
Killed in Action: 11th April 1917
Arras Memorial, France.   Bay: 9

Patrick was born in Cookstown but lived at Lislea, County Armagh. He enlisted in Armagh, joining the 1st Battalion of the Royal Irish Fusiliers. On the morning that he was killed in action it was snowing. At 9.00am the 1st Battalion were ordered to proceed to their assembly position, which was a sunken road running north and south and situated to the north of Fampoux. They were in position by 11.00am but unfortunately they had been spotted by an enemy aeroplane and the position was heavily shelled. There were many casualties from this shelling. Their attack that day proposed an advance of 2,000 yards. At 12.00 noon the attack commenced, and the troops advanced with great gallantry but were met with heavy machine gun fire from the north, south and in front. They advanced through this and some of them got to within 200 yards of their objective before they had to retire. It was during this attack that Patrick was killed in action. There is no known grave and Patrick is commemorated on the Arras Memorial, Bay 9.

195380-Private John McGarvey

52nd Battalion Canadian Infantry (Manitoba Regiment)
Died: 19th April 1917
Age: 24
Aubigny Communal Cemetery Extension, France. Grave: 2-B-21

John McGarvey was born on 9th December 1893. He was a son of Michael and Mary McGarvey of Dirnan, Lissan, Cookstown.

He emigrated to Canada and enlisted at Peterborough, Ontario, on 1st December 1915 when he was twenty-two years of age. His enlistment papers state, he was five feet seven inches tall with blue eyes, light brown hair and a fresh complexion. He worked as a labourer and was single. He listed his father as next of kin. John McGarvey died on 19th April 1917 and is interred in plot 2, row B, grave 21 at Aubigny Communal Cemetery Extension, France. The exact nature of his death is unknown. He may have died of wounds as a result of the Candian Offensive nearby at Vimy Ridge, between 9th and 12th April 1917. No.42 Casualty Clearing Station buried many of their dead in the cemetery at Aubigny.

Aubigny-en-Artois is a village 15 kilometers north-west of Arras on the road to St. Pol. The village was held by commonwealth forces from March 1916 until the Armistice.

21390-Lance Corporal James Creighton

Machine Gun Corps, 87th Company
Died of Wounds: 27th April 1917
Age: 36
Etaples Cemetery, France.   Grave: 19-L-8a.

James Creighton was a son of John Creighton of Coagh, and educated at Tamlaght National School. He enlisted in the Royal Inniskilling Fusiliers in Cookstown, army Number: 9559. He later transferred to the 87th Company Machine Gun Corps and was seriously wounded in April 1917. He was taken to Etaples General Hospital where he died on 27th April 1917 and is buried in plot 19- row L- grave 8a at Etaples Cemetery, France.

James Creighton is commemorated on Coagh War Memorial (Royal British Legion, Cookstown).

"He fell at his post like a soldier brave
He answered his Master's call
He sleeps far away in a hero's grave
For his country's cause he did fall

But we shall meet him yonder
As we travel one by one
Through the valley of the shadow
And the land of endless sun"

Submitted by his family to the Mid Ulster Mail on the anniversary of his death.

875269-Private William Hogg
8th Battalion Canadian Infantry
Killed in Action: 28th April 1917
Age: 36
Vimy Memorial, France.

William Hogg was born on 12th October 1883 and was a son of Thomas and Mary Hogg of Tullyconnell, Tullyhogue, and husband of Margaret A. Hogg of Tullyconnell. As a young man he emigrated to Canada where he worked as a farmer. He enlisted at Winnipeg on 19th February 1916, and gave his address as Swan Lake, Manitoba and named his brother Thomas as next of kin. His attestation papers describe him as five feet nine inches tall with blue eyes, fair hair and a fair complexion. He gave his religion as Presbyterian. William was killed on the morning of the 28th April 1917 during the Battle of Arras, in an attack on a village near Vimy Ridge. He has no known grave and is commemorated on Vimy Memorial, France.

He is also commemorated on Cookstown Cenotaph and First Presbyterian Roll of Honour, Cookstown.

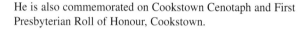

20/420-Private Henry James Kilpatrick

25th Battalion Northumberland Fusiliers
Killed in Action: 28th April 1917
Age: 38
Canadian Cemetery No2, Neuville St Vaast, France.   *Grave:*
17-E-23

Henry James Kilpatrick was born at Moymore, Pomeroy. He was a son of Benjamin and Jane Kilpatrick (nee Miller) of Moymore. He enlisted at Newcastle-upon-Tyne, where he was working. He joined the 20th Battalion Northumberland Fusiliers (Tyneside Scottish) but later transferred to the 25th Battalion Northumberland Fusiliers (Tyneside Irish). He had been wounded at the Battle of the Somme and returned home to recover from his wounds. After returning to the front line he was killed in action on 28th April 1917 during the Battle of Arras. His body was lost and for almost twenty years he was commemorated on the Arras Memorial, France.

His remains were later discovered along with two of his colleagues on 11th May 1936 and all were interred at Canadian Cemetery No2, at Neuville St. Vaast, which is close to Vimy Ridge. Henry James Kilpatrick is buried in plot 17- row E- grave 23. His name is still inscribed on the Arras Memorial to the Missing.

Second Lieutenant George Henry Powell

Machine Gun Corps, 5th Company
Killed in Action: 29th April 1917
Age: 27
Arras Memorial, France. Bay: 10

George Powell was a son of Mr. G.H. Powell M.D., of Nenagh, County Tipperary and of Mrs. Powell, who, after the death of her husband, moved to live in Cookstown. George Henry Powell joined the 5th Company Machine Gun Corps and was killed in action on 29th April 1917. He has no known grave and is commemorated on the Arras Memorial, Bay 10.

28157-Private James Gibson
1st Battalion Royal Inniskilling Fusiliers
Killed in Action: 18th May 1917
Arras Memorial, France. Bay: 6

James Gibson was born in the parish of Derryloran, Cookstown. On enlistment he named his brother, Henry, as next of kin, which would indicate that both parents were dead by then. Henry lived at 13 Alaska Street, Belfast. James enlisted in Hamilton while he was living and working in Scotland. He joined the 1st Battalion Royal Inniskilling Fusiliers. James was killed in action on 18th May 1917. There is no known grave and James is commemorated on Arras Memorial, Bay 6. He was twenty years of age.

Three men were killed in action on this day and their bodies couldn't be recovered. None of them has a known grave and are commemorated on the Arras Memorial, Bay 6. The others were John Veysey, an Englishman from Berkshire, who had transferred to the Royal Inniskillings, and John McCullough from Ardstraw, County Tyrone.

6678-Private Paul McGuckin
Machine Gun Corps-141st Company
(formerly: 24755 Royal Irish Fusiliers)
Killed in Action: 20th May 1917
Age: 24
Bedford House Cemetery, Belgium. Enclosure 4 – Special Memorial: 35

Paul McGuckin was a son of Paul and Eliza McGuckin of Lower Mullin, Ballinderry Bridge. He was born at Kinturk, County Tyrone. He enlisted with the Royal Irish Fusiliers in Armagh but later transferred into the 141st Coy Machine Gun Corps. On 20th May 1917 Paul McGuckin was killed along with nine of his comrades. When the Commonwealth War Graves Commission came to build the Cemeteries after the war, they misplaced the location of Paul McGuckin's, burial plot. He is commemorated on Special Memorial 35 at Bedford House Cemetery, Belgium.

8285 - Lance/Sergeant Samuel Magee

1st Battalion East Lancashire Regiment
Died of Wounds: 24th May 1917
Age: 33
Greenock Town Cemetery, Greenock, Scotland.   Grave: O-142

Samuel was a son of Samuel and Annie Magee who moved to 38 Main Street, Greenock from Cookstown. He and his wife Sarah Jackson Magee lived in Belfast and he enlisted there. In May 1917 he was seriously wounded and brought back to Britain for treatment. He was taken to hospital in Greenock, to be close to his parents, but his condition gradually worsened and eventually he died there on 24th May 1917. He was buried in Greenock Cemetery with full military honours in grave, O 142.

17811 - Private James Corbett
9th Battalion Royal Inniskilling Fusiliers
Killed in Action: 7th June 1917
Menin Gate, Ypres, Belgium. Panel: 22

James was a son of John and Eliza Corbett of Killymoon Street, Cookstown. He enlisted in the Army at Finner Camp, Ballyshannon, County Donegal.

James was seriously wounded on the 1st July 1916 at the Battle of the Somme. He had been struck four times, two bullets in his body and had shrapnel wounds to his hand and knee. He spent a few weeks recovering at Edmunton Military Hospital and needed an operation. On Monday 21st August 1916 he was sent to Tipperary where he had to undergo further surgery for the wound to his hand. James was quoted at the time as saying, *"I hope to get back to my comrades at the front."*

James was killed in action on 7th June 1917 during the opening phase of the Battle of Messines. There is no known grave and James is commemorated on the Menin Gate Memorial, panel 22. He is also commemorated on Cookstown Cenotaph and Second Presbyterian Roll of Honour (at Molesworth).

"This day brings to our memory our dear son who has gone to rest,
And those who think of him tonight are those who loved him best,
But the hardest part is still to come when the heroes do return,
And we, missing among the cheering crowd the face of our dear son."

Submitted for publication to the Mid Ulster Mail, By John and Eliza Corbett, 1917

Second Presbyterian Roll of Honour at Molesworth, Cookstown

14885-Corporal William George Hill
14th Battalion Royal Irish Rifles
Killed in Action: 7th June 1917
Spanbroekmolen Cemetery, Belgium. Grave: B-10

William George Hill was a son of Alexander and Ellen Hill of The Doons, Tullyhogue. William was born in Cookstown and enlisted in Belfast just after the start of the First World War and survived many of the early engagements. He was killed at the Battle of Messines on 7th June 1917. William is buried in row B, grave 10 in Spanbroekmolen Cemetery, Belgium.

After the war when the family were asked if they wanted an inscription engraved on his headstone they asked for the following.

"Greater love hath no man. That a man lay down his life for his friends"

Inscriptions cost the family, one old penny per letter.

17495-Private Samuel Junk
9th Battalion Royal Inniskilling Fusiliers
Killed in Action: 7th June 1917
Irish House Cemetery, Belgium. Grave: A-8

Samuel Junk was born at Ardboe, County Tyrone and was living in Stewartstown at the outbreak of war. He enlisted in Cookstown and had served with the 9th Battalion Royal Inniskilling Fusiliers for nearly two years when he was killed at the Battle of Messines on the 7th June 1917.

The Battle of Messines was launched on 7th June 1917 by British General Herbert Plumer's second army, which included the 36th (Ulster) and the 16th (Irish) Divisions, near the village of Mesen in Belgium. The target for the offensive was a ridge running north from Mesen village past Wytschaete village (which the Ulster and Irish Divisions eventually overran). The ridge was a natural stronghold southwest of Ypres.

For more than a year the allies had tunnelled under the German trenches and placed 455 tonnes (1,000,000 lb) of ammonal explosive. Twenty one mines were eventually placed under the German front lines. The detonation of the mines were all timed to go off at 3.10am on the morning of 7th June 1917, this was preceded by a heavy artillery bombardment. When 19 of the original 21 mines exploded, the noise was said to have been heard as far away as London, and was possibly the loudest man made noise up to that date. In Switzerland the explosions registered as an earthquake. Some estimates put the German casualties of the initial mine explosions at 10,000 men.

The explosions were followed by 9 Divisions of infantry advancing under the cover of a creeping barrage of artillery fire.

The task of the 9th Inniskillings that day was to support the 11th Inniskillings in the advance and to push through to the far side of the village of Wytschaete.

18 men of the 9th Inniskillings were killed in action at the Battle of Messines, including Samuel Junk, who is buried in row A, grave 8 at Irish House Cemetery.

The two mines which failed to detonate on the morning of 7th June 1917 remained undetected until years after the war as details of their placements were lost, much to the discomfort of people who lived in the region. During a thunder storm on 17th June 1955 one of the mines detonated, the only casualty was a cow grazing in a field nearby. The second mine is thought to have been recently pinpointed, but is yet to be recovered. Samuel Junk is commemorated on Coagh War Memorial (RBL, Cookstown)

20815-Private Joseph Mitchell

9th Battalion Royal Inniskilling Fusiliers
Killed in Action: 7th June 1917
Wytschaete Military Cemetery, Belgium. Grave: 2-E-17

Joseph Mitchell was the second son of Thomas Mitchell of Coagh. He was killed in action at the Battle of Messines on 7th June 1917. He is buried in plot 2- row E- grave 17 at Wytschaete Military Cemtery, Belgium. He is commemorated on Coagh War Memorial (Royal British Legion, Cookstown). Soon after his death the ladies of Coagh Dancing Class submitted a short poem in his honour in the local press. It read as follows.

He fell at his post like a soldier brave
He answered his Master's call
He sleeps far away in a hero's grave
For his country's cause he did fall

Far away from all who loved him,
The soldiers gently laid him to rest
In the low grave he lies sleeping
One of God's brightest and best.

The following verse was submitted by his father to the Mid Ulster Mail on the anniversary of his death.

We submit to our God who did give us the lend
Of the child who now from us is taken again
For we know that in love He has taken our son
Away from Life's sorrow and evil to come
Soon from times changing scene we shall follow him home
At the bright city's gate he will watch till we come
In the home of the Saviour we shall meet with our boy
And we know he will greet us with fullness of joy

17354-Corporal John Rush
8th Battalion Royal Inniskilling Fusiliers
Killed in Action: 7th June 1917
Menin Gate, Belgium   Panel :22

John was a son of Frank and Mary Rush of Clare Bridge,
Cookstown. He enlisted at Cookstown. John had attained the
rank of Corporal when he was killed at the Battle of Messines.
He had by this time seen action in many of the major battles and
was well used to life in the trenches. He was first reported
missing and the family at home had an anxious wait before news
of his death was confirmed. There is no known grave and John is
commemorated on the Menin Gate Memorial, panel 22. He is
also commemorated on Cookstown Cenotaph. He was twenty-two
years of age.

23/1023-Lance Corporal William John Crooks

1st Battalion Trentham Regiment
3rd New Zealand Infantry Brigade, N.Z.E.F.
Killed in Action: 8th June 1917
Age: 23
Messines Ridge (NZ) Memorial. Mesen, Belgium.

William John Crooks was born 5th November 1893. He was the son of James Crooks (formerly of Ballybriest, Cookstown) and Louise Sheldon, Barrow-in Furness, England.

As a young man, William immigrated to New Zealand and lived there with his aunt and uncle Jane Crooks and Crooks Mitchell at Northbrook Road, Rangiora, and brother of Annie (Crooks) of Black Grouse Lodge, Ballybriest, Cookstown.

At age 22 he enlisted at Rangiora in the New Zealand Expeditionary Force, joining 'D' company 1st Battalion Trentham Regiment. He was promoted to Lance-Corporal on 8th September 1915. He was described in regimental records as 5' 6" in height.

On September 15th 1916 he was wounded in action, but remained on duty with his battalion. For some months prior to Messines, William acted as a sniper and observer for his battalion. On the 7th June 1917, the first day of the Battle of Messines, William Crooks was acting as an observer attached to his battalion headquarters. The day went well for the battalion, but the following day the enemy bombardment was fierce and persistant in the New Zealand sector of the line. At about 11.30 hours a shell burst in the trench that William's company were holding, he and three others were killed instantly.

He was buried according to reports at the time but his grave is now lost and he is commemorated on Messines Ridge (NZ) Memorial, Mesen, Belgium.

He is also commemorated on Cookstown Cenotaph and at Claggan Presbyterian Church.

130272-Pioneer Frederick Dowie
Royal Engineers
Died of Wounds: 18th June 1917
Age: 28
Calais Southern Cemetery, France. Grave: G-4-9

Frederick Dowie was born at Unagh, Lissan, Cookstown. He was working in Glasgow before the outbreak of the First World War and enlisted there with the Royal Inniskilling Fusiliers but transferred to the Royal Engineers. He was seriously wounded at the Battle of Messines and sent to a hospital in Calais, where he died of his wounds. He is buried in plot 4- row G- grave 9 at Calais Southern Cemetery, France. He is commemorated on Cookstown Cenotaph and Molesworth Presbyterian Roll of Honour.

16082-Private James Watson
10th Battalion Royal Inniskilling Fusiliers
Killed in Action: 23rd June 1917
Messines Ridge Cemetery, Belgium. Grave: 6-B-33

James Watson was born in Moneymore. He is described as having enlisted in Donegal probably Finner Camp. He joined the 10th Battalion Royal Inniskilling Fusiliers and went to France in October 1915. James was killed in action during the later stages of the Battle of Messines and is buried in plot 6- row B- grave 33 at Messines Ridge Cemetery, Belgium. He was the only man in the 10th Battalion killed on this day. He was possibly killed by sniper fire.

James Watson is commemorated on Moneymore War Memorial (Assembly Rooms).

28498-Private Samuel Young

9th Battalion Royal Inniskilling Fusiliers
Killed in Action: 26th June 1917
Age: 19
Messines Ridge Cemetery, Belgium. Grave: 6-B-23

Samuel Young was born at Tamlaght and was a son of Robert and Elizabeth Young of Lower Coagh. Samuel enlisted in Omagh with the 9th Battalion Royal Inniskilling Fusiliers. He went out as a battle casualty replacement after the battalion was decimated at the Battle of the Somme and had served with them for six or eight months. He survived the battle at the beginning of June but was killed in action on 26th June 1917. He was buried in plot 6- row B- grave 23 at Messines Ridge Cemetery, Belgium.

He is commemorated on Coagh War Memorial, (Royal British Legion Cookstown).

41582-Gunner William Brown

270th Siege Battery, Royal Garrison Artillery
Died of Wounds: 1st July 1917
Poperinghe Cemetery, Belgium   Grave: 2-A-37

William Brown was born in Moneymore and enlisted in Cookstown. As a young man he joined the Royal Garrison Artillery. He died of wounds on 1st July 1917 and is buried in Plot 2, Row A, Grave 37 at Poperinghe Cemetery, Belgium. He is commemorated on Cookstown Cenotaph.

33166 - Private Richard Bell

10th Battalion Cameronians (Scottish Rifles)
Died of Wounds: 22nd July 1917
Etaples Cemetery, France. Grave: 25 - K - 3

Richard Bell was born in Cookstown, and at the outbreak of the
First World War he was living and working in Glasgow. He
enlisted in Glasgow with the 10th Battalion Cameronians
(Scottish Rifles). In July 1917 Richard was seriously wounded
and taken to hospital in Etaples. It had been hoped to get him to
hospital in England but by the time of his arrival at Etaples he
was considered too ill to travel. He died there on 22nd July 1917
and is buried in plot 25- row K- grave 3 at Etaples Cemetery,
France. The town of Etaples is about 27 kilometres south of
Boulogne and during the First World War the area around the
town was the scene of immense concentrations of
Commonwealth reinforcement camps and hospitals. The area was
chosen for this purpose as it was considered remote from enemy
attack, except from aircraft, and was accessible by railway from
both the northern and southern battlefields. By 1917 there were
an estimated 100,000 troops camped among the sand dunes here.
There were 11 General Hospitals, one stationary, 4 Red Cross
hospitals and a convalescent depot which could deal with 22,000
wounded or sick. The cemetery at Etaples is the largest
Commonwealth cemetery in France with 10,773 burials from the
First World War. It also contains 658 German burials and 119
burials from World War 2.

106464-Corporal Henry McDonald Glasgow

Royal Engineers (Gas Section)
Died of Illness: 24the July 1917
Age: 20
Derryloran Old Cemetery, Sandholes Road, Cookstown

Henry McDonald Glasgow was the youngest son of William James and Rebecca J. Glasgow of 52 James Street, Cookstown. William James Glasgow managed the Post Office in Cookstown. Henry was a Scholar of the Royal College of Science and was attached to the Royal Engineers (Gas Section) in France from August 1915, where he was involved in the maintenance, inspection and production of gas materials.

He died of illness at home on 24th July 1917 and is interred in the Glasgow family plot at Derryloran Old Cemetery, Sandholes Road, Cookstown. He is commemorated on Cookstown Cenotaph and on First Cookstown Presbyterian Church Roll of Honour.

Inscription on grave surround at Derryloran Old Cemetery

25832 - Private William V. McGaw

9th Battalion Seaforth Highlanders
(Formerly- Highland Light Infantry)
Died of Wounds: 25th July 1917
Age: 21
Mont Huon Military Cemetery, Le Treport. France.
Grave: 3-M-5B

William McGaw was born at Ballymoyle, Coagh. County Tyrone.
He was a son of William and Mary Keightly McGaw of
Ballylifford, Ballinderry Bridge. At the outbreak of the First
World War, he enlisted in Glasgow, joining the Highland Light
Infantry. He later transferred to the 9th Battalion Seaforth
Highlanders, 9th (Scottish) Division. He was wounded in action
and taken to No: 3 General Hospital at Le Treport and died there
on 25th July 1917. He is buried in plot 3- row M- grave 5B at
Mont Huon Military Cemetery, Le Treport, France. There are
2,357 burials in this cemetery including 200 German soldiers.
During the First World War, Le Treport was an important hospital
centre and by July 1916, the town contained three General
Hospitals (the 3rd, 16th and 2nd Canadian), No: 3 Convalescent
Depot and Lady Murray's BRCS Hospital.

21296-Corporal Robert Mitchell

9th Battalion Royal Inniskilling Fusiliers
Killed in Action: 6th August 1917
Age: 24
Menin Gate, Ypres (Ieper), Belgium. Panel: 22

Robert Mitchell was born at Tamlaght, County Tyrone, and was a
son of James and Lizzie Mitchell who later moved to live at
Greenfield Street, Govan, Glasgow. Robert enlisted at
Randalstown with the Royal Inniskilling Fusiliers and had
attained the rank of Corporal. He survived the Battle of Messines
and was killed in action on the eve of the Third Battle of Ypres,
on 6th August 1917. The weather was extremely wet and this part
of Belgium is low lying and the drains had been destroyed by the
constant shelling. For the next three weeks soldiers would
struggle through this morass with wounded men often drowning.
Robert Mitchell was lost in this dreadful environment. There is
no known grave and Robert is commemorated on panel 22 on the
Menin Gate Memorial, Ypres, Belgium. He is commemorated on
Coagh War Memorial (Royal British Legion, Cookstown).

15317-Private William Miller

7/8th Battalion Royal Irish Fusiliers
Killed in Action: 8th August 1917
Menin Gate, Ypres (Ieper), Belgium. Panel: 42

William Miller was born and lived in Pomeroy. He was killed in action during the Third Battle of Ypres, on 8th August 1917. There is no known grave and William is commemorated on panel 42 on the Menin Gate Memorial, Ypres (Ieper), Belgium.

29900-Private Hugh Ashfield

10th Battalion Royal Inniskilling Fusiliers
Died Of Wounds: 11th August 1917
Lijssenthoek Cemetery, Belgium.   Grave: 17 J 10a.

Hugh Ashfield was the son of Hugh Ashfield and Mrs. Annie Ashfield (nee Greer) and lived at Killymoon Street, Cookstown. Hugh was a brother of Eliza-May and Lydia Ashfield.

He enlisted in the army at Omagh and went out with a draft of men after the Battle of the Somme. He was wounded at the Battle of Pilkhem Ridge and taken to a casualty clearing station (C.C.S.) where he died of his wounds on 11t August 1917. Private David Armstrong from Stewartstown was taken to the same C.C.S. and also died. Hugh was buried with full military honours in plot 17- row J- Grave 10a at Lijssenthoek Military Cemetery, Belgium. David Armstrong is buried just a few graves away in the same row.

Hugh Ashfield is commemorated on Cookstown Cenotaph and on St. Luran's Church of Ireland Roll of Honour, Derryloran, Cookstown.

27459-Private David Armstrong

9th Battalion Royal Inniskilling Fusilers
Died of Wounds: 12th August 1917
Lijssenthoek Cemetery, Belgium. Grave: 17-J-20

David was a son of Mary Jane Armstrong of Chapel Street, Cookstown. The family had previously lived in Stewartstown, where David was born. David's story is similar to that of Hugh Ashfield. They had enlisted at much the same time in Omagh and both went to France as battle casualty replacements to bring their individual battalions back up to strength following the Battle of the Somme. Both were wounded at the Battle of Pilkhem Ridge and taken to the same hospital. They died a day apart. David died from his wounds on 12th August 1917. They are buried nearby each other in Lijssenthoek Military Cemetery, Belgium. David is buried in plot 17- row J- grave 20. When the war was over and these cemeteries were being erected the families were asked if they wanted anything special engraved on the headstone. David's family chose:

"O Lord is daily, with thine eye of love,
And bring us safely, to our house above. Amen".

David Armstrong is commemorated on Stewartstown Cenotaph and Donaghendry Church of Ireland Roll of Honour, Stewartstown.

**PTE. THOMAS LESLIE,
of Kawakawa.
Killed in action.**

21215-Rifleman Thomas Leslie
2nd Battalion, 3rd New Zealand Rifle Brigade
Killed in Action: 12th August 1917
Age: 22
Prowse Point Military Cemetery, Belgium.   *Grave: 4-A-2*

Thomas Leslie was a son of Mrs. A Leslie of Donaghey, Sherrygroom, Cookstown.

He later emigrated to New Zealand, and at the out break of the First World War, he enlisted with the 3rd New Zealand Rifle Brigade (Earl of Liverpool's Own), who were affectionately known as The Dinks'.

1st and 2nd Battalion of 3rd Rifle Brigade left Wellington, New Zealand on 8th October 1915 and arrived in Alexandria, Egypt on 14th November. They were joined by the 3rd and 4th Battalions in March 1916 and after a period of major reorganisation the Brigade left Alexandria for France on 7th April 1916. After a period of training the brigade entered the front line on the 13th May 1916, east of Armentieres. It participated in the vast majority of the battles of 1916 and 1917. Most notably it's first major offensive at the Somme on 15th September 1916 when it attacked the German front lines as part of the Battle of Flers-Courcelette. At the Battle of Messines on 7th June 1917 the Brigade successfully attacked from the town of Nieuwkerke in a mission to seize control of a series of German pill-boxes. The brigade next saw action during the Third Battle of Ypres, 31st July -10th November 1917.

Thomas Leslie was killed in action on 12th August 1917 and is interred in plot 4- row A- grave 2 at Prowse Point Military Cemetery, Belgium. This cemetery is close to Ploegsteert and a lane close by leads to Ploegsteert Wood which was eventually captured. Hundreds of men lost their lives in the struggle.

Thomas Leslie is commemorated on Cookstown Cenotaph.

923-Sergeant John Suffern Scott

8th Battalion Canadian Infantry
Killed in Action: 15th August 1917
Rue-Petillon Military Cemetery Fleurbaix, France.
(8th Canadian Cemetery Lens Memorial 4)

John Suffern Scott was a son of James Scott of Bellagharty,
Ballyronan, Magherafelt. He was born on 15th July 1896. He
emigrated to Canada, where he worked as a labourer and was
unmarried. He enlisted at Valcartier Camp in Quebec on 21st
September 1914 and joined the 8th Battalion Canadian Infantry.
He was described as being five feet nine inches tall, with blue
eyes, red hair and a fair complexion. He was twenty-one years of
age and was part of the Canadian Expeditionary Force sent to
Europe in early 1915, and served alongside his cousin, Jack Scott.
They were part of a force of 18,000 Canadians who suffered a gas
attack at what is now known as Vancouver Corner. This was the
first occasion a large Canadian force had been exposed to gas. A
35 foot high memorial of a Canadian soldier with his head bowed
stands on the spot to commemorate the 2,000 Canadians who died
there on 22/23rd April 1915. John Suffern Scott survived the
Battle of the Somme but was killed in action north of Lens on
15th August 1917. He was buried in Eighth Canadian Cemetery at
Lens, which was subsequently destroyed by shellfire. He and
fourteen of his comrades were re-interred in Rue Petillon Military
Cemetery, Fleurbaix, France. He is commemorated on Woods
Church Roll of Honour near Ballyronan. His brother George also
served throughout the war.

13600-Private Thomas John Gibson
9th Battalion Royal Inniskilling Fusiliers
Killed in Action: 16th August 1917
Tyne Cot Memorial, Belgium. Panel: 70-72

Thomas Gibson was born in Coagh and went to Finner Camp to enlist in the 9th Battalion Royal Inniskilling Fusiliers.

By mid-August 1917 the 9th Inniskillings had been resting for a few days on the wet ground at Vlamertinghe, before moving up to Capricorn Trench in support of 11th Inniskillings and 14th Royal Irish Rifles on the evening of August 15th . At 4.45pm on the afternoon of August 16th the first company moved out of Capricorn trench to support the 11th Inniskillings, during the Battle of Langemarck. A heavy barrage of enemy artillery came down, but there were no immediate casualties. They advanced in line over ground already pitted with shell holes, enemy machine gun fire stopped them in their tracks and they were forced to dig in. Although the planning for the advance was well arranged, the deep mud hampered the effort. Men sank in the mud as they struggled to aid their wounded comrades. The valley of Steenbeck was shelled intensely during the next day and night and many wounded men were forced to lie in 'No Man's Land'. Thomas John Gibson was lost during the Battle of Langemarck, and has no known grave. He is commemorated on panel 70-72 at Tyne Cot Cemtery Memorial, Belgium.

He is also commemorated on Coagh War Memorial (Royal British Legion, Cookstown).

Inscription on Tyne Cot Memorial

16589-Corporal Thomas Henry
14th Battalion Royal Irish Rifles
(109th Trench Mortar Battery)
Killed in Action: 16th August 1917
Age: 20
Tyne Cot Memorial, Belgium.   Panel: 138-140, 162, 162a, 163a,

Thomas was born at in the parish of Derryloran, Cookstown, about 1897. He was a son of Richard and Elizabeth Henry, who, at the outbreak of the First World War were living at 88 Mountpottinger Road, Belfast. Thomas enlisted in Belfast, joining the 14th Battalion Royal Irish Rifles. Some time before the Battle of Langemarck he was attached to the 109th Trench Mortar Battery and was serving with them when he was killed in action on 16th August 1917. The ground in this area of Belgium became a quagmire, following the incessant rain. Thomas has no known grave and is commemorated on Tyne Cot Memorial, Panels, 138-140, 162, 162a, and 163a. He was twenty years of age.

Inscription on Tyne Cot Memorial

28393-Private Alexander McKinney
8th Battalion Royal Inniskilling Fusiliers
Killed in Action: 16th August 1917
Age: 19
Tyne Cot Memorial, Belgium. Panel: 70-72

Alexander McKinney was born at Loup, Moneymore, and was the son of Mr. A. McKinney of Salterstown.   He enlisted in Omagh, joining the 8th Battalion Royal Inniskilling Fusiliers and after training he was sent with the draft to France in the autumn of 1916. Alexander was killed in action during the Third Battle of Ypres on 16th August 1917. He has no known grave and is commemorated on panel 70-72 on Tyne Cot Memorial, Belgium. He was a member of Saltersland Presbyterian Church and is commemorated on Moneymore War Memorial (Assembly Rooms).

23183-Sergeant John Milligan
11th Battalion Royal Inniskilling Fusiliers
Killed in Action: 16th August 1917
Tyne Cot Memorial, Belgium. Panel: 70-72

John Milligan was born at Tullyrusher, County Tyrone. He enlisted in Cookstown, with the Royal Inniskilling Fusiliers. During his time in the Army he had attained the rank of Sergeant. Six Officers including the Commanding Officer Lieutenant Colonel Audley Pratt D.S.O. and 91 other ranks including Sergeant John Milligan were killed in action at the Battle of Langemarck on 16th August 1917. John Milligan has no known grave and is commemorated on panels 70-72 on Tyne Cot Memorial, Belgium.

42495-Private James Tanney
2nd Battalion West Yorkshire Regiment
Killed in Action: 16th August 1917
Tyne Cot Memorial, Belgium. Panel: 42-47-162

James Tanney was born in Pomeroy and went as a young man to England in search of work. He enlisted in Newcastle-upon-Tyne with the 2nd Battalion West Yorkshire Regiment. He arrived in France in 1916 and survived many engagements. By the time of Passchendaele, August 1917, the weather had changed to almost continuous rain. The drainage of the Belgian countryside had been destroyed by the constant shellfire. Every hollow on the battlefield was full to overflowing with stagnant water. Wounded soldiers were often lost in these conditoins. James was killed in action at Passchendaele and has no known grave. He is commemorated on panels 42-47 and 162 on Tyne Cot Memorial, Belgium

Inscription on Tyne Cot Memorial

9416 - Sergeant Hugh Benjamin Haslam
6th Battalion Connaught Rangers
Died of Wounds: 26th August 1917
Age: 27
Boulogne Eastern Cemetery, France. Grave: 8-I-19

Hugh Benjamin Haslam was born at Sherrygroom, Cookstown. He was the son of Mrs James Greer, The Park, Priestland, Bushmills, County Antrim, and husband of Georgina M. Haslam, 18 St. Vincent Street, Shore Road, Belfast.

He enlisted in Clydebank, Scotland and served with the 6th Battalion Connaught Rangers. Records show that he received a wound to his hand and spent some time in hospital as well as a spell on home leave.

His battalion served with the 16th Irish Division in July and August 1917 and were fighting North-East of Ypres, Belgium, where he was severely wounded. He was taken to hospital in Boulogne where he had his right arm amputated but died later from his wounds.

He is buried in plot 8, row I, grave 19 at Boulogne Eastern Cemetery, France.

His brother, Robert, served throughout the war and was taken prisoner in March 1918 and arrived home in January 1919.

20235-Private John (Jack) McAllister
9th Battalion Royal Inniskilling Fusiliers
Killed in Action: 9th September 1917
Age: 23
Hermies British Cemetery, France.   Grave: H-3

John McAllister was a son of Daniel and Elizabeth McAllister of Ballymultrea, Magherafelt. He was a member of Salterstown L.O.L. 482.

He enlisted in Randalstown, joining the 9th Battalion Royal Inniskilling Fusiliers. John was killed in action on 9th September 1917. The exact nature of his death is unknown as he was the only death suffered by the 9th Battalion on this day and is listed as killed in action. He is interred in row H, grave 3 at Hermies British Cemetery, France. This Cemetery is in open countryside a few kilometres west of Bapaume.

He is also commemorated on Ballinderry Church of Ireland Roll of Honour.

3288-Lance Corporal Patrick Bradley
2nd Battalion Royal Scots
Killed in Action: 25th September 1917
Perth Cemetery (China Wall), Belgium. Grave: 11-A-12

Patrick Bradley was born at Kildress, Cookstown. He enlisted in
Cookstown with the 2nd Battalion Royal Scots. During his
service Patrick attained the rank of Lance Corporal. He was
killed in action close to the village of Zillebeke in Belgium on
25th September 1917. He is buried in plot 11- row A- grave 12 at
Perth Cemetery (China Wall), Belgium. Patrick Bradley is
commemorated on Cookstown Cenotaph.

31237- Private Thomas Bell
2nd Battallion Royal Inniskilling Fusiliers
Died of Wounds: 28th September 1917
Coxyde Military Cemetery, Belgium. Grave: 4-B-23

Thomas was a son of James and Mary Bell of Chapel Street,
Cookstown.

He was employed by Mr. Bayne of Letteran, Lissan before going
to work in Glasgow. He enlisted with the 2nd Battalion Royal
Inniskilling Fusiliers in Glasgow in January 1917. His brother
James Bell had previously been wounded and returned to the
Western Front. Thomas was seriously wounded in September
1917 and was with his close friend Private Francis Hampsey
when he fell. He was taken to hospital in Vuerne and died of his
wounds there on 28th September 1917. He is buried at Coxyde
Military Cemetery, Belgium, in Plot 4, row B, grave 23. Private
Francis Hampsey survived the war and returned to Cookstown.
Thomas Bell is commemorated on Cookstown Cenotaph.

12/3299-Private Francis Donaghy
1st Battalion Auckland Regiment, New Zealand
Died of Wounds: 6th October 1917
Aged: 28
Nine Elms British Cemetery, Belgium.   Grave: 4-A-3

Francis Donaghy was a son of Francis and Maggie Donaghy of Dunnamore, Cookstown.

Some years before the First World War Francis had emigrated to New Zealand and settled in Auckland. He enlisted into the 1st Battalion Auckland Regiment and was seriously wounded at the beginning of October 1917. He died of wounds on 6th October and was buried in plot 4, row A, grave 3 at Nine Elms British Cemetery, Belgium. During the First World War New Zealand raised 110,368 troops - of which 16,697 lost their lives.

24217-Private Peter Mallon
7th Battalion Royal Inniskilling Fusiliers
Killed in Action: 9th October 1917
Age: 22
Croisilles British Cemetery, France.   Grave: 2-C-2

Peter Mallon was a son of John and Catherine Mallon of Church Street, Cookstown. The family had previously lived in Belfast where he enlisted. Peter was killed in action on 9th October 1917. He is buried in plot 2- row C- grave 2 at Croisilles British Cemetery, France. This cemetery is situated between Bapaume and Arras and is quite easy to find and is immaculately maintained. The Battalion War Diaries tell us that the 9th October was a quiet day as only two soldiers lost their lives. The other man killed on this day was David O'Hara who was born in Newry and lived in Lisburn. The two men were killed in separate incidents. David has no known grave and he is commemorated on Bay 6 on Arras Memorial to the Missing, France.

Peter Mallon is commemorated on Cookstown Cenotaph

32788-Private Thomas Alexander McReynolds
16th Battalion Warwickshire Regt
Killed In Action: 9th October 1917
Age: 25
Tyne Cot Memorial, Belgium. Panel: 23-28-163a.

Thomas Alexander McReynolds was the son of T.A. McReynolds, (Rural District Councilor), Kingsmills, Stewartstown, and Mrs. Mary E. McReynolds. Thomas volunteered for service when war was declared having previously served with the North Irish Horse before the war. He enlisted in Glasgow with the Dragoon Guards and was sent to France in 1914 where he was wounded twice. He transferred to the Royal Warwickshire Regiment in the autumn of 1917 during the Third Battle of Ypres and shortly after joining he was reported missing during an advance at Polygon Wood, Belgium. This advance led to very heavy casualties with sixty-one men, killed or missing from the 16th Battalion. A witness observed him being wounded and he was later declared dead. He has no known grave and Thomas is commemorated on Tyne Cot Memorial. He was twenty-five years of age. At the time of Thomas's death his younger brother, Austen McReynolds was serving with the Royal Garrison Artillery. Austen had seen service in Gallipoli, Egypt, France and Italy. Thomas is commemorated on St. Andrew's, Ardtrea Church of Ireland Roll of Honour and on Coagh War Memorial (RBL, Cookstown).

St. Andrew's Roll of Honour, Ardtrea

10490-Private Edward Leo Phair

1st Battalion Irish Guards
Died of Wounds: 10th October 1917
Age: 25
Dozinghem Cemetery, Belgium. Grave: 9-J- 4

Edward Leo Phair was born in Cookstown. He was the only son of Richard and Margaret Phair. The family later moved to live at 4, Brookvale Terrace, Portrush. Edward worked as a gardener at the Northern Counties Hotel in Portrush prior to enlisting with the Irish Guards in Coleraine.

Edward Phair joined the Battalion in 1915 and took part in the Battles of La Bassee and Leventie, and Loos. The Irish Guards were moved to the Somme region and took part in the capture of the village of Guillemont in September 1916. In the winter of 1916 he was given leave while suffering from a bad case of trench foot. He went home to recuperate and later rejoined his Battalion which was still based around Gouazeaucourt on the Somme. The Irish Guards were later moved to Belgium and in the fighting near Poperinghe on the 9th October 1917, Edward Phair was seriously wounded. He was taken to a casualty clearing station were he died of his wounds the next day. He is buried in plot 9- row J- grave 4 at Dozinghem Cemetery, Belgium.

He is commemorated on Cookstown Cenotaph, Coleraine War Memorial and Holy Trinity Church Roll of Honour, Portrush.

47464-Rifleman William Hunter

1st Battalion Royal Irish Rifles
Killed in Action: 24th October 1917
Age: 23
Prowse Point Cemetery, Belgium. Grave: 3-D-2

William was a son of Samuel and Rebecca Ann Hunter, who had lived for a time at Ballyronan, where William was born. They later moved to live in Magherafelt. Later still they moved to Belfast and settled at 23 Donegore Street. William enlisted in Belfast, joining the Royal Army Service Corps. He later transferred to 1st Battalion Royal Irish Rifles and was killed while serving with them on 24th October 1917. The family asked for the following inscription to be engraved on his headstone.

"Ever remembered by his loving Father and Mother".

William Hunter is buried in plot 3, row D, grave 2 at Prowse Point Cemetery, Belgium.

134797-Gunner William George Scott
328th Siege Battery Royal Garrison Artillery
Died of Wounds: 24th October 1917
Age: 21
Brighton (Bear road) Borough Cemetery. ZHN 4.

William George Scott was a son of William and Sarah Ann Scott (nee Scott) of Ballygrooby, Moneymore. He was born at Drumenagh Hill, near Ballyronan, where the family had a farm. The family moved to Ballygrooby, near Moneymore in1909. William and Sarah eventually had a family of nine children, Rachel, Harry, Jack, Ruth, Sarah, James, William-George, Alfred and May.

William George Scott enlisted in Cookstown with the Royal Garrison Artillery soon after the Battle of the Somme. He never returned home to Ballygrooby. He was still serving with the Artillery when he was seriously wounded on 2nd September 1917. He was brought back to hospital in Brighton, where he was visited by his sister Ruth just before he died. He passed away on 24th October 1917 and was buried in Brighton (Bear Road), Borough Cemetery, ZHN 4. He was twenty-one years of age. He is commemorated in Moneymore War Memorial (Assembly Rooms).The family believe that he enlisted only six months before he was wounded. Two of his brothers, Jack and Harry, also enlisted, both joining the Canadian Army. Jack enlisted in 1914, Harry in 1916. Harry was famous for being an excellent shot with a rifle, and served in France and Belgium as a sniper. During leave in England he won various competitions at Bisley. Jack joined the 90th Winnipeg Rifles alongside his cousin, John Sufferin Scott, at Valcartier Camp in September 1914. Despite being gassed, having his rifle smashed by shrapnel and bullet holes in his trousers and tunic, Jack survived the war, as did Harry. Their cousin, John Sufferin Scott, was killed in action on 15th August 1917. His story is also told in this book.

487453-Private James Davison

Princess Patricia's Canadian Light Infantry
(Eastern Ontario Regiment)
Died: 31st October 1917
Age: 30

Nine Elms British Cemetery, Belgium. Grave 8 B 20

Private James Davison was born on 3rd June 1887. He was the
son of Andrew and Clara Davison, of Drumrot, Moneymore,
County Londonderry and later of, 1817- 4th Avenue East,
Vancouver, British Columbia. James lived and worked in Calgary,
Canada as a travelling salesman before his enlistment.

He died on 31st October 1917 and is buried in grave 8-B-20 at
Nine Elms Cemetery, Belgium. He is commemorated on
Moneymore War Memorial (Assembly Rooms) and First
Presbyterian Roll of Honour, Moneymore.

Lieutenant Eric Wallace Harris

213 Siege Battery Royal Garrison Artillery
Died of Wounds: 4th November 1917
Age: 20
Lijssenthoek Military Cemetery, Belgium. Grave: 21- H-13

Lieutenant Eric Wallace Harris was born in Dublin and was the
only son of William Wallace Harris, Solicitor and Gertrude May
Harris, of "Chelmsford", Avoca Avenue, Blackrock, Dublin. He
entered Trinity College, Dublin prior to enlisting. He gained the
rank of Lieutenant and was attached to 213th Siege Battery, Royal
Garrison Artillery. He was seriously wounded in early November
1917. He died on 4th November and was interred in plot 21- row
H- grave 13 at Lijssenthoek Military Cemetery with full military
honours. After the war when the cemeteries were being put in
place his family asked for the following inscription to be placed
on his headstone.

"Death cannot sever love, and remembrance lasts for ever".

Eric Wallace Harris is commemorated on Stewartstown Cenotaph
and Donaghendry Church of Ireland, Stewartstown. He is also
commemorated on the War Memorial in Trinity College, Dublin.

22946-Private James Treanor
2nd Battalion Royal Irish Fusiliers
Killed in Action: 7th November 1917
Gaza War Cemetery, Israel. Grave: 20-B-12

James Treanor was born in Clogher, County Tyrone. The family later moved to live in Pomeroy. James enlisted in Portadown, where he joined the 2nd Battalion Royal Irish Fusiliers. In 1917 he was serving in the Middle East, and was killed in action there on 7th November 1917. At roll call later that day, twenty men were found to be either killed or missing.

James Treanor is interred in plot 20- row B- grave 12 at Gaza War Cemetery, Israel.

437103-Private James Hegan
7th Battalion Canadian Infantry
Killed in Action: 12th November 1917
Age: 23
Dozinghem Cemetery, Belgium. Grave: 13-F-16

James Hegan was a son of William John and Mary Hegan of Ballysudden, Cookstown, and was born on 27th March 1894. As a young man he emigrated to Canada and settled at Edmonton. He worked in Canada as a farmer and was still single when he enlisted at Edmonton on 6th May 1915. James was described as being five feet nine and a half inches tall, with grey eyes, light brown hair and a ruddy complexion. He joined the 7th Battalion Canadian Infantry and was killed in action on 12th November 1917. He was twenty-three years of age. James is interred in plot 13, row F, grave 16 at Dozinghem Cemetery in Belgium. He is also commemorated on Cookstown Cenotaph and his name was added to the family headstone in Cookstown Cemetery, where it is inscribed that he died of wounds on 12th November 1917. His father, William John, died at on 20th June 1930, age 79.

281545-Gunner William Thompson
237th Siege Battery Royal Garrison Artillery
Died: 12th November 1917
Noeux-les-Mines Communal Cemetery Extension, France.
Grave: 3-A-18

William Thompson was born at Meenan, County Down and lived for a while in Tandragee, County Armagh. He moved to Cookstown to work and lived for a number of years at 12 Fortview Terrace, Chapel Road, with his wife Mary and their five children, William, Samuel, Alice, Jean and Violet. William Thompson enlisted with the Royal Garrison Artillery in Belfast.

He is described as having died at the front on 12th November 1917. He was buried in plot 3- row A- grave 18 at Neoux-les-Mines Communal Cemetery Extension, France.

The cemetery at Noeux-les-Mines was chiefly used by 6th and 7th Casualty Clearing Stations between, August 1917 and December 1918.

William Thompson is commemorated on the Tandragee War Memorial.

40651-Private Alexander Martin

10th Battalion Royal Inniskilling Fusiliers
Killed in Action: 20th November 1917
Age: 27
Cambrai Memorial, France. Panel: 5-6

Alexander Martin was the fifth born son of James and Sarah
Martin of Killycolpy, Stewartstown and a nephew of Mrs.
Straghan of 14 Cromwell Road, Belfast. Alexander was lodging
with his aunt in Belfast as he was working in the city with the
firm of Rennick, Robinson & Co. Alexander had originally
enlisted in the North Irish Horse on 25th May 1915 at Antrim and
later transferred to the Royal Inniskilling Fusiliers. He went
overseas in a draft to bring the 10th Battalion up to strength on
9th January 1917. One of his brothers was wounded in action on
16th August 1917 at the Third Battle of Ypres, but recovered.
Another brother was serving in the Royal Navy. Alexander was
Worshipful Master of Magdalene Church Defenders Temperance
L.O.L. 615 and a member of R.B.P. 12.

On 20th November 1917, three hundred and eighty one tanks,
followed closely by infantry, attacked along a six mile front and
at 6.20am 1,000 guns opened up with an intense bombardment on
the German lines. The 10th Inniskillings went into attack at the
Battle of Cambrai with 27 officers and 430 other ranks. Their
objective was to bombard the German machine gun posts on a
slag heap near the Canal-du-Nord. This slag heap was the by
product of the Canal that the French had been building before the
start of the war. This advance took on a different style to that used
at the Somme. The infantry didn't advance across open country.
Instead they fought their way through the German communication
trenches rather than straight through the German lines, this effort
gave better cover from small arm and artillery fire. No tanks were
assigned in the sector held by the 10th Inniskillings and the
hurricane bombardment by heavy artillery on the slag heap
commenced instantaneously at 8.30am. The Trench Mortar
Battery pounded the front German trenches and machine gun
posts and after a few minutes, switched back and forth to other
targets as the infantry fought their way through. After a short but
fierce fight the 10th Inniskillings had seized their objective by
9.30am in the middle of a blizzard, clearing over 1.5 miles of the
front line trenches of the Hindenburg Line. The allied artillery had
started a programme of hitting prearranged targets as the infantry
advanced through the German lines.

The 10th Inniskilling's gains were considerable and casualties were light. 1 officer and 45 other ranks were wounded in the advance. Only one man, Private Alexander Martin was killed. Sadly he has no known grave and is commemorated on panel 5-6 on Cambrai Memorial, France.

Alexander Martin is commemorated on Albany Presbyterian Roll of Honour. His name is missing off Stewartstown Cenotaph.

14160-Rifleman Charles Campbell
10th Battalion Royal Irish Rifles
Killed in Action: 22nd November 1917
Cambrai Memorial. France Panel: 10

Charles Campbell was born in Stewartstown and enlisted in Belfast, joining the 10th Battalion Royal Irish Rifles. He had been with them almost from the beginning of the war, and had been through most of the earlier engagements. He was killed at the Battle of Cambrai on 22nd November 1917. There is no known grave and Charles is commemorated on panel 10, on the Cambrai Memorial, France.

28158-Private William James McMinn

1st Battalion Royal Inniskilling Fusiliers
Died of Wounds: 22nd November 1917
Age: 19
Rocquigny-Equancourt Road Cemetery, France. Grave: 3-B-27

William James McMinn was a son of John and Mary Jane McMinn of Coalisland, County Tyrone. He was born in the parish of Derryloran, Cookstown. He was living in Motherwell and enlisted in Hamilton, Scotland with the 1st Battalion Royal Inniskilling Fusiliers some time in late 1916. William was wounded at the Battle of Cambrai and removed to hospital and later died of his wounds. He is buried in plot 1, row C, grave 20 at Rocquigny-Equancourt Road Cemetery, France.

15452-Private Robert Davison

Royal Inniskilling Fusiliers Depot
Died of Illness: 2nd December 1917
Age: 21
Desertlyn Churchyard, Moneymore, County Londonderry   335

Robert was a son of Robert and Sarah Jane Davison of Lisalbanagh, Magherafelt, and was born there in 1896. He enlisted at Finner Camp in County Donegal joining "D" Company of the 10th Battalion Royal Inniskilling Fusiliers but due to his state of health was employed at the Depot. Robert died of an illness on 2nd December 1917 and is buried in Desertlyn Churchyard, Moneymore and is commemorated on Moneymore War Memorial, (Assembly Rooms) and at Union Road Presbyterian Church Roll of Honour in Magherafelt.

362346-Gunner Andrew Duncan
Royal Garrison Artillery 393rd Siege Battery
(Lancashire and Cheshire)
Killed in Action: 5th December 1917
Age: 20
Bedford House Cemetery, Belgium. Enclosure 4: Grave: 2-D-18

Andrew was a son of Andrew and Margaret Duncan of Drumquin,
County Tyrone. He was born in Pomeroy and enlisted into the
Royal Garrison Artillery, 393rd Siege Battery. He was working
and living in Liverpool where he enlisted, joining the Lancashire
and Cheshire Regiment. Andrew was killed in action on 5th
December 1917 and is buried in Enclosure 4- plot 2- row D-
grave 18 at Bedford House Cemetery, Belgium.

D.6281-Private Thomas Cullen
6th Inniskilling Dragoons, Household Cavalry and Cavalry of the
Line
Died of Wounds: 6th December 1917
Age: 25
Tincourt Cemetery, France. Grave: 4 - A - 17.

Thomas Cullen was a son of David and Elizabeth Cullen of
Pomeroy. The family later moved to live at 363 Northcross
Street, Leadgate, Durham.

Thomas enlisted with the Household Cavalry and Cavalry of the
Line, at Chester-le-Street, County Durham. At the beginning of
December 1917 Thomas was seriously wounded. He was
removed to one of the Casualty Clearing Stations situated at
Tincourt but died of his wounds on 6th December 1917. He is
buried in plot 4- row A- grave 17 at Tincourt Cemetery, France.

The Halifax Tragedy
6th December 1917

Halifax, Nova Scotia was the headquarters of No: 6 Military District during both world wars. The extensive harbor in Halifax was heavily defended and was the main port of embarkation for Canadian troops serving abroad. In the First World War, the city had nine military Hospitals with almost 1,500 beds.

On the morning of 6th December 1917, a collision took place in the harbour between the Imo a Norwegian vessel employed in the Belgian relief effort (which was on it's way to New York to pick up supplies) and Mont Blanc a French vessel loaded with ammunition. The ships collided at the narrowest point of the harbour, just outside of the large Bedford Basin staging area. The Mont Blanc was carrying over 35 tons of benzol fuel, 200 tons of TNT, 2,300 tons of picric acid and 10 tons of gun cotton. It is believed that immediately after the collision, the on deck stores of benzol began to leak and ignited soon after. The crew, knowing the danger that they were in, abandoned ship and headed for Dartmouth while the ship drifted towards Pier 6 on the Halifax side of the port. A large group of bystanders, unaware of the volatile cargo, started to gather near the pier to watch the Mont Blanc as the ship drew closer. Barely twenty minutes after the initial collision the ship exploded. In the resulting explosion, half a square mile of the city was destroyed with 1,600 lives lost in the blast, rising to 2,000 later on. Two hospitals were ruined and one was badly damaged. The explosion immediately severed all lines of communication, and was reported to be heard as far away as Prince Edward Island.

In the aftermath, varying accounts argued as to the exact number of wounded there were, the figure was put in the region of 9,000 injured, including 200 - 600 people blinded by the blast. One of the longest running measures of assistance to victims of the explosion was the Halifax Relief Commission, more recently administered by the Federal Department of Veterans Affairs, Canada.

Robert Donnelly from Cookstown was discharged from Army service after 2 years in 1915 and took his wife Sarah (nee McCrae) and daughter Mary Freda to live in Ottowa, Canada, where he subsequently joined the Royal Navy in Halifax, Nova

Scotia, with the rank of Able Seaman. Sarah was the daughter of Mr. and Mrs. Andrew McCrae, of Lisnanane, Sandholes, Cookstown. Robert's duties with the Royal Navy included service on a submarine and was based on, HMCS Niobe assisting with mine sweeping in Canadian waters. Robert and Sarah had another child while living at 6 Veith Street, Halifax. Ethel Elizabeth was 11 months old at this time and Sarah was 8 months pregnant on the morning of 6th December 1917. Robert was on board his ship, Niobe when he heard the explosion on the Mont Blanc.

After he returned to shore, he searched the ruins of his home at Veith Street to find the body of his pregnant wife Sarah with still born child and daughters, Mary, aged 6 and Ethel, aged 11 months. They had been killed in the blast.

Five days after the disaster, the Officers and men of HMCS Niobe paid the funeral expenses for Robert. Sarah was buried with her two children and still born child in the same casket on 11th December 1917, at St. John's Cemetery, Halifax, Nova Scotia.

The Halifax Fort Massey Memorial stands within the grounds of Fort Massey Cemetery and commemorates the names of two servicemen who were killed in the explosion but whose bodies were never found.

751-Rifleman John White
14th Battalion Royal Irish Rifles
Killed in Action: 7th December 1917
Cambrai Memorial, France 10

John White was born in the Shankhill district of Belfast and went to live in Lower Coagh just before the start of the First World War. He went back to Belfast to enlist with 14th Battalion Royal Irish Rifles. John was killed in action on 7th December 1917 after the Battle of Cambrai. He has no known grave and is commemorated on the Cambrai Memorial, panel 10. He is also commemorated on Coagh War Memorial (RBL, Cookstown).

G/36955 Private Robert Reid
36th Battalion Royal Fusiliers
Transferred to (63968), 107th Battalion, Labour Corps
Died of Wounds: 12th December 1917
Tincourt New British Cemetery, France. Grave. 4 B 22

Robert Reid was born Plumstead in Kent, but lived for a time at Drumgornal, Stewartstown; County Tyrone. He was living in East Ham before he enlisted with the Royal Fusiliers in East Ham, Essex. He later transferred to the Labour Corps and died of wounds on the 12th December 1917. He is buried in plot 4- row B- grave 22 at Tincourt New British Cemetery, France. He is commemorated on Stewartstown Presbyterian Church Roll of Honour and Stewartstown Cenotaph.

6500-Rifleman Thomas John Graham
14th Battalion Royal Irish Rifles
Killed in Action: 16th December 1917
Thiepval Memorial, France. Panel: 15A-15B

Thomas John Graham was born in Pomeroy. When he enlisted in Belfast he did not name his parents as next of kin, so they may have passed on. He joined the 14th Battalion Royal Irish Rifles and following a number of years spent at the front Thomas was killed in action on 16th December 1917. He was the only man from his Battalion killed on this day. He has no known grave and is commemorated on panel 15A-15B on the Thiepval Memorial, France.

202071-Private Andrew Colvin M.M.
(Military Medal / Belgian 'Croix de Guerre')
3rd Battalion Canadian Infantry
(Central Ontario Regiment)
Died: 23rd December 1917
Bruay Communal Cemetery Extension, France. Grave L 3

Andrew Colvin was born 5th February 1888 and was the son of Elizabeth Colvin, Ballynenagh, Moneymore, County Londonderry.

Andrew emigrated to Canada and lived at 15 Gwynne Avenue, Toronto, where he worked as a carpenter.

He enlisted with the Canadian Infantry on 10th November 1915 and his attestation papers say that he was unmarried. He was 5 feet 4 inches tall, grey eyes, black hair and a dark complexion. He had a half inch scar on his upper lip and a scar on the first finger of his left hand.

He served as a dispatch rider with his battalion in France, carrying messages to and from the front lines. During one of his missions he came under attack from the enemy positions and was seriously wounded but managed to stay conscious until he got the message through to his destination. For the action, Andrew was awarded the Military Medal. He was also the recipient of the Belgium 'Croix de Guerre'.

Belgian 'Croix de Guerre'

Andrew Colvin is buried at Bruay Communal Cemetery Extension, France in grave L 3

Nearly half the 443 burials in this small cemetery extension are of men from the Canadian Corps who occupied this sector of the front line from early 1917.

Andrew Colvin (M.M. Croix de Guerre) is commemorated on Moneymore War Memorial (Assembly Rooms).

The Military Medal (or M.M.) was established in wartime Britain by King George V on 25th March 1916. The Medal was initially awarded to non-commissioned officers and men of the Army (including Royal Flying Corps and Royal Naval Division) for individual or associated acts of bravery which were insufficient to merit an award of a Distinguished Conduct Medal (or D.C.M.). Awards of the Military Medal were announced in the London Gazette but without a citation describing the act of bravery for which it was issued. As many as 115,600, were awarded during World War One.

Military Medal

The Belgian Croix de Guerre (or War Cross) was instituted on 25th October 1915 as a means of formally recognizing acts of heroism performed by individuals of any of the allied powers during World War One.

Lieutenant William John McVeigh

7th Battalion Royal Munster Fusiliers
Killed in Action: 28th December 1917
Age: 24
Jerusalem War Cemetery, Israel Grave: F-31

William John McVeigh was a son of James McVeigh of Loy Hill, Cookstown.

He was a past student of St. Mary's College, Dundalk and had studied at University College, Dublin between 1910 and 1911. After five months training as a Cadet he was gazetted Second Lieutenant in March 1915. After seeing a great deal of active service on the Western Front and being wounded on three occasions he was gazetted Lieutenant and sent to Salonika. He also served in Egypt and Palestine. He was killed in action on 28th December 1917 and is buried in Jerusalem War Cemetery, in grave F-31. An Officer commanding the 6th Royal Munster Fusiliers sent a letter from Palestine to Mrs. McVeigh on 31st December 1917, in which he said:

"I regret very much that your son was killed in action near Abu Dineen on 28th, while gallantly leading his platoon over the walls into Alay in face of heavy rifle and machine-gun fire. The loss of your son is deeply felt by us all, he was such a fine officer, especially keen on machine-gun work, and we cannot spare him. May I offer you, in your great sorrow, on behalf of myself and the officers of the battalion, our sincere regret in your great loss."

Lieutenant William J. McVeigh is commemorated on Cookstown Cenotaph and the family headstone in St. Luran's Roman Catholic Graveyard, Cookstown as William John McVeagh.

Miss Anderson of Cookstown received a letter of thanks from Private Francis White, a native of Coalisland, who happened to obtain one of the scarves sent out by her to soldiers at the Front. He mentions the interesting fact that Lieutenant McVeigh, Cookstown, is platoon Commander. He happily expresses the men's opinion of that young officer as follows.

Dear Miss, I'm sure you'll be surprised to get a line from me
A lonely Munster Fusilier from the green isle o'er the sea
It's just a word or two of thanks for the gift I had today
I mean the scarf you kindly sent, which came, by chance, my way

Tonight as I was standing near the Quarter Masters store
"Fall in" and "Cover off", I heard our Sergeant loudly roar
We toe'd the line and "numbered off", then quickly marched away

to the billet of our Officer, Lt. J McVeigh.

Before proceeding further, just a word or two, I'll say
In praise of this same officer, Lt. J McVeigh
He never bully-rags his men, or orders them about
He's just a perfect gentleman, a sportsman out and out.

He never sees us short of fags or tobacco for a smoke
And, another thing, he's always gain to give or take a joke
He doesn't swank, or put on "side", Oh no, he's not that sort
Just ask "D Coy" what he is and they'll tell you he's a sport

We halted at his billet door, when he told his servant Fox
To open out that parcel, and to hand him out the socks
He gave a pair to every man, and the socks we needed bad
There were neither legs, nor heels, nor toes in the only pair I had

Well, after we received the socks, he told us all to stay
As he said he had some mittens, and some scarves to give away
He hadn't quite sufficient scarves to go around the lot
But I don't care, I'm satisfied, for the splendid one I got.

Reprinted from: Mid Ulster Mail 1918

Menin Gate Memorial, Ypres, Belgium.

The Menin Gate Memorial was formerly known as the Antwerp Gate and records the names of 54,416 men who have no known graves and were lost in the Ypres Salient.

It includes the names of 40,244 British (who died before 16th August 1916). 6,983 Canadians, 6,198 Australians, 564 South Africans, 421 Indians, 6 British West Indians. Men from Cookstown District Council area are commemorated here.

The town of Ypres was totally destroyed during the First World War and was restored throughout the 1920's. Winston Churchill had suggested leaving the town as a ruin, as a reminder of the devastation of war, he said, "Ypres, Britain's most hallowed ground." Only one cemetery lies within the walls of the gate and it can be reached by walking along the ramparts.

The Cloth Hall and Cathedral were also restored. St George's Anglican Chapel was built there for the ex patriots who stayed to work in Belgium and help with the war graves restoration, it too is a memorial.

The Last Post has been sounded by Ypres Fire Service every night since 11th November 1929, except when the town was under occupation by German forces during World War 2, between 20th May 1940 and 6th September 1944.

Building work on the Menin Gate in the 1920's

2739-Corporal Thomas Espey
4th Regiment, South African Infantry
Died: 7th January 1918
Fins New British Cemetery, Sorel-Le-Grand, France.
Grave: 3 F 13

Corporal Thomas Espey was born and lived at Gortreagh, Cookstown.

He emigrated to South Africa and enlisted with the 4th Regiment, South African Infantry on 16th August 1915.

South Africa raised a brigade of 4 Infantry Battalions for the Western Front, in addition to 5 Batteries of Heavy Artillery, a Field Ambulance, a Royal Engineers Signal Company and a General Hospital. It is also estimated that around 3,000 South African men joined the Royal Flying Corps. The Infantry battalions were raised from the four main provinces of the South African Union. 1st Regiment (Cape Province), 2nd Regiment (Natal and Orange Free State), 3rd Regiment (Transvaal and Rhodesia) and the 4th Regiment was unique in it's formation, known as the South African Scottish, it was raised from the Transvaal Scottish and Cape Town Highlanders and wore the Atholl Murray tartan as part of their uniform. While in France the entire Brigade came under orders from the 9th Scottish Division and their first major engagement there, was at the Somme in July 1916, where the 4th Regiment was involved in the fighting at Trones Wood. Then the entire brigade attacked at Longueval (Delville Wood) on the afternoon of 14th July 1916. Longueval is the site, where the South African Memorial and Museum are today.

The Brigade went on to serve in the Battle of Arras and Third Battle of Ypres in 1917 and Gauche Wood in March 1918 during Operation Michael/German Spring Offensive.

When the Germans launched their second major offensive in 1918 during the second phase of the Battle of Lys, the Brigade was ordered to counter attack at Messines.

On the 24th April 1918 the 1st, 2nd, and 4th, Regiments were amalgamated, temporarily becoming South African Regiment and were reformed again in September 1918.

On the 11th September 1918, the brigade finally parted with the 9th Scottish Division and joined the 66th (2nd West Lancashire) Division and aided in the recapture of Le Cateau on the 17th - 18th October 1918. Over 146,000 men served with South African Units during World War 1 with 18,600 casualties including 6,600 dead.

Thomas Espey is buried in plot 3, row F, grave 13 at Fins New British Cemetery, Sorel-Le Grand, France. He is also commemorated on Cookstown Cenotaph.

4583-Private Joseph Mayne
6th Battalion Connaught Rangers
Died of Wounds: 10th January 1918
Age: 21
Tincourt New British Cemetry, France. Grave: 4-E-12.

Joseph Mayne was the youngest son of James and Mary Mayne, Ardcumber, Tullywiggan, Cookstown. He was working as a barman in Belfast at the outbreak of the First World War. On the formation of the Irish Brigade, he joined the 6th Connaught Rangers on the 19th July 1915 at 61 Mill Street, Belfast, giving his home address as 10 Anne Street, Belfast. Joseph Mayne was described as 5 feet 8 inches tall and 140 lbs in weight. He named his mother, Mary as next of kin. He proceeded to Fermoy, County Cork for training with the 6th Connaught Rangers on 21st July 1915.

Following training, the Battalion with the strength of 36 Officers and 952 other ranks sailed from Southampton to Le Harve on the 17th December 1915. He had been on active service in France since Christmas 1915.

The 6th Connaught Rangers fought at the Somme in September 1916 and lost 23 officers and 407 other ranks, almost half its strength. Joseph Mayne was home on leave in Cookstown a number of times, including a period between 18th to 24th August 1917.

On the 10th January 1918 the Battalion was in the front line at Lempire, east of Peronne and came under attack from an enemy raiding party under the cover of a bombardment. The Germans attempted to enter the advanced Lewis-gun post in the Lempire Road, which they bombed, wounding three men but were repulsed. A few minutes before 4.00am the enemy tried to raid one of the Lewis-gun posts, which was placed, necessarily, in an isolated position, well out in 'No Man's Land', about 150 yards in front of the fire trench, in a sunken road that crossed both lines of trenches. The raiders came across the snow in the dark, camouflaged in white overalls. The double sentries on duty in the sunken road heard, but in the darkness could not see any movement in front of them. Hesitating to shoot, they challenged. The immediate reply was a volley of hand grenades. Joseph Mayne, who was in charge of the Lewis-gun, was wounded in many places, including his stomach, his left arm severely damaged. Mortally wounded, and with blood pouring from his arm, he struggled up, and leaning against the parapet, with his unwounded hand discharged a full magazine (47 rounds) into the enemy, who broke and ran. Not one of them reached the Connaught lines. Joseph Mayne then collapsed unconscious across his gun. He was taken to No.55 Casualty Clearing Station situated at Tincourt and died of his wounds a short time later. He is buried in plot 4, row E, grave 12 at Tincourt New British Cemetery, France.

Tincourt was used by these Casualty Clearing Stations throughout 1917 and they were still based there at the end of the war. At the time of his death, Joseph's elder brother, John, was serving in the Medical Department of 9th Infantry, American Army, in France. Joseph Mayne's Commanding Officer, Rowland Fielding, recommended that Private Mayne be awarded the Victoria Cross for his outstanding bravery, but this was not awarded and he was posthumously 'Mentioned in Dispatches' by Sir Douglas Haig's dispatch on 7th April 1918.

His personal effects, including a letter, 15 photographs, a wallet, a religious medal and a book along with his identity disc were sent home to his family on 11th May 1918.

Joseph Mayne is commemorated on Cookstown Cenotaph.

56984 - Private David Crooks Mitchell

1st Battalion Canterbury Regiment,
New Zealand Expeditionary Forces
Died: 11th January 1918

David Crooks Mitchell was the son of Crooks Mitchell and Jane Mitchell (nee Crooks), of Northbrook Road, Rangiora, Australia and formerly of Ballybriest, Cookstown.

He has no known grave and is commemorated at Buttes New British Cemetery (NZ) Memorial, Polygon Wood, Belgium, and on Claggan Presbyterian Roll of Honour, Lissan, Cookstown.

32499-Lance Corporal William John Albert Bell
Otago Regiment, New Zealand
Died of Wounds: 21st February 1918
Age: 29
Lijssenthoek Cemetery, Belgium.   Grave: 27-E-8a

William John Albert Bell was a son of John Bell and Margaret
Ann Bell of Ballygoney, Coagh, and brother of Harper Bell and
Adelaide Bell, Coagh, Miss Laura Bell and Mrs. Margaret
Lamont of New York, USA.

William J.A. Bell was formerly a Royal Irish Constabulary, Police
Officer and had served in Fermanagh and at Brown Square
Barracks in Belfast. He resigned from the police in 1912 and
emigrated to New Zealand, where he joined the New Zealand
police, and was soon promoted to the fingerprint office of the
criminal investigation department. His mother passed away on
29th June 1914. When war broke out, he volunteered and enlisted
in the army. During his training with the army he was promoted
to Sergeant, finally gaining the rank of Sergeant Major at the time
of his arrival back in England where he passed the examination
for commissioned rank but he decided not to accept it. He was
deputed to training work in England, but was so anxious to get to
the front that he gave up his rank and went as a private. Soon
after, however, he earned promotion on the field. He was twice
wounded, once in the leg and again in the neck. He was home on
leave in Coagh in the summer of 1917. It was while in action on
17th February 1918 that he received severe wounds and was
taken to No2 Canadian Casualty Clearing Station where he died
on 21st February. His father, Sergeant John Bell received a letter
from one of the nursing sisters at the Clearing Station which said.

*Dear Mr Bell. Before this reaches you, you will have heard that
sad news of your boy's great sacrifice. I know the Chaplain here
has written to you already, but because your boy especially asked
me to write, I want to send you this letter and express my
sympathy for you in your grief, though could you have seen how
splendid he was in those last few hours, I am sure there could be
room for nothing in your heart but pride that your son was so
much of a man, and had taken his courage and his manhood
home with him to his God. As you probably know, he was shot
through the chest, and from the first his condition was a very
critical one. Later the doctors knew it was hopeless, and he was
not allowed to suffer. He too, knew towards the end that he could
not live, and spoke to me of dying, and asked me if, after he had*

gone I would write to his father. I asked him if he had any special messages to send, and he said, just tell him how and when I died. He told me that you were in hospital in Ireland. He is buried in the Cemetery here. It is called Lijssenthoek Cemetery and is about a mile from Poperinghe. The graves are carefully tended and during the last year the cemetery has become a very large one. The few personal effects your boy brought here with him will be sent to you through the war office in England.

Your son came into our ward during the night at 2.20am, Feb 17th and he passed away at 5.00am on the morning of the 21st. He was so sweet and grateful for every little thing we did for him, and his beautiful character was so clearly marked on his face and fine physique, that my heart aches for you in the loss of such a son.

I remain yours, very sincerely. **Claire Gass, Nursing Sister.**

W.J.A. Bell is commemorated on Coagh War Memorial (R.B.L. Cookstown)

The Soldiers and Sailors Memorial Hall, Coagh, built in 1921.

Photo courtesy of Tom Jebb

18158 - Private Edward Magee
5th Battalion Royal Irish Fusiliers
Killed in Action: 10th March 1918
Jerusalem War Memorial, Israel. Panel 45

Edward Magee was born in Portadown and lived at Milburn Street, Cookstown, with his wife Roseanne and their two boys, William and Joseph.

He came to Cookstown to work at Wilson's Mill. He enlisted in the army in February 1915 and was subsequently wounded in action at Gallipoli. While recovering from his wounds he was allowed home on leave to see his family before going back to active service. He was killed in Action on 10th March 1918 in Palestine.

He has no known grave and is commemorated on panel- 45 on Jerusalem War Memorial, Israel. He is also commemorated on Cookstown Cenotaph.

He leaves behind an aching heart,
That loved him very dear;
A heart that will never forget
His memory written here.

Oh! Never, never, can we part
For in my heart thou dost remain,
I'll cherish him within my heart,
Till we united, meet again.

Forget him! No, I never will
As years roll on, I love him still.
On his soul, Sweet Jesus, have mercy.

Submitted for publication (Mid-Ulster Mail, 1918) by his wife Roseanne

Major Hubert Maxwell Lenox-Conyngham D.S.O.
(Distinguished Service Order)
Army Veterinary Corps
Died of Illness: 15th March 1918
Age: 47
Kilgobbin Old Church Cemetery, Dublin, Ireland

Hubert Maxwell Lenox-Conyngham was born in Dublin. He was
a son of Sir William and Lady Lenox-Conyngham of Springhill
House, Moneymore, and the brother of John Staples Molesworth
Lenox-Conyngham. He was married to Eva Darley of The
Paddocks, Kilsby, Rugby and lived at Fernhill, Sandyford,
Dublin.

He joined the Army Veterinary Service Corps in 1897 and served
in East Africa (Somaliland Campaign) in 1902-03. During the
First World War, he attained the rank Major and was 'Mentioned
in Despatches' and awarded the D.S.O. (Distinguished Service
Order). He gained the rank of Brevet-Lieutenant Colonel in June
1917. He died of illness on Friday the 15th March 1918 at
Chester and was brought home to Dublin, where he is buried in
the north-west part of Kilgobbin Old Church Cemetery, Dublin.

He is commemorated on Coagh War Memorial (Royal British
Legion, Cookstown), on Moneymore War Memorial (Assembly
Rooms) and Kilternan Church of Ireland Roll of Honour, Dublin.

11701- Private Patrick Barton
2nd Battalion Royal Inniskilling Fusiliers
Killed in Action: 21st March 1918
Essigny -le-Grand German Cemetery, Memorial 10
Grand Seracourt Cemetery, France.

Patrick was born in Broxburn, Linlithgow, and enlisted in Coatbridge, Scotland. The family lived in Lisburn and Cookstown.

On the morning of 21st March 1918, the Germans launched the Spring Offensive or Kaiserschlact beginning with Operation Michael on a fifty mile front between the Sensee and Oise Rivers, penetrating deep into the lines of the British Fifth Army and the right wing of the British Third Army. At this point in the war, the German army had developed Stormtrooper units. Their tactic was to attack and disrupt enemy headquarters, artillery units and supply depots, pushing through the British lines and leaving the strong points to be mopped up by follow up troops. Although the British were aware of an imminent attack, the weight of the enemy bombardment and ferocity of the advance was a surprise. The attack was made under the cover of fog. Within a matter of days the Germans had advanced over twenty miles into Allied held territory. By 5th April 1918 Operation Michael was called off. The allies had lost an estimated 255,000 men (British, Commonwealth, French and American). They also lost 1,300 artillery pieces and 200 tanks as they withdrew. German losses amounted to an estimated 239,000 men, largely the specialist shocktroops or Stosstruppen.

Patrick Barton was reported missing, killed in action in fierce hand to hand fighting, when the enemy, under the cover of a thick fog, attacked the British lines. He was most likely a wounded prisoner of the Germans, dying later of his wounds. He was interred in Essigny-le-Grand German Cemetery at Memorial 10. Grand Seracourt Cemetery is only a short distance away, and his remains were later moved to there. Patrick Barton is commemorated on Cookstown Cenotaph

20321-Private Hugh Hagan

7th/8th Battalion Royal Inniskilling Fusiliers
Killed in Action: 21st March 1918
Pozieres Memorial, France. Panel: 38-40

Hugh Hagan was born at Tamlaghtmore and worked at Greenvale
Mill (Adair's), Cookstown. He enlisted in Omagh, with the 7th
Battalion Royal Inniskilling Fusiliers. The 7th Battalion went to
France in February 1916 and had seen many fierce engagements
by the time of the German Spring Offensive in March of 1918.
The Battalion first seen action at the Battle of Hulluch in April
1916, followed by action on the Somme (Guillemont and
Guinchy) in September 1916, and the Battle of Messines
(Inniskilling Wood) in June 1917, followed by the Third Battle of
Ypres (Delva Farm), Langemarck, in August 1917. It was after
Langemarck that the 7th and 8th Battalions of Inniskillings were
amalgamated.

On the morning of the 21st March 1918, The Germans launched a
massive offensive along a 50 mile front, which in a few days
would drive the allies back over twenty miles. Hugh Hagan was
killed in action on the first day of the offensive. He has no known
grave and is commemorated on panel 38-40 on the Pozieres
Memorial, France.

He is also commemorated on Cookstown Cenotaph.

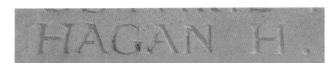

Inscription on Pozieres Memorial

29851-Private Patrick McCann

7th/8th Battalion Royal Inniskilling Fusilers
Killed in Action: 21st March 1918
Pozieres Memorial, France. Panel: 38-40

Patrick McCann was born at Ardtrea, Stewartstown and at the
outbreak of the First War his family were living in Moneymore.
He enlisted at Omagh, with the 8th Battalion Royal Inniskilling
Fusiliers. He was killed in action during the German Spring
Offensive on the 21st March 1918. He has no known grave and
he is commemorated on panel 38-40 on Pozieres Memorial,
France.

24715-Lance Corporal Laurence McKenna
7/8th Battalion Royal Inniskilling Fusiliers
Killed in Action: 21st March 1918
Pozieres Memorial, France. Panel: 38 - 40

Laurence was born at Kildress, County Tyrone. He enlisted with
the 7th Battalion Royal Inniskilling Fusiliers at Pomeroy. On
23rd August 1917 the 7th Battalion and 8th Battalion
amalgamated to form the 7/8th Battalion. Laurence had been
promoted to Lance Corporal and had gained vast experience. By
the time of the German Spring Offensive he had been through
many of the main engagements of the First World War. A surprise
attack came on the morning of the 21st March 1918. A dense
clinging mist enveloped everything and visibility was limited. The
Battalion became involved in heavy hand to hand fighting. It was
during the fighting that Laurence McKenna was lost. The
battalion were routed and forced to withdraw, leaving wounded
and dying men where they lay.

Laurence McKenna is commemorated on panel 38-40 on Pozieres
Memorial, France.

20325-Private Charles O'Neill
7/8th Battalion Royal Inniskilling Fusiliers
Killed in Action: 21st March 1918
Age: 26
Pozieres Memorial, France. Panel: 38-40

Charles O'Neill was a son of Mary O'Neill of Ballyrogully, Loup,
Moneymore. He enlisted with Royal Inniskilling Fusiliers in
Magherafelt.

Charles O'Neill was killed in action on 21st March 1918, during
Operation Michael, the first day of the German Spring Offensive,
also known as the Lundendorf Offensive. He has no known grave
and is commemorated on panel 38-40 on Pozieres Memorial,
France.

Inscription on Pozieres Memorial

9958-Private Joseph Stewart

7th /8th Battalion Royal Inniskilling Fusiliers
Killed in Action: 21st March 1918
Age: 24
Pozieres Memorial, France. Panel: 38-40

Joseph Stewart was born in Pomeroy and was a son of Mrs. Annie Mabin.

He lived with his wife Lily Stewart at Church Street, Cookstown. He enlisted in Omagh with the Royal Inniskilling Fusiliers.

Joseph Stewart was killed in action on 21st March 1918, the first day of the German Spring offensive. He has no known grave and is commemorated on panel 38-40 on the Pozieres Memorial, France. He is commemorated on Cookstown Cenotaph and St. Luran's Church of Ireland Roll of Honour, Derryloran, Cookstown.

Inscription on Pozieres Memorial

27687-Corporal William (Billy) Mayne

9th Battalion Royal Inniskilling Fusiliers
Killed in Action: 21st March 1918
Savy British Cemetery.
Roupy Road German Cemetery Memorial 34, France.

William Mayne was born at Anaghananam, Sandholes, Cookstown.

He joined the ranks of the Inniskiliing Fusiliers along with his friends, Isaac Black, Sandy Little, Robert Hogshaw and John Kerr from the village of Sandholes. They trained at Finner Camp, Ballyshannon, County Donegal and Shane's Park Camp, Randalstown, County Antrim. Soon after William enlisted he was promoted to the rank of Corporal.

The late Mrs. Jane Swail, Sandholes, recollected, when she was a child, seeing her brother Isaac Black, Sandy Little, Billy Mayne and Robert (wee Bob) Hogshaw walking out from Cookstown train station to the Sandholes village when they came home on leave wearing their uniforms, and all the local children going out to greet them. The following letter was sent to his sister Cissie, after the Somme Offensive, July 1916:

My Dear Sister, Just a few lines in answer to your most welcome letter. Sorry to see by it that you weren't doing so well. I hope you are keeping well now. Well Cissie, I was speaking to John Kerr the other day, I just happened to meet him in the trenches. He was showing me a letter he had from Dr. Logan enquiring about poor Isaac and Sandy, poor lads. I think they were killed in 'No Mans Land'. I am sure you would see some sights in Belfast. Is Johnny's knee mending? Remember me to him.

In the above letter Billy Mayne refers to his friends Isaac Black and Sandy Little who were killed in action on 1st July 1916, and Dr. Logan who was the Presbyterian Minister at Sandholes during that time.

Billy Mayne is also mentioned by the late Jim Donaghy who served with him in 109 Trench Mortar Battery during the Battle of Cambrai, details of which are published in the book, "Three Cheers for the Derry's" by Gardiner S. Mitchell.

William (Billy) Mayne was killed in action on the first day of the German Spring Offensive, and was buried in Roupy Road German Cemetery at Mem 34. After the war when the Commonwealth War Graves Commission came to erect the

British Cemeteries he was re-interred in Savy British Cemetery. The cemetery is situated on the south-western outskirts of the village of Savy, on the west side of the road to Roupy, about 6.5 kilometres west of St. Quentin.

William Mayne is commemorated on Cookstown Cenotaph and on Sandholes Presbyterian Roll of Honour.

20439-Private John Slevin
1st Battalion Royal Inniskilling Fusiliers
Killed in Action: 22nd March 1918
Age: 20
Pozieres Memorial, France. Panel: 38-40

John Slevin was a son of James and Elizabeth Slevin of Killymoon Street, Cookstown. He was born at Fintona, County Tyrone, and when in his late teens enlisted in Omagh with Royal Inniskilling Fusiliers. He was killed in action in the retreat from St Quentin, during the German Spring Offensive. He has no known grave and is commemorated on panel 38-40 on Pozieres Memorial, France. He is also commemorated on Cookstown Cenotaph.

Inscription on Pozieres Memorial

26124-Private John McVeigh
1st Battalion Royal Irish Fusiliers
Killed in Action: 23rd March 1918
Pozieres Memorial, France. Panel: 76-77

John McVeigh was born at Ardboe, County Tyrone. He enlisted in Ballymena while his family were living in Draperstown. John was reported killed in action on 23rd March 1918, two days after the start of the German Spring Offensive. The morning of the 23rd March was again foggy and soon after dawn the enemy captured Ham and advanced on Brouchy, to the rear of the position held by the 1st Royal Irish Fusiliers. . By 2.00pm it became necessary to draw back the left flank, but by 8.00pm the enemy had captured Cugny. Orders were issued that if a man was wounded and couldn't walk; he was to be left behind to fall into the hands of the enemy. It was considered better to lose a wounded man rather than lose three or four men who might be trying to save one. John has no known grave and is commemorated on panels 76-77 on Pozieres Memorial, France.

Inscription on Pozieres Memorial

29816-Private Thomas Cheevers
9th Battalion Royal Inniskilling Fusilers
Died of Wounds: 26th March 1918
Noyon New British Cemetery, France. Grave: 4-D-10

Thomas Cheevers was born in Cookstown and was the son of James and Margaret Cheevers of Millburn Street, Cookstown. He was working in Scotland at the outbreak of the First World War and enlisted in Glasgow in early 1917 and returned home for training. He joined his Battalion at the front as a battle casualty replacement, in late 1917. Thomas was wounded in the retreat from St.Quentin during the German Spring Offensive of March 1918. He died of his wounds on 26th March 1918 and is buried in plot 4- row D- grave 10 at Noyon New British Cemetery, France. He is commemorated on Cookstown Cenotaph and St. Luran's Church of Ireland, Roll of Honour, Derryloran, Cookstown.

41401-Lance Sergeant George Adams Henry.M.M.
9th Battalion Royal Irish Fusiliers
Died of Wounds: 26th March 1918
St. Sever Cemetery, France. Grave: 6-H-12b

George Henry was the youngest son of Mr. W. J. Henry, (Rural District Councillor), of Cloghog, Cookstown.

He joined the North Irish Horse prior to the war as a trooper and went to France at the outbreak of the First World War. For some months he was the bodyguard of Sir John French when he was Commander-in-Chief, and afterwards of General Smith-Dorrien. Several months before he died he was transferred to the Royal Irish Fusiliers and took part in several engagements. On 13th January 1918, Sergeant Henry was awarded the Military Medal along with Lance Corporal A.C. Clarke. He received severe wounds in action on 14th March 1918 and died on the 26th March at the Australian General Hospital at Rouen. He is interred in plot 6- row H- grave- 12b at St. Sever Cemetery, France. During the morning service in Second Cookstown Presbyterian Church on Sunday 31st March 1918, the Reverend David Maybin B.A., made touching references to the death of Sergeant Henry.

George Henry is commemorated on Cookstown Cenotaph and on Second Presbyterian, Roll of Honour (at Molesworth) Cookstown.

21645-Private Thomas John Gerald Haire

9th Battalion Royal Irish Fusiliers
Killed in Action: 27th March 1918
Age: 20
Pozieres Memorial, France. Panel: 76-77

Thomas was a son of David and Sarah Jane Haire. He was born in Stewartstown and the family later moved to Cloverhill, County Cavan. Thomas enlisted there, joining the 9th Battalion Royal Irish Fusiliers. By the time of the Great German Spring Offensive of March 1918 the battalion was in withdrawal and on the 26th March passed through Avrilcourt, Tilloloy, Grivillers, Guerbigny and arrived at Erches at about 11am. On the morning of the 27th the enemy attacked and the 9th Irish Fusiliers were forced back to a position south of Arvillers. It was here that Thomas was killed in action. There is no known grave and Thomas is commemorated on the Pozieres Memorial, panels 76-77. He was twenty years of age. The battalion were forced to remain here for the night. They lost two men on that day of retreat. The other man was George Gilroy of 50 Stanhope Street, Belfast. He was thirty-one years of age and is also commemorated on Pozieres Memorial, France.

29112-Corporal John Gilmour McGee

14th Battalion Highland light Infantry
Formerly 23371-Cameronians, (Scottish Rifles)
Killed in Action: 27th March 1918
Arras Memorial, France. Bay: 8

John Gilmour McGee was a son of Alexander McGee of Toberlane, Cookstown. He was employed with his father at Wellbrook until early 1916. He was a prominent member of the Ulster Volunteers and of Orritor L.O.L. After leaving his position at Wellbrook he went to work in Glasgow where he joined the Cameronians (Scottish Rifles) and subsequently transferred to the Highland Light Infantry. He was in France from June 1916 and took part in many engagements, notably at Cambrai and Arras. He was home on leave twice during active service. At the time of his death John had two other brothers serving in the army. George McGee was serving with the Inniskillings, and Robert with a Labour Battalion of the Royal Scots. John Gilmour McGee was one of 14 men of the 14th Highland Light Infantry who were killed in action on 27th March 1918. He has no known grave and is commemorated on bay 8 on the Arras Memorial to the Missing, France. He is also commemorated on Cookstown Cenotaph.

21923-Private Robert J. Patterson

10th Battalion Royal Inniskilling Fusiliers
Died of Wounds: 28th March 1918
Age: 18
Namps-au-Val Cemetery, France Grave: 1-A-19

Robert J. Patterson was a son of Rachel Patterson of 91 Donegal
Road, Belfast. He was born at Ballymacarrett but lived for a time
in Moneymore. Robert enlisted in Belfast and joined the
Battalion in late 1917. He was wounded during the retreat from
St. Quentin and removed to one of the many hospitals at Namps
for treatment. He died of his wounds on 28th March 1918 and is
buried in plot 1- row A- grave 19 at Namps-au-Val Cemetery,
France. He is commemorated on Moneymore War Memorial
(Assembly Rooms).

11083-Private James Mitchell

9th Battalion Royal Inniskiling Fusiliers
Killed in Action: 29th March 1918
Age: 28
Pozieres Memorial, France. Panel: 38-40

James Mitchell was a son of John and Nancy Mitchell of Coagh.
He was born in Tamlaght, County Tyrone and when war broke out
went to Omagh to enlist into the 9th Battalion Royal Inniskilling
Fusiliers. James survived many of the earlier battles of the war
but was killed in fierce hand to hand fighting during the German
Spring Offensive on 29th March 1918. The 9th Battalion suffered
very badly and by the end of the day seventy-two men had given
their lives. James has no known grave and is commemorated on
panel 38-40 on the Pozieres Memorial, France. He is
commemorated on Coagh War Memorial (Royal British Legion,
Cookstown).

The inscription on Pozieres Memorial, France.

T.F.291027-Sergeant Robert Henry Lewis Steele

1st/7th Middlesex Regiment (Duke of Cambridge's Own)
Died of Wounds: 29th March 1918
Aubigny Communal Cemetery Extension, France. Grave: 3-C-41

Sergeant Robert Henry Lewis Steele was born and raised in Middlesex. He was the son of Robert R. Steele and Mrs. Caroline Steele and Grandson of Mr. Robert Steele of Grange, Tullyhogue, Cookstown, and Husband of Lucy Steele of "Raewood", Baring Road, Lee; London. He died of his wounds received in action during the German Spring offensive, on 29th March 1918, and is buried plot 3- row C- grave 42 at Aubigny Communal Cemetery Extension, France.

PTE. MICHAEL CORRI-
GAN, of Utiku,
Killed in action.

13/2027-Private Michael Corrigan

2nd Battalion Auckland Regiment
New Zealand, Rifle Brigade.
Killed in Action: 30th March 1918
Age: 33
Grevillers Cemetery, New Zealand Memorial. France

Michael Corrigan was a son of Bernard and Sarah Corrigan of Dirnan, Lissan, Cookstown. As a young man he had emigrated to New Zealand and settled in Auckland. At the outbreak of the First World War, Michael enlisted with the 2nd Battalion Auckland Regiment, New Zealand Rifle Brigade. He was killed in action on 30th March 1918. There is no known grave and Michael is commemorated on Grevillers Cemetery, (New Zealand) Memorial, France.

The inscription on the New Zealand Memorial at Grevillers Cemetery, France

21890-Private Robert McNichol, M.M.
(Formerly 29639-Royal Garrison Artillery)
1st Battalion Royal Dublin Fusiliers
Killed in Action: 30th March 1918
Pozieres Memorial, France. Panel 79 - 80

Robert McNichol was the son of Daniel and Brigid McNichol, Killycurragh, Cookstown, and husband of Elizabeth McNichol.

He had previously served with the Royal Garrison Artillery before transferring to 1st Battalion Royal Dublin Fusiliers. During his years of service Robert was awarded the Military Medal. The Military Medal was awarded to men and women who had shown individual or associated acts of bravery and at least 115,000 were awarded during the First World War. Awards of the Medal were announced in the London Gazette (without an accompanying citation). Robert's brother Daniel was severely wounded in action during the First World War, resulting in the loss of one of his legs. He survived the war and returned to Killycurragh. Robert McNichol was listed as missing, killed in action on 30th March 1918, during the German Spring Offensive. He has no known grave and is commemorated on panel 79 - 80 at Pozieres Memorial, France. He is also commemorated on Cookstown Cenotaph.

Robert was survived by his parents, his wife Elizabeth and his brothers, Daniel and William and his sisters, Mary-Jane, Martha, Margaret and Lilly.

The inscription at Pozieres Memorial, France.

4420-Private Andrew McClintock Graham.

19th Battalion Australian Imperial Force, 11th Regiment
Died of Illness: 7th April 1918
Rockwood Cemetery, Sydney, Australia.

Andrew was born 7th September 1875 at Meenlougher, Castlefin, County Donegal. He was the son of Robert Graham and Barbara Mary Graham (nee McClintock).

His father, Robert, was known as 'Master' Graham and the family came to live at Claggan, Cookstown, where Robert Graham was a school teacher.

Robert and Mary had 10 children, of which Andrew (named after his maternal grandfather, Andrew McClintock) was the 4th born child. He immigrated to Australia in 1909-10 and had been a regular soldier serving with the Cape Mounted Rifles (Colonial Forces) before enlisting with 1st Australian Imperial Forces at Casula, Liverpool, New South Wales, on 13th December 1915 when he was forty years of age. Just before he enlisted he had undergone an operation in hospital for varicose veins in both legs.

He embarked at Sydney on board His Majesty's Australian Transport "Nestor" on 9th April 1916 and disembarked at Alexandria. On 29th May 1916 he left Alexandria on board His Majesty's Transport "Migantic" and arrived at Plymouth on 7th June.

On 9th September of that same year he sailed for France. Andrew marched out of Etaples on 24th September and was taken on strength of the 19th Battalion in the field on 30th September. Six weeks later, on 14th November, he was wounded in action. On 18th November he was admitted to hospital in Rouen suffering from a gunshot wound to the left foot which turned out to be serious. On 14th December 1916 he embarked on H S Western Australia at Rouen and was removed to hospital in England.

Much hospital treatment followed but on 1st March he was transferred from the Royal Victoria Hospital, Netley, to 3rd Auxiliary Hospital, Dartford, seriously ill. Three weeks later, on 23rd March he was discharged to the Depot, at Weymouth.

After boarding Transport ship "Euripides" 10th April 1917, his wounds were serious and he was admitted to the Montevideo Camp hospital. The foot injury was still giving trouble and on 3rd August he was returned to Australia to be discharged.

He arrived in Australia on 18th September 1917 and was finally discharged from the army on 18th March 1918.

Andrew died at Sydney Hospital on 7th April 1918, from a heart condition. He was 43 years old, and was buried at Rockwood Cemetery, Sydney, Australia. His name does not appear with the Commonwealth War Graves, even though his death is certainly related to wounds received in action.

In later years his grave fell into disrepair and it was only in recent years that members of the Salvation Army took it upon themselves to restore it.

His name is commemorated on Claggan Presbyterian Church Memorial, Cookstown and on Cookstown Cenotaph.

17756-Corporal Thomas Graham
12th Battalion Royal Irish Rifles
Killed in Action: 14th April 1918
Age: 22
Wulverghem-Lindenhoek Road Cemetery, Belgium. Grave: 4-C-1

Thomas Graham was the son of William and Mary Jane Graham of 12 Milfort Avenue, Dunmurry. He was born in Cookstown but his family moved to Dunmurry to live before the start of the First World War. Thomas enlisted in Lisburn, joining the 12th Battalion of the Royal Irish Rifles. He was sent to Belgium in a draft to bring the Battalion back up to strength after the Battle of the Somme. Thomas was killed in action on 14th April 1918 and is interred in Wulverghem-Lindenhoek Road Cemetery. He is buried in plot 4- row C- grave 1. He was twenty-two years of age. The Battalion lost a total of ten men on this day. The first, Edward Davidson of Bangor had been seriously wounded in a previous incident and died of his wounds at the Dressing Station. He is interred in Lijssenthoek Cemetery and lies in plot 26, row F, grave 9. The other eight have no known graves and are commemorated on Tyne Cot Memorial. Thomas' burial took place in the nearby Wulverghem-Lindenhoek Road Cemetery and was conducted by a Chaplain to the Forces.

19446-Corporal Charles Edward Crooks
12th Battalion Royal Irish Rifles
Killed in Action: 16th April 1918
Age: 22
Tyne Cot Memorial. Belgium. Panel: 138-140 (162-162a-163a)

Charles Edward Crooks was born in Moneymore and following the start of the First World War he enlisted in Antrim. Charles was a son of John Crooks of 61 Mill View, Muckamore, County Antrim. He was killed in action on 16th April 1918 and has no known grave. He is commemorated on Tyne Cot Memorial, panels 138-140 (162-162a-163a). He was twenty-two. The 12th Battalion lost three men on the 16th April 1918 and none of them have a known grave.

126191 - Gunner Joseph Wylie Neill
Royal Field Artillery
Killed in Action: 17th April 1918
Aged: 22
Le Grand Hasard Military Cemetery, Hazebrouck, Belgium. 4 - B - 15

Joseph Wylie Neil lived in Oldtown Street, Cookstown up until about 1914 and before leaving home for work in Scotland he was a member of Cookstown Company of the Ulster Volunteers. He went to Clydebank to work in the shipyards of Mr. John Brown & Company. His next of kin was listed as his father, James Neill of 126 Glasgow Road, Clydebank. He joined the Royal Field Artillery in early 1916 and was sent to France in July of that year.

It was reported at the time of his death on 17th April 1918, that he had been killed by shellfire while having his tea. He is buried in plot 4, row B, grave 15 at   Le Grand Hasard Military Cemetery, Hazebrouck in Belgium.

We shall know his voice in the lamb's sweet song,
His step in the streets of Gold,
The same sweet smile on his loving face,
as he wore in the days of old.
Oh why was he taken, so young and so fair?
When earth held so many it better could spare;
Hard, was the blow that compelled us to part!
with a loved one, so near, and so dear to our heart.

Submitted to the Mid Ulster Mail by his Uncle and Aunt, Mr & Mrs Beattie, Clydebank, at Easter 1927.

446191-Private Michael McGurk
Labour Corps-712th Company
Died of Wounds: 18th April 1918
Age: 32
Wimereux Communal Cemetery, France. Grave: 11-B-10a

Michael McGurk was born in Pomeroy, County Tyrone.

Michael and his wife, Mary Ellen McGurk, lived at 61 Norfolk Street, Belfast. He enlisted in Belfast, joining the Leinster Regiment, but later transferred to the 712th Company, Labour Corps. In early April 1918 Michael was seriously wounded and taken to hospital at Wimereux. He died of his wounds there, on 18th April and is interred in plot 11, row B, grave 10a, at Wimereux Communal Cemetery, France

29062-Private Robert Mitchell
9th Battalion Royal Inniskilling Fusiliers
Killed in Action: 30th May 1918
Canada Farm Cemetery, Belgium. Grave: 4-A-4

Robert Mitchell was born in Coagh. Before the war Robert was employed by Duff Brothers in Coagh. At the time of Robert's death his father and his younger brother were on active service as well as three cousins. News of his death was first conveyed to Robert's mother by his cousin, Sergeant Joseph Mitchell, who was also his Platoon sergeant, and who stated in a letter that Robert was killed instantly by a shell in a rest camp where they were just settling down to a period of rest after getting out of the trenches. Mrs. Mitchell also received a letter from the Chaplain, Rev Edwin Fleming, conveying the sympathy of the Officers and men of the Battalion and adding that he buried Robert on the 1st June 1918. Robert is buried in plot 4- row A- grave 4 at Canada Farm Cemetery, Belgium. Robert was the only casualty in his battalion that day. He is commemorated on Coagh War Memorial (Royal British Legion, Cookstown).

Lieutenant (Quartermaster) John Rogers D.C.M.
Gordon Highlanders
Died: 13th June 1918
Age: 41
St. Kentigern's Roman Catholic Cemetery, Glasgow. Grave I - 311

John Rogers was the son of Francis and Mary Rogers, Cookstown, County Tyrone, and husband of Mary J. Rogers, 685 Garscube Road, Glasgow.

It is not known how he died. He is buried at home in St. Kentigern's Roman Catholic Cemetery, Glasgow.

Staff Nurse-Rachel Ferguson

Queen Alexandra's Imperial Military Nursing Service
Q A I M N S
Died of Illness: 26th June 1918
Bordighera Cemetery, Italy Grave: 2-B-7

Rachel was born on 29th December 1886. She was the daughter of John Stewart Ferguson and Annie Ferguson of Lanebrook House, Ballygoney, Coagh. Rachel was educated at Ballygoney National School and Lady's School, Cookstown. She trained at the Royal Victoria Hospital in Belfast from 16th August 1911 to 23rd April 1915 where she qualified as a Staff Nurse. When asked to give the details of one lady to whom application could be made for a reference she nominated Mrs. George Wilson, The Manse, Ballygoney.

Notified of acceptance for service on 10th September 1915 she arrived in Salonika on 6th June 1916 where she was posted to No: 28 General Hospital.

While in service, she became unwell and was admitted to the Red Cross Convalescent Home on 15th June 1917 before being transferred to a hospital ship on 29th June. She re-joined No: 28 General Hospital for duty on 8th July 1917, and with her contract due to expire on 12th November, she submitted an application on 9th October to extend her service by six months "Or until my services are no longer required, whichever should happen first." This application was accepted.

She embarked on H.M. Transport "Abbassich" for Italy to work in No: 62 General Hospital on 7th November 1917. They disembarked at Taranto eight days later. She was serving in Italy until May of 1918 when she was given leave for fourteen days. She re-joined No: 62 General Hospital on 25th May 1918 but on 26th June she was admitted there as a patient, suffering from bronco-pneumonia. She was by now dangerously ill and died later that day. She is buried in plot 2- row B- grave 7 at Bordighera Cemetery in Italy. She is also commemorated on Coagh War Memorial (Royal British Legion, Cookstown) and on the memorial plaque in St Ann's Cathedral, Belfast to Irish nurses who died in the Great War.

6895 - Private Patrick Hughes
1st Battalion Royal Irish Rifles
Died: 6th July 1918
Age: 33
Bertenacre Military Cemetery, Fletre, France. Grave: 1- A - 1a

Patrick Hughes was born in Stewartstown, County Tyrone, the son of Michael and Mathilda Hughes, later of, 49 Atcar Street, Mount Pottinger Road, Belfast.

He enlisted in the army in Belfast and served with the 1st Battalion Royal Irish Rifles

Patrick died on the 6th July 1918 and is buried in plot 1- row A- grave 1a at Bertenacre Military Cemetery, Fletre, France. This cemetery was originally made by French troops, and used by the 36th Ulster Division in July-September 1918 after the Battle of the Lys.

Private-Patrick Grimes
United States Army (American Expeditionary Force)
Died of Wounds: 1918
Age: 28
St Joseph's Roman Catholic Churchyard, Kileenan, Kildress,
County Tyrone.

Private Patrick Grimes was born on 29th June 1891 at Cloughfin, Kildress, County Tyrone. He was the son of Charles Grimes and Mary Grimes (nee Donnelly), and brother of Sarah, Kate, Anne, Joseph, Charles and Reverend Father Michael Grimes.

He immigrated to the United States, settling in New York where he worked as a barman for Robert Byrne in Manhattan.

When the United States of America entered the First World War he was among the 24 million men eligible for the draft. Patrick Grimes's draft card shows that he was 5 feet, 8 and half inches tall, blue eyes, brown hair and lists his mother, brothers and sisters as his dependants, and was signed by Peter Cusack, (registrar) on the 5th June 1917.

The U.S. Army mobilized an estimated 4,355,000 personnel during the First World War.

The American Expeditionary Force began arriving in France in June 1917 and by March 1918 there were 250,000 service personnel there; this number increased to 1 million by July and 2 million by November and the armistice. Two thirds of American service personnel would see action in 29 Divisions. Patrick Grimes is thought to have died of wounds received in action sometime around June or July 1918. He is listed among the casualty list of the American Expeditionary Force published on 18th August 1918, but his date of death is not determined. Many of the records of U.S. service personnel who served during the First World War were lost as the result of a fire at the National Personnel Records Centre, St. Louis Missouri on 12th July 1973. An estimated 16-18 million official military personnel files were lost.

His remains were returned home to Kildress, where he was buried in the Graham / Grimes family plot, in St Joseph's, Kileenan Roman Catholic Churchyard.

He is commemorated in United States of America, Soldiers of The Great War - Volume 2 -NEW YORK.

23160- Private George Bleakes
9th Battalion Royal Inniskilling Fusiliers
Died: 1st August 1918
Age: 40
Glageon Cemetery, France. Grave: J-7

George was a son of Elizabeth Bleakes of North Street, Stewartstown. He was born in Dungannon about 1878. He enlisted in Cookstown with the 9th Battalion Royal Inniskilling Fusiliers.

George Bleakes died on 1st August 1918. He is interred in Glageon Cemetery and lies in row J, grave 7. This Cemetery is about 56 kilometres east of Cambrai.

The village of Glageon was in German occupation for most of the First World War. The communal cemetery was used for the burial of German soldiers and allied prisoners of war from September 1914 to August 1918. There are 54 Commonwealth war dead buried here out of a total of 220 graves. George Bleakes was almost certainly a prisoner of war and most likely captured during the German Offensive of 1918. He is commemorated on Stewartstown Cenotaph and Donaghendry Church of Ireland Roll of Honour (as George Bleeks). The Surname 'Bleakes', is more commonly spelt as 'Bleeks'. It is not known which way the family spelled the name but records show it spelled in both forms.

192477 - Lieutenant Ernest Creighton
13th Battalion Canadian Infantry
Killed in Action 8th August 1918
Age: 27
Hangard Wood Cemetery, France. Grave: 1-A-2

Ernest Creighton was the youngest son of James and Sarah
Creighton (nee Black) of Doons, Orritor, Cookstown. He was
born on 21st May 1891 and after leaving school joined the Royal
Irish Constabulary. In 1913 he emigrated to Canada and
transferred to the local police. He enlisted in the Army at Toronto
on 30th August 1915. He was described as being five feet eleven
and a quarter inches tall, with blue eyes, light brown hair and a
ruddy complexion. His uprightness of character and his ability
soon made themselves felt and in a very short time he was
promoted to the rank of Sergeant and qualified as an instructor of
infantry. For over a year he served in the trenches of France and
took part in several major actions. Again his worth attracted the
attention of his superiors and he was selected for a Commission,
being sent to England to qualify himself for that position. Ernest
was killed in action on 8th August 1918 and is interred in plot 1,
row A, grave 2 at Hangard Wood Cemetery, France. His close
friend, William Black of Doons, Orritor named is grandson
Ernest after Lieutenant Creighton.

12/1885 - Gunner Alexander Law Bell
New Zealand Field Artillery
Died of Wounds: 9th August 1918
Age: 21
Couin New British Cemetery, France. Grave: G 10

Alexander Law Bell was the son of Edward and Mary Bell of
Coagh, County Tyrone.

He emigrated to New Zealand where he joined the New Zealand
Field Artillery.

He is listed as having died from wounds received in action on 9th
August 1918 and is buried in row G, grave 10 at Couin New
British Cemetery, France. He is also commemorated on
Ballygoney Presbyterian Roll of Honour.

PTE. ALEX. L. BELL
of Ngaruawahia,
Died of wounds.

An estimated 16,697 New Zealanders died and 41,000 were
wounded in World War 1.

31267-Private Alexander Duff Harkness

2nd Battalion Wellington Regiment, New Zealand Expeditionary Force
Died of Wounds: 16th August 1918
Age: 28
Bagneux Cem, Gezaincourt, France. Grave: 4-C-25

Alexander was the son of Adam and Margaret Harkness of Drumconvis, Coagh. He had emigrated to New Zealand in 1914. He enlisted with the Wellington Regiment in 1916. After training he arrived back in England in January of 1917. In May he was allowed home on leave and visited his old home in Drumconvis. He was again given leave in August of 1917.

Alexander Harkness died of wounds received in action on 16th August 1918 while serving with the 2nd Battalion Wellington Regiment. He is interred in plot 4., row C, grave 25 at Bagneux British Cemetery, Gezaincourt, France.

He is also commemorated at Coagh Presbyterian and on Coagh War Memorial (Royal British Legion, Cookstown).

In a letter to his mother, one of his friends said.

"Your boy was a Company stretcher bearer and while going forward with three others a shell landed very close. One chap was killed, and the others, including your son, received nasty wounds. Company stretcher bearers do splendid work here. They are right up at the front with their companies and carry from the front line to the Regimental Aid post."

Mrs. Harkness also received letters of sympathy from Mr. Milner, Secretary of State for war, Mr. J. Allen, Minister of Defence, Wellington, New Zealand, and the Governor of New Zealand.

In 1999 the Naval and Military Press published a Roll of Honour naming every man from New Zealand who had given his life in the First World War.

71062-Private Wesley McClelland

North Irish Horse (5th Cyclist Battalion)
Killed in Action: 16th August 1918
Ancre British Cemetery, Beaumont-Hamel, France.
Grave: 7-E-56

Wesley McClelland was born in the parish of Derryloran, and lived with his family in Cookstown. He enlisted in Cookstown with the North Irish Horse. A Regiment which, formed part of the original British Expeditionary Force that arrived in France in August 1914. While in France, the Regiment went through many changes. From the original Regiment of North Irish Horse, two Battalions were formed. 1st Battalion were formed on 10th May 1916 and was made up of A, D and E squadrons. 2nd Battalion was raised on 21st June 1916, from the ranks of the original B and C squadrons along with a service squadron from the 6th Inniskilling Dragoons. At the end of August 1917 the 2nd Battalion were temporarily dismounted and became part of the 9th (NIH) Battalion Royal Irish Fusiliers. By the beginning of March 1918 the 1st Battalion North Irish Horse became the 5th Cyclist Battalion (North Irish Horse) with its original squadrons unchanged. After taking part in the action of the German Spring Offensive of March 1918, the Regiment was further reduced when an officer and 13 men were attached to 64th Brigade, 21st Division on 14th August 1918. Two days later, on the 16th August 1918, Wesley McClelland was killed in action as the division prepared for another attack on the Somme. He is buried in plot 7-row E- grave 56 at Ancre British Cemetery, Beaumont-Hamel, France.

He is commemorated on Cookstown Cenotaph as Charles Wesley McClelland.

49824 Private Joseph James Simpson
1st Battalion Royal Irish Fusiliers
Killed in Action: 16th August 1918
Age: 29
Bertenacre Cemetery, France. Grave: 1-D-7

Joseph James Simpson was born on the 9th October 1889 at Ballymully, Moneymore. He was the son of John and Matilda Simpson (nee Kennedy). John Simpson was a farmer, and he and his wife and seven children lived at Ballydawley, Moneymore.

Joseph James Simpson enlisted at Finner Camp, County Donegal with the 10th Royal Inniskilling Fusiliers (army number 16006). He served with them at the Battle of the Somme. In the spring of 1918 the Battalion were disbanded and he transferred to the 1st Battalion Royal Irish Fusiliers and was serving with them when he was killed in action on 16th August 1918. He is buried in plot 1- row D- grave 7 at Bertenacre Cemetery, France.

In later years, his brother Edward would often recollect seeing his brother Joseph James leave home for the last time.

We walked to the train station at Moneymore, and had only gotten down the road a bit when he stopped and told me to go no further with him, as he wanted to take one last look at the old homestead. – Edward Simpson.

Joseph James Simpson is commemorated on Moneymore War Memorial (Assembly Rooms) and on First Presbyterian Moneymore Roll of Honour.

24260-Private Robert Walls

7/8th Battalion Royal Inniskilling Fusiliers
Killed in Action: 24th August 1918
Age: 29
Tyne Cot Memorial, Belgium. Panel: 70-72

Robert was a son of Mrs. Bridget Walls of Moneymore and the late John Walls. He was born at Ballyrogully, Loup, Moneynore, County Londonderry. Robert enlisted in Moneymore and served during most of the battles of the First World War after the spring of 1916. On 23rd August 1917, the 7th and 8th (service) Battalions of Royal Inniskilling Fusilers were amalgamated to form the 7th/8th Battalion. This was due to the fact that both Battalions had suffered serious casualties over the past year and in particular in The Battle of Langemarck. It was getting more difficult to find recruits for these two Battalions. Robert Walls spent another year with the Battalion before he was killed in action on 24th August 1918. He has no known grave and Robert is commemorated on panels 70-72 at Tyne Cot Memorial, Belgium. He is commemorated on Moneymore War Memorial (Assembly Rooms).

206121-Private Henry Cobain (formerly-9th Battalion Durham Light Infantry)
6th Battalion East Kent Regiment (The Buffs)
Killed in Action: 27th August 1918
Age: 29
Peronne Road Cemetery, Maricourt, France. Grave: 4-C-27

Henry (Harry) Cobain was the son of Joseph and Sarah Cobain, of Dunnisk, Pomeroy, County Tyrone.

He was working in the North of England when he enlisted at Chopwell, County Durham, joining the Durham Light Infantry and subsequently transferred to the 6th Battalion East Kent Regiment (The Buffs).

The East Kent Regiment, known as The Buffs, obtained the name when they were the 3rd Regiment of Foot in 1743 while on campaign in Holland and the Low Countries.

The name refers to the 'buff coats'- armour made of soft leather that the regiment was issued with. Regiments at that time were often called after the Colonel's commanding them and as 3rd Regiment and 19th Regiment of Foot were commanded by Thomas Howard and Charles Howard respectively, both regiments became known as Howard's Regiment of Foot. To avoid any confusion the Regiments took the colours of their facings as part of their names, so the 19th Regiment of Foot became known as the 'Green Howards' and the 3rd Regiment became known as Howard's Buffs, this was eventually shortened to The Buffs.

In World War 1, the 6th Battalion East Kent Regiment (the Buffs) seen service and action at Loos, Somme, Albert, Poziers, Le Transloy, Ancre, Arras, Cambrai, St. Quentin, Amiens, The Hindenburg Line 1918, Epehey and St. Quentin Canal.

At the Battle of Albert, (first phase, second Battles of the Somme 1918), 37 Brigade, including the 6th East Kents took up the attack on the 9th August 1918 and by the next day they had advanced almost two miles. After a brief rest, the Division attacked again on 22nd August, pushing right across the wilderness of the old Somme Battlefields, capturing Meault, Mametz, Carnoy, Hardecourt and Faviere Wood, which it reached after a week's, continuous fighting. The Division had made another advance of 15,000 yards.

During World War 1, the village of Maricourt was close to the front lines, at a point of junction between British and French Forces. The village fell into German hands during the great advance of March 1918 but was recaptured at the end of August.

On the 27th August 1918 the 6th East Kent's were given the objective of taking the east edge of Trones Wood, east of the town of Albert. Captain L. P. Figgis and 10 men were killed in the action, including Henry Cobain. He is buried in grave 4-C-27 at Peronne Road Cemetery, Maricourt, France.

3080100-Private Patrick O'Neil
24th Battalion Canadian Infantry (Quebec Regiment)
Died of Wounds: 27th August 1918
Age: 34
Wancourt British Cemetery, France. Grave: 3 B 10

Patrick O'Neil was the son of Edward and Sarah O'Neil, Cookstown, County Tyrone, and husband of Fannie O'Neil, Higgins Court, Andover, Mass., USA.

The town of Wancourt was captured on 12th April 1917 after very heavy fighting and the advance was continued in the following days. The Area then fell into German hands in March 1918, during the Spring Offensive. On 26th August 1918, the Canadian Corps (including the 24th Battalion) recaptured the area. Patrick O'Neil was seriously wounded during the taking of Wancourt and died of his wounds the next day.

He is buried in plot 3, row B, grave 10 at Wancourt British Cemetery, France and is commemorated on Coagh War Memorial (RBL, Cookstown).

201602-Private George Greer
75th Battalion Canadian Infantry
Killed in Action: 2nd September 1918
Age: 28
Dury Mill Cemetery, France. Grave: 2-B-24

George Greer was born on 10th January 1890 at Tievenagh, Parish of Ardtrea. He was a son of William and Letitia Greer (nee McIvor). In 1901 he was living on the family farm at Tamlaght, Coagh. George worked in a hardware shop in Maghera before emigrating to Toronto where he worked in the famous hardware shop of Eatons. He married a Canadian girl, Annie, in December 1915 and they had one son, George, who was born in 1917. He originally enlisted in the 95th Battalion Canadian Infantry in October 1915. His height is recorded as five feet five inches and his weight as 126lbs.

The Battalion embarked for England in October 1916. The Canadian training camp was at Bramshott and it was here that he subsequently transferred to the 157th, then the 116th and finally 75th Canadian Regiment. On 17th May the Regiment embarked for France.

During August 1918 the Canadians attacked the German front lines near the village of Dury. The offensive lasted from 26th August to 5th September and it was during this offensive that George was killed in action on 2nd September. On the day he died the 4th Division, which included the 75th Battalion, attacked close to the village of Dury. This is very open countryside over flat farm land and enemy machine-gun fire caused heavy losses. He is buried in plot 2- row B- grave 24 at Dury Mill Cemetery, France. George Greer is commemorated on Cookstown Cenotaph and Orritor Presbyterian Roll of Honour, Cookstown. After his death his wife Annie and son George returned to Tamlaght.

201341-Private James Spratt

Highland Light Infantry
1st/5th (City of Glasgow) Battalion (Territorial)
Died of Wounds: 3rd September 1918
Age: 27
Mons Communal Cemetery, Belgium.   Grave: 6 B 4

James Spratt was the son of George and Margaret Spratt, Chapel Street, Cookstown.

James was born in Dundee, Scotland and was living in Glasgow when he enlisted.

He died of wounds on 3rd September 1918 and is the only man from the battalion to die on this day. He is buried in plot 6, row B, grave 4 at Mons Communal Cemetery, Belgium.

Mons holds a unique place in the history of the First World War, as the first shots of the war were fired near here and likewise the last shots also.

The British Expeditionary Force first encountered the Germans here and the first British soldier to be killed in the 'Great War' was Private G Parr of the 4th Middlesex Regiment who was killed on the 21st August 1914. The last British soldier to be killed in action on 11th November 1918 just moments before the armistice was 12643- Private George Edwin Ellison of 5th Lancers (Royal Irish) Corps of Lancers, Household Cavalry.

767 -Rifleman Thomas McMahon
2nd Battalion Royal Irish Rifles
Killed in Action: 6th September 1918
Ploegsteert Memorial, Belgium. Panel: 9

Thomas McMahon was born in Cookstown. He enlisted in Belfast with the Royal Irish Rifles. He remained with them throughout the war and was killed in action on 6th September 1918 close to Ploegsteert Wood, during an attack that was aimed at dislodging the enemy from trenches they had recently taken in the area around Armentieres and Ploegsteert Wood. The Battalion lost thirty-three in the action.

Thomas McMahon has no known grave and is commemorated on panel 9 on Ploegsteert Memorial, Belgium.

534010-Private William Henry
Labour Corps
Died: 9th September 1918
Age: 39
Bralo British Cemetery, Grave: 9

William Henry was the son of Mr. and Mrs. William Henry of Cookstown. He was born in Cookstown but had gone to live and work in Blantyre, Scotland. He enlisted in Hamilton, joining the Royal Inniskilling Fusiliers with the number 13240. He later transferred to the Labour Corps. Prior to the outbreak of war he lived with his wife, Annie, at 5 Kirkgate, Saltcoats, Ayrshire. William was a brother of Johnny Henry of Waterloo Terrace, Cookstown. William died from Malaria having served for over three years in Salonika. He is interred in Bralo British Cemetery, Grave 9.

5079-Sapper John Crilly

Australian Royal Engineers (Tunnelling Company)
Died of Illness: 25th September 1918
Age: 48
Brisbane General Cemetery, Australia.

John Crilly was born in Pomeroy, County Tyrone. He was the son of James and Mary Crilly.

He emigrated to Australia and lived with his wife Esther in Brisbane.

He had served for three years in the Australian Light Horse before enlisting for overseas service on 15th July 1916 at the age of 45. His attestation papers show that he was 5 feet six and three quarter inches tall. He served as a Sapper with 6th Australian Tunnelling Company, Royal Engineers and was transferred to France on 15th October 1916.

On the 30th December 1916 he was transferred from the Australian Base Hospital in Rouen, France to Middlesex County Hospital, England suffering from bronchitis and influenza. He was making good progress until 14th February 1917 when he had a number of epileptic fits. His Consultants found on the 7th March 1917 that he was suffering from Epilepsy and Cardio Vascular damage, due to wear and tear. He was also diagnosed with Fibrosis of the lungs and Emphysema and it was suggested his service had aggravated this condition. It was recommended that he was no longer fit for Military Service and this was confirmed by Doctors on 28th March 1917. He was sent home to Australia on 8th April 1917 and upon arrival was transferred to hospital from early June 1917 until August 1918. He was discharged from the army on 13th July 1918, as his health was in decline. His wife and family were awarded a pension.

John Crilly died in Hospital in Brisbane on 25th September 1918 and is buried in Brisbane General Cemetery, Brisbane, Australia.

26413-Private James Ferguson
2nd Battalion Royal Inniskilling Fusiliers
Killed in Action: 29th September 1918
Age: 21
Dadizeele New British Cemetery, Belgium. Grave: 3-E-13

James Ferguson was born in the parish of Ardtrea. He was the son of Mr John Ferguson and lived at The Hermitage, Ballyronan.

James enlisted in Newtownards, County Down some time during 1915 and was involved in a number of engagements during the First World War. He was killed in action on 29th September 1918. The Battalion had marched to fresh billets, skirting Courtrai to St. Anne, where they were accommodated in and around a convent. Twenty men from the Battalion were killed on this day. James Ferguson is buried in plot 3- row E grave 13 at Dadizeele New British Cemetery, Belgium. He was twenty-one years of age. When the cemeteries were being put in place the families at home were asked if they wanted a personal inscription on the headstone. James's family chose "Safe in the arms of Jesus".

Dadizeele (now Dadizele) village was in German controlled territory for much of the First World War until it was reached by the 36th Ulster Division, and taken by the 9th Scottish Division on 29th September 1918.

237471-Private James Ferson
4th Battalion Canadian Machine Gun Corps
Killed in Action: 1st October 1918
Canada Cemetery, Tilloy-les-Cambrai, France. Grave: 2-A-7

James Ferson was a son of William Ferson of Drumnacross, Cookstown and was born on 4th September 1889. He emigrated to Canada as a teenager and found work as a tramway conductor in Toronto, where he lived at 6 Chesley Avenue. He enlisted in Toronto on 10th April 1916 and was described as being five feet four and three quarter inches tall, with blue eyes, brown hair and a fresh complexion. He was not married. James was attached to the Canadian Machine-Gun Corps. At Easter 1918 he was home on leave in Cookstown recovering from being gassed in an attack by the enemy. He was killed in action on 1st October 1918 by a machine gun bullet through the heart as he was getting his own machine gun into action. Lieutenant Parsons was with him at the time and later wrote a very touching letter to the family in Cookstown. In it he said *"I was with him during all of the recent fighting and he did splendid work, and he will be missed by all of the battery. He did his duty nobly"*.

James Ferson is buried in plot 2, row A, grave 7 at Canada Cemetery, Tilloy les Cambrai, France, and is commemorated on Cookstown Cenotaph

Private-Thomas George Doris

United States Army
Killed in Action: 7th October 1918
Old Cross Abbey and Cemetery, Ardboe, County Tyrone

Private Thomas George Doris was born 28th April 1893, the son of Michael Doris and Maryann Doris (nee Corr), of Farsnagh Coagh.

His father, Michael was a fisherman, and Thomas immigrated to the United States and settled in Milford, Connecticut.

No United States Military draft details can be found for Thomas Doris, as not all men eligible for military service actually registered for the draft in 1917. He served with the American Expeditionary Force in France and was killed in action during the Muese Argonne Offensive, on the 7th October 1918.

His remains were returned home to the "Old Cross", Ardboe, where his body is interred in the Doris Family plot at the Old Cross Abbey and Cemetery, Ardboe, County Tyrone.

He is commemorated in United States of America, Soldiers of The Great War - Volume 1 - Connecticut.

21933-Private James Edward Lavery

2nd Battalion Royal Dublin Fusiliers
Killed in Action: 7th October 1918
Age: 34
Vis-en-Artois Memorial, France. Panel: 10

James Edward Lavery was the son of Joseph and Mary Lavery of
31 Lagan Street, Belfast. He enlisted in Cookstown, joining the
Royal Innsikilling Fusiliers with number: 18467 but later
transferred to the 2nd Battalion Royal Dublin Fusiliers. Although
the family were living in Belfast, James was probably working in
Cookstown. He was killed in action on 7th October 1918. He has
no known grave and is commemorated on Vis-en-Artois
Memorial, France.

10788-Private William Long

5th Battalion Royal Inniskilling Fusiliers
Died of Wounds: 8th October 1918
Tincourt Cemetery, France. Grave: 7-F-10

William Long was born in the parish of Derryloran and lived at
Milburn Street, Cookstown. He worked at Gunning's Factory
(Milburn) prior to enlisting with the 5th Battalion Royal
Inniskilling Fusiliers in Omagh. His wife died in 1916 and his
young daughter was cared for by relatives.

By October 1918 he had survived a number of engagements of
the First World War but was seriously wounded at Le Catelet
when the enemy put down a barrage. The leading Company were
caught in this onslaught and the column halted. William was
seriously wounded and removed to the Casualty Clearing Station
at Tincourt. He died there later that evening and is buried in plot
7- row F- grave 10 at Tincourt Cemetery, France. He is
commemorated on Cookstown Cenotaph, St Luran's Church of
Ireland, Roll of Honour Derryloran, Cookstown and on Gunning's
Factory Memorial (Royal British Legion Cookstown).

William Long's brother Samuel also served during the First World
War.

Lieutenant Commander George Richard Colin Campbell

Royal Navy
Died: 10th October 1918
Age: 34
Grangegorman Cemetery, Dublin, Ireland.

A month before the war ended, the R.M.S. Leinster, a city of Dublin Steam Packet Company ship, was torpedoed by German Submarine UB 123, having just left Kingstown (now Dun Laoghaire). 501 of the 771 people on board died, including crew, postal workers, civilians, Voluntary Aid Nurses and eight Royal Dublin Fusiliers. Many were Irish men and women returning from leave. There were 25 members of the Royal Navy on board.

George Richard Colin Campbell was the second highest ranking member of the Royal Navy on the ship. Known as Colin, the thirty-four year old Lieutenant Commander was born at Ballyeglish, Moneymore, County Londonderry, the son of a clergyman. A career naval officer, he had been promoted to Lieutenant Commander in 1916. He joined the Admiralty Compass Department, rising to become superintendent of the Magnetic Compass Branch. With Dr. G.T. Bennett he invented the Campbell-Bennett Aperiodic Compass. Travelling with Campbell was his wife, Eileen, and four and a half year old daughter, also named Eileen. All three were lost in the sinking. Eileen Campbell's body was recovered from the sea with her baby still tightly clutched in her arms. They were brought to the mortuary of St Michael's Hospital, Kingstown, (now Dun Laoghaire), County Dublin where Colin's father, the Rev Edward Campbell identified them. Colin's body was recovered later. All three are buried in Grangegorman Military Cemetery, Dublin. Their grave has a headstone with a sculpted ships anchor.

The headstone reads:

1. Lieutenant Commander George Richard Colin Campbell, RN. Compass Dept, (Slough), HMS President. Born Ballyeglish, Moneymore, County Londonderry. Aged 34. Son of Rev Edward and Lydia Campbell, Sheskburn, Ballycastle, County Antrim.

2. Eileen Hester Campbell, (nee Knox-Browne), Aughentaine, Fivemiletown, County Tyrone. Wife of George Richard Colin Campbell. Mother of Eileen Campbell.

3. Eileen Elizabeth (four and a half) only child of George and Eileen Hester.

Lieutenant Commander Campbell is commemorated on Dungannon War Memorial

Lieutenant John Carruth
6th Battalion Royal Dublin Fusiliers
Died of Wounds: 10th October 1918
Tincourt New British Cemetery. France. Grave: 8-B-13

John Carruth was the forth son of Mr. E. Carruth, The Haven, Mallusk, Belfast, and the husband of Vera Maude Louise Carruth of Bona Vista, Stewartstown, County Tyrone, (whom he married in July 1915), the daughter of Mr. J.E. and Mrs. Vicker, Stewartstown.

He obtained his commission as an officer through Queens University Officer Training Corps in September 1915 and was gazetted to the 6th Battalion Royal Dublin Fusiliers on 15th October 1915. He served at the Battle of the Somme and was invalided home with trench fever. After his return to health, he was promoted Lieutenant and subsequently was attached to the 1st Royal Irish Rifles on 13th August 1916. He acted as a bombing officer at the Curragh camp until November 1917 when he was posted to Palestine to join his regiment. He was home on leave in August 1918. On the night of 7th October 1918, the Battalion was attacked by a bombardment of shell fire and he was badly wounded and taken to No.50 Casualty Clearing Station and died of his wounds there on 10th October 1918. He is buried in plot 8 - row B -grave 13 at Tincourt New British Cemetery, France. Lieutenant Carruth's brother, Matthew was killed in action on 9th September 1916 serving with the 16th Irish Division.

Vera Carruth received her pension until she remarried a former officer in her husband's regiment in 1931.

Corporal - John Charles McKeown

327th Infantry Regiment, 82nd Division (American Expeditionary Force)
United States Army
Killed in Action: 10th October 1918
Meuse-Argonne American Cemetery, Romagne, France. Grave: G - 16 - 2

Corporal John Charles McKeown was born at 'The Beeches', Killygonland, Ardboe, County Tyrone.

On 18th May 1917, the Selective Service Act was passed authorizing the President of The United States Of America to increase temporarily the military establishment of the U.S. The Selective Service System, under the office of the Provost Marshal General, was responsible for the process of selecting men for induction into military service, from the initial registration to the actual delivery of men to military training camps.

During World War 1 there were three registrations. The first, on June 5th 1917, was for all men between the ages of 21 to 31. The second draft, on June 5th 1918, registered those men who attained the age of 21 after June 5th 1917, and a supplemental second draft was ordered on August 24th 1918 for those men who turned 21 after June 1918. The third draft registration was held on September 12th 1918, for men between the ages of 18 to 45.

The information included on each registration differs somewhat but the general information shown includes order and serial numbers, full name, date and place of birth, race, citizenship, occupation, personal description and signature.

John Charles McKeown was one of the 24 million men (about 23% of the population in 1918) eligible for the draft when the United States of America entered the First World War. His Draft Card states that he was born 21st June 1894, Stewartstown, County Tyrone, Ireland. He worked was a Clerk in Providence, Rhode Island, and had no dependants, was unmarried, caucasian, and had no previous military experience.

He was described as tall, medium build, blue eyes and black hair. When he enlisted he was a resident of Lonsdale district, Providence, Rhode Island.

Details were signed on behalf of the draft board by William Davie on 6th June 1917.

It is important to note that not all those who registered for the draft actually served in the military and not all men in the military registered for the draft.

John Charles McKeown was listed as killed in action on 10th October 1918 during the U.S. Army's biggest engagement in World War 1, the Meuse-Argonne Offensive, which was the largest U.S. engagement of the war and began on the 26th September 1918 and ended with the Armistice on 11th November 1918. In those few weeks of fighting the U.S. Army had lost 18,000 men.

John Charles McKeown is buried in plot G, row 16, grave 2 at Meuse-Argonne American Cemetery, Romagne, France

He is commemorated in United States of America, Soldiers of The Great War, Volume 3 Rhode Island.

A/203561-Rifleman William McCann
12th Battalion Kings Royal Rifle Corps
Died of Wounds: 11th October 1918
Houchin Cemetery, France   Grave: 3-B-14

William McCann was born in Stewartstown. When he enlisted in Belfast he joined the Royal Army Service Corps but later transferred to the 12th Battalion of the King's Royal Rifle Corps. William died of wounds on 11th October 1918. He is interred in plot 3 - row B - grave 14 at Houchin British Cemetery, France.

The cemetery is situated 5 kilometres south of the town of Bethune.

27534-Private Edward Ferguson

9th Battalion Royal Irish Fusiliers
Killed in Action: 14th October 1918
Age: 20
Dadizeele New British Cemetery, Belgium. Grave: 3-D-5

Edward Ferguson was born in County Londonderry. He was the son of Michael and Elizabeth Ferguson of New Cottages, Coolnafranky, Cookstown. He enlisted in Greenock, Scotland where he was living and working during the First World War.

He is thought to have been killed during an attack on the Terhand-Kezelberg area on 14th October 1918. At 5.35am the attack began under a very heavy artillery barrage.

He is buried in plot 3, row D, grave 5 at Dadizeele New British Cemetery, Belgium.

When the war was over and the cemeteries were being put in place, Edward's family were asked if they would like to have a personal inscription added to the headstone. They chose. "May He Rest in Peace"

He is commemorated on Cookstown Cenotaph.

31184-Lance Corporal George Usher

2nd Battalion Royal Inniskilling Fusiliers
Died of Wounds: 16th October 1918
Age: 19
Duhallow (ADS) Cemetery: Grave: 4-H-23

George Usher was a son of James and Margaret Usher of Milburn Street, Cookstown. He was born in Cookstown and worked at Gunning's (Milburn) Factory.

George enlisted in Omagh with Royal Inniskilling Fusiliers. After a period of training he was promoted Lance Corporal and joined his battalion in a draft during 1916.

He died of wounds on 16th October 1918 and was interred in plot 4- row H- grave 23 at Duhallow (Advanced Dressing Station) Cemetery. He was nineteen years of age. When the war was over and the cemeteries were being put in place, George's family were asked if they would like a personal inscription added to the headstone. They chose the following.

"I shall go to him but he shall not return to me".

Samuel 2, Chapter 12, Verse 26.

George Usher is commemorated on Cookstown Cenotaph and St. Luran's Church of Ireland Roll of Honour, Derryloran, Cookstown and Gunning's (Milburn) Factory Memorial, Royal British Legion Cookstown.

Gunning's (Milburn) Factory
Memorial (RBL, Cookstown)

61888- Private William Thomas Bleeks
Machine Gun Corps (Infantry) 3rd Indian Division
Died of Illness: 17th October 1918
Age: 28
Cairo War Memorial, Cemetery. Egypt. Grave: O-322

William Thomas Bleeks was born in Stewartstown and was a son of James and Elizabeth Bleeks, of North Street, Stewartstown. He enlisted in Dungannon, joining the Connaught Rangers, army number: 9457. He then transferred to the Machine-Gun Corps and by 1918 was serving in Palestine where he fell ill and was transferred to hospital in Cairo. He died on 17th October 1918 and is interred in row O- Grave 322 in Cairo War Memorial Cemetery, Egypt.

During the First World War, Cairo was the headquarters to the United Kingdom garrison in Egypt. Along with Alexandria, it became a main hospital centre for the receipt and treatment of casualties from Gallipoli and later in the war it dealt with the sick and wounded from operations in Palestine and Egypt. William Thomas Bleeks is commemorated on Stewarstown Cenotaph and Donaghendry Church of Ireland Roll of Honour.

71398-Private Matthew Hagan

(formerly of North Irish Horse)
Household Cavalry & Cavalry of the Line
Staffordshire Yeomanry
Died of Illness: 17thOctober 1918
Beirut War Cemetery, Lebanon. Grave No. 31.

Matthew was a son of William and Matilda Hagan of Aughavey, Coagh, and was educated at Tamlaght National School.

Before Matthew enlisted in Antrim he was employed by his brother John in the fowl and egg business in Coagh. He joined the North Irish Horse in the early months of the war, and after training in Antrim, went to France, where he took part in some major engagements for 18 months. He was invalided home suffering from pleurisy, and after spending some time in Hilden Hospital in Belfast, and visiting his parents, he returned to his unit and volunteered again for overseas service. In late 1917 the North Irish Horse were temporarily disbanded and in January 1918 he was transferred to the Staffordshire Yeomanry. He contracted malaria while serving in Palestine and died on 17th October 1918, aged 24. He is buried in grave 31 at Beirut War Cemetery, Lebanon.

Matthew Hagan is commemorated on Coagh War Memorial (Royal British Legion Cookstown). A memorial to the men of the North Irish Horse can be found in Belfast City Hall, Matthew Hagan is named there.

Far away from all who loved him
Soldiers gently laid him to rest
In a heroes grave he lies sleeping
One of God's brightest and best
As He rose again he shall also rise
From the quiet bed where he now safely lies
Cheer ye fond mourners who sadly weep
For happy are they who in Jesus sleep

Obituary inserted by his family to Mid Ulster Mail *1918*

4325-Private John Sloan

5th Battalion Royal Inniskilling Fusiliers
Killed in Action: 17th October 1918
Vis-en-Artois Memorial, France. Panel 6

John Sloan was born at Tullyconnell, Cookstown. He enlisted in Cookstown with the Royal Inniskilling Fusiliers. He was killed in action along with four comrades on 17th October 1918. There is no known grave. John is commemorated on Vis-en-Artois Memorial, which forms the back wall of Vis-en-Artois Cemetery, France. John Sloan is commemorated on Cookstown Cenotaph.

44404 - Private Thomas Darragh

1st Battalion Royal Inniskilling Fusiliers
(Formerly - 87520 Royal Irish Rifles)
Died of Wounds: 19th October 1918
Terlincthun British Cemetery, Wimille, Boulogne, France.
Grave: 6-A-33

Private Thomas Darragh was born in Ballymena. County Antrim and appears to have enlisted there with the Royal Irish Rifles. He served with the Rifles before being transferred to the 1st Battalion Royal Inniskilling Fusiliers.

He died of wounds at a base hospital near Boulogne and is interred in grave 6-A-33 at Terlincthun British Cemetery, Wimille, Boulogne, France. He is also commemorated on Cookstown Cenotaph.

Terlincthun British Cemtery is situated on the Northern outskirts of Boulogne, France. The first rest camps for commonwealth soldiers were established near Terlincthun in August 1914 and during the whole of the First World War, Boulogne and Wimereux housed numerous hospitals and medical establishments.

The cemetery at Terlincthun was begun in June 1918 when the space for service burials in the civilian cemeteries of Boulogne and Wimereux was exhausted.

Some of the burials here were brought from surrounding cemeteries where they could not be maintained. There are 4,378 commonwealth burials from World War 1 and more than 200 of other nationalities, mostly German. The cemetery also contains 149 burials from World War 2. Of the total burials there, only 3880 can be identified.

44264-Private David George Curran

1st Battalion Royal Inniskilling Fuiliers
Died of Wounds: 23rd October 1918
Age: 19
Duhallow A.D.S Cemetery, Belgium.
Grave: 4-J-7

David Curran was a son of David and Elizabeth Curran of Oldtown Street, Cookstown and was employed at Gunnings Factory. He enlisted in Cookstown late in 1916 and had been through many of the campaigns towards the end of the First World War. He was seriously wounded in both legs on 14th October 1918, and was taken to No 44 Casualty Clearing station where one of his legs was amputated. David was seriously ill and spent much of his time in the company of the Chaplain of the station where he spoke of his love for his Mother and the other members of the family at home.

David died of his wounds on 23rd October 1918.

Following his death the Chaplain wrote to the family and the letter concludes:

I know how sore your heart will be, and that your hope will be desolate without him. But I hope you will try to remember that your loss is His gain and it is well with your boy. Everything was done for him that was humanly speaking possible but his wounds were so severe that he passed away at 4.00pm on 23rd October 1918.

David Curran is buried in plot 4- row J- grave 7 at Duhallow A.D.S Cemetery

He is commemorated on Cookstown Cenotaph, Gunning's Factory Memorial (Royal British Legion Cookstown) and St. Luran's Church of Ireland Roll of Honour Derryloran, Cookstown.

31893-Private Peter Quinn
Royal Inniskilling Fusiliers (Depot)
Died at Home: 25th October 1918
St. Mary's Roman Catholic Cemetery, Stewartstown, County Tyrone.

Peter Quinn was born in Newcastle-upon-Tyne and enlisted in Dublin, joining the Royal Inniskilling Fusiliers. He was assigned to work around the Inniskilling Depot. Before he enlisted Peter had lived for some time in County Tyrone. He died on 25th October 1918 and is interred in Stewartstown R.C. Churchyard. He is commemorated on Stewartstown Cenotaph.

306732-Private 2nd Class- William Hamilton Tomb
Royal Air Force
Died of Illness: 2nd November 1918
Age: 17
Kildress Church of Ireland Churchyard, Clare, Kildress, Cookstown.

William Hamilton Tomb was the son of Hamilton and Mrs. Martha Tomb of Killycurragh, Cookstown. He served his apprenticeship with Mr. McKinney, Pharmaceutical Chemist in Cookstown. William was regarded as a smart and obliging lad and although only seventeen years of age when the call came for recruits for the Royal Air Force he volunteered. He died of complications from pneumonia at the Royal Air Force Hospital at Landford training camp, Dorset on 2nd November 1918. His body was brought home to Cookstown and taken to 3rd Presbyterian Church (Molesworth). The coffin was covered in wreaths and draped in the Union Jack and was borne to the hearse by members of Montober R.B.P. of which William was a member. The Lodge marched in front of the hearse to Clare Churchyard, Kildress. Behind the chief mourners also marched the Cookstown Comrades of the Great War. Owing to the uncertainty of the time of the funeral the authorities could not provide a regular military funeral. The chief mourners at the funeral were his mother and sister and his brothers, John and Henry. The funeral service at the graveside was conducted by the Rev. Stanley Thompson, B.A. Dungannon (for Rev J. Johnston B.A. Orritor), and the Rev. J. Entrican B.A. led the prayer. Funeral arrangements were conducted by Mr. Robert Steenson.

William Hamilton Tomb is commemorated on Cookstown Cenotaph.

"The End In Sight."

*Christmas Card 1918.
Image depicts the
sentiments of the men still
at the front.*

Courtesy of Tom Jebb.

37102-(Worker) S. Moore

Queen Mary's Army Auxiliary Corps
Died: 1st April 1919
Age: 19
Desertlyn Old Graveyard, Moneymore, County Londonderry.

The Women's Auxiliary Army Corps was established in March 1917 and made up of volunteers of whom 57,000 were eventually employed. The first WAAC's moved to France on 31st March 1917 and by early 1918 there were some 6,000 WAACs based there, though most woman served at the home front. It was officially renamed Queen Mary's Army Auxiliary Corps (QMAAC) in April 1918 although the title was not generally accepted by the WAACs. The Organization mirrored the military model, their officers were ranked as Controllers and Administrators, non-commissioned officers were ranked as Forewomen and the equivalent of an army private was ranked as a Worker. The women were tasked with duties such as, cooking, catering, cleaning, telephony, motor vehicle maintenance and administration work etc. WAAC / QMAAC were formally under the control of the War Office and were a part of the British Army.

'Worker' S. Moore died on 1st April 1919 and is buried in Desertlyn Old Graveyard, Moneymore, County Londonderry. She has a Commonwealth War grave headstone.

Temporary- Captain Edward George Francis Gunning

Royal Field Artillery and Royal Army Ordnance Corps
Died: 10th June 1919
Age: 29
Les Baracques Cemetery, Sangatte, Calais, France. Grave: 18-A-15

Edward Gunning was the son of Francis Portes Gunning J.P. of Cookstown County Tyrone (late Lieutenant, Irish Guards) and Mrs. Kate Francis Gunning, of 11b Cromwell Place, South Kensington, London.

Captain Edward Gunning is thought to have died as the result of an accident and is buried in plot 18, row A, grave 15 at Les Baracques Cemtery, Sangatte, Calais, France.

In April 1915, No 6 Base Supply Depot was started at Calais to help relieve the pressure on Boulogne and to provide a base nearer to the front than Le Harve or Rouen. The base remained open until the last of the Commonwealth Forces left France in March 1921. The 30th, 35th, and 38th General Hospitals, No 9 British Red Cross Hospital and No 10 Canadian Stationary Hospital were based in the town, providing about 2,500 beds. For three years, Commonwealth burials were made in Calais Southern Cemetery, but it became necessary to start a new site at Le Baracques and the first burials took place here in September 1917. It was in continued use until 1921 and now contains 1,303 Commonwealth burials from the First World War, together with 250 other nationalities, most of them German.

17230 - Regimental Quartermaster Sergeant, J.A.B. Barlowe

19th Battalion Royal Irish Rifles
Died: 16th July 1919
Age: 23

Donaghendry Church of Ireland Churchyard, Stewartstown, County Tyrone.

J.A.B. Barlowe was the son of James A. Barlowe and Martha Barlowe, Dundiven, Craigavad, Belfast. He is buried in Donaghendry Church of Ireland Churchyard and is commemorated on the Roll of Honour in the church, He is also commemorated on Stewartstown Cenotaph.

First World War - Addendum

This addendum has been included to provide details of soldiers who enlisted in Cookstown or who lived within or close to the Cookstown district boundary. Some are named on Cookstown district memorials and in many cases further details are uncertain particularly in relation to their place of burial or nature of death.

3066- Sergeant J. Burns lived in Cookstown and died on 7th August 1920. He is interred in Cookstown New Cemetery.

J. Burns

19859- Private James Campbell, age 20, was the son of William and Jane Campbell, of Magherafelt. He enlisted in Cookstown and served with the 2nd Royal Inniskilling Fusiliers. He died as a Prisoner of War in France on 15th October 1918 and is buried in grave: A-4 at Sarrable Military Cemetery, France.

9949-Private Francis Eccles, age 27, was born in the parish of Drumglass, Dungannon and was the son of Francis and Mary A. Eccles, of Carland, Dungannon. He enlisted in Cookstown and served with the 1st Royal Inniskilling Fusiliers at Gallipoli where he was wounded in action. He died of his wounds at hospital in Malta on 3rd August 1915 and is buried in grave: E-EA-E 658 at Addolorata Cemetery, Malta. He is commemorated on Dungannon War Memorial.

58599-Rifleman W Hobson served with the King's Royal Rifle Corps. He was the son of Benjamin and Eliza Hobson of Stewartstown, Co. Tyrone. He died on 13th June 1919 aged 34. He is buried at Donaghendry Church of Ireland Churchyard, North Street, Stewartstown.

W. Hobson

4419-Private John Hughes was born in Magherafelt and lived in Belfast. He enlisted in Cookstown and served with the 1st Royal Inniskilling Fusiliers. He was killed in action on 1st July 1916, during the Battle of the Somme and is buried in grave: 1-C-39 at Ancre British Military Cemetery, Beaumont Hamel, France.

9214-Private Robert Irwin M.M. (Military Medal) was born and lived in Castledawson. He enlisted in Cookstown and served with the 1st Royal Inniskilling Fusiliers. He was killed in action on 1st July 1916, during the Battle of the Somme at is buried in grave: C-50 at Y-Ravine Cemetery, Beaumont Hamel, France. He is commemorated on Castledawson War Memorial.

17812-Private Thomas Jeffrey was born in Muckamore, County Antrim and lived in Belfast. He enlisted in Cookstown and served with the 9th Royal Inniskilling Fusiliers. He was killed in action on 1st July 1916, during the Battle of the Somme. He has no known grave and is commemorated on panel: 4D-5B on Thiepval Memorial, France.

10569-Private William Johnston, age 24, was born in Moneymore and lived in Magherafelt. He was a brother of Andrew Johnston, Coolshinney, Magherafelt. William enlisted in Cookstown and served with the 2nd Royal Iniskilling Fusiliers. He was killed in action at the Battle of Festubert on 16th May 1915. He has no known grave and is commemorated on panel: 16-17 at Le Touret Memorial, France.

4354-Lance Corporal Hugh John Kearns was born and lived at Brackaville, Coalisland. He enlisted in Cookstown and served with the 2nd Royal Inniskilling Fusiliers. He was killed in action during the Battle of Festubert on 16th May 1915. He has no known grave and is commemorated on panel: 16-17 at Le Touret Memorial, France.

4476-Private William Kirkpatrick, was born in Portstewart, and lived in Maghera. He enlisted in Cookstown with the Royal Inniskilling Fusiliers as Private 19745. He later transferred to the 5th Connaught Rangers. He was killed in action at Gallipoli on 28th August 1915. He has no known grave and is commemorated on panel: 181-183 on Helles Memorial, Turkey. He is also commemorated on Portstewart War Memorial.

18090-Lance Corporal Francis John Lennox served with the 11th Battalion Royal Irish Rifles. He was the son of Mr. W.S. Lennox of Aughrim, County Londonderry, and brother of Andrew and James Lennox, The Arcade, Cookstown, County Tyrone and W.G. Lennox of 550 Rushton Road, Toronto, Canada. He was killed in action on 1st July 1916. He is commemorated on Thiepval Memorial, France, Panel: 15A-15B

12080- Private Joseph Logan, age 20 was born in Maghera and lived at Knockloughrim. He was the son of Patrick and Rose Logan, of Lemnaroy, Castledawson. He enlisted in Cookstown and served with the 9th Royal Inniskilling Fusiliers. He was killed in action in Belgium on 29th September 1918 and is buried in grave: 3-D-1 at Birr Cross Roads Cemetery, Ieper (Ypres), Belgium.

28406- Private Leslie Martin was born and lived in Upperlands, County Londonderry. He enlisted in Cookstown and served with the 1st Royal Inniskilling Fusiliers. He was killed in action during the German Spring Offensive on 22nd March 1918. He has no known grave and is commemorated on Pozieres Memorial, France.

9197- Private James McAnary, M.M., (Military Medal). He was born and lived in Desertmartin, County Londonderry. He enlisted in Cookstown and served with 1st Royal Inniskilling Fusiliers. He was killed in action during the Battle of Cambrai on 30th November 1917. He has no known grave and is commemorated on panel 5-6 on Cambrai Memorial, France. He is also commemorated on Castledawson War Memorial.

30745- Private William McCord was born at Desertlyn, Moneymore. He was the son of William and Lucinda McCord, Carmean, Moneymore. He enlisted in Cookstown and served with the 9th Royal Inniskilling Fusiliers. He was killed in action during the German Spring Offensive on 29th March 1918. He is buried in Grave 1-C-2 at Grand Seraucourt British Cemetery, France. He is commemorated on Moneymore War Memorial (Assembly Rooms).

27419- Private George McCracken, age 21. He was born in Castledawson and was the son of Joseph and Elizabeth McCracken, of Castledawson, County Londonderry. He enlisted in Cookstown and served with 'D' company, 9th Royal Inniskilling Fusilers. He died on wounds on 19th September 1918 and is buried in grave: 4-A-1 at La Kreule Military Cemetery, Hazebrouck, France. He is commemorated on Castledawson War Memorial.

24582- Private Brown Vance, age 21, was the son of Mrs. Marshall, of Killyfaddy, Magherafelt, County Londonderry. He enlisted in Cookstown under an assumed name, the alias: Patrick McFalls and served with the 9th Royal Irish Fusiliers. He was killed in action during the Battle of Langemarck (Third Battle of Ypres) on 16th August 1917. He has no known grave and is commemorated on panel: 140-141 at Tyne Cot Memorial, Belgium.

4155- Private James McMaster, age 33. D.C.M. (Distinguished Conduct Medal). He was the son of Alexander and Catherine McMaster, of Corlecky Maghera, and husband of Mary McMaster, of Hall Street, Maghera, County Londonderry. He enlisted in Cookstown and served with the 7th (South Irish Horse) Battalion Royal Irish Regiment. He was killed in action during the German Spring Offensive on 21st March 1918 and is buried in grave: 1-B-32 at Templeux-le-Guerard British Cemetery, France.

11753- Private William Montgomery, age 18 was the son of Robert and Agnes Montgomery, of Upperlands, County Londonderry. He enlisted in Cookstown and served with the 1st Royal Inniskilling Fusiliers. He died of wounds at home on 29th June 1915 and is buried in Ahoghill Second Presbyterian Churchyard (South-West part of Cemetery).

108944- Private James Moran, age 35 was born in Desertmartin and lived at Bracanaslea, County Londonderry. He enlisted in Cookstown with the Royal Irish Regiment and served as Private 29829 before transferring to the 182nd Battalion Labour Corps. He died of wounds on 20th November 1917 and is buried in grave: 4-A-25 at St. Hilaire Cemetery, Frevent, France.

28408- Private William Patton was born and lived in Upperlands, County Londonderry. He enlisted in Cookstown and served with the 9th Royal Inniskilling Fusiliers. He was killed in action in an attack on the village of Gulleghem during the Battle of Lys, on 15th October 1918. He has no known grave and is commemorated on panel 70-72 at Tyne Cot Memorial, Belgium. He is also commemorated on Kilrea War Memorial.

16411-Private John Quinn was born at Brackaville, Coalisland. He enlisted in Cookstown and was subsequently posted to the 11th Royal Inniskilling Fusiliers. He was killed in action on 30th January 1917 and is buried in grave: 1-N-5 at Berks Cemetery Extension, Belgium.

16559- Private William Teaney was born and lived in Magherafelt. He enlisted in Cookstown and served with the 1st Royal Inniskilling Fusiliers. He was reported, killed in action due to enemy fire while the Battalion was doing some routine work in the Somme area, on 6th February 1917. He has no known grave and is commemorated on panel: 4D-5B on Thiepval Memorial, France.

3246- Private Francis Tohill was born and lived in Magherafelt. He enlisted in Cookstown and served with the 1st Royal Inniskilling Fusiliers. He was killed in action during the Battle of Arras on 19th May 1917. He has no known grave and is commemorated on bay: 6 on the Arras Memorial, France.

9272- Sergeant (QMS) Robert James Williams was born in Dundalk, County Louth and lived in Dublin. He enlisted in Cookstown and served with the 7th Royal Inniskilling Fuiliers. He was killed in action during the Third Battle of Ypres on 16th August 1917 and is buried in grave: 1-A-39 at Douchy Farm New British Cemetery, Belgium.

4429- Private John Wright, age 20 was the son of Mrs. Susan Wright, of Rosegarland, Magherafelt. He enlisted in Cookstown and served with the 1st Royal Inniskilling Fusiliers. He was killed in action in the assault on Scimitar Hill during the Gallipoli Campaign on 21st August 1915. He has no known grave and is commemorated on panel: 97-101 on Helles memorial, Turkey.

John Bradley commemorated on Cookstown Cenotaph. Listed as R.I.F.

A.E. Brown commemorated on Moneymore War Memorial. No further details are available.

W.J. Corr (Royal Inniskilling Fusiliers)- Coagh War Memorial, Royal British Legion, Cookstown. There was an alias W J Corr who served with the Royal Welch Fusiliers in 1919 (died 10th April 1919) his real name was W L Rankin, buried at Grangegorman Miltary Cemetery, Dublin Ireland.

Marvyn Jack McGeown is commemorated on Cookstown Cenotaph and on St. Luran's Church of Ireland Roll Of Honour (as M.J. McGeown) Derryloran, Cookstown. No other details are available.

J.McWilliams is commemorated on Moneymore War Memorial, Assembly Rooms as War Dead. It is thought that McWilliams survived the war but did not return home. No other details are available.

Charles Montgomery is commemorated on Cookstown Cenotaph, no regimental details are given. No other details available.

Private Samuel Rice served with the Royal Inniskilling Fusiliers. He married Mrs. Mary Kempton, the wife of the late Henry Kempton, of Urbal, Coagh, on 20th April 1915, Private Rice had been training and based at Randalstown Camp at the time of his marriage. He was home on leave from France in February 1916, shortly after spending a couple of months in hospital at Brompton and Liverpool as a result of a discharge from his ears that appeared soon after an enemy bombardment. He was by this time partially deaf. He is commemorated on Coagh War Memorial as having died in the First World War. No other details are available.

Sergeant William Scilly, served with the South African Expeditionary Forces. He came from Killybaskey and is listed on First Presbyterian, Moneymore, as killed in action and commemorated on those who served in the Great War Memorial Roll of Honour at the Assembly Rooms, Moneymore. No other details are available

6972309 – Lance Sergeant Edward Joseph Timoney was the son of Edward and Brigid Timoney, of Loy Street Cookstown and husband of Catherine Timoney, of 45 Churchtown Cottages, Dundrum, County Dublin. Lance-Sergeant Timoney served with the 1st Battalion Royal Inniskilling Fusiliers (11582), attached to the 36th Division Signals Company. He died while in service in India on 17th September 1920.He was buried at Malakand Cemetery 116 and is commemorated on face 1 on Dehli Memorial (India Gate), Rajpath, Kingsway, Dehli, India.

He was a brother of John Timoney who was killed in action on 11th July 1916 and is commemorated on Thiepval Memorial, France.

Corporal Hugh Henry Watters, served with the Highland Light Infantry. He came from Tamnavalley, Ardboe, County Tyrone. He is listed on Albany Presbyterian Memorial as having served during the First World War. He is commemorated on Stewartstown Cenotaph as war dead. This appears to be an error as he subsequently emigrated to America.

1784 – Private James WOODS, age 36, served with the 19th Battalion Middlesex Regiment attached to the 144th company, Labour Corps (382735). He was the son of Henry and Sarah Woods of Derryganard, Lissan, Cookstown. He died on 25th November 1919 while in service in France. He is buried in grave 19- A- 13a at Les Baraques Military Cemetery, Sangatte, Calais, France.

J.W. Silkstone is commemorated on Stewartstown 479 Masonic Roll of Honour. No further details are available.

J. Woods

150090 Private William J R Gorman
8th Battalion Canadian Infantry (Manitoba Regiment)
Died of Wounds: 7th February 1917.
Age: 25.
Fosse no:10 Communal Cemetery Extension, Sains-en-Gohelle,
France. 1 B 38

William J.R. Gorman was born on 23rd December 1892 in
Bangor, County Down, he was the son of Thomas B. Gorman, of
19 Bridge Street, Bangor.

William emigrated to Canada where he worked as a Salesman
before enlisting with the 8th Battalion Canadian Infantry.

He died of wounds at is buried in grave 1 B 38 at Fosse No: 10
Communal Cemetery Extension, Sains-en-Gohelle, France.

William Gorman signed the Ulster Covenant in 1912 at
Sandholes Cookstown listing his home address as Bangor, Co.
Down. He is commemorated on Cookstown Cenotaph.

The Roll of Honour at St. John's (Woods Chapel), Ballyronan,
Magherafelt

There are four names on the memorial that are not included
elsewhere in this book:

James Gilmour from Aughrim who served with the 9th Royal
Inniskilling Fusiliers, killed on 1st July 1916. He is buried in
Connaught Cemetery, Thiepval, France.

Frederick William Fordes of Laurel Cottage, Magherafelt, was
serving as Chief Engineer on.board SS "Myrtle Branch" when the
ship was torpedoed by the Germans off the Irish Coast on 11th
April 1918. He is commemorated on Tower Hill Memorial,
London.

Humprey Wilson from Ballymaguigan emigrated to Canada and
served with the 75th Canadian Infantry (Central Ontario Reg.) He
died on 2nd September 1918 and is buried Dury Mill Cemetery
in France

Thomas John Richardson from Ballynagarve served with the 2nd
Battalion, Royal Inniskilling Fusiliers and was killed in action on
21st July 1917 He is buried at Longuenesse Cemetery, St. Omer,
France.

Gracefield church is now attached to the Woods Church
(formerly Moravian church), these men would probably have
worshipped there.

World War 2

Germany took control of Austria in 1938 and in March 1939 invaded Czechoslovakia. This was the last straw for the then British Prime Minster Neville Chamberlain. He had appeased Hitler during the annexation of Austria because of its large German population and very few people at home had the political will to contemplate war again.

After Germany's annexation of Czechoslovakia, Britain declared it would defend Poland if Germany invaded.

On 1st September 1939 Germany invaded Poland, on 3rd September. Britain and France declared war on Germany and within a week Canada, Australia, South Africa, India and New Zealand declared their support for Britain and France.

The United States of America declared it would remain neutral; it was over 2 years before they would join the Allies cause.

Southern Ireland remained neutral through out the war but this did not prevent a large number of men from joining the British armed forces. Northern Ireland became a base for thousands of men from the Royal Navy, Royal Air force and Army personnel. Upwards of 300,000 American G.I.'s would turn Northern Ireland into a giant base in the fight against Germany.

Whilst many men from the area joined the Royal Inniskilling Fusiliers, Royal Ulster Rifles and Royal Irish Fusiliers, many also joined mainland regiments. Larger numbers joined the Navy, with many men joining the Royal Air Force, reflecting the giant strides made in aircraft design and its role in warfare in comparison to World War 1

1939

This was the period known as the "phoney war". Britain biggest tragedy was the sinking of the H.M.S "Royal Oak" by a German submarine in Scapa Flow off Scotland. At the Battle of the River Plate the British Navy trapped the German battleship "Graf Spee" forcing her to be scuttled. This was a big boost to morale. The "Blackout" all over the land led to many accidents and people fined for not closing their curtains at home. Motor vehicles lights where turned down towards the ground.

"Dig for victory" was the slogan chosen to encourage people from all over Britain to grow their own food. Public parks, tennis courts, golf courses were under cultivation in an effort to achieve self sufficiency and free up space on Merchant ships for munitions. Over 1,400, 000 allotments by the end of 1943 led to over 1, 000,000 tons of vegetables being grown annually. Farmers were forced to cultivate as much land as possible and encouraged by government received grants to buy tractors. This led to the slow demise of the work horse in the countryside. Double summer time was introduced and remained throughout the war.

1940

Food rationing was introduced to Northern Ireland, but many people in border areas could go "South" to add to their meagre rations.

In March Italy joined the war forming and Axis with Germany. Germany invaded Denmark and Norway in April. Britain sent help but was unable to prevent Germany occupying both countries.

Neville Chamberlain resigned as Prime Minster and was replaced by Winston Churchill on 10th May. World War 2 had started in earnest, and as Winston Churchill predicted in his famous speech "blood, sweat and tears" would be endured by many over the coming years.

May 10th seen the invasion of Belgium, Luxembourg and Holland followed shortly by the invasion of France. The speed of the German attack surprised the British and the French leading to the evacuation from Dunkirk at the beginning of June.

The evacuation known as "Operation Dynamo" succeeded in returning over 338,000 men to Britain (over 100,000 of them Frenchmen).

Whilst the main evacuation was carried out by the Royal Navy, all sorts of sea craft played their part such as fishing vessels, pleasure craft and lifeboats.

Often overlooked was the large number of men who were evacuated after Dunkirk mainly from the North West of France but the most infamous "event" was the loss of SS Lancastria lying of St Nazaire (Brittany) with troops, RAF personnel, and civilian refugees, including women and children, on board. She was attacked by German Bombers and one of the bombs when down the funnel. The number on board may never be known, but almost certainly exceeded 6,000; some estimates were as high as 9,000. The ship sank rapidly and, according to the estimate of the Captain, only 2,500 of those on board were saved.

Owing to the scale of the tragedy, Winston Churchill forbade publication of the news, in the interests of public morale, and hence the story of the Lancastria has never been generally known, although it is Britain's worst maritime disaster.

Local men died during the defence of Dunkirk and the subsequent evacuation.

Italy declared war on France and Britain on June 10th and France signed an amnesty with Germany on 22nd June.

On July 10th the Battle of Britain began and many local men in the Royal Air Force would play their part. Radar played a big part in the winning of the "Battle of Britain". The Germans failed to destroy the Royal Air Force and changed to the bombing of British cities. This failure led Hitler to postpone the invasion of Britain, codenamed Operation "Sea Lion".

The Northern Ireland Government believed that they were outside the range of German bombers so many of the Anti Aircraft guns protecting Belfast were removed to the British mainland.

The decryption of the German Enigma Cypher Machine at Bletchley Park in England would prove decisive in the outcome of the war. The forerunner of today's computer would allow the Allies to break the German codes.

1941

The British drove the Italians out of the Western desert and back to the city of Torbruk. This led to the famous German General Rommel and the African Corps arriving in Africa, they succeeded in pushing the British and the Australians back into Egypt.

Belfast paid a heavy price for having very little anti-aircraft protection, searchlights or balloon barrages as German Bombers attacked on 7th April, Easter Tuesday 18th April, 4th May and 5th May. Over 1,100 died, more than 50% of houses were destroyed in some areas and over 100,000 made temporarily homeless. During the Easter Raid the Stormont government asked President De Valera for help. This resulted in Fire brigade crews from Dublin, Drogheda and Dundalk coming north for the first time.

The Belfast Blitz resulted in many people especially children moving out to towns and country areas. Cookstown and the surrounding areas had Belfast children in the community and many stayed until the end of 1944 or to finish their education.

On 24th May the German battleship the "Bismarck" sank H.M.S "Hood" causing the loss of over 1400 men, only 3 survived. The loss of the pride of the British Navy caused large scale shock in Britain but the Bismarck had been damaged and needed to return to France for repairs. Her rudder was damaged again by Swordfish aircraft from H.M.S. Ark Royal resulting in her sinking on 26th May. Only 100 of her crew survived. This welcome news could not disguise the fact of the ever increasing menace of German U-Boats in the North Atlantic. Britain was dependant on the United States of America for most of its food supplies and many other resources. The Royal Navy and in particular the Merchant Navy would pay a heavy price in the following years.

On the 22nd June the Germans attacked Russia (known as "Operation Barbarossa") and by early December they were almost at the "gates of Moscow" but like Napoleon they had not reckoned on the Russian winter.

On the 7th December Japan attacked The United States Navy at Pearl Harbour, and the next day The United States and Britain declare war on Japan.

Germany declared war on the United States on 11th December, the whole world was now at war.

1942

The first American troops arrive in Northern Ireland on 25th January.

February 15th saw the British, Australian and Indian forces surrender to the Japanese at Singapore in what is seen as the most humiliating defeat ever of the British Army. The Japanese captured almost 100,000 men, many of whom died in the Japanese death camps.

The Germans pushed the Allies back to El Alamein near Cario in Egypt by 30th June. The Donegal born General Montgomery takes command of the Allies in North Africa and launches the Battle of El Alamein in October which leads to the Germans being driven back into Tunisia by the end of the year. The United States Army invades North Africa on November 8th.

The bombing of Germany by the Royal Air Force intensifies, Churchill believes it to be the best way Britain can attack mainland Europe. The first all America bombing of Germany begins on 17th August. The

Battle of the Atlantic continues, and the large naval base at Londonderry plays a very important part in the battle. The flying boat base at Castle Archdale also plays a big part in the Battle of the Atlantic. They are helped by neutral Eire ignoring their flight path out to the Atlantic over South Donegal.

British Foreign Secretary tells of the mass execution of Jews by the Nazis on December 17.

The German army began to fall back in Russia. German victories have largely halted and the Allies begin to plan the invasion of mainland Europe.

1943

The Russians pushed the Germans back and re-took Stalingrad in February which had been under siege from the summer of 1942. More than one million Russians died during the siege. Many remains were left in the centre of the city for other families to eat.

By May the German and Italian armies surrender in North Africa.

The Allies invaded Italy (via Sicily) in July and the long hard road of forcing the Germans back on mainland Europe began. Italian surrender is announced in September and in October changes sides and declared war on Germany.

The Japanese occupy large swathes of South East Asia and numerous Pacific islands.

The "death railway" in Thailand-Burma is completed by Allied and Asian prisoners of war. The dreadful conditions and cruelty of the Japanese led to 110,000 deaths during the railway construction. The bombing of Germany by Royal Air Force and the United States air Force continued. The Battle of the Atlantic continues, and assisted by the breaking of the German codes (enigma cypher) the battle begins to turn slowly in the Allies favour.

1944

January sees the Russians push the Germans back on all fronts. The Allies invade the Italian mainland at Anizo and begin the push to liberate Rome.

The month of June begins with the Allies liberating Rome on the 5th and invading France on the 6th ("Operation Overlord") - a day known subsequently as D-Day.

D-Day began the Battle of Normandy which lasted from 6th June to 31st August.

The landings marked the beginning of 11 months of hard struggle to liberate France, Belgium, and the Netherlands.

On D-Day British and Canadian forces landed over 60,000 and 22,000 men respectively. The Americans landed 73,000 men, other nations which were involved were Free French, Norway, Greece, Poland, Belgium, the Netherlands, Czechoslovakia, Australia and New Zealand.

On the 13th June the Germans launched the first V-1 rocket against England. This unmanned rocket plus the later V-2 version caused many deaths in the South of England, the Belgian cities of Antwerp and Brussels and the French towns of Lillie, Arras and Cambrai.

The Allies encircled approximately 250,000 Germans in the Faliase pocket in Normandy and either captured or killed 90,000 forcing the Germans to fall back quickly towards Belgium during the last 10 days of August.

Paris is liberated on 25th August and during the first week of September Brussels the capital of Belgium is liberated.

The Americans begin the liberation of the Japanese held Pacific islands, the Japanese fight to virtually the last man causing the Americans thousands of casualties. The Allies begin to force the Japanese out of Burma, Thailand, and Malaya.

Operation "Market Garden", the Allied plan to capture the bridges over the Rhine in Holland was launched on 17th September. The British paratroopers holding the north side of the bridge at Arnhem held out until 24th September.

The failure of XXX corps led by the Guards Armoured division to arrive in time condemned a large part of Holland to a long hungry winter.

The Russians crossed into Germany for the first time on 20th October. The Germans launched "The Battle of the Bulge" on 16th December in a desperate attempt to cut off Allies Forces and reach the channel ports. The

attack initially has success but by the end of the year the
Germans were struggling due to lack of fuel.

The battle for Normandy was the first time penicillin was readily
available; many causalities survive due to the availability of this
drug.

1945

A surprise German attack on the allied air bases in Europe in the
New Year was repulsed with the loss of over 200 German
aircraft. The Allies actually lost 300 aircraft but easily replaced
them. German industry was being bombed day and night. The
German Air Force no longer posed a great threat to the Allied
Forces.

The Royal Navy had wrested control from the German
submarines after a long struggle for supremacy; more and more
of the convoys were getting to their destinations. It is often
forgotten that the British Merchant Navy supplied part of the
Russian War effort usually via the port of Archangel.

The Russians liberated Warsaw on 17th January followed shortly
afterwards by Auschwitz concentration camp. The Germans
fought bravely to defend the "Fatherland" especially against the
Russians who like the Germans in the early part of the war
commit many atrocities.

The Americans slowly drive the Japanese from the Pacific
islands; Iwo Jima is taken at the cost of over 6,000 American
lives. The British and Commonwealth armies forced the Japanese
out of Burma and Borneo.

The British and Americans crossed the Rhine in March. On 25th
March the last V-2 rocket is launched against Britain, they had
caused almost 3,000 civilian casualities. The total loss to civilian
life caused by air bombardment against German occupied Europe
was over 67,000.

Allied troops begin to liberate the concentration camps inside
Germany. The world was stunned by the pictures and scale of
this genocide.

Over 11,000,000 people lost their lives in the Holocaust, over
half of whom were Jews.

On the 12th April President Roosevelt dies and is succeeded by
Harry Truman.

The American and Russian forces meet up on the 25th April; Hitler commits suicide on the 30th April. Germany signs an unconditional surrender, an armistice was not contemplated at this time.

V-E day is celebrated on the 8th May; Europe is free from Nazi tyranny after almost 5 years.

America wins the race to develop the atomic bomb. Truman delivered an ultimatum to the Japanese on 25th July, surrender or face destruction.

Japan rejected the offer and the first bomb falls on Hiroshima on 6th August. One minute afterwards 66,000 people die. Another atomic bomb is dropped on Nagasaki and 33,000 die. War and how future generations might fight had changed for ever.

Japan surrenders and Victory over Japan is celebrated on 15th August.

Britain had lost 450,000 men and women during the course of the war and her Commonwealth Allies another 150,000.

World War Two Roll of Honour

6976709 – Fusilier John CRAWFORD

2nd Battalion Royal Inniskilling Fusiliers
Died: 30th December 1939
Le Grand Luce War Cemetery, France.

Fusilier John Crawford was the son of Mrs. McMahon, Coagh Street, Cookstown.

The 2nd Battalion Royal Inniskilling Fusiliers were patrolling the front line between Comines and Devlemont in late December 1939. At this time John Crawford is thought to have taken ill with hypothermia and was taken to a field hospital where he died later. Exact details of his death are unknown.

He is buried at le Grand-Luce War Cemetery, France and is commemorated on Cookstown Cenotaph.

6976709 – Able Seaman William DARRAGH

Royal Navy, HMS Grenville
Lost at Sea: 19th January 1940
Portsmouth Naval Memorial.

Able Seaman William Darragh was the son of the late Thomas Darragh & Sarah Jane Darragh, Killymoon Street, Cookstown, and husband of Catherine Darragh, Cookstown. William Darragh's father, Thomas, served with the Royal Inniskilling Fusiliers and the Connaught Rangers during the First World War and was killed in action in France in 1916.

William Darragh served his apprenticeship to the joinery trade with Joseph Crilly & Sons, Building Contractors, Cookstown and was highly regarded and popular among his friends and acquaintances.

He joined the Navy in 1934, and the first ship he joined was the HMS 'Iron Duke'. He had the honour to be one of the naval ratings to be chosen to represent the Fleet at the funeral of the late Admiral Earl Jellicoe in 1935. HMS 'Iron Duke' was slightly damaged by a bomb at Scapa Flow in October 1939. He later served on HMS Royal Oak, which was torpedoed at Scapa Flow, the same month.

After periods of service in other ships he was transferred to HMS Grenville, a flotilla leader, and served on her in the Mediterranean prior to the outbreak of the Second World War. HMS Grenville (H03) was a British Royal Navy Ship named after Vice Admiral Sir Richard Grenville. HMS Grenville was a G class destroyer laid down by the Yarrow Shipbuilding Company Limited, at Scotstoun in Glasgow on 29th September 1934, launched on 15th August 1935 and completed on 1st July 1936.

HMS Grenville was in Spanish waters during the Spanish Civil War, and while lying in Barcelona harbour one of her motor pinnace which had gone to collect Consular Mail, was fired upon. When the ship returned to home waters in November 1939 Seaman Darragh came home on short leave. This was to be the last time he saw his native town. His period of active service in the Navy would have been completed in another year. The destroyer Grenville had been engaged in convoy patrol duty, and it was stated that she was responsible for the sinking of at least one U-boat. HMS Grenville sunk after striking a mine in the North Sea on 19th January 1940 in which William Darragh was killed.

William Darragh was popular among his ship mates. He often spoke highly of Captain Creasy, the ships Commander who was among the survivors of the January attack on the vessel.

At the time of his death, William was survived by his mother, Mrs. Lagan, Orritor Street, Cookstown, and his brother Joseph Darragh, a joiner, who during the Second World War was engaged on Government work in Scotland. He was survived by another brother, Thomas Darragh who at the time was a painter and lived in Cookstown.

William Darragh is commemorated on Portsmouth Naval Memorial and Cookstown Cenotaph.

6976636 – Sergeant Thomas James GILDEA
2nd Battalion Royal Inniskilling Fusilers
Killed in Action: 17th May 1940
Age: 28
Halle Communal Cemetery, Vlaams-Brabant, Belgium.

Sergeant Thomas James Gildea was the son of Robert and Hester Gildea, Cookstown, Co. Tyrone, and the husband of Sally Gildea, 12 Sandhurst, Cookstown. Sergeant Gildea was born on 6th April 1913 and prior to active service he worked as a printer and also worked at the Vauxhall Car Plant at Luton, England. Before returning home at the outbreak of war, he had previously served 7 years in the army and had been in India, retiring from the army to get married to Cookstown girl, Sally Crane on 28th March 1937. They had 2 children, Nancy-Joyce who died in infancy and Maureen who was 10 months old when her father died. He was killed in action on the night of 17th May 1940 aged 28. It is believed that Sgt. Gildea was killed close to the Senne Canal at Halle in an action to support Royal Engineers who were demolishing bridges over which the B.E.F. had passed and to prevent them from falling intact to the advancing German troops.

He is buried at Halle Communal Cemetery, Vlaams-Brabant, Belgium, and is commemorated on Cookstown Cenotaph and on the family memorial in Cookstown New Cemetery.

At the time, the date of his death was difficult to ascertain and for a number of years his wife Sally persisted in making enquiries. The following is a letter in response to Mrs. Gildea's request. It was sent by The British Red Cross Society to Mrs. Gildea on 5th June 1942 when she lived at 44 Union St, Cookstown:-

Dear Mrs. Gildea,

You asked us in your letter if P/S/M McDaids mentioned the date in which your husband was killed; we did not tell you this as it seems a little uncertain, and I am sure you will realise how difficult it must have been in the fierce fighting and confusion to be quite accurate about dates.

P/S/M McDaid says that your husband was killed on 14th or 15th of May, but another man, L/CPL Graham who has written to us since then (he gives no further details and only corroborates McDaid's statements), says that the date was May 17th.

Perhaps later on, when it is possible to question them personally and not by writing, it may be possible to make certain which of these 3 dates are correct.

Thank you so much for your letter, I only wish we had not been obliged to send you such sorrowful news.

6976036 – Fusilier Joseph BURNS
1st Battalion Royal Irish Fusiliers
Killed in Action: 19th May 1940
Age: 28
Heverlee War Cemetery, Leuven, Vlaams-Brabant, Belgium

Fusilier Joseph Burns was the son of John & Margaret Burns of Morgan's Hill Road, Cookstown, Co. Tyrone.

On Sunday19th May 1940 the 1st Battalion Royal Irish Fusiliers were acting as part of the rear guard before the retreat to Dunkirk and were holding a 5000 yard front North East of Ninove near the River Dendre, in Belgium. It is believed that Fusilier Burns was killed when the Luftwaffe carried out a bombing and strafing attack on the 1st Battalion's positions on the 19th May 1940.

He is buried at Heverlee War Cemetery, Leuven, Vlaams-Brabant, Belgium, and is commemorated on Cookstown Cenotaph.

We smile with the world, but never forget,
In our garden of memories, you live with us yet.

Submitted to Mid-Ulster Mail by his family, Morgan's Hill Road Cookstown

7042852 – Fusilier William SLAINE
1st Battalion Royal Irish Fusiliers
Killed in Action: 23rd May 1940
Age: 35
Dunkirk Memorial, France

Fusilier William (Billy) Slaine was the son of William & Elizabeth Slaine, and husband of Annie Slaine, Cookstown, Co. Tyrone. At the time of his death he was survived by his wife Annie and 2 children, Billy & Lilly.

Fusilier Slaine was part of a reserved demolition guard defending the La Bassée Canal, near Bethune over which friendly forces were retiring. Royal Engineers blew the bridge as German groups attempted to storm it. This action resulted in significant loss of lives on both sides including that of Fusilier Slaine who was killed in this action on 23rd May 1940 aged 35.

William Slaine is commemorated on Column 129, Dunkirk Memorial and Cookstown Cenotaph.

43157 - Pilot Officer, James Hamilton GORDON

Royal Air Force, 15 Squadron
Killed in Action: 25th May 1940
St. Inglevert Churchyard, France.

Pilot Officer (Air Gunner) J.H. Gordon was the son of James and Matilda Gordon and husband of Virtue O. Gordon of Holywood, County Down. He was serving with 15 Squadron, Royal Air Force, based at R.A.F Wyton. On 25th May 1940 he was detailed to bomb troops, vehicles and vital bridges just behind the German front line, which was closing in on the main body of the British Expeditionary Force. His aircraft, a Blenheim Mark IV serial number P6913 LS was shot down near St. Inglevert, midway on the main road between Calais to Boulogne-sur-Mer and Marquise, with the loss of all of the crew. Pilot Officer D.S.R. Harriman and Sergeant P. Bloomer were also killed.

Pilot Officer J.H. Gordon is buried at St. Inglevert Churchyard, France. He is commemorated on Stewartstown Cenotaph.

6976614 – Fusilier John GALLOWAY

2nd Battalion Royal Inniskilling Fusilers
Killed in Action: 28th May 1940
Dickebusch Old Military Cemetery, Belgium

Fusilier John Galloway was born on 3rd April 1908 and enlisted 13th January 1930 in Omagh. He was the son of John & Kathleen Galloway, Killymoon Street, Cookstown, and husband of Mary Galloway, of Stewartstown, Co. Tyrone. Prior to enlistment John Galloway worked as a labourer.

At dawn on the 28th May 1940, B Company of 2nd Inniskillings were ordered to patrol forward to the St. Elo area and came under heavy German artillery and small arms fire. It is believed that Fusilier Galloway and 2 others were killed in this action.

He is buried at Dickebusch Old Military Cemetery, Belgium and is commemorated on Stewartstown Cenotaph.

At the time of his death he was survived by his wife Mary (Minnie) who later married Joe Quinn, who was a P.O.W. in the Second World War.

6976397 – Fusilier Joseph CONLON

2nd Battalion Royal Inniskilling Fusiliers
Killed in Action: 18th May – 8th June 1940
Age: 25
Gavrelle Communal Cemtery, Pas de Calais, France.

Fusilier Joseph Conlon was born in 1915, and came from Annetermore, Ardboe, Cookstown, Co. Tyrone. Prior to service Joe worked as a labourer.

The German Army invaded Belgium, Holland and France on 10th May 1940. The French and British armies where taken by surprise and their positions overran by the invasion. The confusion led to the evacuation to the coast. The 2nd Battalion Inniskillings fought in a rear guard action as part of the withdrawal to Dunkirk. Fusilier Joseph Conlon was killed sometime between 18th May and 8th June 1940.

He is buried at Gavrelle Communal Cemetery, Pas de Calais, France.

D/SSX 20220 – Able Seaman Andrew CURRAN

Royal Navy- H M S Glorious
Killed in Action: 9th June 1940
Age: 22
Plymouth Naval Memorial, Panel 37 – Column 2.

Able Seaman Andrew Curran was the son of Francis & Minnie Curran, Cookstown, Co. Tyrone, and brother of Mrs. Evelyn Millar of Belfast.

HMS Glorious was returning from Norway on route to Scapa having assisted in the evacuation of British and allied forces from the 5th – 8th June 1940. HMS Glorious, an aircraft carrier, had on board 20 RAF Fighters and 10 Fighter and 5 torpedo bombers from the fleet Air arm. On 9th June HMS Glorious and its escorting destroyers HMS Acasia and HMS Ardent were intercepted in the Norwegian Sea by the German Battle Cruisers, Gneisenau and Scharnhorst and sunk in little over two hours with the loss of over 1500 officers and men, including Andrew Curran. He is commemorated on Panel 37, Column 2, Plymouth Naval Memorial, Cookstown Cenotaph.and St. Andrew's Church of Ireland Roll of Honour, Ardtrea

May the sunshine he missed on life's highway
Be his in that Heaven of rest

Submitted to Mid-Ulster Mail by his sister Evelyn Millar

625299-Aircraftman William Charles IRVINE
Royal Air Force, 220-Squadron
Died on active service: 11th June 1940
Age: 19
Thornaby-On-Tees Cemetery, Yorkshire, England

Aircraftman, 1st Class (Wireless Operator), William Charles (Billy) Irvine was the son of William & Ethel Victoria Irvine (nee Appelby), Doorless, Tullyhogue, Cookstown, Co. Tyrone.

Billy Irvine's mother Ethel came from Henley-on-Thames, Oxfordshire, where she met her husband William Irvine, a WW1 Veteran and Poet. They returned to Tullyhogue where they run a cobblers shop and raised 7 children, Jack, Albert, Victor, Percy, Margaret, Violet & William (Billy)

Billy Irvine was on board a coastal command aircraft, Hudson P5127 that veered after takeoff and dived into the ground 1 mile north of Thornaby, Yorkshire, on 11th June 1940. He is buried at Thornaby-On-Tees Cemetery, Yorkshire, England and is commemorated on Cookstown Cenotaph and St. Andrew's Church of Ireland Roll of Honour, Ardtrea.

13003876 - Private John Joseph MURPHY
Pioneer Corps, 50th Company.
Killed in Action: 17th June 1940
Age: 43
Dunkirk Memorial, France. Column 153.

Private John Joseph Murphy was the husband of Mary Ann Murphy, (nee Quinn) Cookstown, Co. Tyrone. The had 7 children, Kathleen, Joseph, John, James & Anthony (twins), Freddie and Patricia. John Murphy had been a veteran of WW1.

During the withdrawal of troops from Northern France, Soldiers and Airmen, uncluding John Joseph Murphy were being evacuated from the Port of St. Nazaire, Brittany, France. He was on board the S.S. Lancastria when it was attacked by German Junkers 88 Bombers on 17th June 1940. One of the bombs went down the funnel of the Lancastria and she sank within 30 minutes, there were approximately 6,000 troops, crew, and civilian personnel on board. Enormous uncertainty remains to the actual loss of life and it is estimated that somewhere between 2000-4000 were drowned. Sir Winston Churchill felt that the country's morale could not bare such news so ordered the press not to reveal the story. The story of the tragedy later broke in the U.S.A., and the papers on the event are not to be released until the year, 2040. John Murphy was aged 43 when he died. He is commemorated on Dunkirk Memorial, Column 153, and Cookstown Cenotaph.

13007917 – Private William NELSON

Pioneer Corps
Killed in Action: 17th June 1940
Age: 42
Rennes Eastern Communal Cemtery, Ille-et Vilaine, France.
Grave: 1-A-61

Private William Nelson was the husband of Elizabeth Nelson and father of Victor Nelson, Fountain Road, Cookstown, Co. Tyrone and brother of James Nelson who died during the First World War. William was also a First World War veteran.

The Germans bombed the troop train on which he was travelling in on 17th June 1940 causing many casualties. Of the 252 Commonwealth Burials from the 1939-45 war in Rennes Eastern Communal cemetery the majority come from this troop train, including Private Nelson who was aged 42.

Private Nelson is buried at Section 18, Plot 1, Row A, Grave 61, Rennes Eastern Communal Cemetery, Ille-et-Vilaine, France. He is commemorated on Cookstown Cenotaph.

638353 – Aircraftman Frederick STEWART

Royal Air Force
Died on active service: 27th July 1940
Age: 22
East Bridgford (Saint Peter) Churchyard, Nottinghamshire,
England

Aircraftman Frederick Stewart was the son of Robert & Rebecca Stewart of 6 Louisville, Cookstown, Co. Tyrone.

Frederick Stewart was killed at R.A.F. Station, Newtown in Nottinghamshire when fire broke out in a stationary aircraft followed by a bomb explosion.

He is buried in East Bridgford (Saint Peter) Churchyard. Nottinghamshire, England and is commemorated on Cookstown Cenotaph.

We think of him in silence and often speak his name;
There's nothing left to answer, just a photo in a frame.

Submitted to Mid-Ulster Mail on his anniversary in 1948

First Radio Officer Samuel John Jackson SCOTT

Merchant Navy, M.V. Upwey Grange
Died at Sea: 8th August 1940
Age: 40
Tower Hill Memorial, London.   Panel 113

Seaman Samuel J.J. Scott was the son of William John and
Martha Scott. Samuel JJ Scott served with the Royal Navy
during the First World War as a Marconi Radio Operator.

On 8th August 1940 the Greaser, M.V. Upwey Grange (London)
which was fully laden and bound for London from Buenos Aires
was torpedoed 200 miles west of Achill Head, Co. Mayo, Eire.
First Radio Officer, Samuel Scott (aged 40), was killed as a result
of this action.

He is commemorated on Panel 113, Tower Hill Memorial,
London. He is also on Cookstown Cenotaph and on First
Cookstown Presbyterian Church Roll of Honour.

C/SSX 29509 - Ordinary Signalman Richard CURRY

HMS Jervis Bay, Royal Navy
Killed in Action: 5th November 1940
Age: 19
Chatham Naval Memorial, Kent, England. Panel 37

Ordinary Signalman Richard Curry was the son of Thomas &
Mary Curry, Coagh, Co. Tyrone.

He was serving on board HMS Jervis Bay, a converted passenger
ship which was taken over by the Admiralty in 1939. The Jervis
Bay was equipped with seven 6 inch guns and redesignated as an
armed merchant cruiser.   On 5th November 1940 HMS Jervis
Bay was acting as sole escort for the 37 Freighter Convoy HX84,
when the convoy was located and engaged by the German pocket
Battle Ship "Admiral Scheer". In an effort to protect the convoy,
HMS Jervis Bay ordered the convoy to scatter and attacked the
Admiral Scheer alone. This gallant but unequal action which
lasted for 24 minutes resulted in the loss of HMS Jervis Bay and
the deaths of her Captain and 198 of her crew including Richard
Curry (aged 19). Their sacrifice however was not in vain as 32
freighters from the convoy escaped into the closing darkness.
Richard Curry was posted missing, presumed killed. The Captain
of the Jervis Bay, Edward Fegen was posthumously awarded the
Victoria Cross.

Richard Curry is commemorated on Panel 37, Chatham Naval
Memorial, Kent.

623929 - Sergeant William Edward CALLAGHAN

Royal Air Force - 220 Squadron
Died on active service: 27th December 1940
Age 19
Runnymede Memorial, Surrey, England

Sergeant William Edward Callaghan was the son of Edward and Evelyn Callaghan, of Portadown, Co. Armagh. He was a member of Ballindrum Pipe Band, Moneymore.

William Callaghan was serving with 220 Squadron R.A.F, Coastal Command as a member of the aircrew onboard a Hudson II (T9373), along with Sergeant J.L. Rees, Sergeant Lane and Squadron Leader (Pilot) Rogenhagen. During a night patrol on the evening of 27th December 1940, the aircraft overstayed its prudent limit of endurance and ran out of fuel on the return to base. The crew abandoned the aircraft by parachute 2 to 3 miles south-east of Trevose Head. The Hudson II finally crashed at 9.29pm near Towan Head, Newquay, Cornwall. Squadron Leader (Pilot) Rogenhagen fractured an arm and a leg during the bale-out and Sergeant Lane survived the jump. Sergeant Lees and Sergeant William Callaghan were thought to have been lost at sea.

William Callaghan is commemorated on Runnymede Memorial, Surrey, England.

Master - Arthur Hill Coates WATERSON

Merchant Navy, SS Atheltemplar
Killed in Action: 1st March 1941
Age: 37
Tower Hill Memorial, London

Arthur H.C. Waterson was second cousin to Arthur Killips of 78 Chapel Street, Cookstown. Master A.H.C. Waterson was killed on active service on 1st March 1941 as Master of the oil tanker, SS Atheltemplar.

The SS Atheltemplar as Vice-Commodore ship led the Starboard Column of the outward bound convoy EN79. EN79 departed from Methil at 0630hrs on 1st March 1941 bound for Buenos Aires. EN79 met the inbound convoy WN91 off the Aberdeenshire coast.

Whilst air cover had been provided by 3 Hurricane Fighters during the daylight hours this was withdrawn at last light. The Luftwaffe had charted the progress of both convoys during daylight hours and 45 minutes after sunset convoy EN79 was attacked by 3 Heinkel III German Bombers. Their bombs hit the Atheltemplar destroying the Navigation Bridge and bridge deck house causing an immediate devastating fire. Captain Waterson and most of the executive officers were killed in the blast. The fires on board the Atheltemplar were eventually brought under control and she was taken under tow to the Tyne for major repairs. One of the aircraft was shot down with the crew of 4, taken as Prisoners of War.

Captain Waterson was aged 37 and is commemorated in Tower Hill Memorial, London.

Fireman – Brice HARKNESS

Auxiliary Fire Service
Killed: 7th/8th April 1941
Belfast County Borough Cemtery, Belfast.
Brice Harkness was the son of Thomas Harkness, Lismoney,
Cookstown.

Brice Harkness served with the Auxiliary Fire Service during the
Second World War and was on duty in Belfast on the night of the
7/8 April 1941 when the German Luftwaffe attacked Belfast for
the first time. Belfast was almost completely undefended. The
Northern Ireland Government believed that Belfast was beyond
the line of German Bombers. Brice Harkness was killed on
active duty, aged 25. The Germans attacked Belfast 3 more times
within the next 5 weeks causing severe damage and almost 1000
deaths. It is thought that Brice Harkness was the first fireman to
die in the Belfast Blitz. He died in the docks area of Belfast.

He is buried at Belfast County Borough Cemetery and is
commemorated on the Roll of Honour for the Auxilliary Fire
Service at Belfast City Hall.

633907- Flight Sergeant John NEWELL

Royal Air Force, 37 Squadron
Died on active service: 23rd May 1941
Age: 21
Ismalia War Memorial Cemetery, Egypt. Grave: 3-D-5

Flight Sergeant, (W.Op./Air Gunner), John Newell was the son of
Samuel & Elizabeth Newell, Stewartstown, Co. Tyrone.

Flight Sergeant John Newell was on board a Wellington Bomber
Mark 1, serial number T2812 that encountered technical problems
after taking-off for a test flight and dived into ground attempting
a forced landing at Shaullufa in the Middle East.

He is buried in grave 3-D-5 at Ismailia War Memorial Cemetery,
Egypt.

754377 - Flight Sergeant Thomas Colqhoun Edmonds BERKELEY

Royal Air Force Volunteer Reserve, 85 Squadron
Killed in Action: 14th June 1941
Age: 24
Runnymede Memorial, Surrey, England.   Panel 35

Flight Sergeant Thomas C.E. Berkeley was born on 2nd October 1916. He was the second son of James Lowry Berkeley and Eleanor Berkeley, and brother of Lowry, Mona, Eleanor, Gladys and James Berkeley of Poplar Hill, Tullyhogue, Cookstown, Co. Tyrone.

Thomas Berkeley worked at Gallaghers Tobacco Factory in York Street, Belfast and served as a pre-war member of the RAF Reserve. He was an all round sportsman and considered quite a proficient Tennis player. He joined 85 Squadron R.A.F on 2nd September 1940 and piloted a Hurricane during the Battle of Britain. During a night operation on 14th June 1941 Flight Sergeant Berkeley was flying a Boston Havoc against German intruders. His aircraft illuminated a German Heinkel 111 with its search light, the enemy responded with fire from the mid upper gunner. The Havoc was hit and went out of control and crashed killing both of the crew.

He is commemorated on Panel 35, Runnymede Memorial, Surrey, England. He is also commemorated on Cookstown Cenotaph and on Molesworth Presbyterian Roll of Honour.

Flt Sgt. Tom Berkely, second from right, pictured beside
Squadron Leader Peter Townsend with walking stick.

Merchant Seaman Lewis JOHNSON

Merchant Navy - S.S. River Lugar
Lost at Sea: 26th June 1941
Age: 47
Tower Hill Memorial, London. Panel: 87

Merchant Seaman Lewis Johnson was the husband of Annie Johnson, of Cookstown, Co. Tyrone.

Lewis Johnston (aged 47) was killed on active service while serving as a fireman and trimmer on board SS River Lugar (Glasgow) on 26th June 1941. SS. River Lugar was carrying a load of Iron ore from Pepel, West Africa and was bound for Liverpool as part of a 60 ship convoy, SL76. She was torpedoed and sunk by the German U-boat, U69, 300 miles South West of the Canary Islands. The Captain, 36 crew and 2 passengers were lost. 6 members of the crew survived the sinking and were rescued by the corvette HMS Burdock.

Seaman Johnston is commemorated on panel 87 of Tower Hill Memorial, London.

6984428 – Private William John HENRY

Reconnaissance Corps, R.A.C
Died: 7th September 1941
Stewartstown Roman Catholic Churchyard, Stewartstown

Private William John Henry was the son of Joseph and Elizabeth Henry, of Stewartstown.

He died on 7th September 1941.

He is buried in the Roman Catholic Churchyard, West Street, Stewartstown and commemorated on Stewartstown Cenotaph

7046163 – Fusilier Andrew ARTT

5th Battalion Royal Irish Fusiliers
Died: 1st November 1941
Age: 51
Cookstown New Cemetery, Cemetery Road, Cookstown

Fusilier Andrew Artt was the son of Andrew and Maria Patterson Artt, and husband of Elizabeth Murray Artt, of Cookstown.

He had previously served in the 1914-18 War and was wounded in action.

He died at home on 1st November 1941, aged 51, and is buried in Cookstown New Cemetery, Westland Road, Cookstown . He is commemorated on Cookstown Cenotaph.

95219 – Lieutenant Francis Richard CHARLES

Royal Armoured Corps, 8th King's Royal Irish Hussars
Killed in Action: 19th November 1941
Age: 22
Alamein Memorial, Egypt.   Column: 17

Francis Richard Charles was born on 12th April 1919. He was the son of Dr. Richard Charles, O.B.E., F.R.C.S. and Mrs. Charles of Ipswich, Suffolk. He was the Grandson of Mr and Mrs. Richard Charles, Loy Hill, Cookstown, County Tyrone.

Francis Richard Charles was educated at the Royal Military Academy, Woolwich, London. He received a commission with the 8th Royal Irish Hussars on 1st July 1939 and was promoted to the rank of Lieutenant on 1st January 1941.

The 8th Royal Irish Hussars were part of the 7th Armoured Division, better known as the Desert Rats. The division took part in the British offensive in late 1940 which recaptured Sidi Barrani and Bardia from the Italians and later in February 1941 the division took part in the decisive Battle of Beda Fomm which led to the capture of most of the Italian forces in North Africa at the time.

After Operation Battleaxe failed to relieve the siege of Tobruk in June 1941, General Archibald Wavell was replaced as Commander-in-Chief of the Middle East campaign by General Claude Auchinleck. On 18th November 1941, Operation Crusader was launched. The objective was to relieve Tobruk. It was during this action that Lieutenant Francis Richard Charles was killed in action on 19th November. He is commemorated on column 17 on the Alamein Memorial, Egypt. 30th Corps continued to advance through the southern desert, aiming to engage and destroy enemy tanks before turning north-west to rendezvous with the breakout at Tobruk. By 21st November, both 30th Corps and 70th Division were pinned down by the enemy artillery of Rommel's 90th Light Division. The situation was saved by the advance of 13th Corps, which began engaging enemy positions along the coast on 22nd November. By 26th November, 13th Corps, New Zealand Division had cleared the corridor between Tobruk and 30th Corps positions. The German Afrika Korps withdrew on 6th December 1941, creating a new frontline at Gazala, west of Tobruk. Later in December further skirmishes in western Cyrenaica caused heavy British losses. This was followed by the German withdrawal to Tripolitan.

1873670 – Sapper Robert John CARDWELL

Royal Engineers, 2nd Field Company
Killed in Action: 9th December 1941
Age: 23
Alamein Memorial, Egypt. Column: 46

Sapper Robert John Cardwell.was the son of Alexander & Mary Cardwell, Gortfad, Sandholes, Cookstown, Co. Tyrone. Prior to service with the Royal Engineers Robert Cardwell worked at home at Gortfad Glebe, Sandholes, Cookstown as a farmer. The following is a letter dated 4th December 1941 which he sent from North Africa:

Dear Mother,

Just a few lines hoping to find you all well as I am keeping well myself. I had two papers and a postcard last week. I haven't had a letter for 4 weeks now.

I haven't been able to write many letters lately, so don't worry if you have to wait a few weeks. The weather is colder now and there has been a lot of rain, there hasn't been any sand storms lately.

Have you been down to Lislea lately, how is everyone there, does Harry like to serve in the R.A.F. Does Mrs. Boyd come down often. This is all for the present, so I wish you all a happy Christmas and new year.

Best of luck,

From Robert John.

(Reference in letter to Harry, his brother, also reference to Mrs. Boyd, his father's cousin.)

Robert John Cardwell was killed in action on 9th December 1941 at El Alamein.

His brother Harry served with the R.A.F., his brother William served with the R.U.C., and his sister Gretta served with Queen Alexandra's Royal Nursing Corps during the Second World War.

Sapper Robert J. Cardwell is commemorated at Alamein Memorial, Egypt, column 46 and on Cookstown Cenotaph.

He was survived by his brothers Joseph & Frank, and sister Mary.

16951- Private Walter Thomas DUFF
New Zealand Infantry, 23rd Battalion
Killed in Action: 11th December 1941
Age: 37
Alamein Memorial, Egypt. Column: 102

Private Walter Thomas Duff was the son of William James Duff and Sara Jane Duff, of Hanover Square, Coagh, Co. Tyrone, and husband of Ella Duff. Mrs. Sarah Duff was a teacher at Coagh National School.

He served with the New Zealand Infantry in Greece when they withdrew in April 1941. The New Zealand Infantry fought throughout the Western Desert Campaign in the Summer and Winter of 1941. Walter Thomas Duff was killed in action on 11th December 1941, aged 37.

He is commemorated at Alamein Memorial, Egypt, Column 102.

509519 - Sergeant William ANDERSON
Royal Air Force, 151 Maintenance Unit
Died: 26th January 1941
Age: 33
Singapore Memorial, Kranji War Cemetery. Column: 414

Sergeant William Anderson was the son of Samuel Reid and Elizabeth Ann Anderson. He served as an instrument maker with No. 151 Maintenance Unit, Royal Air Force, based at Java. He died from natural causes on 26th January 1942 and was reported buried in Singapore Cemetery. However, all burial records were lost during the Japanese invasion and because it was impossible to identify his grave, Sergeant Anderson's name is commemorated on Singapore Memorial.

He is commemorated on First Moneymore Presbyterian Roll of Honour.

652473 – Sergeant Edward BROWN

Royal Air Force – 224 Squadron
Died: 6th February 1942
Age: 23
Runnymede Memorial Panel 79

Sergeant Eddie Brown was the son of Mr. Edward (Ned) Brown & Sarah Jane Bradford (nee Crooks) of Mullaghmoyle, Stewartstown. He was born 27th August 1918.

Sergeant Brown was serving as a Wireless Operator / Air Gunner with 224 Squadron, R.A.F Coastal Command. He was onboard the Hudson aircraft AM692 during a night patrol on 6th February 1942 along with four other crew. He is commemorated on Runnymede Memorial, Stewartstown Presbyterian Memorial Window and Cookstown Cenotaph.

Sergeant J. Blight. Sergeant T.E. Orr and Sergeant L. Hamilton. The Hudson failed to return from patrol and was posted missing.

The family received a telegram dated 8th February 1942 stating:

We regret to inform you that your son, 652473 Sgt. Brown is missing as a result of our operations on 6th February 1942. Any further information received will be immediately communicated to you.

244 Squadron.

Memorial Window Stewartstown Presbyterian Church commemorating the names of Edward Brown and Richard David Millar

D/SSX 17378 – Able Seaman John McGUCKIN
Royal Navy, H.M.S. Jupiter
Lost at Sea: 27th February 1942
Plymouth Naval Memorial. Panel: 65, column 3

Able Seaman John McGuckin, was born on 23rd Feb 1914 and was the son of Michael and Bridget McGuckin, Ballinderry Bridge, Cookstown. Prior to joining the Navy he was serving his apprenticeship as a tailor. He died whilst serving on H.M.S. Jupiter on 27th February 1942. During the battle of the Java Sea the ship struck a mine and sank shortly afterwards.

The following are extracts from 2 letters from John McGuckin to his mother on 6th December and 28th December, though the year is not specified:

Dear Mother,

Just another chance of wishing you all the best for Christmas. This is supposed to arrive before then if nothing untoward happens it on the way. I have the privilege to get to let you know some of the places we have visited since leaving, they are, Azores, St. Helena, Freetown, Capetown, Durban, from there to the Mediterranean and as far as Columbo. No further information can be given.

Could you in some way let Mrs. Curry know that her letter has been delivered though I have not met him yet, but I will in a few days from now. The weather is very warm here though it is the cool season, in fact the sweat is dropping from my nose at present. Never the less, I feel good and am as brown as a berry all over, the fair skin has to go first. I would like to send Maureen a cable for Christmas but I couldn't be sure whether she is at the same address or not. I hope to be free to get to Mass, and receive Holy Communion. If I am so unlucky as to not, I hope you will all remember me that morning.

All the best for now and don't worry, I couldn't be better.

Your loving son, Johnny.

Dear Mother,

*This is suppose to be the best chance for sea mail we have had in
the last 5 or 6 weeks so I am hoping it gets to you in a shorter
time than the others.*

*I have just been wondering how you all spent Christmas.
Personally I have had a very good one, perhaps I had something
you hadn't, that was sunshine. Sorry to say I didn't hear mass
that day though no fault of my own.*

John McGuckin is commemorated on Plymouth Naval Memorial,
Panel 65, column 3, and the family headstone in Ballinderry
Roman Catholic Cemetery.

D/SSX 26862 – Able Seaman Patrick Joseph TYRE
Royal Navy, H.M.S. Stronghold
Lost at Sea: 2nd March 1942
Age: 21
Plymouth Naval Memorial. Panel: 66, column 3

Able Seaman Patrick Tyre was the son of Patrick & Elizabeth
Tyre, Belfast, formerly of Cookstown.

On 2nd March 1942 a Japanese task group consisting of the
heavy cruiser Maya and the destroyers Arashi and Nowaki
discovered and sank HMS Stronghold as she tried to escape the
south of Java for the safer waters of Northern Australia. Maya
later took on board 50 survivors from HMS Stronghold. Patrick
Tyre's body was lost at sea, he was aged 21.

He is commemorated on Plymouth Naval Memorial, Panel 66,
column 3, and Cookstown Cenotaph.

6977628 – Fusilier William Thomas CAMPBELL

1st Battalion Royal Inniskilling Fusiliers
Died on active service: 10th April 1942
Age: 30
Rangoon Memorial, Burma.   Face: 11

Fusilier William Thomas Campbell was born at Ballyronan, Moneymore on 17th January 1916 and the son of Mr. William Campbell and Mrs. Rachel Campbell (nee Glendinning).   He enlisted in Omagh on 29th January 1934 and died10th April 1942, aged 30. The following letter is dated 8th August 1939 one can get an indication of his sense of humour:

Dear Mother,

In answer to your last two letters and which I was glad to get, glad to see you are all keeping well as this leaves me just as usual. Well mother, Mary must have kept her marriage a bit of a secret, for Tillie was telling me in the last letter that she thought she was getting married. So I see she has now already done so. Dawson never writes or neither does Mary so you see I will have no bother calling her by her new name, but I would like a letter from Dawson very much. The time here is very dull and I am beginning to think my time long of going in, it is just like home here plenty of rain and cold weather and nowhere to go and it gets a fellow like me down being used to plenty of life. You need not be scared of me getting married for I think that I will remain single as I am still pretty much of a woman hater and they always get a fellow in a lot of trouble.

Well mother, it is just a little bit chancy yet whether I get home this year or not but they have got to let me home next year. I hope that it all goes well and Hitler does not declare war before that. I hear that fags are very dear at home now, I don't know what a fellow will do for smokes around here now. I have had no reply as yet from Tillie and I was expecting one from her before I got yours, but you answered first. Tell Mary I said to drop me a line sometime and let me know how she is keeping. Well mother, I will have to close as this is all at present, so write soon.

From Willie to mother, with love. Xxx

He is commemorated on face 11 on the Rangoon Memorial, Burma.

Not a day do we forget you, in our hearts you are always near,
We, who loved you, sadly miss you as it dawns another year.

Submitted to Mid-Ulster Mail by his family, Ballyronan and Duneane, Randalstown.1946

6979112 – Fusilier Samuel John PURVIS

2nd Battalion, Royal Irish Fusiliers
Killed in Action: 25th April 1942
Age: 23
Pembroke Military Cemetery, Malta. Grave: 6-5-11

Fusilier Samuel Purvis was born in 1919 and was the son of George Purvis, and Jane Purvis (nee McMaster), of Cookstown, Co. Tyrone. The family lived near the Red Bridge, Drapersfield, and then Church Street, Cookstown. He joined the Royal Irish Fusiliers in 27th December 1937 and had seen service in Egypt and Palestine.

It was during the Battle of Malta that he lost his life in one of the many air raids on the island on 25th April 1942, aged 23. He is buried in grave 6-5-11 at Pembroke Military Cemetery, Malta. He is commemorated on Cookstown Cenotaph.

1180125 – Aircraftman 1st Class, Stephen George KIRKHAM

Royal Air Force Volunteer Reserve, 976 Balloon Squadron
Died of Wounds: 30th April 1942
Age: 34
Heliopolis War Cemetery, Cairo, Egypt. Grave: 1.F.8

Stephen George Kirkham was the son of Mr and Mrs. T. Kirkham and husband of Mrs. Mary Agnes Kirkham of Hammond Street, Moneymore, County Londonderry.

He served with the Royal Air Force Volunteer Reserve 976 Balloon Squadron in Egypt. The 900 series number was allocated to Barrage Balloon units of the Auxiliary Air Force.

The North African campaign covered a vast front, and as expected, many areas lacked sufficient Air defences. Balloons provided protection at several important ports and coastal landing areas, effectively enhancing the existing anti-aircraft defences and preventing low level attacks by enemy aircraft.

Stephen George Kirkham appears to have died from wounds received in action. He is buried in grave 1.F.8 at Heliopolis War Cemetery, Cairo, Egypt. The cemetery at Heliopolis was opened in October 1941 for burials from the many hospitals in the area coping with sick and wounded, mainly from the Western Desert campaigns.

6985550 – Fusilier Victor George PURVIS
70th (Young Service) Royal Inniskillings Fusiliers
Died on active service: 3rd June 1942
Age: 18
Cookstown New Cemetery, Cemetery Road, Cookstown.

Fusilier Victor Purvis was born on 12th August 1923. He was the fourth son of William and Annie Jane Purvis, and brother of Robert and Jean Purvis of Kingsbridge, Cookstown. Prior to enlistment he worked as an apprentice Plumber.

He joined the Inniskillings at the age of 18, on the 27th November 1941 at Omagh. The 70th (Young Soldiers) Battalion, Royal Inniskilling Fusilers was raised in Donaghadee, County Down on 24th December 1940 and moved to Craigavon on 18th January 1941 and then to Larne on the 24th October 1941. Further training took place in England where Victor George Purvis died as a result of drowning near Cornwall while training on 3rd June 1942. His remains were returned home and he is buried in Cookstown New Cemetery, Cemetery Road, Cookstown. He is commemorated on Cookstown Cenotaph.

The 70th (Young Soldiers) Battalion was disbanded in 1943.

1035372 - Leading Aircraftman William James BLEEKS

Royal Air Force Volunteer Reserve
Died by Accident: 20th June 1942
Age: 24
Seagoe Cemetery, Portadown, County Armagh.

Leading Aircraftsman William Bleeks was born on 28th May 1918 and prior to service with the R.A.F. he worked in the Seagoe Hotel, Portadown. He was the eldest son of Robert and Elizabeth Anna Bleeks (nee Wright), Hawthorn Cottage, Stewartstown, Co. Tyrone and husband of Mary Jane Bleeks (nee McCann) of Portadown, Co. Armagh.

He was killed on active service as a result of an accident at Skeabrae, Scotland on 20th June 1942, aged 24, and was returned home for burial at Seagoe Cemetery, Portadown, Co. Armagh. He is survived by his 2 children, Roberta May Leonard, and William James Bleeks, Stewartstown, Co. Tyrone.

He was the nephew of William T. Bleeks, who was killed in action on 17th October 1918 while serving with the 3rd Indian Division.

Yes, I heard an Angel whisper, he is here the one you love;
Just a little while before you, in our Father's home above.
He will rise to walk in Heaven's own light.

Submitted to Mid-Ulster Mail by his family

William James Bleeks is commemorated on Stewartstown Cenotaph

1939 — 1945

11TH HUSSARS
Lt. D.A.N. VISCOUNT STUART
9TH LANCERS
2/Lt. R.J.O. VISCOUNT STUART
ROYAL INNISKILLING FUSILIERS
FUS. E. MᶜGUCKIEN
ROYAL AIR FORCE
F/Sgt. J. NEWELL
·· J. GORDON
L.a.c. W.J. BLEEKS
U.S. ARMY
Pte. P. ANDERSON

Donaghendry Church of Ireland Roll of Honour

Assistant Steward Norman Dennis (Den) RIGLEY

H.M.S. Palomares (Naval Auxiliary Personnel (Merchant Navy)
Killed in Action at Sea: 9th November 1942
Age: 22
Liverpool Naval Memorial. Panel 17, Column 2

Norman Dennis Rigley was the husband of Amy Rigley (nee Somerville), Coagh, Co. Tyrone, and the son of George William and Elizabeth Alice Rigley of 53 Stainburn Avenue, West Derby, Liverpool.

Norman Dennis Rigley served as an Assistant Steward on board the Armed Merchant Cruiser, HMS Palomares. At the outbreak of the Second World War, the Royal Navy wasn't able to man all the auxiliary vessels which served with it and to deal with the shortfall in manpower, a number of officers and men of the Merchant Navy agreed to serve with the Royal Navy under the terms of a T.124 agreement. Under this agreement Merchant Navy personnel were subject to Royal Naval discipline while generally retaining their Merchant Navy rates of pay and other conditions. The manning port established to administer these men (including Norman Dennis Rigley) was at Liverpool.

When HMS Palomares docked in Belfast 'Den' Rigley and his friend, Jim Sheen met up with Amy Somerville and Evelyn Thompson. The two girls worked in the cafeteria of FW Woolworths, High St, Belfast. Romance blossomed between 'Den' & Amy and a few months later 'Den' proposed on board a tram in Belfast City Centre. Amy later joined 'Den' in Liverpool where they married on 13th March 1942. Jim Sheen was the Best Man, and Evelyn Thompson was Bridesmaid.

While in service on HMS Palomares, 'Den' Rigley and his friend Jim Sheen saw significant action with the Russian Convoys to Archangel and Murmansk including the disastrous convoy PQ17 where 25 vessels out of 36 were lost to enemy action.

During 'Operation Torch', the British-American invasion of French North Africa, HMS Palomares acted as an Anti-Aircraft artillery vessel. The landings commenced on 8th November 1942. On 9th November the ship was badly damaged by enemy action. Assistant Steward, Norman Dennis (Den) Rigley was killed in this engagement.

Jim and 'Den' made a promise to each other that in the event of either's death the other would visit the 'widow'. His friend Jim Sheen kept the promise.

Mrs. Amy Rigley gave birth to their daughter, Norma Denise a few months later.

Norman Dennis Rigley is commemorated on Liverpool Naval Memorial.

The memorial commemorates 1,400 officers and men of the Merchant Navy who died on active service aboard more than 120 ships with the Royal Navy. The majority of Merchant Navy personnel who died at sea and did not serve with the Royal Navy are commemorated at Tower Hill Memorial in London.

232729 – Lieutenant David Andrew Noel STUART

Royal Armoured Corps, 11th Hussars
Killed in Action: 10th November 1942
Age: 21
Alamein Memorial, Egypt. Column: 19

© *Earl Castle Stewart*

Viscount D.A.N. Stuart was the son of Arthur Stuart, M.C., 7th Earl Castle Stewart, and Eleanor the Countess of Castle Stewart, of Nutley, Sussex, and Stewartstown, County Tyrone.

Viscount D.A.N. Stuart received his education at Eton College and Trinity College, Cambridge where he studied languages prior to joining the services. He joined the squadron of 11th Hussars on 15th July 1942 and was described as a fine and extremely promising troop leader, much liked by his men.

The War diaries for the 11th Hussars state that: Enemy Aircraft including ME 109's and CR 42's attacked them at 1300 hrs on the 10th November 1942. They came under a further attack at 1500 hrs, by 7 ME 109's. The attack lasted for 25 minutes, the enemy bombing with bouncing bombs and machine gunning from low-level. Lieutenant D.A.N. Stuart was killed in this action and his driver – operator, Trooper Cahill was severely wounded. Three lorries were also destroyed in the attack. The diaries go on to say that Lieutenant Stuart will be greatly missed by his squadron and that he was buried near Bir Bibni 376354 by Major Wainman and Captain Wright (Doctor).

He is commemorated on Alamein Memorial, Egypt, Column 19, and on Stewartstown Cenotaph and on the Memorial Plaque in Donaghendry Church of Ireland, Stewartstown.

© *By kind permission 8th Earl Castle Stewart*

978191- Sergeant John Samuel ORR–
Royal Air Force Volunteer Reserve
Died by Accident: 30th December 1942
Age: 21
Irvinestown Church of Ireland, Churchyard, County Fermanagh.

Sergeant (Pilot) John Orr was the son of Samuel & Evelyn May Orr, of County Armagh, formerly of Pomeroy, Co. Tyrone.

John Orr was based with the RAFVR at Castle Archdale, County Fermanagh, which was the largest flying boat base during the Second World War. Situated on Lower Lough Erne the base was used by the flying boats to patrol the Western Atlantic waters and the sea approaches of the United Kingdom. As part of Coastal Command, a Catalina reconnaissance aircraft from 209 Squadron left the base at Lough Erne in the early hours of the morning of 26th May 1941 through the "Donegal Corridor" (a stretch of air space secretly provided by the Irish Government). By mid morning the Catalina had spotted the oil slick of the stricken German Battleship, Bismarck, and reported the ship's position to the Admiralty. By 10.30 am the next morning the Bismarck was sunk.

On 30th December, 1942, while piloting the aircraft Catalina Mark 1B, serial number FP239 of 131 Operational Training Unit as part of Coastal Command, the aircraft flew into a hill in bad visibility one mile north west of Omagh, Co. Tyrone. Sergeant Orr was killed, aged 21.

He is buried at Irvinestown Church of Ireland Churchyard, Co. Fermanagh.

7046141 - Fusilier Leonard (Leo) O'NEILL
1st Battalion Royal Inniskilling Fusiliers
Killed in Action: 7th January 1943
Age: 20
Rangoon Memorial, Myanmar, Burma.

Fusilier Leonard (Leo) O'Neill was born on 18th July 1922 and was the son of Harry J. & Elizabeth O'Neill, Stewartstown. He enlisted with the Inniskillings on 30th July 1940, shortly after his 18th birthday at Omagh, Co. Tyrone. He had previously worked as a brick worker/labourer.

It is believed he died in an action near Donbaik, Burma when a patrol from D Company, 1st Inniskillings engaged a much stronger force of Japanese troops resulting in many casualties, some from sniper fire. Leo O'Neill was killed in this action on 7th January 1943, aged 20.

He is commemorated on Rangoon Memorial, Burma, and Stewartstown Cenotaph.

The following verse appeared in the Mid Ulster Mail on the 4th anniversary of Leo's death, submitted by his father, Harry O'Neill:

Oh, why was he taken, that one we loved so fair.
And the world had so many it could better spare.
Hard was the blow that caused us to part,
But his memory, it is written in gold within our hearts.

Stewartstown War Memorial

FX76845 – Petty Officer Airman, Alan Millar Cameron BAYNE

Royal Navy, H.M.S. Condor
Died: 17th February 1943
Age: 23
Cookstown New Cemetery, Westland Road – Cemetery Road, Cookstown

Petty Officer Airman Alan Bayne was the son of William James Bayne, and Mrs. Selina Bayne, of Tinwald, Canterbury, New Zealand and formerly of Moneymore County Londonderry.

Allen Bayne served with the Royal Navy as part of Fleet Air Arm which was formed in 1937. He was based at H.M.S. Condor, a Royal Naval Air Station at Arbroath in Scotland. The base was used as No: 2 Observers School and deck landing training school, used by 753, 778 and 783 Squadrons. It later became a Naval Air Signals School. Flying ceased from the base in 1954. It was later taken over in 1971and renamed R.M. Condor Barracks, the base for 45 Commando, Royal Marines.

Allen Bayne died while in service on 17th February 1943, aged 23. No details of his death are available. His remains were returned home and he is buried in Cookstown New Cemetery, Westland Road, Cookstown.

He is commemorated at First Moneymore Presbyterian Roll of Honour.

6982776 - Fusilier Hugh O'NEILL

1st Battalion, Royal Inniskilling Fusiliers
Killed in Action: 7th/8th April 1943
Age: 21
Rangoon Memorial, Myanmar, Burma.

Fusilier Hugh O'Neill was born on 23rd January 1922 and was the son of Hugh & Bridget O'Neill, Chapel Street, Cookstown. He had worked as a message boy prior to enlisting with the Inniskillings on the 26th June1940 at Omagh.

The 1st Battalion Royal Inniskilling Fusiliers were stationed in India prior to the outbreak of World War Two. When the Japanese swept through South-East Asia and into Burma, the 1st battalion Royal Inniskilling Fusiliers where rushed north of Rangoon to destroy oil wells in March 1942. They succeeded, but less than a third of the battalion eventually returned to India.

On 7th / 8th April 1943 Hugh O'Neill was part of a patrol from 1st Battalion, Inniskillings which engaged a much stronger Japanese force in Padana Chaung area, Burma. The patrol suffered heavy casualties as the enemy seemed to be in strength. A decision was made that the Battalion lay up in the undergrowth for a whole day. Any sign of movement was met with indiscriminate firing from the Japanese in which the Medical Officer was killed. The plan was made to move at dusk southwards and then strike due west to come out on the beach south of Indin. Movement that night through enemy lines was extremely difficult. Fusilier O'Neill was killed in action during one of these engagements, aged 21.

He is commemorated on Rangoon Memorial, Myanmar, Burma, and is also commemorated on Cookstown Cenotaph.

7047221- Fusilier Isaac HENRY

1st Battalion Royal Irish Fusiliers
Killed in Action: 15th/16th April 1943
Age: 30
Medjez-el-bab War Cemetery, Tunisia

Fusilier Isaac Henry was born in June 1912 at Magheraglass, Cookstown. He was the son of Robert Henry and Mrs Anne Henry (nee McGaughey). Prior to joining the army he was a steel erector and went to live in Coventry with his wife, Margaret. He was conscripted in 1940.

1st Battalion Royal Irish Fusiliers were part of the 38th (Irish Brigade) who fought in North Africa and later in Itlay.

On 15th / 16th April 1943 his battalion was tasked with capturing the Djebelang, one at a series of barren rocky hills north of Medjez in Tunisia. Whilst the Battalion made good progress in capturing what was a hill fortress subsequent artillery fire and mortaring and sniping killed 2 officers and 3 other ranks. It is believed Fusilier Isaac Henry was one of these casualties.

He is buried at Medjez-El-Bab War Cemetery, and commemorated on Cookstown Cenotaph and at Kildress Parish Church.

6978607 – Sergeant William John HERON

6th Battalion Royal Inniskilling Fusiliers
Killed in Action: 27th April 1943
Age: 21
Medjez-el-bab Memorial, Tunisia. Panel: 19

Sergeant William John Heron was the son of John and Annie Heron, of Coagh, Co. Tyrone.

The 38th (Irish Brigade) was formed in 1942 and included the 6th Battalion Royal Inniskilling Fusiliers, 1st Royal Irish Fusiliers and 2nd London Irish Rifles. They served in North Africa and later in Sicily and on the Italian mainland.

Sergeant William John Heron was killed in an action involving A & C Company's of the 6th Battalion, Royal Inniskilling Fusilers on 27th April 1943. In an attempt to seize high ground in the Gollcah Gully in Tunisia, advancing troops came under very heavy and accurate machine gun and mortar fire as they assaulted crest after crest. The battalion suffered significant casualties in this action. Sergeant Heron was aged 21.

He is commemorated on panel 19 at Medjez-El-Bab Memorial, Tunisia,

2718459 – Guardsman Thomas Megaw
1st Battalion Irish Guards
Killed in Action: 27th April 1943
Medjez-el-Bab War Cemetery, Tunisia, North Africa. Grave: 9 G 20

Thomas Megaw was the son of Robert and Mary Megaw, and husband of Florence Elizabeth Megaw, Moneyhaw, Moneymore, County Londonderry.

Thomas had been training for the Police Service when he was persuaded to join the Irish Guards in 1937/38. He joined the Irish Guards with the intention of serving for 3 years but his plans were interrupted by the outbreak of World War 2.

His battalion embarked for Norway 10th April 1941, taking part in the Battle of Norvik. As part of the 1st Army, the 1st Irish Guards embarked for North Africa on 10th March 1943. Sadly Thomas was killed in action on 27th April 1943, just prior to the Axis forces being defeated in May 1943.

He is buried at Medjez- el Bab War Cemetery, Tunisia, North Africa., in grave 9 G 20.

There are 2,903 commonwealth servicemen buried or commemorated in the cemetery. 385 of the burials are unidentified. Special memorials commemorate 3 soldiers in Tunis, Tunisia (Borgel Cemetery) and one in Youks-les-Bains Cemetery, whose graves are now lost.

Within Medjez-el-Bab Cemetery stands the Memorial bearing the names of 2,000 men of the 1st Army who died during operations in Algeria and Tunisia between 8th November 1942 and 19th February 1943. It also commemorates the names of men who died with the 1st and 8th Armies who died in operations between 20th February 1943 and 13th May 1943, who have no known graves.

There are also 5 men from World War 1 buried there, their remains were brought here in 1950 from Tunis (Belvedere cemetery) and Carthage (Basilica Karita cemetery).

The following inscription was supplied by the family:

In life we love you very dear, and in death we do the very same.

13009152 – Lance Corporal George STIRRUP
Pioneer Corps
Died of Illness (P.O.W): 13th June 1943
Age: 50
Berlin War Cemetery, Charlottenburg, Berlin, Germany. Grave: 11.D.10

Lance Corporal George Stirrup was born on 21st November 1892 in Enniskillen and later moved to Cookstown where he married his wife Annie. He was the son of James & Catherine Stirrup, Cookstown, Co. Tyrone. He had previously seen action while serving with the Royal Dublin Fusiliers between the 22nd February 1909 and 7th August 1920 seeing service throughout the First World War. George and Annie Stirrup had two children, George Albert (jnr) who died on the 15th August 1919, aged four months, and another son named Victor.

The following verse appeared in the Mid Ulster Mail in 1919 submitted by George and Annie Stirrup:

We dream, we see your dear kind face and kiss your cold still brow,
But in our hearts we know, we have no Geordie now,
Home to Jesus, home to many
Every wave of trouble o'er
He is with those other loved one's
On that happy peaceful shore.

George Stirrup re-enlisted with the Auxiliary Military Pioneer Corps on 6th January 1940 in Omagh, Co. Tyrone. He was posted on 5th March 1940 and appointed Lance Corporal on 30th March 1940, being shipped out with the British Expeditionary Force on 29th March 1940. He was listed as 'Missing in Action' in May of that year during the withdrawal to Dunkirk. He was later found to be a Prisoner of War in June 1940.

While he was a Prisoner of War, George Stirrup died as a result of Coronary Sclerosis, damage to the cardiac muscle on 13th June 1943, aged 50. Originally buried in Frankfurt New Cemetery his body was then moved to Berlin 1939 – 1945 War Cemetery, Charlottenburg, Berlin. The cemetery is in the district of Charlottenburg and holds a total of 3,860 military burials. It was used in the post war years to bury the remains of Airmen and P.O.W's who were buried throughout Germany in other cemeteries.

George Stirrup's remains were buried under the name of George

Sterrit, the name inscribed on his headstone. According to the Commonwealth war graves commission, the family had been contacted after the war to confirm the details for the inscription. The war grave commission's records show the name to have been spelt Sterrit. This however is the wrong spelling of the surname and measures have now been undertaken to correct the error.

George Stirrup's son Victor also served throughout the Second World. George was also the great uncle of Air Chief Marshal Sir Graham Eric (Jock) Stirrup.

The following verse appeared in the Mid Ulster Mail in 1950, on the anniversary of George's death, submitted by his wife Annie and son Victor:

Far away from his native land, with a simple cross at his head,
He fought and died for Britain, one of God's honoured dead.
Sleep on dear George, as days roll by, no flowers on the grave
you lie.
For the broad wide ocean keeps us apart, your smiling face
forever in my heart.

George Stirrup is commemorated on Cookstown Cenotaph.

George Stirrup's grave in Berlin wrongly inscribed as G. Sterritt.

PLY/X3717 - Marine Samuel George DUNCAN

Royal Marines, H.M.S. Repulse
Died: 19thJuly 1943.
Age: 20
Kanchanaburi War Cemetery, Thailand. Grave: 8.M.3

Marine S.G. Duncan was son of Samuel and Lucy Duncan, of Soarn Cottage Stewartstown, Co. Tyrone.

HMS Repulse together with HMS Prince of Wales had left Singapore shortly after the outbreak of war with Japan on 8th December 1941 in an attempt to intercept a Japanese invasion convoy going towards Malaya. After no such invasion no force was found 'Force Z' turned south only to be attacked by 86 Japanese torpedo bombers flying from Saigon. Repulse evaded 14 Torpedo's but received 5 direct hits sinking within 20 minutes. HMS Electra and HMS Vampire both destroyers in Force Z rescued 385 of the crew, 327 died. HMS Prince of Wales, a new battleship was sunk in the same action less than an hour later by the same torpedo bombers with a loss of 513 of her crew.

Marine Duncan was on board HMS Repulse and survived her sinking by Japanese war planes dropping torpedo's on 10th December 1941. Although he was rescued, Marine Duncan was subsequently taken prisoner and died as a prisoner of war at Konue Camp on 19th July 1943, aged 20.

Marine Duncan is buried at Kanchanaburi War Cemetery, Thailand, grave, 8.M.3. He is also commemorated on Cookstown Cenotaph

6980686 – Fusilier Robert GILDEA

2nd Battalion, Royal Inniskilling Fusiliers
Killed in Action: 19th July 1943
Age: 36
Catania War Cemtery, Sicily, Italy. Grave: 4.B.48

Fusilier Robert Gildea was born in 1907, and was the son of Robert & Esther Gildea, Cookstown, Co. Tyrone and the brother of Sergeant Thomas Gildea (killed in action 19th May 1940).

Tragically he lost his younger sister Jane who was burnt to death at home, aged 9.

Prior to enlistment Robert worked as a farm labourer with the Espie family, Lismoney, Cookstown. While in service he was 'batman' to Colonel Pennyfeather-Evans.

Robert served with his cousin, Jim McCullough with the 2nd Royal Inniskilling Fusilers in France before evacuation to Dunkirk, when they where then posted to Madagascar, India.

The Battalion took part in the invasion of Sicily and mainland Italy.

Fusilier Robert Gildea was killed in action at the Battle of Lemon Bridge, Sicily on 19th July 1943, aged 36. He is buried at Catania War Cemetery, Sicily, grave 4.B.48. He is also commemorated on Cookstown Cenotaph and the family burial plot in Cookstown New Cemetery, Westland Rd, Cookstown.

After his death his sister, Mrs. Maggie Hudson received a letter from Colonel Pennyfeather-Evans in which he stated "Bob was a fine little Irishman". His sister Maggie said "In God's good time we'll meet again".

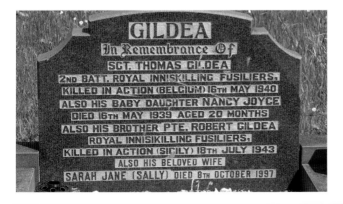

6982809 – Fusilier William J. HARKNESS
2nd Battalion, Royal Inniskilling Fusiliers
Killed in Action: 19th July 1943
Age: 26
Catania War Cemetery, Sicily, Italy. Grave: 3.F.10

Fusilier William J. Harkness was the son of Willam Harkness and Susan Harkness (nee Harrison) of Killycolp, Tullyhogue, Cookstown, and husband of Mary J. Harkness, Coalisland, Co. Tyrone.

On 10 July 1943, following the successful conclusion of the North African campaign in mid May, a combined allied force of 160,000 Commonwealth and American troops invaded Sicily as a prelude to the assault on mainland Italy. The Italians, who would shortly make peace with the Allies and re-enter the war on their side, offered little determined resistance but German opposition was vigorous and stubborn. The campaign in Sicily came to an end on 17 August when the two allied forces came together at Messina, but failed to cut off the retreating Axis lines.

Fusilier William Harkness was killed in action at the Battle of Lemon Bridge, Sicily on 19th July 1943, in the same action that took the life of Fusilier Robert Gildea.

Fusilier William Harkness is buried in grave 3.F.10. at Catania War Cemetery, Sicily, Italy.

Catania War Cemetery contains burials from the later stages of the campaign, from Lentini northwards. Many died in the heavy fighting just short of Catania (the town was taken on 5 August) and in the battle for the Simeto river bridgehead. Catania War Cemetery contains 2,135 Commonwealth burials of the Second World War, 113 of them unidentified.

The following obituary appeared in the Mid Ulster Mail on the anniversary of his death in 1950:

When Last I saw your smiling face,
You looked so bright and well.
I little thought dear son,
It was our last farewell

1533637 – Sergeant Alan John TAIT

Royal Air Force Volunteer Reserve, 103 Squadron
Died by Accident: 3rd October 1943
Age: 28
St. John's (Woods) Church of Ireland, Ballyronan, County
Londonderry.

Sergeant Alan J. Tait was the son of Robert & Margaret, and husband of Joy Olivia Tait, Portstewart, who was residing in Ballyronan at the time of her husband's death.

He died on 3rd October, 1943, aged 28. While serving as a Navigator on board a heavy bomber Lancaster Mark III, serial number JB436 the aircraft crashed shortly after take off at Elsham Wolds, England. His remains were returned home and he is buried in the family plot, at St. Johns Church of Ireland, Woods, Ballyronan.

D/JX 158782 – Telegraphist Edward Henry Sidney CARSON

Royal Navy, H.M. Submarine Usurper
Killed in Action: 3rd/12th October 1943
Age: 20
Plymouth Naval Memorial. Panel: 81, Column: 1

Telegraphist Edward H.S. Carson was the son of William J. & Olive V.M. Carson, Ballyronan.

On 3rd October 1943 HMS Usurper, a 'U' class submarine was believed to have been sunk by depth charges after being attacked by the German anti submarine vessel, UJ-2208/Alfred, in the gulf of Genoa. Failing to return to Algiers, HMS Usurper was posted missing presumed lost with all hands on 12th October 1943. On board was Telegraphist Edward H.S. Carson, aged 20.

He is commemorated at Plymouth Naval Memorial, Panel 81, Column 1.

1874237 – Sapper David BRIMAGE

Royal Engineers, 42 Field Coy
Killed in Action: 29th October 1943
Age: 26
Minturno War Cemetery, Italy. Grave: 8.G.23

Sapper David Brimage was the son of Hugh & Jane Brimage, Pomeroy, County Tyrone.

Sapper Brimage served with the allied forces that had made rapid progress throughout Southern Italy after landing on 3rd September 1943. By late October British Forces were moving with determined persistence at the German winter defensive position known as the Gustav Line. During this fighting Sapper Brimage was killed on 29th October 1943 aged 26.

He is buried at Minturno War Cemetery, Italy, grave 8.G.23.

14415058 – Fusilier Alexander (Sandy) JEFFERS

6th Battalion Royal Inniskilling Fusiliers
Killed in Action: 3rd November 1943
Age: 19
Sangro River War Cemetery, Italy. Grave: 8.E.6

Fusilier Alexander (Sandy) Jeffers was the son of Alexander &
Annie Jeffers, Coagh, Co. Tyrone.

He was killed on 3rd November 1943, aged 19, during the
Battalion assault on the town of San Salvo, west of the River
Trigno. The assault commenced at 0400hrs on 3rd November and
by 1300hrs with the support of artillery and armour the battalion
was firmly established. The battalion lost 2 officers who were
killed and 3 were wounded, with 15 other ranks killed (including
Sandy Jeffers) and 45 wounded.

The following was placed in the local paper the following year:

In loving memory of our dear son, Sandy, who was killed in
action on 3rd November, in the central Mediterranean, and was
buried in the Sangro River Cemetery Italy.

Far away from his native land,
With a simple cross at his head:
He fought and died for Britain,
One of God's honoured dead.
Sleep on dear Sandy, as the days roll by;
No flowers can we lay on the grave where you die;
For the broad wide ocean keeps us apart,
But your smiling face is ever in our heart.

Still sadly missed by his loving father, mother, brother and sister,
Main Street, Coagh.

Fusilier Alexander Jeffers is buried at Sangro River War
Cemetery, Italy, grave 8.E.6.

The site of this cemetery was selected by the 5th Corps. The
graves of men who had died in the fierce fighting on the Adriatic
sector of the front in November-December 1943, and during the
static period that followed were brought here. In addition, the
cemetery contains the graves of a number of escaped prisoners of
war who died while trying to reach the Allied lines. SANGRO
RIVER WAR CEMETERY contains 2,617 Commonwealth
burials of the Second World War.

Alexander (Sandy) Jeffers in also commemorated on the family
headstone at Old Eglish Cemetery, Ballinderry Bridge.

13805100 – Staff Sergeant Eugenio PELLEGRINI
Pioneer Corps
Died: 12th December 1943
Derryloran Roman Catholic Graveyard, Chapel Hill, Westland Road, Cooktown

Staff Sergeant Eugenio Pellegrini was an Italian Immigrant who lived with his family at Church Street in Cookstown.

He is thought to have died as a result of an accident whilst on home service in England on 12th December 1943. His remains was returned home and buried at Derryloran Roman Catholic Churchyard, Chapel Hill, Westland Rd, Cookstown.

D/KX143149 – Leading Stoker George Usher JOHNSTON
Royal Navy, H.M.S. Kenya
Died on active service: 13th December 1943
Age: 21
Trincomalee War Cemetery, Sri Lanka. Grave: 2.B.2

Leading Stoker George Usher Johnston was the son of William & Annie Johnston, Cookstown. He was born on 21st January 1923 at 'Orange' Row, in Coagh Street, Cookstown. George had 5 sisters and went to Oldtown School. Prior to joining the Navy he worked as a shop boy in Faulkners, Cookstown. He had tried to join the Navy on a couple of occasions before his 18th birthday but was unsuccessful. His two sisters, Ivy and Sadie had joined the ATS during the Second World War.

He died as a result of a tragic accident on 13th December 1943, aged 21 on board HMS Kenya. He was buried in an iron casket on the shore close to where he died. A few years later his body was reinterred at Trincomalee War Cemetery, Sri Lanka in grave 2.B.2., He is commemorated on Cookstown Cenotaph.

2204122 – Sergeant Edward Colhoun McLAUGHLIN

Royal Air Force Volunteer Reserve, 100 Squadron
Killed in Action: 2nd/3rd January 1944
Runnymede Memorial, Surrey

Sergeant Edward (Ted) Colhoun McLaughlin was the son of Edward & Jeanie McLaughlin, Ballyronan. Prior to the war he worked in Walsley, England with his uncle in his grocer's shop. During the war he flew numerous missions over Hanover, Bocum, Hagen, Munich, Kassel, Stuttgart, Dusseldorf and Berlin. The following letter was received by Ted's father Edward, dated 4th January 1944 written by Wing Commander J.F. Dilworth, R.A.F. Station, Grimsby, Lincolnshire.

Dear Mr. McLaughlin,

Further to my telegram to the 3rd. instant, it is with the deepest regret that I write to you confirming that up to the present, no news has been received of your son, Sergeant Air Gunner Edward Colhoun McLaughlin who did not return from an operational sortie on the night of Sunday, 2/3 January 1944.

Unfortunately, there is very little information that I can give you as nothing was heard from the plane after it took off from Base at 1140pm on 2nd January, to attack targets in Berlin. Although nothing was heard, there is, of course, a possibility that the crew were forced to abandon their aircraft over enemy territory, and they may be safe, although Prisoners of War.

"Ted" had been with us 4 months and during this time he had proved himself to be a very capable and efficient member of a gallant crew. They had taken part in many successful sorties against the most heavily defended targets in Germany. He was very popular with his colleagues, and we all desire to express our deepest sympathy and share with you the hope that he and his crew will soon be reported safe.

Ted's sister, Margaret was serving with the Royal Navy, based on H.M.S. Caroline during the later years of the war and received a letter from the Red Cross stating that the whereabouts of Ted's grave were unknown.

Edward (Ted) McLaughlin is commemorated at St. John's (Woods) Church of Ireland, Ballyronan, County Londonderry and at Runnymede Memorial, Surrey.

The Air Forces Memorial at Runnymede commemorates the names of over 20,000 airmen who were lost and have no known graves during the Second World War. The memorial overlooks the River Thames on Cooper's Hill at Englefield Green about 4 miles from Windsor to Egham on the A308.

D/SMX268 – Blacksmith, William Hugh FREEMAN
Royal Navy, HMS Leonian
Died: 7th February 1944
Age: 23
Cupuccini Naval Cemtery, Malta. Grave: Protestant Section
(Men's) Plot F, grave 111

Blacksmith William Hugh Freeman was the son of William Hugh & Mary Freeman, Church Street, Cookstown, the husband of Iris Elvina Freeman, Devonport, England. William (Billy) Freeman was well known in the Cookstown area as his father, William (Hughie) was a very popular Blacksmith. Prior to the war young William worked with his father as a Blacksmith and was a keen motor cyclist, having taken part in the Cookstown 100 motorcycle race in 1938.

Billy Freeman joined the Royal Navy in the summer of 1938. He was a member of the crew of HMS Exeter, with the rank of Seaman. HMS Exeter played a heroic part in the battle with the 'Pocket' Battleship Graf Spee off the River Plate on 13th December 1939. On the morning of 13th December, shortly after 6am Billy was lying on deck when the order came for "action stations". Distant guns flashed and soon HMS Exeter had received her first baptism of fire. Seaman Billy Freeman was a member of the crew of one of the 4.7 inch guns that returned fire until the gun itself was disabled by a hit that killed and wounded many men, a piece of shrapnel cutting a hole in Billy's cap and a slight cut to one hand. While serving on board HMS Exeter, Billy served with 14 men from Northern Ireland as well as men from the Republic of Ireland.

He arrived home on leave on 2nd March 1940 for 28 days to visit his parents in Cookstown. It is recorded that there were very enthusiastic scenes in Cookstown when he stepped of the bus from Belfast at the Transport Board's parcel depot in William Street where he was surrounded by a large crowd of well-wishers. That evening he was met by the members of Killymoon & Derryloran bands and paraded to his home carried on the shoulders of some of his neighbours. There was much loud cheering and Billy Freeman was heard to say "I hope I live to see Hitler scuttle himself too".

William (Billy) Freeman was in service on board HMS Leonian when he died on 7th February 1944, aged 23. The details of his death are unknown.

He is buried at Cupuccini Naval Cemetery, Malta, Grave Prot. Sec. (Men's) Plot F, Coll. Grave 111.

Malta (Capuccini) Naval Cemetery, which once belonged to the Admiralty, is divided into two sections, Protestant and Roman Catholic. Most of the 351 Commonwealth burials of the First World War form a triangular plot in the Protestant section, the rest are scattered elsewhere. Among those buried in the cemetery are 44 men from HMS "Egmont", the Depot ship at Malta, and 22 who died when HMS "Russell" was sunk by a mine off Malta in April 1916. Most of the 694 Commonwealth burials of the Second World War are also in the Protestant section in a plot near the entrance, but there is another group in the Roman Catholic section.

William Freeman is commemorated on Cookstown Cenotaph.

William Freeman with his wife Iris Elvina Freeman

623923 – Sergeant Thomas NELSON

Royal Air Force Volunteer Reserve 158 Squadron
Killed in Action: 20th February 1944
Age: 23
Hanover war Cemetery, Germany. Grave: 5.C.6

Sergeant (Air Gunner) Thomas Nelson was born in Cookstown. He was the son of Thomas J. & Sarah Nelson, Larne, and the husband of Mary Nelson, and nephew of Mrs. E. Scott, Moneymore Road Cookstown.

He was killed on 20th February 1944, aged 23.

He is buried at Hanover War Cemetery, grave 5.C.6., and commemorated on Cookstown Cenotaph.

1796421- Sergeant Robert Thomas Garth LOUGHRIN

Royal Air Force Volunteer Reserve
Died by Accident; 29th February 1944
Age: 20
Harrogate (Stonefall) Cemetery, Yorkshire. Grave: F.B.17

Sergeant (Flight Engineer) Robert Garth Loughrin was born on 25th July 1923 and was the son of Joseph Geddes Loughrin and Maud Evelyn Loughrin (nee Sharpe), of Mackney Road, Cookstown. Prior to the war Garth was an engineer. He joined the Royal Air Force Voluntary Reserve as a flight engineer on a Halifax J.D. 386 (heavy bomber) with the 1666 Heavy Conversion Unit which was formed on 5th June 1943 at Dalton, England. He was attached to the Royal Canadian Air Force.

Ministry of Defence records show that Sgt. R.T.G. Loughrin was a flight engineer on Halifax J.D. 286. While the aircraft was on a cross country exercise on 29th February 1944 the aircraft did a spiral dive to 800 feet, the pilot tried to recover the aircraft from the dive and lost control. The aircraft crashed at Bridge Farm near Broughton, Lincolnshire at 1820hrs and caught fire. It is thought that the aircraft developed rudder stall and the pilot was unable to gain control. All 7 crew members were killed. The full crew were as follows:-

1796421 Sgt. R.T.G. LOUGHRIN – Flight Engineer

J.19620 P/O J. SIGURDSON – Pilot

J.26289 F/O G.L. MUSKETT – Navigator

J.28076 F/O J.B. EATON – Air Bomber

R.96219 W/O J.M. HEALY – Wireless Operator / Air Gunner

R.124095 Sgt. P. ZAYETS – Air Gunner

R.192018 Sgt. F.E. WILT – Air Gunner

Garth Loughrin is buried at Harrogate (Stonefall) Cemetery, Yorkshire, grave F.B.17., and is commemorated on Cookstown Cenotaph, the family headstone in Cookstown Cemetery and on Orritor Presbyterian Church Roll of Honour, Cookstown.

IA/ 966 - Major, Gilbert William NANGLE
2nd Battalion, 7th Gurkha Rifles, Indian Army
Killed in Action: 2nd March 1944
Age: 41
Cassino War Cemetery, Cassino, Frosinone, Italy.   Grave: 28 C 8

Gilbert Nangle was the son of retired Colonel Kenlis E. and Sybil B. Nangle.

They lived at Ballyeglish Rectory, Moneymore, County Londonderry.

Colonel Nangle worshipped at Ballyeglish parish church and read the lesson every Sunday. During World War 2 he was the Comanding Officer with Ballyeglish Home Guard.

Gilbert Nangle enlisted in the Indian Army at the outbreak of World War 2. The Indian Army at the beginning of the War, numbered in the region of 205,000 men, this would rise later in the war to 2.5 million men, making it the largest all volunteer force in the world.

Major Gilbert Nangle is remembered around Ballyeglish to this day. When he came home on leave he would often go on long walks around the area.

He was Mentioned in Dispatches and was killed in action on March 2nd 1944, during the Battle for Monte Cassino, Italy and is buried in grave, 28 C 8 at Cassino War Cemetery, approximately 80 miles from Rome.

The site for Cassino War cemetery was originally selected in January 1944, but the development of the Battle during the first 5 months of that year made it impossible to use until after the German Army had withdrawn from Cassino.

During the early months of 1944, Cassino witnessed some of the fiercest fighting of the Italian campaign. The town of Cassino and the dominating Monastery Hill proved the most stubborn obstacles encountered in the advance towards Rome.

There are 4,271 service personnel buried at Cassino War Cemetery, 289 of which are unidentified. Within the cemetery stands the Cassino War Memorial which commemorates a further 4,000 Commonwealth servicemen who were lost during the Italian Campaign and have no known grave.

After the War, Major Gilbert Nangle's parents moved to live in Portstewart.

3129096 – Fusilier William KELLY

1st Battalion Royal Scots Fusiliers
Killed in Action: 6th March 1944
Age: 33
Taukkyan War Cemetery, Burma.   Grave: 5.H.6

Fusilier William Kelly was born on 3rd July 1910, the son of Mary Kelly, Factory Square, Cookstown, and formerly of Gortagilly, Moneymore. William Kelly worked as a farm labourer prior to enlisting in the army on 14th December 1933. He had seen service in Egypt Palestine and India.

William's mother received a telegram dated 2nd February 1943 stating that her son had died of wounds in Madagascar. Further notification was sent on that he had been wounded and taken to hospital from where he was discharged and returned to his unit. The telegram stated that the War Office sincerely regretted the misinformation and the anxiety it may have caused.

Fusilier William Kelly was killed in action a year later when defending Brigade Headquarters.

After William Kelly's death on 6th March 1944 (aged 33), the following letters were sent to Mrs Kelly, Factory Square, Cookstown:

Reverend Peter Mayhew, C.F.
2nd Battalion East Lancs Regiment,
India Command (Burma)

8th March 1944.

Dear Mrs. Kelly,

You will have heard long before this reaches you of the loss of your son, Fusilier Kelly. May I tell you how deeply we feel for you, and how sorry are all his comrades in the Brigade. We buried him in the shade of a tree in a green valley in Burma. Later on, his body will be put in a war cemetery and a beautiful stone will be put up in place of the little cross which now marks his grave. May God bless you and strengthen and comfort you in your loss until the day of reunion. With our very deep sympathy to you and all who mourn your son.

Yours Sincerely,

Peter Mayhew. C.F.

Capt. Davies
H.Q. 29 Infantry Brigade Group
India Command (Burma)
18th March 1944

My dear Mrs Kelly,

I am writing to offer you on my own behalf and on behalf of all ranks of this Headquarters our deepest sympathy in the heavy loss you have sustained in the death of your brave son, Fusilier Kelly. He was killed at his post bravely resisting an attack by the Japanese on this Headquarters. He died instantaneously doing his duty well and conscientiously as he has always done it since I have known him. I can assure you that no man was more liked by all who came into contact with him than your son and his quiet willingness earned him the respect of everyone with whom he came into contact. By his death we have all lost a friend and the British Army a fine soldier. Our Padre will have written to you telling you of your son's burial, and a suitable cross has been erected to mark his resting place and that of the brave fellows who died with him. We shall all mourn his loss but our sorrow will be slight compared to yours, but believe me you have the deepest sympathy of us all.

Yours sincerely,

Capt. Davies

Fusilier William Kelly is buried at Taukkyan War Cemetery, Burma, Grave 5.H.6.

Taukkyan War Cemetery is the largest of the three war cemeteries in Burma (now Myanmar). It was begun in 1951 for the reception of graves from four battlefield cemeteries at Akyab, Mandala. The cemetery now contains 6,374 Commonwealth burials of the Second World War, 867 of them unidentified. In the 1950s, the graves of 52 Commonwealth servicemen of the First World War were brought into the cemetery from the following cemeteries where permanent maintenance was not possible: Henzada (1); Meiktila Cantonment (8); Thayetmyo New (5); Thamakan (4); Mandalay Military (12) and Maymyo Cantonment (22). Taukkyan War Cemetery also contains: The Rangoon Memorial, which bears the names of almost 27,000 men of the Commonwealth land forces who died during the campaigns in Burma and who have no known grave.

2114030 – Sapper Thomas William WATTERSON
102 Field Company, Royal Engineers
Killed in Action: 21st March 1944
Age: 23
Naples War Cemetery, Italy.   Grave: 1.H.1

Sapper Thomas William Watterson was the son of Thomas and Mary Watterson, Coagh, and husband of May Watterson, Old Easwick, Yorkshire, England. Prior to enlisting, he worked as a farm labourer for Jack Wilson, Coagh.

He was killed in action on 21st March 1944, aged 23.

He is buried in Naples War Cemetery, Italy, grave 1.H.1.

131970 -Flying Officer Andrew Alexander HENRY
Royal Air Force Volunteer Reserve, 50 Squadron
Killed in Action: 10th May 1944
Age: 22
Forest-sur-Marque Communal Cemetery, Nord, France. Grave: 1. 3

Flying Officer (Air Bomber) Andrew Alexander Henry was born on 22nd April 1922 to Robert James Henry and Elizabeth Ewing Henry (nee Tennant), of Montober, Cookstown, Co. Tyrone. Prior to the Second World War he worked as a Petroleum Officer in the Civil Service, joining the Royal Air Force Volunteer Reserve as a Flying Officer.

He died on 10th May 1944, aged 22 years. He is buried at Forest-Sur-Marque Communal Cemetery, Nord, France, grave 1.3.

During his service one letter survives which he wrote home to his mother:-

Dear Mother,

I don't think I have written since I was in Glasgow and that seems quite a time ago. Even so, there is not a great deal to say except that I wont be able to get home until the travel ban is lifted, and that wont be until everything has gone up in smoke.

As you see by my new address I am on the move again. I came here last Sunday week but it is only temporary and I expect to be off again somewhere else next week. I have done a few hours in the air around here, the first time I have been off the ground since the end of last November. I have been pretty lucky getting a move like this as I managed to get with my old pilot, navigator, and our engineer again. Our rear gunner hasn't done any, but the mid-upper has done 44 trips. Our wireless operator is new. He's a very amusing bloke and comes from Mauritius. He can speak English fairly well and seems good at his work.

Well I don't think there is much else to say at the present time so I will stop and go out in the sun for a while.

Alec

Written while training in Nottinghamshire with the R.A.F.

Alec was flying his 34th sortie when his bomber was shot down over east of the city of Lille in France.

In a letter to his father dated, 13th May 1944 from Wing Commander A.W. Heward expresses:

Dear Mr Henry,

It is with deep regret that I have to confirm that your son, Flying Officer A.A. Henry has been reported missing from operations carried out on the night of 10/11th May 1944.

He was the air bomber of a Lancaster aircraft captained by Warrant Office J.H. Mason, which was detailed to attack LILLE, and, unfortunately nothing further has been heard of the aircraft since take off.

This was your son's 4th sortee of his second operational tour, 34 in all and he was one of our most experienced air bombers. He carried out his duties with the up most accuracy and precision. He was popular with his crew and his absence will be sadly felt in the Officers Mess.

With regard to his personal belongings, these are being collected and listed and will be forwarded to the R.A.F. Central Depository, Slough, Bucks as soon as possible, in accordance with regulations. You will receive a letter from that unit asking your wishes as to the disposal of these personal effects and any enquiry regarding them should be direct to the Officer Commanding, R.A.F. Central Depository.

All 7 crew members were killed. The full crew were as follows:-

1216353 W.O. J.H. Mason – Pilot

650776 Sgt. T. Harris – Flight Engineer

1561612 F/Sgt. J.J. Waters – Navigator

1681254 Sgt. R.J. Becherel – W.O.P./Air

641825 F/Sgt. W.C. Bull – M/U Gunner

1450790 Sgt. W.G. Wood – R/Gunner

131970 F/O A.A. Henry – Air Bomber

14418439 – Lance Corporal George ROLLINS
6th Battalion Royal Inniskilling Fusiliers
Killed in Action: 15th May 1944
Age: 19
Cassino War Cemetery, Italy. Grave: 11.K.20

Lance Corporal George Rollins was born on 30th June 1924, the son of George Rollins (snr) and Mrs. Lena Rollins (nee McCollum), Ardtrea, Cookstown. George was a member of Drumbonaway L.O.L 241. Prior to enlisting he had worked as a labourer. About 10 days before he was killed in action George received his promotion to Lance Corporal.

He was killed in action on 15th May 1944, aged 19 as a result of enemy action at the village of Vendittis, near Cassino, Italy. The Battalion assaulted the village capturing it by 0500hrs. The battalion with armoured support achieved its objectives for the day capturing approximately 25 prisoners. The Battalions casualties for the day included 2 Officers killed and 2 wounded, and 9 other ranks killed, including George Rollins and 50 wounded.

Lance Corporal George Rollins is buried in grave 11.K.20. at Cassino War Cemetery, Italy. He is commemorated on Cookstown Cenotaph, Stewartstown Cenotaph and at St. Andrew's Church of Ireland, Ardtrea, Cookstown.

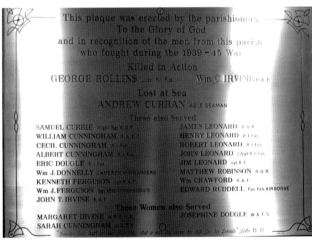

St. Andrew's Church of Ireland Roll of Honour, Ardtrea

1670597 – Sergeant Alexander Henry FREEBURN
Royal Air Force Volunteer Reserve, 514 Squadron
Killed on Operations: 22nd May 1944
Cookstown New Cemetery, Cemetery Road-Westland Road,
Cookstown

Sergeant (Navigator) Alexander Henry Freeburn, was the son of David & Margaret Freeburn, Cookstown, and the nephew of Alexander Freeburn who died in WW1.

Alexander Henry Freeburn flew with 514 Squadron during the Second World War.

Records show that on the night of 21/22 May 1944, 1670597 Sergeant A.H. Freeburn (R.A.F. V.R.) was the navigator of Lancaster D.S. 633 of 514 Squadron (Bomber Command) based at R.A.F. Waterbeach.

The aircraft was returning from operations against Duisburg and was seen to circle Waterbeach at 0303hrs. At 0309hrs the crew were instructed to jettison their bombs out at sea, but nothing more was heard of the aircraft after that time. It was presumed that the aircraft went down in the sea on 22nd May 1944, and all 7 crew were lost. Sergeant Freeburn's body was later washed ashore at Snettisham, Norfolk on 19th June 1944.

Alexander Freeburn's remains were returned home. He is buried at Cookstown New Cemetery, Cemetery Road - Westland Road, Cookstown.

THE WINDOWS IN THE FRONT
ELEVATION OF THIS CHURCH ARE
PLACED HERE AS A MEMORIAL TO
THE FOLLOWING WHO MADE THE
SUPREME SACRIFICE IN THE
WORLD WAR 1939-1945

THOMAS C. E. BERKELEY
EDWARD BROWN
ALEXANDER FREEBURN
BRICE HARKNESS
GEORGE JOHNSTON
GORDON REID

Molesworth Presbyterian 1939-45 Roll of Honour

6984370 – Fusilier William McCORMICK

2nd Battalion, Royal Inniskilling Fusiliers
Killed in Action: 29th May 1944
Age: 25
Cassino Memorial, Cassino War Cemetery, Italy.   Panel: 6

Fusilier William McCormick was the son of Alexander and Annie McCormick, Conygnham Street, Moneymore and brother of Mrs. Watterson, Urbal Road, Coagh.

The British Army in Italy at this time where given the erroneous title of, the D-Day Dodgers, an unfair description, given that they encountered some of the fiercest fighting of the Italian Campaign at this time in and around Cassino.

William McCormick was killed in action on 29th May 1944, aged 25.

He is commemorated at Cassino Memorial, Italy, panel 6.

The following verse was submitted by his sister Mrs. Watterson to the Mid Ulster Mail on the anniversary of his death:

I often speak your name, dear brother,
And wonder how you died;
It was sad we could not say goodbye
Before you closed your eyes

6985178 Lance Corporal Henry GREER
1st Royal Ulster Rifles, 6th Air Landing Brigade
Killed in Action: 8th June 1944
Age: 21
Ranville War Cemetery, Calvados, France. Grave: 4A.G.2

Henry Greer was a close friend of Joe Hall and Lance Corporal Ruddell

On the 6th June 1944, the day the allies invaded German occupied Europe. The Allied plan was to land on the beaches of Normandy at Utah and Omaha Beaches (United States Forces), Juno Beach (Canadian Forces) and Gold and Sword Beaches (British Forces).

The 1st Royal Ulster Rifles were part of 6th Air Landing Brigade (6th Airborne Division) who landed by gliders in and around the town of Ranville in Normandy on the 6th June 1944. Their objective was to capture and hold the bridges over the River Orne and the Caen Canal, a strategy to prevent the Germans from reinforcing the Normandy defences.

During the Normandy Invasion, Ranville was the first village to be liberated in France when the Caen Canal Bridge was taken intact on the 6th June by Parachute and Glider borne troops of the 6th Airborne Division.

The 1st battalion Royal Ulster Rifles captured the small town of Longeuval and spent the next two days strengthening their positions. Lance Corporal Henry Greer was killed in action fighting for the battalion's next objective, the town of St. Honorine, on 8th June 1944. He is buried at Ranville War Cemetery, Calvados, France. Grave: 4A.G.2. Many of the Division's casualties are buried here. The cemetery contains 2235 commonwealth burials from the Second World War.

Henry Greer is commemorated on Cookstown Cenotaph.

14410593 Private Gordon REID

7th Battalion Parachute Regiment, A.A.C.
Killed in Action: 7th July 1944
Age: 20
Ranville War Cemetery, Calvados, France.   Grave: 3A.E.3

Private Gordon Reid was the son of John & Elizabeth Reid, Cookstown.

Gordon was a member of 7th Battalion Parachute Regiment, 5th Parachute Brigade, 6th Airborne. The reason the 6th Airborne were given the number 6, was to mislead the Germans into thinking the British Airborne had 6 Divisions, when in fact they had only two. The Army Air Corps was formed to administer the Glider Regiments and Parachute Regiments in 1942. The Special Air Service (S.A.S.) was included in 1944.

Prior to D-Day Gordon parachuted into France as part of a joint operation with the S.A.S, led by Lieutenant Colonel Blair Mayne, Captain Pat Garstain and four other Ulster born soldiers including Cookstown man, Tot Barker. Their objective was to destroy railway tracks and rolling stock. Their operation was successfully completed. While being airlifted the group came under heavy enemy fire and Tot Barker was hauled on to the plane by Blair Mayne.

Gordon parachuted into France again with the 7th Battalion Parachute Regiment on the 6th June 1944. Their objective was to secure the Eastern flanks of the British landings and to secure the village of Benoville and subsequently the area around Ranville. The 6th Airborne spent the next 2 months consolidating their position in this area.

Gordon Reid was killed on 7th July 1944, aged 20. He is buried at Ranville War Cemetery, Calvados, France in grave 3A.E.3. Heis commemorated on Cookstown Cenotaph.

The following verse appeared in the Mid Ulster Mail in 1947 on the anniversary of his death, submitted by his family:

Sleep on, dear son, in a far off grave,
A grave we may never see;
But as long as life and memory last,
We will remember thee

6211647 Albert Victor SYMONDS

1st Battalion Middlesex Regiment
Killed in Action: 15th July 1944
Age: 26
Bayeux Memorial, Normandy, France. Panel: 16, column 2

Corporal Albert Victor Symonds was born on 21st November 1917 in Islington, North London, the son of Mr. Herbert & Mrs. Louisa Symonds (nee Bailey), later of Barnet, Hertfordshire. Albert was the husband of Gertrude Symonds (nee Stewart), Cookstown, Co. Tyrone.

Prior to enlisting in the Army, he worked in the retail clothing business and was an accomplished musician. While based with the Middlesex Regiment in Portrush, N. Ireland in 1941 Albert met and romanced Gertrude Stewart from Magherafelt. Gertrude worked for the Ministry of Finance, whose offices were moved from Stormont to the Metropole in Portrush. They married on 6th June 1942 and had 1 child, Elizabeth Laverne born 3rd May 1943.

He was killed in action on 15th July 1944, aged 26 during Operation Greenline, in Normandy. Operation Greenline was a night attack across the Odon Valley. All the companies of the battalion moved up on the night of 14th July 1944 to take up their positions. Casualties were severe, particularly in D (mortar) Company with their bombs exploding on enemy targets with great accuracy. This in turn incurred the wrath of the enemy and casualties were high as all the platoons in D Company were concentrated close together because of the narrowness of the valley they crossed.

He is commemorated at Bayeux Memorial, Normandy, France, Panel 16, column 2.

The Bayeux Memorial stands opposite the Bayeux Cemetery and bears the names of more that 1,800 men of the Commonwealth land forces who have no known grave and who died in the early stages of the campaign in Normandy. The inscription is in Latin and is translated: "We, once conquered by William, have now set free the conquerors land."

The Memorial was unveiled by the then Duke of Gloucester on 5th June 1955.

CRANE Thomas –

1532034 - Royal Air Force Volunteer Reserve, 101 Squadron.
Killed in Action: 28th July 1944
Age: 22
Rebrechien Communal Cemetery, France.

Sergeant (Air Bomber) Thomas Crane was the second son of Thomas and Maud Crane, of Cookstown, County Tyrone and later of Belfast. He was a brother of John, James, Richard, Madge, Ethel, Violet, Marina, Elizabeth, George, Maureen, Doreen and Noel.

He joined the Royal Air Force Volunteer Reserve when he was under the age of enlistment, by forging his father's signature. He eventually passed training as a Spitfire pilot but was later posted to Canada for training with Bomber Command. He served as a bomb aimer and front gunner with 101 Squadron.

On the night of 28th July 1944, while on a bombing raid to Stuttgart, Germany, the Lancaster Bomber was attacked by Luftwaffe fighter planes over France. The plane burst into flames before crashing into a crop field near the village of Rebrechien. One of the villagers, Gaston Jahier, who was 23 years old at the time recalled:

"The explosion scattered parts all around us. As I got to the crash site I saw the whole area on fire. I can remember the sheaves of wheat burning in the fields. The next morning I went back to see the wreckage and I found an identification picture 50 metres from the crash site. It was a photograph of a young, brown haired, beardless man and one could read the name Smith written on the back".

Gaston Jahier was referring to Flight Sergeant Clifford Ernest Smith who was one of the 8 men on the plane. The villagers recovered all the bodies and buried them at Notre Dame de Rebrechien Cemetery. They have maintained the graves ever since. Two pieces of propeller are placed either side of the headstone as a memorial to the men they refer to as, *"Liberators of France".*

Thomas Crane's sister, Mrs. Marina Ferguson recalled:

"I remember when Thomas came home on leave and I used to have to wait in a long queue of family members to kiss him goodbye when he had to go back. My mother made sure his memory never faded and I remember how heartbroken she was

when we were told he was missing in action. She kept a huge photograph of him on the wall which we surrounded with poppies every year. When we all left home she made sure we all had a photo of him to keep his memory alive.

Sergeant Thomas Crane is buried in Rebrechien Communal Cemetery, France along with the rest of his crew, Sergeant (Air Gunner) Eric Ronald Brown, age 21. Sergeant (W. Op. Air) Wolf Herman Engelhardt. Sergeant (Flight Engineer) John Hodgson, age 27. Pilot Officer Peter Joseph Hyland, age 21. Sergeant (W.Op. Air) John Thomas Victor Moore, age 21. Flight Sergeant (Navigator) Clifford Ernest Smith and Pilot Officer (Air Bomber) Albert William Turri, age 30, Royal Canadian Air Force.

Rebrechien is a village and commune some 9 miles (14 kilometres) north-east of Orleans. The cemetery is situated east of the village on the road to Loury.

Thomas Crane is commemorated on Cookstown Cenotaph.

6986237 – Private Thomas James (Tot) BARKER
Special Air Service Regiment, A.A.C. 1st
Killed (P.O.W.): 8th August 1944
Marrisel French Communal Cemetery, Oise, France. Grave: 326-329

Private Tot Barker was born in 1924 and the son of John & Florence Barker, Cookstown, Co. Tyrone. Prior to enlistment Tot worked with Messrs David Anderson & Son Grocers, Cookstown. At the age of 17 he joined the Royal Inniskilling Fusiliers. A month before his 18th birthday he transferred to the Royal Ulster Rifles.

The following letter was written by Tot whilst serving with the Royal Ulster Rifles addressed to his sister, Mrs. Evelyn Nelson and her husband Lowry. It refers to the death of their daughter, Avril Nelson.

To my dear sister Evelyn, and Lowry,

I got your telegram on Thursday evening and honestly I am very sorry for your trouble. I still can't believe it. Lowry if you are reading this letter will you write and let me know how Evelyn is doing. I know Evelyn and you are in a very bad state but I know you are a man and that you will be better than Evelyn so you can let me know about you and Evelyn. I hope you got my telegram all right. I had to get a fellow to send it, as I was out on a school and didn't get back until Saturday evening. I tried to get home but the Adjutant wouldn't let me as we are all going home in January on leave. I can't believe that wee Avril is away. The last time I saw her was in our house when I was going back the last time and she was laughing and I feel like crying when I'm writing this letter. Will you give me a photo of wee Avril when I go home Lowry because I never liked a kid as much as I liked wee Avril. I'm getting on fine. So dear Evelyn and Lowry, I'll close now wishing that you are well and hope that you will soon be happy again.

From your ever loving brother, and brother in law

Tot.

P.S. Write soon and let me know how you're getting on.

He later became a paratrooper with the 6th Airborne Division and finally joined the Special Air Service where he was under the command of Colonel Blair "Paddy" Mayne. On the night of 4/5th July 1944 a unit of paratroopers commanded by Captain Pat

Garstin were dropped south of Paris behind the German lines. Their mission was to damage German Aircraft on the French Airfields and to blow up ammunition dumps. The Germans were ready and waiting for them, as it was later revealed that they were betrayed by some locals. The party of soldiers were taken prisoner. Tot Barker and Captain Garstin were wounded and taken to hospital. The remaining five were taken to Gestapo Headquarters in Paris and all were horribly tortured. Tot Barker and Captain Garstin were reunited with their comrades on the night of the 7th/8th of August. During the 8th of August they were told they were going to be exchanged for German agents and were being transferred to Switzerland. After midnight they were taken to a field of the roadside near the village of Noailles. The soldiers were dressed in civilian clothes and all were handcuffed. Just outside Beauvais they were taken to a wood and put before a firing squad. Captain Garstin whispered to his comrades that when he shouted they were to make their dash for freedom. When the Gestapo stated that they had been condemned to death and were to be shot, French soldier, Serge Vaculik became hysterical and took the opportunity of escaping as Captain Garstin gave the command. They all started running except for Captian Garstin. Two men escaped but Trooper Thomas James (Tot) Barker and 4 others including Joseph Walker from Moira near Belfast, William Pearson Young from Randalstown, and Captain Garstin from Cork were killed. The French people from the village nearby erected a memorial near the spot where they were murdered. Sergeant Serge Vaculik and Ginger Jones escaped and were sheltered by the French Resistance and eventually sent back to British lines.

Tot Barker is buried at Marissel French National Cemetery, Oise, France, grave 326-329. He is also commemorated on Cookstown Cenotaph.

In February 1947 at the War Crimes trials at Wuppertal, Germany, six S.S.men were found guilty of murder, the two witnesses were Serge Vaculik and Ginger Jones. Four were hanged and two imprisoned.

Tot's brother Louis served with the Royal Ulster Constabulary as a Sergeant at Comber R.U.C. Station for many years. In September 1964 he travelled to France with his wife Eileen and their nephew Thomas (Tot) joined them there to take part in a memorial service commemorating the death of this group of soldiers. The Barker family met one of the survivors Serge Vaculik.

2723871 Guardsman Peter McCALLAN
3rd Battalion Irish Guards
Killed in Action: 11th August 1944
Age: 25
St. Charles De Percy War Cemetery, Calvados, France. Grave: 3.D.12

Guardsman Peter McCallan was the son of James & Brigid Ann McCallan, Pomeroy, Co. Tyrone. He was killed in action on 11th August 1944, aged 25.

Guardsman McCallan was killed in heavy fighting serving in the Guards Armoured Division between Caumont L'Evente and Vire, France, in the major allied trust to drive a wedge between the German 7th Army and Panzer Group West in the latter part of the Normandy Campaign.

He is buried at St. Charles De Percy War Cemetery, Calvados, France in grave 3.D.12

© Earl Castle Stewart

311623 – Lieutenant Robert John Ochiltrie STUART
Royal Armoured Corps, "B" Squadron., 9th Queen's Royal Lancers
Killed in Action: 17th September 1944
Ancona War Cemetery, Italy. Grave: 4.C.7

Viscount R.J.O. Stuart was the son of Arthur Stuart, M.C., 7th Earl Castle Stewart, and The Countess Castle Stewart, of Nutley, Sussex, and Stewartstown, Co. Tyrone.

Prior to enlistment Viscount R.J.O. Stuart received his education at Eton College.

Lieutenant R.J.O. Stuart was killed in action on 17th September 1944, aged 20.

He is buried at Ancona War Cemetery, Italy in grave 4.C.7.

© By kind permission 8th Earl Castle Stewart

5437164 – Corporal James DUNN

5th Battalion Duke of Cornwall's Light Infantry
Killed in Action: 23rd November 1944
Age: 25
Groesbeek Memorial, Gelderland, Holland.

Corporal James Dunn was born in 1919, the son of Robert & Margaret Dunn (nee McKeown). When he was 10 years old his mother passed away and he was then looked after by his grandparents, Robert & Lucinda Dunn.

James joined the army as a boy soldier in the 1930s. He then joined the Duke of Cornwall Light Infantry. In 1942 he transferred to the Military Police and after a year returned to his old regiment attached to the 1st Airborne in 1944. The 5th Battalion, the Duke of Cornwall Light Infantry served at Arnhem as part of 214 Brigade, 43rd Wessex Division and had seen action from the 17th – 27th September. Corporal James Dunn was killed in action on 23rd November 1944, aged 25.

He is survived by his brother William Dunn, Cookstown.

He is commemorated on Groesbeek Memorial, Gelderland, Holland and Cookstown Cenotaph.

164836 - FLACK – George Gaston

Flying Officer (Air Gunner) Royal Air Force Volunteer Reserve
Died: 30th December 1944
Beckenham Crematorium and Cemetery, Section: W 11, grave 16884

George Gaston Flack was born and lived on the family farm between Loup and Ballyeglish, Moneymore, County Londonderry. The family worshipped at Saltersland Presbyterian Church.

He is buried at Beckenham Crematorium and Cemetery (once, Crystal Palace District Cemetery) in grave 16884. Section: W 11

128 war graves are scattered throughout this cemetery, a number of them from the Royal Naval Depot, HMS 'Crystal Palace' and the Army Service Corps, Motor Transport Depot at Grove Park. Many of the graves could not be individually marked and 26 casualties are commemorated on a screen wall. There were 40 other graves that could not be satisfactorily maintained and these headstones were moved to a small World War 2 plot, which contains only 10 of the 127 World War 2 burials.

2324118 – Signalman Richard David MILLAR
Royal Corps of Signals 12th Indian Infantry Brigade (Signal Section)
Killed in Action: 5th January 1945
Age: 27
Singapore Memorial. Column 44

Signalman David Millar was the son of Robert and Margaret Millar, Stewartstown, County Tyrone. He was born on 28th February 1917. David had been in service for a number of years prior to the war. He joined up as a boy soldier at about 15 years old, and was later posted to Palestine, in May 1937 – February 1938. He was posted to India in June 1939 and then to Malaya in January 1940 with the Royal Corps of Signals. In July 1940 he wrote the following letter to his mother dated 21st July 1940:-

Dear Mother,

Just a few lines to let you know, that I am still getting along quite well. I hope that everyone is keeping well at home now. I have been rather worried just lately as it is ages since I last had a letter from you. It takes the mail a terrible while getting here now since the regular airmail was stopped. To send a letter to England by airmail now, it costs over two dollars which is about five shillings and I am afraid that that is rather expensive for me.

There has been quite a lot of changes in the war since the last time I wrote what with France signing an armistice with Germany and Italy declaring war. Still, there is no use getting down hearted as they shall never beat Britain. I have been rather worried lately about Bobby and Willie as I still have not had a letter from either of them. I don't know their address otherwise I would write to them.

How did you get the 12th of July over you, I suppose it was a lot quieter this year due to the war. I expect that most of my chums around Stewartstown have joined the army now since war was declared. How did Johnny Ferguson get on, did he join up at all, he was always very keen to join the Signals.

Have you still got Iris and Pat living with you, I bet they are just about fed up with Stewartstown by now. Still, they will be a lot safer there than they would be in Scarborough. By the time that I get home Margaret and Pat will have grown so big that I won't know either of them. I suppose they will have both forgotten all about me. Do you realise it is scarcely two years since I was home on leave but it does not seem half that time. Before I know where I am I will have finished my 8th and I hope that the war will be over by then. Still, I shall probably sign on in the army anyway as I don't think I could settle down to civilian life now. Well, this is all I have to say just now, don't forget to write by notion. With all my love, Davy.

The following letter was written by F.G. Lee, Okehampton, Devon after the war, F.G. Lee was a comrade in the Royal Corps of Signals and served with David in Malaya prior to them becoming Prisoners of war:-

David Millar in Palestine 1937/38

Dear Mrs. Millar,

Forgive me for opening which may be old wounds but I am fulfilling a sacred promise made to your son Signalman R.D. Millar – Royal Signals.

We have been buddies for years and were taken prisoners at Singapore in 1942. Up until approximately May 1944 we were together – but we were parted and he was sent to Labuan. Nothing was heard until we were relieved by the Australians in August 1945 when I was sent to their hospital at Labuan. After very extensive inquiries from every possible source it can be considered definitely that none was left as those who did not die were shot by the Japanese when the Australians arrived. Your son was very brave – took everything with a smile, and may God help you in your sorrow.

David's brother William found the above letter while searching through papers in 1976. Wanting to find out more about his brother's experiences he replied to Mr. Lee. The following letter is Mr. Lee's reply, dated Monday 16th February 1976:-

Dear Sir,

Ref: a letter written to me on 6th January 1976.

What a surprise! – What memories revived! A lot of water has gone under the bridge my friend but I will try and do what you ask of me. I first met David who was known to all his friends as 'Paddy' at a place called Trimoqevy, Southern India in 1938 when the war clouds in England were gathering. A number of us were told do parade and being good soldiers David and I fell in the rear rank.

The last rank they called Force Heron! And sent them too North Africa. The rear rank, called Force Emu! And were sent to Singapore and made up the signal unit for the 11th Indian Division which were sent to Penang on the outbreak of the Japanese war. Our life at Singapore until the Far Eastern war, was one of plenty, not a lot of work and plenty of time for sport, etc. Prices in the canteens were very cheap. Players No. 3 were 40 cents, (one Singapore dollar was 2/4d). Whisky 6 dollars, beer 20 cents. Fresh food was very cheap, we all paid one dollar a week and lived like fighting cocks.

Then came the day of reckoning and off to Penang, and as you know we came down through Malaya like a dose of salts. Our 11th Division was cut off at a place in the jungle called 'Slim River' and after wandering around for weeks we eventually went in the bag and sent to Singapore.

Things were not too bad to start with, it was a novelty and we did not until late realise what we were in for. Geneva Convention, and Red Cross, etc. We thought we would see that we were looked after, how wrong we were and it wasn't long before we were sent out on working parties pinching food from anywhere we could and being beaten up for doing so! But doing the same the next chance because we were hungry. They then came around for volunteers – army style, "you, you, you, you, you !!!!" etc., to make an air strip in the jungle of Sarawak (part of Borneo). So off we went in the tank of a dirty little old oil tanker. Thank God that trip wasn't too long, about a week and so to Kutching. From this base we were sent as a party of 150 men and 12 'Nips'. The work was hard but the Jap Officer in charge was really different. He had been forced back from America to fight under duress because of his family and relations in Japan, you know the sort of set up? Beatings were not allowed and a slapping party organised, etc, and life wasn't too bad. Then of course trouble - malaria, tropical ulcers, and sceptic scabies, the lot and no medication. The Jap O.C. could not give us what he didn't have. When we were down to about 20 men we went back to Kutching. Everything there was in a sorry state, skeletons walking around and then out of the blue we were sent to Labuan, a little island of the coast of Borneo. The Australians were advancing a bit and unknown to us Labuan was going to be their objective for a base camp. As they landed we were hounded down to the sea on the other side of the island and then the guards opened up with their machine guns. I was not in the near vicinity of David at this period. We were scattering everywhere trying to hide, etc. When they had finished with us they turned to go into the little jungle that there was but they could not hide either and were killed by the Aussies. David was among the ones I saw buried by the Australian Burial Party.

A brave and fine man, a pal to me, we shared even our snails when we were fast enough to catch them and I am proud to have known him. Under the conditions we lived under everything was different but believe me, it did sort the men from the boys.

Thank you for writing – God what memories you have stirred up.

Sincerely Yours,

F.G. Lee.

Richard David Millar was executed along with other prisoners on 5th January 1945, aged 27. He is commemorated on Singapore Memorial, column 44. He is also commemorated on Stewartstown Presbyterian Church Memorial Window, and Stewartstown Cenotaph.

*Memorial Window at Stewartstown Presbyterian commemorating
Edward Brown and Richard David Millar*

32923639- Private (Radio Operator) John Percy ANDERSON

United States Army, 172 Infantry Regiment, 43rd Infantry Division
Killed in Action: 10th February 1944
Age: 24
Manila American Cemetery, Manila, Philippines. Grave: A.7. 202

Private John Percy Anderson was born in 1919. He was the son of David Anderson, Stewartstown, Co. Tyrone.

David Anderson owned the local Paragon Stores in the Square, Stewartstown. Originally from Co. Cavan, he came and settled in Stewartstown, where he and his wife had 6 children, including John.

After his mother's death, John emigrated to the United States alone when he was 11 years old and settled with his aunt, Mrs. Nelson in Middlesex, New Jersey. He finished High School before working as a machine operator prior to enlisting in the US Army on 22nd May 1943 in Newark, New Jersey.

John would have been in service at Guadalcanal, New Guinea and training in New Zealand. The 172nd Regiment, 43rd Division were part of the US invasion fleet whose objective was the taking of Lingayen Gulf on the island of Luzon, Philippines. John Anderson acted as a radio operator with the forward command before the invasion. At 0930hrs on 9th February 1944 the Infantry's 2nd Battalion landed at Beach White One amidst fierce Japanese mortar and artillery fire. During the taking of the island John Percy Anderson was killed in action on 10th February 1944.

He was awarded the Bronze Star and Purple Heart.

The following Citation for his Bronze Star was sent home to his aunt Mrs. Nelson in New Jersey:

For Heroic achievement in connection with Military Operations against the enemy at Luzon, during the period of 10th – 30th January 1944. Private John Anderson, a radio operator for his battalion Commander, excelled in the performance of his duty during this entire period. No matter what acute situation the forward command group encountered, Private Anderson kept radio communications in operation. He also excelled in his alertness by keeping his battalion Commander informed of all radio messages accurately.

Private John Anderson is buried at Manila American Cemetery, Manila, Philippines. Plot A, Row 7, grave 202.

John Percy Anderson is commemorated on Stewartstown Cenotaph.

T/6985220 – Driver Frank McGEOWN
Royal Army Service Corps
Died on active service: 17th March 1945
Age: 21
Derryloran Roman Catholic Churchyard, Chapel Hill, Cookstown

Driver Frank McGeown was the son of Bernard & Sarah McGeown (nee Murphy), Loy Street, Cookstown. Prior to active service he worked in Cookstown Pork Factory.

He died on 17th March 1945, aged 21 as a result of a road accident. While acting as a dispatch rider his motorcycle collided with a lorry in England. His remains were returned home to Cookstown.

He is buried in the family plot at St. Luran's Roman Catholic Churchyard, Chapel Hill, Cookstown, and is commemorated on Cookstown Cenotaph.

6972028 – Sergeant William NEILL
5th Battalion (Home Defence) Royal Inniskilling Fusiliers
Died of Illness: 22nd April 1945
Age: 51
Cookstown New Cemetery, Westland Road, Cemetery Road, Cookstown

Sergeant William Neill was the son of William & Jane Neill of Clare, Cookstown, and the husband of Elizabeth (Bessie) Neill (nee McFarlane), Gortgonis, Coalisland, Co. Tyrone. He was the father of George, Margaret, Clyde, June, James and William (jnr) who served with the British Army on the Rhine (B.A.O.R) after the war.

Sergeant William Neill served in the First World War at Salonika, Egypt and France and was wounded on 8th November 1918. His army service number was 3881. He re-enlisted on 3rd March 1919 in Le Harve and transferred to Army Reserve on 5th March 1919 in Dublin. He was discharged on 14th December 1922 in Hamilton, Scotland with the rank of Corporal. Before the outbreak of the Second World War he worked as a Mill worker in Cookstown, and re-enlisted with the 5th (Home Defence) Battalion, Royal Inniskilling Fusiliers on 5th August 1940.

He died of illness while in service at Southend General Hospital in Essex on 22nd April 1945, aged 51 and is buried in Cookstown New Cemetery, Westland Road, Cookstown He is commemorated on Cookstown Cenotaph.

6979734 – Fusilier Ernest McGUCKIN

2nd Battalion Royal Inniskilling Fusiliers
Died on active service: 27th December 1946
Age: 25
Klagenfurt War Cemetery, Austria.   Grave: 7.A.12

Fusilier Ernest McGuckin was born in Stewartstown on 21st October 1919, and was the son of the late Robert McGuckin, Low Cross, Tullyhogue, and Emily Morrison, Dennistoun, Glasgow, formerly of Stewartstown, Co. Tyrone.

Prior to enlisting in the army on 8th September 1938, Ernest worked as a farm labourer.

He died as a result of a road traffic accident while in service in post war Austria, on 27th December 1946, aged 25. He is commemorated on Stewartstown Cenotaph and Donaghendry Church of Ireland Roll of Honour.

He is buried at Klagenfurt War Cemetery, Austria in grave 7.A.12.

Klagenfurt, the only Commonwealth war cemetery in Austria, was begun in June 1945 by the British occupying forces, which moved graves into it from all over the country. It now contains 589 Commonwealth burials of the Second World War. Between 1950 and 1954, eight First World War graves (three of them unidentified) were moved into the cemetery from small cemeteries at Innsbruck, Mauthausen, Muhldorf and Vienna. At the same time, special memorials were erected to two other First World War casualties whose graves at Muhldorf and Vienna could not be found.

The following appeared in the Mid Ulster Mail on the second anniversary of his death, it was submitted by his mother Mrs. Morrison:

There is no night that can hide you from sight,
In drifting clouds, in passing crowds, there is you.
You spent too few years upon this earth,
Just long enough to show your worth.
You left a memory, no one can steal,
And heartache, only time can heal.

Second World War Addendum

Two further names are included on the Second World War panel on
Cookstown Cenotaph.

P. Bell no further details are available.

M. Crawford no further details are available.

It is uncertain as to whom these inscriptions refer.

Air Force Memorial

The Air Forces Memorial at Runnymede commemorates by name over
20,000 airmen who were lost in World War 2, during operations from
bases in the U.K. and North and Western Europe, who have no known
graves.

These men served in Bomber, Fighter, Coastal, Transport, Flying,
Training and Maintenance Commands, and came from all parts of the
Commonwealth. Some airmen were from occupied countries in
continental Europe (Polish, Czech, etc) who continued to fight while
serving with the R.A.F.

The memorial was designed by Sir Edward Maufe and sculptured by
Vernon Hill. The engraved glass and painted ceilings were designed by
John Hutton and the poem inscribed on the gallery window was written
by Paul H. Scott.

The Memorial is located 4 miles from Windsor, overlooking the River
Thames.

Naval Memorials

Plymouth, Portsmouth and Chatham Naval Memorials

After the First World War, an appropriate way had to found of commemorating those members of the Royal Navy who had no known grave, the majority of deaths having occurred at sea where no permanent memorial could be provided. An Admiralty committee recommended that the three manning ports of Great Britain, Chatham, Portsmouth and Plymouth, should each have an identical memorial of unmistakable Naval form, an Obelisk, which would serve as a leading mark for shipping. The memorials were designed by Sir Robert Lorimer and sculptured by Henry Poole

After the Second World War it was decided that Naval memorials should be extended to provide space for commemorating the Naval dead of that war.

In addition to commemorating the seamen of the Royal Navy who sailed from Plymouth, the First World War panels also bear the names of sailors from Australia and South Africa. The governments of other commonwealth countries chose to commemorate their dead elsewhere, for the most part these memorials are in their home ports.

After the Second World War, Canada and New Zealand again chose to commemorate at home, but the Plymouth Naval Memorial lists those sailors from other parts of the commonwealth.

Plymouth Naval Memorial commemorates 7,251 sailors from World War 1 and 15,933 sailors from World War 2 who have no known grave. The memorial is situated centrally on The Hoe which looks directly toward Plymouth Sound

Chatham Naval Memorial commemorates 8,515 sailors from World War 1 and 10,098 sailors from World War 2 who have no known grave. The memorial overlooks the town of Chatham and is approached by a steep path from the Town Hall Gardens.

Portsmouth Naval Memorial commemorates 9,667 sailors from World War 1 and 14,918 sailors from World War 2 who have no known grave.

The memorial is situated on Southsea Common, overlooking the promenade at Portsmouth.

Medals and Awards

Victoria Cross

The Victoria Cross (VC) is a military decoration awarded for valour "in the face of the enemy" to members of armed forces of some Commonwealth countries and previous British Empire territories. It may be awarded to a person of any rank in any service and civilians under military command, and is presented to the recipient by the British monarch during an investiture held at Buckingham Palace. As it is the highest award for bravery in the United Kingdom, it takes precedence over other postnominals and medals.

The VC was introduced in 1856 by Queen Victoria to reward acts of valour during the Crimean War. Since then the medal has been awarded 1,356 times to 1,353 individual recipients. Only 14 medals have been awarded since the end of the Second World War. The medal itself is made from the gunmetal of a weapon supposedly captured at the siege of Sevastopol.

Distinguished Service Order (DSO)

The Distinguished Service Order (DSO) was instituted in 1886. Following various 19th Century campaigns, it was realised that no adequate award for distinguished service was available to junior officers apart from the VC and, in the case of Majors and above, the CB. Since 1886 the basic design has remained the same apart from the obverse central crown and the reverse royal cypher, which changes with each sovereign.

Conspicuous Gallantry Medal (CGM)

The CGM was instituted in 1855 as a reward for gallantry for the Royal Navy. The first issues was made to recipients for gallantry in the Baltic and Crimea. After a lull of some 18 years, the medal was re-instituted in 1874 with a batch of awards for Ashantee. From this date the medal was issued with the following obverses: Victoria, Edward VII, George V and George VI. About 50 of the second Victoria issue were awarded, with 2 Edward VII medals, 110 George V issues, and 72 George VI issues. There is only one instance of someone winning a bar to his CGM.

In 1943 the CGM was exended to the RAF to recognise gallantry whilst flying in operations against the enemy.

Distinguished Service Cross (DSC)

Instituted in June 1901 as reward for Warrant and Subordinate officers of the Royal Navy. In October 1914, the rules of eligibility were changed to so that all officers were eligible for the DSC. In 1931 the Merchant Navy officers were eligible in certain situations. From 1940, the year of its award is engraved on the lower part of the cross.

During World War One approximately 1700 DSCs were awarded, with about 90 first bars and 10 second bars. In World War Two, approximagely 4500 DSCs were awarded, with 430 first and 44 second bars. One medal was issued with three bars; the equivalent of being awarded the DSC four times.

Distinguished Service Medal (DSM)

Instituted in October 1914 to supplement the CGM, and was to be awarded for act of bravery which were deemed not sufficient for the award of the CGM. During World War Two, eligibility was extended to Army and RAF personnel serving on board ship, and to the Merchant and Dominion Navies.

All DSMs are issued named to the recipient, the details are impressed (Word War I), engraved or impressed (World War II) around the medal's rim 4,100 DSMs were issued during World War I, with 67 first bars and 2 second bars. In World War II, approximately 7,100 DSMs were issued, with 152 first bars and 3 second bars. One DSM was issued with 3 bars. About 50 DSMs were issued, during World War II, to the Maritime Royal Artillery, and 23 to the RAF.

Distinguished Conduct Medal (DCM)

The DCM was instituted in 1854 to recognise "distinguished, gallant and good conduct" by troops in the Crimea. All DCMs are issued named to the recipient, usually with impressed details around the medal's rim.

Nearly 25, 000 DCMs were issued during World War I, compared to 1,900 for acts during World War II. The majority of World War I DCMs have citations in the London Gazette. Since 1939, DCMs are listed in the London Gazette but don't have citations.

Military Cross (MC)

The MC was instituted in December 1914 as a reward for gallantry for officers of the rank of Captain or below, and for Warrant Officers. Officers over the rank of Captain (Major and above) were eligible for the DSO. From 1940, the date of the award is engraved on the lower part of the cross.

In World War I there were 37,000 MCs awarded, with 3,000 firs bars, 170 second bars and 4 third bars. During World War II, approximately 10,000 MCs were awarded and 500 first bars.

All awards of the MC are listed in the London Gazette. Citations exist for the First World War awards.

Military Medal (MM)

The MM was instituted in March 1916 as an award for non-officer rank of the Army for acts of braery. In the First World War the MM was awarded to a few recipients from the Royal Navy and Royal Airforce. Some RAF personnel were awarded the MM during World War II. All MMs are issued named with the recipient's details impressed around the medal's rim.

During World War I, 115,000 MMs were awarded with 5,800 first bars and 180 second bars. There was 1 award of the MM and 3 bars. World War II saw the award of 15,000 MMs with 164 first bars and 2 second bars.

Although all MMs awarded are listed in the London Gazette, the First World War MMs don't have citations. The Second World War MMs generally do have citations.

Distinguished Flying Cross (DFC)

The DFC was instituted in 1918 as an award to officers and warrant officers who displayed courage or devotion to duty whilst flying in active operations.

During World War 1, a total of approximately 1,000 DFCs were awarded, with 70 first bars and 3 second bars. During World War II, approximately 20,000 DFCs were awarded (the most of any award), with approximately 1,500 first bars and 42 second bars. Second World War DFCs have the year of issue engraved on the reverse of the bottom section of the cross.

Citations are generally available in the London Gazette for the Second World War DFCs. Some of the First World Ward DFCs also have citations.

Air Force Cross (AFC)

The AFC was instituted in June 1918 as an award to officers and warrant officers for courage or devotion to duty while flying, though not in active operations against the enemy. It was not officially named (as other officer's medals).

During World War I, approximately 680 were awarded. During World War II, approximately 2,000.

Distinguished Flying Medal (DFM)

The DFM was instituted together with the DFC in 1918, and was awarded to NCOs and men for bravery whilst flying on operations against the enemy. All DFMs were named witht he recipient's details around the rim of the medal. The World War One medals had the details impressed. The Second World War DFMs had the details engraved.

During World War I, approximately 105 DFMs were awarded, with 2 first award bars. During World War II, approximately 6,000 DFMs were awarded, with 60 first award bars and 2 second award bars.

Air Force Medal (AFM)

The AFM was instituted, with the AFC, in June 1918, and was awarded to NCOs and men for courage or devotion to duty whilst flying, though not in active operations against th eenemy. All AFMs are name: large capitals during World War One or engraved during World War Two.

Approximately 120 AFMs and 2 bars wre issued during World War One, and 259 AFMs issued during World War Two.

Mention-in-Dispatches

The award of a Mention-in-Dispatches or a Commendation was published in the London Gazette, though not much information was published aside from the Despatch which mentioned the recipient's name. A spray of bronze oak leaves to signify a Mention in Despatches was introduced during World War One and continued to be awarded for active service up to 10th August 1920. The oak leaf pin was worn on the ribbon of the Victory Medal.

The 1939-45 Star

Awarded for service as follows:

• Navy - awarded for six months service afloat in areas of active operations from 3 September 1939 to 2 September 1945.

• Army - awarded for six months service in an operational command during the period 3 September 1939 to 2 September 1945.

• Air Force - awarded to all aircrew who have taken part in operations against the enemy, subject to at least two months in an operational unit and to all non-air crew who served six months in the area of an Army operational command. A gold rosette worn on the ribbon signifies participation in the Battle of Britain, 1 July 1940 to 31 October 1940.

• Merchant Marine - awarded under the same conditions as Navy provided that at least one voyage was made through a specified area of active operations.

The Atlantic Star

Awarded for service as follows:

• Navy - awarded for six months service afloat in the Atlantic or Home waters between 3 September 1939 and 8 May 1945, after qualifying for the 1939-45 Star.

• Army - awarded under the same conditions as Navy.

• Air Force - awarded to air crew for operations against the enemy at sea within the areas and dates defined for Navy, subject to completing two months service in an operational unit, after qualifying for the 1939-45 Star.

• Merchant Marine - awarded under the same conditions as Navy, but requiring six months service at sea anywhere provided one voyage is made in the defined area.

A person qualifying for this Star and the Air Crew Europe Star and the France and Germany Star is awarded only the first earned, plus Clasps for the others. A silver rose emblem is worn on the ribbon bar to denote the award of a bar.

The Air Crew Europe Star

Awarded for two months operational flying from United Kingdom bases over Europe and the United Kingdom between 3 September 1939 and 5 June 1944. The 1939-45 Star must be earned first.

A person qualifying for this Star and the Atlantic Star and the France and Germany Star is awarded only the first earned, plus Clasps for the others. A silver rose emblem is worn on the ribbon bar to denote the award of a bar.

The Africa Star

Awarded for service as follows:

• Navy and Merchant Marine - service at sea in the Mediterranean between 10 June 1940 and 12 May 1943, or in support of Army operations in Abyssinia, Somaliland and Eritrea or for shore service as for Army.

• Army - entry into the operational area on the posted strength of a unit or formation in the area between the Suez Canal and the Straits of Gibraltar between 10 June 1940 and 12 May 1943 or for service in operations in Abyssinia, Somaliland, Eritrea, Malta or Syria.

An arabic numeral '1' or '8' may be worn on this ribbon to denote service with the British 1st Army or 8th Army respectively.

The Pacific Star

Awarded for service in the Pacific theatre between 8 December 1941 and 2 September 1945 as follows:

• Navy and Merchant Marine - service in the Pacific Ocean, South China Sea and part of the Indian Ocean, or for shore service under same criteria as Army. The 1939-45 Star must be earned first.

• Army - operational service in territories, not including Burma, that have been invaded by the enemy or the allies.

• Air Force - air crew service in operations against the enemy (one operational sortie qualifies)

A person qualifying for both the Pacific Star and the Burma Star is awarded only the first Star earned. A Clasp is worn denoting service for the other Star.

The Burma Star

Awarded for entry into operational service in the Burma campaign between 11 December 1941 and 2 September 1945 as follows:

• Navy and Merchant Marine - service in the Bay of Bengal and the prescribed area of the Indian Ocean, or for shore service under same criteria as Army. The 1939-45 Star must be earned first.

• Army - operational service in Burma, and, in addition, provinces of Bengal and Assam between 1 May 1942 and 31 December 1943; provinces of Bengal and Assam east of the Brahmaputra between 1 January 1944 and 2 September 1945; China and Malaya between 16 February 1942 and 2 September 1945.

• Air Force - air crew service in operations against the enemy (one operational sortie qualifies).

The Italy Star

Awarded as follows:

• Army - for entry into operational service on land in Sicily or Italy during the campaign there, between 11 June 1943 and 8 May 1945.

• Navy and Merchant Marine - service in the Mediterranean Sea directly connected with active operations in the Mediterranean theatre, or for shore service under same criteria as Army. The 1939-45 Star must be earned first.

• Air Force - air crew service in operations against the enemy within the Mediterranean theatre including sorties from the Mediterranean area over Europe.

The France and Germany Star

Awarded for entry into operational service on land in France, Belgium, Holland or Germany between 6 June 1944 and 8 May 1945.

• Navy and Merchant Marine - One days service afloat in the prescribed areas of the North Sea, the English Channel and the Bay of Biscay.

A person qualifying for this Star and the Air Crew Europe Star and the Atlantic Star is awarded only the first earned, plus Clasps for the others. A silver rose emblem is worn on the ribbon bar to denote the award of a bar.

The Defence Medal

Awarded to members:

• serving for six months in specified non-operational areas subjected to enemy air attack or closely threatened;

• who served for six months at any time between 3 September 1939 and 2 September 1945 in the Northern Territory north of 14° 30' South and the Torres Strait Islands;

• serving for 12 months non-specified non-operational service overseas from or outside Australia; or

• of Mine and Bomb Disposal units employed in areas subjected to enemy air attack or closely threatened for three months within the periods stated.

The War Medal 1939-45

Awarded to members who served full-time in operational or non-operational service between 3 September 1939 and 2 September 1945. The qualifying period is 28 days.

For the Merchant Marine, the 28 days must be served at sea.

A member Mentioned in Dispatches for service during World War 2 wears a bronze oak leaf emblem on the ribbon. Only one emblem is worn no matter how many times a member may have been 'mentioned'.

1914 Star

The 1914 Star was instituted in April 1917 and was awarded to those in the Army who served in France or Belgium on the strength of a unit, or service in either of those countries between 5th August 1914 and midnight on 22/23rd November 1914. The medal was issued with name and details of the recipient impressed on the reverse side. All recipients were also issued with the British War Medal and the Victory Medal. A total of 378,000 1914 Stars were awarded including a small number to Royal Naval personnel who served at Antwerp prior to midnight on 22/23rd November 1914. In October 1919, King George V sanctioned the award of a bar to this medal. The bar was awarded to holders of the medal who had been under fire in either France or Belgium during the dates covered. The exact number of medals issued with a bar is unknown.

1914-1915 Star

The 1914-15 Star was instituted in 1918 and was awarded to those who saw service between 5th August 1914 and 31st December 1915. Those personnel eligible for 1914 Star were not eligible for this one. The medal was issued, named with the recipients details on the reverse side. All recipients of this medal would have also received the British War Medal and the Victory Medal. Approximately 2,366,000 of 1914-1915 Star were issued, of the total issued, included, 283,500 to the Royal Navy and 71,500 to Canadian personnel.

British War Medal 1914-1920

This Medal commemorates some of the bloodiest battles ever fought by British and Commonwealth Forces. The medal was instituted by King George V in 1919 to mark the end of the First World War and record the service given. Although the war ended with the signing of the armistice in 1918, the qualification period to receive this medal was extended to include those in the post war period who were involved in service in Russia and in mine-clearance operations in former theatres of war. Approximately 6,500,000 silver medals were issued to members of the Army who had served overseas and in theatres of operation between 4th August 1914 and 11th November 1918, and awarded to members of the Royal Navy who had served over 28 days in operation or who lost their lives between 4th August 1914 and 11th November 1918.It was also awarded to members of the Royal Air Force after 1st April 1918 and the Royal Flying Corps and Royal Naval Air Service prior to 1st April 1918.110,000 bronze medals were issued to Chinese, Maltese, Indian and other native Labour Corps and other native personnel who were mobilised for war service and received pay at military rates.

Victory Medal 1914-1919

This medal was instituted in 1919 to commemorate the victory of the Allies over the Central Powers. It was resolved that each of the Allies should issue a Victory Medal to their own nationals. Approximately 5,725,000 British Victory Medals were issued and those personnel who had been "Mentioned in Dispatches" between 4th August 1914 and 10th August 1920 would have worn an oak leaf pin on the ribbon of this medal.

Medals were issued to members of the Army and the Royal Navy who were in the establishment of a unit within an operational

theatre of war between 4th August 1914 to 11th November 1918, and to members of the Royal Air Force after the 1st April 1918, and members of the Royal Flying Corps and Royal Naval Air Service prior to 1st April 1918.

Mercantile Marine War Medal 1914-1918

This bronze medal was instituted by the United Kingdom Board of Trade and was awarded to members of the Mercantile Marine (later, Merchant Navy) who served on one or more voyages through a danger zone during the period, 4th August 1914 to 11th November 1918. A total of 133,135 medals were issued.

Memorial Plaque

The 120 millimetre, bronze Memorial Plaque was awarded to the next-of-kin of those who lost their lives whilst on active service during World War One. The inscription around the edge reads: He died for freedom and honour. When commemorating the death of a woman (e.g. a Nurse) it would read: She died for freedom and honour. Over 1million were issued, to Army, Navy and Air Force

Memorial Scroll

The Memorial Plaque was accompanied by a Memorial Scroll. At the top of the scroll was an emblem of King George v, followed by this text:

He whom this scroll commemorates
Was numbered among those who
At the call of King and Country,
Left all that was dear to them,
Endured hardness, faced danger,
And finally passed out
Of the sight of men by the path of duty and
Self-sacrifice, giving up their own lives,
That others might live in freedom.
"Let those who come after see to it that his name be not
forgotten"

The details of the deceased service person are then shown in red ink

Allied Subjects Medal

The Allied Subjects' Medal was a medal issued to those people (not necessarily British) who had helped the Allied cause, by for example, assisting POW's to escape and avoid detection. Due to a disagreement between the British War and Foreign Offices, the Medal was not introduced until November 1920, with additional awards made in 1921 and 1922.

The Medal itself was either Silver or Bronze, and 33 millimetres in diameter. On the obverse side was a profile of King George V. The reverse side had a female humanity figure offering a cup to a British Soldier resting on the ground, against a profile of ruined buildings. All medals were issued, unnamed and almost half of the total issued went to women.

Commonwealth Cemeteries and Memorials.

When the First World War commenced no-one properly understood the enormity of the impending loss of life nor had any structured system been put in place to handle the human consequences of such a catastrophic struggle.

In the early days of the War there was no organisation responsible for marking, recording and registering soldier's graves beyond their own battalion or regiment. Grave registration fell to unit chaplains who recorded each grave, personal details and made the appropriate reports to the appropriate headquarters.

In late 1914, a mobile ambulance unit provided by the Red Cross and headed by Fabian Ware began voluntarily to undertake the work of grave registration. Their work expanded rapidly recording and caring for all the graves they could find.

Official responsibility for graves rested with the Adjutant General's Office and was delegated to the Director of Graves Registration and Enquiries (DRG&E). By 1915, the War Office gave official recognition to Ware's work. He was relieved of Red Cross work and his unit was incorporated into the British Army as the Graves Registration Commission.

As the War progressed, it became evident that the spirit of imperial co-operation with the War itself should be reflected in the Commission. In May 1917 the Imperial War Graves Commission was established by Royal Charter with the Prince of Wales serving as President and Fabian Ware as Vice Chairman.

The French Government on 29 December 1915 provided land that would be maintained in perpetuity for British war dead and by 1918 the enormous task of recording the details had identified 587,000 graves and a further 559,000 casualties with no grave.

The Commonwealth War Graves Commission followed from the Imperial War Graves Commission and pays tribute to 1,700,000 men and women of the Commonwealth Forces who died in two world wars.

Since it's inception, the Commission has constructed 2,500 war cemeteries and plots, erecting headstones over graves and, in instances where the remains are missing, inscribing the names of the dead on permanent memorials. There are now casualties commemorated at military and civil sites in some 150 countries.

The Commission's principles:

That each of the dead should be commemorated by name on the headstone or memorial.

Headstones and memorials should be permanent.

Headstones should be uniform and that no distinction be made on account of military or civil rank, race or creed.

From a single poet's grave on the Isle of Skyros to a cemetery in Belgium with over 11,000 burials, the Commission maintains over a million war graves as well as hundreds of memorials honouring 750,000 war dead who have no known grave.

In British Commonwealth Cemeteries you will find a Cross of Sacrifice, and the altar like, Stone of Remembrance.

The Cross of Sacrifice has four different sizes and this relates to the size of the cemetery.

14 feet high for a cemetery with 40 - 250 burials
20 feet high for a cemetery with 251 - 2,000 burials
25 feet high for a cemetery with over 2,000 burials

And 30 feet high for special cases. The only special cases on the Somme are the British - French Cemetery at Thiepval Memorial and the Australian Cemetery and Memorial at Villers-Bretonneux.

British Cemeteries up until the end of 1945 had no national distinctions. Subsequently cemeteries that contained large numbers of other nationals such as Canadians were distinguished by having a Maple Leaf or appropriate insignia placed over the entrance to the cemetery and on the visitors book.

In some cases Commonwealth Cemeteries will contain German, French and American dead, but no German graves are found in French or American cemeteries.

Only American war dead are found in American Cemeteries.

Commonwealth War Graves in Cookstown District
Cookstown New Cemetery (Cemetery Road), 7 burials
Derryloran Old Cemetery (Sandholes Road), 1 burial
Derryloran (Chapel Hill) Roman Catholic Churchyard, 3 burials
Stewartstown Roman Catholic Curchyard, 2 burials
Donaghendry Church of Ireland Churchyard, 2 burials
Kildress C of I old Churchyard, 1 burial
Kildress Church of Ireland Churchyard, 1 burial
Ballygoney Presbyterian Churchyard, 1 burial
Desertlyn (St John) C of I Churchyard, 1 burial and Desertlyn Old Graveyard, 1 burial.

BURIAL OF THE DEAD

During the First World War life in the trenches was, at best, precarious and whilst being underground offered relative safety, soldiers often died as a result of random shelling, sniper fire or raiding parties. Major assaults exposed waves of infantry to direct machine gun and rifle fire often resulting in huge numbers of casualties. Enemy attack frequently resulted in similar consequences.

The varying nature of men's deaths determined the type of burial ultimately received. Men killed at the Front, whether killed immediately or dying quickly of wounds, were buried by their units close to the Front in temporary graves or existing burial grounds. Those lost during assaults or withdrawals often lay out for long periods because of the risk associated with trying to recover their remains. Soldiers lost in these circumstances were often buried in pits by the enemy with few records kept. Men killed or wounded in the fighting around Ypres in Belgium were often swallowed up by the mire all around them. The Battles of Langemark and Paschendale were particularly dreadful. Shellfire frequently fragmented the living and unearthed those previously buried leaving the work of identification of casualties and proper recording of burials very difficult.

The entire region fought over both in Belgium and France saw a concentration during the period 1915 to mid-1918 in a limited North-South corridor of approximately one hundred miles wide. This ebb and flow of combat over the same areas, particularly so at Ypres and in the Somme area, resulted in most early burial grounds being destroyed by shellfire as the landscape was systematically obliterated.

Those who died of wounds away from the combat zone or at base hospitals were generally assured of a permanent burial place. The area of Etapes in Northern France was used as a transit area and concentration area for general hospitals. There are more than 11,000 permanent burials here.

By November 1918, half of all those killed on the Western Front were recorded as "missing presumed killed".

BATTLEFIELD CLEARANCE

Battlefield clearance and the return of large areas of France and Belgium to agriculture and normal civilian life took many years. Disposal of munitions and recovery of the dead were priorities and this work continues to this day.

After the War large areas of battlefields were taped into grids and systematically searched by exhumation companies who looked for tell tale signs such as helmets and equipment protruding from the ground. Discoloured water (green or black) or lush vivid coloured grass often indicated a human burial close to the surface. Recovery of bodies continued until 1928 with those found being placed in creosote soaked canvas and identification sought from discs, personal affects, watches, regimental buttons, webbing marked with the wearer's name or by whatever means. Bodies often remained unidentified and are buried as "a soldier of the Great War known unto God". During this time many remote or isolated burials were relocated to the larger cemeteries being constructed by the Imperial War Graves Commission. Construction of First World War cemeteries continued until 1938.

Bodies continue to be unearthed to this day largely as a result of development or agriculture and receive a military funeral. If identified, they are removed from memorials to the missing.

The disposal of munitions, largely unexploded artillery rounds and hand grenades, is still a major issue for French and Belgian farmers in these areas. Millions of unexploded rounds remain buried and account for a number of deaths each year when disturbed.

Ulster Tower, Thiepval.

The Ulster Tower, Thiepval was built in 1921, the cost was raised by public subscription from people all over Ulster including Donegal, Cavan and Monaghan. The plan of the Tower was modelled on Helen's Tower at Clandeboye Estate just outside Bangor, County Down, where many of the men of the 36th (Ulster) Division trained before their service on Western Front during World War 1.

The Ulster Tower was the first War Memorial opened on the Western Front and was officially opened in November 1921 by Chief of the Imperial General Staff, Field Marshal Sir Henry Wilson who took the place of Lord Carson who couldn't attend due to illness.

The Tower is a Memorial to the fallen of all the men of Ulster and stands today near the ground where many Ulster men died on the 1st July 1916 during the Somme Offensive.

It was estimated that during the 1920's- 30's the Tower was well attended, seeing something in the region of 300 visit per day. The Tower was manned by personnel who looked after it all year round.

In subsequent years the Tower fell into disrepair and parts of the building needed restoration. The Farset group helped restore the Tower to it's former glory and the Tower was re-dedicated on 1st July 1989. Behind the Tower now is a visitors centre which was opened in 1991 and a memorial stone to the men of the Ulster Division who received the Victoria Cross was unveiled later that year by the Royal Irish Rangers.

The memorial to the fallen brethren of the Loyal Orange Institution worldwide was erected outside the gates of the Tower in 1994 and subsequently moved a couple of years later inside the grounds.

Ulster Tower, Thiepval, France

Archive photo courtesy of Wesley Wright

Stewartstown War Memorial

Stewartstown War Memorial is located in the village square. It is a granite obelisk standing 16 feet (5 metres) high, and surrounded with a substantial railing and is situated at the top of the square. On top of the south face of the obelisk there is a black laurel wreath on the shaft, the names of the First World War dead are listed on the panel below in bronze.The names of the Second World War dead are listed on the east face of the obelisk.

The Memorial was unveiled by the sister of Viscount Charlemont., the Hon. Rachel Caulfield who performed the ceremony on behalf of Viscount Charlemont's wife Lady Charlemont, who was too ill to attend. Viscount Charlemont explained that the obelisk was only part of the Memorial in Stewartstown, as trees were to be planted all around the square in the village. The unveiling ceremony was performed by 38 ex-servicemen and a detachment of soldiers from the Military Depot in Omagh.

The original plan had been to build a memorial Hall similar to that of Coagh village. However by 1924, not enough money had been raised and it was decided to erect an obelisk.

Memorial Rolls of Honour can also be found in Donaghendry Church of Ireland, North Street, Stewartstown and Stewartstown Presbyterian, Hillhead, Stewartstown.

Public Notice, Mid Ulster Mail c 1920

Coagh (Soldiers and Sailors) Memorial Hall

The foundation stone for the building was laid down on 1st July 1920 by Mr. R.J. McKeown M.P.The building was contracted to Mr. J.B. McKeown.

Coagh (Soldiers and Sailors) Memorial Hall was opened on 16th July 1921by Lady Craig (wife of the then, Northern Ireland Prime Minister, Sir James Craig). The tablet to the fallen was unveiled by Mrs Lenox-Conyngham and the names were read out by Captain R.C. Elliot, (Chaplain of Forces). The tablet to those who served was unveiled by Mrs. R.J. McKeown and a dedicatory prayer was read out by Lieutenant Colonel D.H. Hanson C.F. The prayers were laid by Reverend John Entrican B.A. and benediction pronounced by Reverend W.T. McClelland. The hall also included a stained glass window to the fallen.

The two plaques inside the hall hold the names of those who died in the 'Great War' and those who served, and cover the areas of Coagh, Tamlaght, parts of Ardboe and Ardtrea.

31 names are included among the fallen. This however is not a complete list of names.

In recent years the Hall has fallen into disrepair and the stained-glass window and Memorial plaques have been removed for safe keeping. The Memorial plaques can now be found in Royal British Legion Hall, Cookstown.

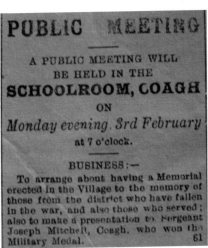

Public notice appeared in Mid Ulster Mail c 1920

Moneymore War Memorial

Moneymore War Memorial is located in Smith Street. It is attached to the side wall of the Assembly Rooms building.

The unveiling ceremony was performed on the 12th October 1922 by Brigadier General Sir William Hacket-Pain, K.B.E., C.B., M.P. The dedicatory prayer was offered by Reverend W.J. McGeagh, B.A., Moneymore Presbyterian Church.

The Memorial surround is made of Irish limestone with a panel made of Aberdeen, red polished granite, which lists the names of 26 men from the district who gave their lives in the First World War. The inscription reads:-"Erected in grateful remembrance of those who made the supreme sacrifice for King and Country during the Great War. 1914-1918," and at the bottom of the memorial:-"Lest We Forget." Another tablet memorial inside the hall includes the names of 162 other men who served during the war. This tablet makes the distinction between those who served overseas and those who served at home.

Two names included on the Memorial are listed in the addendum to this book as they were born and lived outside Cookstown District area. At time of publication we have received no information on A.E.Brown.

William McCord of Carmean, Moneymore, Magherafelt served with the 9th Royal Inniskilling Fusiliers. He was killed in action on 29th March 1918. He is buried at Grand-Seraucourt Cemetery, France.

Other War Memorials

Le Touret Memorial, France carries the names of 15 men from Cookstown District.

Ploegsteert Memorial, Belgium carries the names of 9 Cookstown District

Pozieres Cemetery and Memorial, France carries the names of 10 Cookstown men. There are 2,733 graves here, almost half are marked as unknown. The memorial wall that encases the cemetery contains the names of 14,644 names of missing soldiers, mostly British but also includes 320 South Africans. Most of the names recorded here are men that are missing or have no known grave and were lost between 21st March - 5th April 1918 when the Germans pushed the allies back almost 30 miles.

Also included here are the names of men from the 4th and 5th Armies who were lost here up to August 1918.

The Menin Gate Memorial, Belgium commemorates the names of 7 men from Cookstown as does the Loos Memorial, France.

Tyne Cot Cemetery Memorial, Belgium commemorates the names of 9 men from Cookstown District.

Vimy Memorial, France commemorates the names of 6 men from the Cookstown District.

16th Irish Division Memorial Cross at Wyschaete, Belgium

16th Irish Division Memorial Cross at Ginchy, France

Vimy Ridge Memorial, France

Tyne Cot Cemetery and Memorial, Belgium

Menin Gate, Ypres, Belgium

Helles Memorial, Turkey

Pozieres Cemetery and Memorial, France

World War 1 Alphabetical List

Arbuthnot John
Armstrong David
Ashfield Hugh
Ballentyne Samuel
Barlowe J.A.B.
Barton Patrick
Bates Oliver
Bayne Joseph
Beach John James
Bell Alexander Law
Bell Richard
Bell Thomas
Bell William J.A.
Biggar Peter
Black Isaac
Blair Robert
Bleakes George
Bleeks William Thomas
Booth Andrew Thomas
Boyd William
Boyle Joseph
Boyle Louis
Bradley John *addendum*
Bradley Patrick
Bridgett William R.
Brown George M.M.
Brown William
Burgess Robert King Holmes
Burns J. addendum
Campbell Charles
Campbell Henry
Campell James *addendum*
Campbell Richard Colin
Campbell William John
Campbell William Thomas
Cander Robert
Carron Francis
Carruth John
Carson Patrick
Cassidy James P
Chambers George
Charles Daniel
Cheevers Francis
Cheevers Richard
Cheevers Thomas
Clark William
Clarke James Herbert

Cobain Henry
Collins Newton Henry
Colvin Andrew M.M.
Cooke Archibald
Cooney Charles Richard
Corbett James
Corey Patrick
Corr William John *addendum*
Corrigan Michael
Coyle John
Creighton Ernest
Creighton James
Crilly John
Crooks Charles Edward
Crooks William John
Crossett John
Cullen Thomas
Curran David George
Curran Samuel
Currie Frederick
Currie Hugh
Curtiss Michael
Cuthell Algernon Hubert
Darragh Thomas 1916
Darragh Thomas 1918
Davidson William Norman
Davison James
Davison Robert
Devlin James 1915
Devlin James 1916
Devlin John
Devlin Thomas
Donaghy Francis 1916
Donaghy Francis 1917
Donaldson John
Donnelly Frederick
Donnelly Samuel
Donnelly Sarah, Mary and Ethel
Doris Thomas George
Dowie Frederick
Duncan Andrew
Dunlop George Malcolm
Dunlop John Gunning Moore
Eccles Francis *addendum*
Ekin Frederick William
Ekin Leslie Montrose M.C.
Ekin James